Authority and Sexuality
in Early Modern Burgundy
(1550–1730)

STUDIES IN THE HISTORY OF SEXUALITY
Judith Brown and Guido Ruggiero, *General Editors*

IMMODEST ACTS
The Life of a Lesbian Nun in Renaissance Italy
Judith Brown

THE EVOLUTION OF WOMEN'S ASYLUMS SINCE 1500
From Refuges for Ex-Prostitutes
to Shelters for Battered Women
Sherrill Cohen

AUTHORITY AND SEXUALITY
IN EARLY MODERN BURGUNDY
(1550–1730)
James R. Farr

MASCULINITY AND MALE CODES OF HONOR
IN MODERN FRANCE
Robert A. Nye

THE BOUNDARIES OF EROS
Sex Crime and Sexuality in Renaissance Venice
Guido Ruggiero

Further volumes are in preparation

Authority and Sexuality in Early Modern Burgundy (1550–1730)

JAMES R. FARR

New York   Oxford
OXFORD UNIVERSITY PRESS
1995

Oxford University Press

Oxford   New York   Toronto
Delhi   Bombay   Calcutta   Madras   Karachi
Kuala Lumpur   Singapore   Hong Kong   Tokyo
Nairobi   Dar es Salaam   Cape Town
Melbourne   Auckland   Madrid

and associated companies in
Berlin   Ibadan

Library of Congress Cataloging-in-Publication Data
Farr, James Richard, 1950–
Authority and sexuality in early modern Burgundy
(1550–1730) / James R. Farr.
ISBN 0-19-508907-3 p. cm.—(Studies in the history of sexuality)
Includes bibliographical references and index.
1. Power (Social sciences)—France—Burgundy—History.
2. Sex—France—Burgundy—History.
3. Burgundy (France)—Moral conditions.
I. Title. II. Series.
HN440.P6F37   1995
306.7'0944'4—dc20   93-32702

1 3 5 7 9 8 6 4 2

Printed in the United States of America
on acid-free paper

To the memory of Marcus Wayne Orr,
who taught me the importance of seeing.

Acknowledgments

The inspiration for this book emerged from conversations among Guido Ruggiero, myself, and our spouses aboard a boat portentously named *La Bourguinonne*, plying the canals flanking the Loire river. While regaling them with stories I had gleaned from the criminal records of the Archives départementales de la Côte-d'Or which I had mined for my first book, it became clear that these narratives had a great deal to do with authority and sexuality. Furthermore, I realized that through these documents I could perceive the legal process as a site where authority was deployed, negotiated, appropriated, and resisted. An expanded examination of these records in the various archives of Burgundy and the Franche-Comté—Dijon, Mâcon, Besançon, and Chalon-sur-Saône—thus became the archival basis of this book, and an understanding of the documents as mediated through the legal process its guiding methodology. Whatever the merits of this book, it assuredly would have many fewer without the wise and informed counsel of Guido. I owe him a great debt of gratitude.

I am also thankful for the help of colleagues who graciously offered to read and comment upon the manuscript in its various stages. Al Hamscher spent many more hours with it than could be fairly expected. His unparalleled knowledge of the legal system of France guided me away from several egregious mistakes, and his spirited commentary throughout the manuscript helped me immensely. Likewise, my good friend Mack Holt shared his deep knowledge of the sixteenth and seventeenth centuries with me in his reading of the manuscript, and he no doubt has spared me the embarrassment of some factual errors. Whatever errors remain are of course my responsibility alone. For taking the time from a busy schedule to read the manuscript and comment upon it, I would also like to thank my student Dean Ferguson (who, with Al Hamscher, convinced me to jettison an entire chapter); my painfully honest but eternally helpful former advisor Bill Monter; and one of the editors of the series in which this book appears, Judy Brown. Thanks also go to my colleague John Lauritz Larson who, as a historian of the Early American Republic, brought the critical eye of the outsider to my topic, methodology, and prose and offered trenchant suggestions for the book's improved presentation and argumentation. A special thanks goes to Rachel Fuchs: more than anyone, she has seen this book emerge (having read portions of it more than once). Her selfless, direct criticism provided an accomplished and informed perspective that helped me hone my analysis of gender relations.

While in France, my research was facilitated by the gracious help of various archivists and librarians: the *conservateur* of the Archives municipales de Dijon, Mademoiselle Marie-Hélène Degroise, and her wonderful assistants, Margaret Jacquette and Pierre Berthier; Mademoiselle Françoise Vignier, the director of the Archives départementales de la Côte-d'Or in Dijon, and her staff; and the staffs at the Archives départementales de la Saône-et-Loire in Mâcon, Archives communales de Chalon-sur-Saône, Archives départementales du Doubs in Besançon, and the Bibliothèque nationale. Many agreeable hours were spent poring over manuscripts under the vaulted ceilings in the converted church that now serves as the Bibliothèque municipale de Dijon, efforts made all the more productive by the unfailing support of Mademoiselle Chauney.

My family's several stays in France were made immeasurably more enjoyable by the companionship and intellectual stimulation of our dear friends Michel and Gisèle Baridon. For such friendship, as well as locating accommodations and good-naturedly enduring the chaos my young sons occasionally brought to their house, our gratitude to them is deep.

Financial assistance for the research and writing of this book was provided by the American Council of Learned Societies, the National Endowment for the Humanities, and Purdue University, and valuable time released from teaching was provided by the School of Liberal Arts at Purdue in the form of a fellowship in the Center for Humanistic Studies.

Finally, I wish to thank my spouse Joanne Lax-Farr, and my two sons Quentin and Mason, for enduring the hardships that inevitably and frequently occur when a husband and father is also an author. My gratitude to them is as immeasurable as the depth of my affection.

West Lafayette, Ind.   J. R. F.
1994

Contents

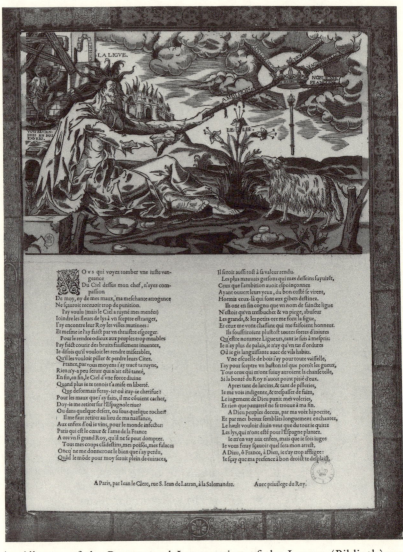

An Allegory of the Poverty and Lamentation of the League (Bibliothèque Nationale)

Authority and Sexuality
in Early Modern Burgundy
(1550–1730)

Introduction

In the early 1590s during the latter stages of the Wars of Religion, a Royalist-inspired woodcut appeared entitled, "An Allegory on the Poverty and Lamentation of the [Holy] League." Dominating the picture space is an old woman, one breast exposed, dark hair flying uncontrollably in all directions. Her hair reproduces the flames blazing from a burning town in the background. This female figure, labelled "The League" (*La Ligue*), is clad in tattered clothes and grasps a frayed rope labelled "ambition," which is tethered to a crown in the upper right of the picture. From a heavenly direction descend four other ropes, labelled "divine will" (*vouloir divin*), "legitimate right" (*droit légitime*), "magnanimity" (*magnanimité*), and "French Nobility" (*noblesse françoise*). Lurking sinisterly behind the woman on the left is a demon playing the lute, under which is inscribed, "you will come back to our hell" (*vous reviendres en nos enfers*).

After the conclusion of the Wars of Religion, the painful and arduous task of mending a torn society commenced. In Burgundy, the final stages of the war had divided the sovereign court, the Parlement, into two entities in 1590, one retaining allegiance to King Henri IV, the other swearing loyalty to the League and the Guise royal pretender, Charles X. With Henri's victory in 1595, the Parlement was reunited, but not without rancor. Indeed, just before the Leaguer parlementaires took the oath of fidelity to Henri, the royal *Procureur Général* Hugues Picardet addressed the judicial body with a scathing and humiliating harangue. He contrasted the loyal Royalist parlementaires to the Leaguers by employing overtly gendered language, identifying the Royalists as masculine and the Leaguers as femi-

3

nine. He sarcastically called upon the Leaguers to recognize the masculine virility of the Royalists—"We are the males"—and the femininity of themselves, since it was the Royalist judges who departed Dijon in 1589 and "vigorously" and "boldly" led its reconquest in 1595. The Leaguers, "those who remained at home while the men were at war, who hatched, bred, gave birth to the surrender of the town, they are the females." After the conquest by the Royalists, Picardet concluded, "since it pleases the Creator, we will now join together in a holy marriage."[1]

Each of these examples are representations of ideas about order—the lack of it in the woodcut, the imposition of it in the harangue. Furthermore, each is constructed from ideas about authority and sexuality: gender relations, the human body, law, and religion. The most striking characteristic about these cultural representations is that both the woodcut and the harangue prominently and centrally employ gendered imagery. In the woodcut, the female represents disorder unleashed upon the world in the form of the League; in the harangue, the female is represented by the dominated League Parlement that is expected to take its subservient place in the marriage to the Royalist Parlement.

Ideas about the human body—both male and female—also guide the visual and verbal representation. Indeed, the human body serves as the "privileged operator" through which biological assumptions are translated into social experience.[2] The female body is portrayed, first, as a symbol of the League (a *corps*) and of disorder and sexual wantonness (note the exposed breast). But in the harangue, this body (the League Parlement) is tamed, domesticated (note the nurturing references to the home and child rearing), and dominated by the "virile male" body, the Royalist Parlement (also a *corps*).

Both representations are Royalist, so depict a certain ideology about proper ordering. Ideas about the law and religion, as both images reveal, played an integral role in this ideology. In the woodcut, the ideas of "legal right" and "divine will" are associated with the French crown, as two of the four cords securing it to heaven. The League clutches at a single frayed rope labelled "ambition," a Royalist statement about the illegitimacy of this body's claim. Picardet is equally concerned to legitimize the Royalist cause against the pretentions of the League, and he does so ultimately by reference to a "holy marriage" willed by the Creator between the two juridical bodies. In his time marriage was both a sacrament and a legally binding contract sanctioned by God and his representative on earth, the king.

Cultural representations like these Royalist examples of authority and sexuality are prescriptive attempts to fix a particular ideology in time and space, and to attach that ideology directly to social experience. Prescription, however, rarely corresponds completely with the social processes of everyday practice, and even in its incompleteness the correspondence is only temporary. As Sally Falk Moore puts it,

> Social processes [should be analyzed] . . . in terms of the inter-relationship of three components: the processes of regularization, the processes

of situational adjustment, and the factor of indeterminacy. The conditions to which these terms allude are ubiquitous in social life. There seems to be a continuous struggle between the pressure toward establishing and/or maintaining order and regularity, and the underlying circumstance that counteractivities, discontinuities, variety and complexity make social life inherently unsuited to total ordering. The strategies of individuals are seldom (if ever) consistently committed to reliance on rules and other regularities.[3]

If the processes of regularization (the "fixing" of an ideology), situational adjustment (the attempted application of that ideology), and the factor of indeterminacy are inherent characteristics of social processes—and it seems to me that the empirical historical record suggests that they might be—then a sociocultural analysis of the relationships among law, religion, and sexual morality in early modern Burgundy, such as the one attempted in this book, might profit from considering the cogency of such methodological assumptions.

Ideology might be regarded as a product of the regularizing or ordering process, and its representations (categories, rules, laws, dogmas, or even woodcuts and harangues) as cultural devices used to attempt to "fix" social reality.[4] Despite the drive to order and to fix, to crystallize and to regularize, however, as Moore writes, "there invariably remains a certain range of maneuver, of openness, of choice, of interpretation, of alteration, of tampering, of reversing, of transforming."[5]

When we enter the world of everyday practice this "certain range of openness, of choice" becomes evident because this is a world of innumerable variables with the inevitable presence of indeterminacy.[6] Rules, laws, or dogmas may frame the choices that individuals can make, but the imposition of such detemporalizing "officialization strategies," so typical of legalism, can only be temporary and partial, because everyday practice unfolds "in temporal, successive frames."[7]

Of course, that the regularization or ordering process can never be complete does not in any way mean that it is irrelevant to the social experience of everyday practice. Indeed, the groups or individuals who guide the ordering process that frames choices are obviously powerful, and the social group or groups that articulate the nature of the order and its manner of application possess the lion's share of power in a given society.[8]

Power in early modern society was certainly asymmetrically distributed, but it was not monolithic. Power relations unfolded in dialectical fashion, simultaneously enabling and constraining the individuals or groups arrayed in its field. Indeed, power relations may be construed as *contests* over the affirmation of a given order that the dominant group attempts to impose upon the less powerful.

As fields of struggle, power relations resemble economies; in both, power is a resource drawn upon by weak as well as strong to optimize a given strategy, and the achievement of that strategy is dependent upon effective negotiation and exchange. The "tactics of consumption" of the resources of power are a way of using dominant or imposed systems, and in turn are guided by and contingent upon the logic of the practice of everyday life.

Arrayed within these "fields of struggle" were bodies. Analytics of the body have attracted considerable scholarly attention in the past decade or so, and responses to disarmingly simple questions—What is the body, and how do we analyze it?—have given rise to complex, far-reaching, and controversial responses from historians, philosophers, and sociologists. These answers fan out into the related issues of epistemology, or ways of knowing; of agency and constraint; and of incorporation, or the cultural uses to which the body is put.

Michel Foucault insisted that the body is a site upon which culture discursively inscribes its values, values that are constituted by that culture's power relations.[9] Furthermore, he maintained that discourses constitute the body as a knowable object and thereby enable the description of the body as a cultural product. Critics deeply interested in and appreciative of the profound implications of analytics of the body like Judith Butler have found Foucault's logic elliptical. If the body is only knowable as a culturally inscribed product, she queries, how can we *know* there is a prediscursive biological body upon which culture inscribes its values?[10]

The epistemological claims of Butler's radical cultural constructivist stance, that there is no knowable body prior to culture, may expose a weakness in Foucault's logic, but it also seems to challenge the phenomenology of embodiment[11] and consequently has proved unattractive to such historians as Caroline Walker Bynum or, indeed, myself, as this study will reflect. Bynum asserts that "all evidence for the doing of history opens out beyond itself to an intractible physicality. . . . What we study—what we can study—is culturally constructed. But we know that we are more than culture. We are body. And, as body, we die."[12] From the premise of the phenomenology of embodiment, scholars, essayists, and artists like Bynum, Haunani-Kay Trask, Adrienne Rich, Robin Morgan, Meredith McGuire, and Audre Lorde have probed epistemology and argued for a somatic or bodily way of knowing.[13] As John Giles Milhaven observes, the epistemological claim of bodily knowing poses a "chilling critique of male-dominated Western Culture . . . [because] males continuing and shaping the culture use only a disembodied 'rational' mode of knowing."[14]

It is, of course, well known that the western epistemological tradition has often separated the rational faculty from bodily materiality, but this dichotomizing nonetheless is relative and thus has a history, and, if we scrutinize this history with gender differential in mind, interesting perspectives open upon the past. Under Aristotelian influence, intellectuals of the late Middle Ages were not particularly concerned with radically distinguishing the body from the soul (in contrast to the Platonic tradition) and assumed the male body as paradigmatic. Consequently, scholars like Aquinas accepted the validity of bodily knowing (although inferior to the rational faculty) while understanding women as essentially inferior versions of men.[15] With the resurgence of Platonism in the late sixteenth and seventeenth centuries (carried, as we will see, with renewed Augustinianism), mind and body were again sharply dichotomized. Furthermore, the former was associated with men and the latter with women, and men assumed that the only legitimate way of knowing was a disembodied rationality.[16] Conversely, materiality was devalued, and the passions were deeply distrusted.

Of course, such assumptions about hierarchical and gendered differential conditions of embodiment were fundamental to patriarchy, and patriarchy arrogated disproportionate power to males. Such an intellectual construct defined an agenda of social order and profoundly influenced the prescriptive authoritarian religious, political, and juridical regimes with which the early modern epoch is associated.

There is ample evidence to demonstrate this "worldly aceticism," but we should not let it blind us to other evidence that shows men even after Rabelais revelling in materiality and the passions. The literature on gallantry and even pornography are cases in point,[17] as is the continued widespread existence of prostitution even after the prohibition of brothels by the king of France in 1561. Of course, neither do gallantry, pornography, or prostitution challenge patriarchy, nor do they alter the public, prescriptive face of order, but their existence does suggest an ambivalence within patriarchy.

By focusing on prescriptive patriarchal attitudes I do not mean to suggest that women had no power over their own bodies. As Bynum cautions us, women were not mere victims of patriarchy.[18] Instead, one must understand the body—female or male, prostitute or king—as an agent cast into fluid situations not of its making, and thereby constrained by its conditions—no matter how gloomy or degrading, or exalted—and simultaneously provided room to maneuver to satisfy its interests. Such a view of "incorporation" allows the body to be an agent of order, a "practical and theoretical operator of social rules," while at the same time a "body of disorder and effervescence, the practical and theoretical operator of a fundamental dimension [flux] of the social aggregate."[19] It also renders highly problematic Foucault's transcendental views on cultural construction, where according to Butler, "inscription . . . is an act initiated by a reified history,"[20] views Dorinda Outram finds reflect a "profoundly coercive understanding of physical experience."[21]

The analysis of the relationships among law, religion, and sexual morality that constitute the substance of this book is framed by these methodological assumptions: the dialectical relations between regularization, situational adjustment, and indeterminacy that inform an understanding of the processes of everyday life, where bodies are arrayed in fields of power and economies. This study spans the nearly two centuries (1550–1730) commonly associated with the Catholic Reformation.

Burgundy serves as an illuminating example for this analysis, not only because of the exceptional holdings of its archives and libraries, but also because of the influential role its powerful inhabitants played in constructing the new moral order. Staunchly Catholic since the 1560s and home to manifold royal courts, it was a prime breeding ground for the reform-minded legal community, the *robins*, that are the social focus of much of this study.

Part I, "The Order of Morality and the Morality of Order," explores the construction of authority, and part II, "The Disposition of Bodies," examines its deployment and appropriation by French men and women. The construction of authority constituted prescriptive attempts by France's increasingly powerful and dominant privileged elite to reorder their world, indeed, to restore a community that they believed had been shattered by the cosmic and mundane disorders that wracked the sixteenth century.[22] The prescriptive attempt to impose moral order upon the world entailed intellectual, religious, legal, and social aspects. This elite did not simply insist on disciplining the passions—especially the concupiscent sort—by the new ethos of civility and enhanced patriarchy within which bodies (especially female) were to be disciplined and controlled according to a social and gender hierarchy. They also negotiated power with their monarch in order to arrive at an accommodation that would ultimately benefit both themselves and their king in the shared task of fashioning a moral order desired by both.

My focus periodically narrows to the ascendant officeholders, the landed *robins*, arguably the most significant group within this dominant elite. As William Bouwsma has pointed out, in this epoch poised on the brink of chaos, law was increasingly viewed as "an antidote to disorder,"[23] and the legal community consequently assumed a prominent position among the forces of order. Paragons of law and order, and ultimately protectors of familial private property so dear to France's privileged elite, the men of the law were essential representatives of their class. They simultaneously served, in Ralph Giesey's words, as "a stabilizing element in the civil order" of France[24] and placed themselves at the frontier between the familiar and conventional world they sought to renew and the howling chaos that they feared lay just beyond it in the future. If a "sense of limit in the social universe" was achieved in French aristocratic culture in the seventeenth century,[25] the thought and behavior of the men of the legal community were in no small measure responsible for it.

In their construction of a new authoritarian moral order, France's—and Burgundy's—privileged elite, including the men of the law, embraced patriarchal intellectual and political programs (the subject of chapter 1, "The Social World and the World of Ideas"). These were inextricably tied to a religious program, that of the Catholic Reformation (the subject of chapter 2, "From the Cloister to the Street"). All three programs—intellectual, political, and religious—propounded a morality of order that rested upon the sacralization of society. Such a sacralization led layman and cleric alike to associate self-discipline and social control—in a word, order—with piety, obedience, and civility.[26] Moreover, this authoritarian ethic constructed sexuality as the epitome of disorder and subversion, a primal force to be controlled and regulated at all cost.

Part II, "The Disposition of Bodies," shifts from the world of prescription to the world of practice, of "situational adjustment" and "indeterminacy," to recall Moore's terminology. How was the order of morality, the morality of order, to be imposed? And how effectively?

The "tactics of consumption" of the resources of power—notably the law—by the common people had a great deal to do with attempted imposition. This book is less about the "success" or "failure" of the Catholic Reformation in Burgundy than the dialectical dynamics of the formulation of the new order, its attempted imposition, and the uses of the law that was so central to it.[27] Of course, in the sixteenth and seventeenth centuries there was nothing new about the desire among the elite for order, discipline, and control, or about the perceived need to regulate and control female sexuality. The influence of Saint Augustine in the Middle Ages and the Renaissance had seen to that. What was new to the early modern period was the *systematic extent* of the early modern vision and the means needed to achieve complete "reform," as well as the expectation that the traditional order could be renewed.

Clerical and lay reformers (led by the *robins*) ultimately agreed that the remaking of society must start with the reform of the parish priest. However, if prescriptive measures were clear enough—shackling the sexuality of the priest was the primary objective—putting them into practice was another matter, as chapter 3 ("The Power of the Holy: Reformers, Priests, and Parishioners") demonstrates. The reform of the priesthood took nearly two centuries, and if it is true that most priests were "reformed" by the early eighteenth century, it is also true that a persistent libidinous minority consistently escaped the strictures designed to regulate their sexual behavior in their parishes. More important, the behavior of this minority provides insights into the everyday world of Burgundians—about what power, sexuality, and holiness meant to them in their daily lives.

The new moral order focused on sexuality, and the imposition of this order involved a contest over the disposition of bodies, both male and female, arrayed in fields of power.[28] Priests' bodies were an essential target, but reformers also recognized that the moral order they envisioned rested upon the institution of marriage and the firm yoking of the *female* body to it. Moralists agreed that control of the body, especially of the female that they looked upon as the cause of sin and thus disorder, was to be achieved through sexual abstinence or strictly regulated monogamy.[29] Chapters 4 and 5 ("Marriage and the Uses of the Law: Legislation, Adjudication, and Litigation" and "Bartered Bodies: Infanticide, Lasciviousness, and Prostitution") are organized around the importance of marriage and constitutive ideas about "proper" gender relations. Chapter 4 explores, first, the formation of the patriarchal marital ethic prescribed by the dominant classes and concentrates on the role law and religion played in it. My emphasis then shifts to the world of practice, where I view law as a power resource to be used, rather than simply as a set of rules to be imposed and obeyed.[30] The question here is how and to what extent the law was appropriated by judge and litigant to achieve the various strategies each had in mind.[31] I focus on cases involving *rapt* (the abduction or seduction of a minor for purposes of clandestine marriage), the essential offense against the marital ethic and the family because it struck at patriarchy. My analysis begins with an examination of the prescriptive literature (notably legislative and juridical) on *rapt* and then shifts to the courtroom as the site where judges and litigants of *rapt* cases appropriated the law for their own purposes. The exploration of the uses of litigation then moves outside the courtroom into everyday life and probes the incorporation of the uses of litigation in the strategies of marital formation.

In chapter 5 the institution of marriage remains the central social fact, but its importance is tacit because my focus now is upon the people who for one reason or another remained outside it. The law and faith of the new morality of order and the order of morality in theory had no place for women who committed infanticide for the preservation of honor in the economy of marriage, nor for women who bartered their bodies in concubinage or prostitution because they had lost their honor and so were excluded from honorable marriage. In practice, however, society did have a place for these women in despair, and the "wages of sin" were no less a part of their calculus of survival than that of their honorable counterparts who carved a niche in marriage.

Throughout this book, a central theme is the contested disposition of bodies caught in fields of power where constant negotiation and exchange were occurring. Sexuality was central to this economy, and law and religion played paramount constitutive roles. Here the "wages of sin" were the common currency, even if what they purchased varied widely throughout Burgundian society.

I

The Order of Morality, the Morality of Order

1

The Social World and the World of Ideas

From the wreckage of the late sixteenth century, France's increasingly powerful and dominant elite embarked upon a systematic and extensive attempt to reorder its world. An authoritarian ethic emerged with the "new" order, an order whose defining and interrelated characteristics were discipline of the passions (especially concupiscent), the reinforcement of social hierarchy, and the maintenance of patriarchy. This new order was voiced in the prescriptive moralistic literature of the age and was adopted by many men, especially in the increasingly powerful and wealthy legal community. Nicolas Brulart, a distinguished and leading judge in Burgundy's Parlement (the prestigious royal court of final appeal in this large and important province) for most of the second half of the seventeenth century, illustrates quite forcefully how a *robin* might embrace and express the new order.

Brulart, First President of the Parlement of Dijon from 1657 to 1691 and author of annual harangues addressed to the legal community of Dijon in which he expressed his views on the "perfect magistrate," was influenced by the philosophy of Stoicism throughout his illustrious career. In this persuasion he was little different from his colleagues on the bench, not just in Dijon but throughout France. Many, indeed most, French parlementaires in the sixteenth and well into the seventeenth centuries had been strongly attracted to Stoicism.[1] The Stoic emphasis on self-discipline over the passions accorded well with the magistrate's concern for order, both for the individual and for society.

Tellingly, at the opening of Parlement in 1658, when Brulart addressed all of his assembled fellow parlementaires, as well as the "Magistrates of the Parquet" (the *gens du roi*), and the *avocats* and *procureurs* licensed to plead before the Parlement, he chose for his subject "the power of interior justice," a classic Stoic theme and one that penetrated the heart of the new moral order. Brulart informed his colleagues that "among the presents that God has given to man, that of interior justice is without doubt the most august and the most divine. . . . It communicates the knowledge of good and evil; it inspires the love of one and the hatred for the other. . . ; it makes known to man his duties and obligations."[2]

But Brulart did not stop with a discussion of the power and importance of self-control by the conscience. He further asserted that "there are two justices on earth, each of which has its own power, the one interior, the other exterior; the first to preserve the calm of each particular man, and the second the repose and tranquility of all men in general, the one to contain the movements of the disordered [*déréglée*] appetite [that is, the passions] before they are produced externally [in behavior], and the other for the regulation . . . of things that regard the Estates, towns, and families."[3] Moreover, he maintained that interior justice, or self-discipline, bears directly upon the exterior, or social, order. Using neoplatonic assumptions about the "sovereign authority" the divinely inspired soul has over the body, he thus reasoned that conscience "is destined to regulate the world."[4]

As was the case with all stoically inspired thinkers, for Brulart the passions posed a very real threat to the individual and to society. Brulart took the destabilizing threat of the passions as the topic of several of his addresses, including his first one as First President in 1657. While discussing "Constancy and the Strength of Courage," he told his fellow magistrates that "the passions . . . seduce man with such force that the light [of reason] is often eclipsed . . . throwing him . . . into disorder and confusion." Justice and the magistrate, however, make war against the passions. Guided by prudence (the "essence of . . . reason" which in turn is "the eye by which the soul distinguishes the true from the false"), justice "comes to [man's] aid to calm this disorder."[5]

So grave did Brulart consider the problem of the passions that he returned to it in 1664 and again in 1681. In 1664, he singled out harnessing the passions as one of the "Combats du Juge," the title of his harangue, and he once again enlisted the Stoic characteristic of prudence in the task.[6] In a 1681 speech defending the hierarchical nature of civil society, he was still concerned about the disorder of passion that threatened it, and to urge *avocats* to do their part, he informed them that their essential function was to counsel reason over passion to their clients.[7]

Order in society was clearly an overriding concern for Judge Brulart, and as the champions of justice, magistrates were warriors for the cause of order. Indeed, he said as much in a harangue in 1678: "jurisprudence . . . is based on the love of order."[8] However much Brulart's ideas on order were informed by his intellectual formation or by his vocation, they were also deeply conditioned by his social station. Honor, hierarchy, social distinction, rank, precedence, *honnêteté*, *bienséance*, and obedience are concepts that continually appear in Brulart's harangues as well as in his letters.[9] Honor was the coin of the realm for all social groups, and the possession of it was clearly of paramount importance to the privileged classes in general and the *robins* in particular. Honor was obtained in a ritualized exchange of recognition of status and was fundamental to both an individual's sense of identity and his place in a sharply stratified society.[10] It is scarcely surprising, then, to find Brulart and others of his social status deeply preoccupied with their honor and its relationship to hierarchical rank and precedence, or that this preoccupation with honor and rank would profoundly stamp their morality of order.

What might appear to modern eyes to be a petty obsession with minor ceremonial detail was of capital significance to men of the *grand siècle*. Consider, for example, the nature of the questions that the inaugural First President of the Parlement of Besançon asked of Brulart in 1679 shortly after Louis XIV created that Parlement. First President Jobelot wanted to know what "the difference [was] between the clothing of the First President and that of the Seconds." This was followed immediately by a question about when hats worn by the parlementaires in session should be removed in honor of the First President. Brulart answered these and 29 other questions meticulously and with apparent deep sincerity.[11]

Ceremonial detail and the all-important perception of honor, rank, and precedence were also at the center of the protracted dispute between Brulart and the *Lieutenant du Roi* d'Amanzé. In 1658, the newly appointed First President Brulart fired off letters to *secrétaires d'état* Chevalier and LaVrillière at the royal court the day after d'Amanzé had deeply offended Brulart by standing at an inappropriate place in Sainte-Chapelle in Dijon during the obsequies for the deceased nephew of His Eminence Cardinal Mazarin, young Louis XIV's first minister. Indeed, d'Amanzé stood in the place that had always been reserved for the king in absentia, and not even royal governors of Burgundy had dared occupy the place in the past. Brulart no doubt was offended personally (he had a very high opinion of the status of First President, and in other letters he made it clear that he deemed it superior to that of the *Lieutenant du Roi*), but he also took umbrage for the Parlement as a whole. D'Amanzé may have been the *Lieutenant du Roi*, but he also was a *Chevalier d'honneur* in the Parlement (and thus inferior to the First President), and Brulart convened all the Chambers immediately to censure d'Amanzé for his "disorder" and "disobedience," which they did.[12] D'Amanzé might have been under the authority of Brulart as a member of the Parlement, but as *Lieutenant du Roi* he wore another hat that, in his mind, ranked him superior to the First President. As Brulart's correspondence with the *secretaires d'état* chronicle, Brulart's and d'Amanzé's dispute over rank was not settled in 1658; indeed, it was still going on in 1674![13]

Brulart's views on honor ran deep precisely because of his sense of order, and this sense of order was intricately interwoven with his judicial, social, even religious and political ideals. All of his harangues in some way touch on these ideals, but none so succinctly and forcefully as that given in 1675 entitled "De L'honnêteté et de la bienséance."[14] Men, he preached, are bound to one another "by a reciprocal commerce of duties," and this social bond is expressed in actions which are "grouped under the name of *honnêteté* and *bienséance.*" *Bienséance* is the spirit of moderation and love of reason that animates virtue, "that elevates and refines in its taste," and *honnêteté*, a quality of the individual of taste and "the brake of the passions," is the virtue that serves as "the foundation of reputation." Brulart moves easily from a social ethic of hierarchy and distinction to his authoritarian juridical and political views when he asserts that the rules of *bienséance* and *honnêteté* "consist principally in the accomplishment of duties," and "the first [in importance] of all is to win esteem because without it authority is enfeebled and dishonored." Furthermore, justice "enlists the aid of *bienséance* and *honnêteté*," and indeed, so does politics and religion. All are bound in a "narrow alliance" with reason and all seek the same goal: a rightly ordered world.

The World in Disorder

By the second half of the seventeenth century the construction of the authoritarian ethic of the new morality of order so well expressed by Brulart, in large measure a response to perceptions of disorder, was effectively complete. For more than a century before, however, perceptions of disorder by society's elite classes were pervasively voiced. Shrill at times, especially from the early sixteenth century through the mid-seventeenth, the alarm over cosmic and mundane disorder was nearly constant in the minds of the dominant wielders of power in society. Fearing they lived in a "contradictory, uncertain, deceptive, and radically insecure world," these baroque elites had a vested interest in putting the world "right" again, at least as they saw it.[15]

What had gone wrong? The Protestant Reformation sundered a united Christendom, and into the breech after 1560 Calvin sent forth his pastors and Satan unleashed his minions, the witches. French judges combated the plague of witchcraft with a legally sanctioned witch hunt (which continued to the mid-seventeenth century), while French Catholics struggled to repel the Huguenot incursion with military force—both judges and Catholics acting in the name of "right order." Many were sure that God's inevitable punishment for such chaotic disunity among His creatures would be the unbridling of the four horsemen of the apocalypse upon the world. Pestilence and dearth were indeed no strangers to France's populace, nor were war and death. The Reformation contributed to the Wars of Religion in France, which doubled as a civil war that raged over the last third of the sixteenth century.

Disorder came in other forms. The horsemen of the apocalypse not only evidenced God's wrath, but also played havoc with the demographic experience of sixteenth- and seventeenth-century French men and women. The population of Burgundy, for example, had been growing since the late fifteenth century and would continue to expand into the seventeenth, but sometime in the 1530s the threshold of poverty began to rise and with it came a swelling of the ranks of vagrants, an expansion that continued intermittently throughout the seventeenth century. The records of town councils are replete with deliberations concerning the threat vagrancy posed to the security of person and property alike.

The Wars of Religion of the sixteenth century and then the invasions by Imperial forces fighting in the Thirty Years' War in the 1630s generated a crisis in the province, stripping the villages of their productive capacity and of their male heads of households, leaving widows, beggars, and transient day laborers to form an estimated 80 percent of the rural population by 1650.[16] Crowds of these rootless people drifted into towns, prompting town councils to issue ordinances aimed to control their flow. Such regulations enjoyed limited success, and the population of indigents in towns periodically swelled.

Town councils responded to the problem of poverty by treating vagrants more severely, perhaps influenced by the recommendations of the Estates General of 1614. The deputies associated indigence and homelessness with criminal activity, demanding that "purse snatchers, thieves, vagabonds, and anyone without a residence or an occupation be branded and marked with the fleur-de-lis, and be condemned to the galleys for five years upon the first offense, and hanged by the neck until dead for the second offense."[17] Such draconian demands notwithstanding, in the sixteenth and early seventeenth centuries indigents were usually expelled from towns. As late as 1626, Dijon attempted to distinguish between worthy and unworthy indigents, lodging the former at Saint-Esprit hospital and, with the help of guards known as the *chasse-coquins* (rogue hunters), expelling the latter. But after 1650 vagrants, though not branded or hanged as the deputies in 1614 had demanded, were often flogged and imprisoned.[18]

Person and property (of society's upper classes) were also threatened by rural and urban revolts that punctuated the sixteenth and seventeenth centuries, often provoked by economic tensions and aggravated by political developments. In the sixteenth century, the economic distress and social conflict that inflation and a widening gap between rich and poor encouraged was compounded by the political chaos unleashed by the Wars of Religion. In the seventeenth century, the taxation policies of the authoritarian state contributed to a wave of rebellions that have been studied in depth by many historians.[19]

If for many people the disorders of the sixteenth and seventeenth centuries entailed material deprivation, for others they offered opportunity. France's—and Burgundy's—economy was being increasingly commercialized, integrated, and centered in cities. The resultant urbanization of the economy provided a context for some people to experience social mobility.[20] Yet urbanization and social mobility met with disapproval in the abundant prescriptive literature authored by philosophers, men of letters, playwrights, novelists, preachers, bishops, and a host of others.[21] These moralists voiced the concerns of the members of society's dominant classes who had a vested interest in order and a fixed hierarchy, despite the paradoxical fact that upwardly mobile families were continually replenishing the ranks of these same classes. Expanding cities were *démesurées* and difficult to control,[22] and the same was being said about upwardly mobile families.

To sixteenth- and seventeenth-century men, then, there was no shortage of phenomena upsetting the imagined equilibrium of right order. Learned males (the masculine must be emphasized here because prescriptive literature voicing these views was almost entirely penned by men, and gender, as we will see, was an important constitutive factor in this ideology of order) longed for a past they believed had existed but which was, in fact, a mythical golden age. This golden age supposedly was characterized by a cosmic, divinely sanctioned hierarchical structure securing the peaceful social relationships that defined the Christian community.

The chaos of the sixteenth and early seventeenth centuries appeared to fracture those peaceful relationships, and into the void left by a shattered community entered "dissociated man,"[23] an unintended consequence first given voice by Michel de Montaigne. Many men, consequently, felt that cultural boundaries were needed to structure the new pattern of human relations, indeed, to protect men from one another. Thus, as William Bouwsma has noted, "much of the worldly wisdom of the early modern age was directed to building fences," to "renewing a sense of limit in the social universe."[24] If the stated goal was shoring up the supposed boundaries of traditional society, the consequence was a new system of order with a new authoritarian definition of the nature of the community, and of the role that church, king, and magistrate would play in it.

The febrile reorientation of world views occurring in the sixteenth and seventeenth centuries reveals a collapse of cultural boundaries, of systems of order, that no longer rendered satisfying meaning to life. The perceived destruction of traditional community-oriented social relationships was one such collapse, but the assault occurred on the intellectual plane too, and prompted men to reorient their entire world view, to recast in important respects the very meaning of order itself. The early modern period witnessed a compulsion for order, but in the sixteenth century intellectual traditions no less than traditional social structures were beginning to disintegrate.

During the sixteenth century relativism made inroads into commonplace norms, nowhere more tellingly, and for our purposes more significantly given our emphasis upon the importance of law, than in French legal scholarship. The onslaught of relativist legal scholarship disseminated widely by printing was corrosive to a traditional normative view of the world. Relativist scholarship undercut assumptions about the universality of Roman law (a position that took well over a century to reestablish), while printing created an information explosion that threatened to scatter the traditional storehouse of knowledge "into decontextualized bits of information" which encouraged the development of new forms of ordering experience.[25]

Innovations in science, as is well known, offered one possibility of re-orientation, but if science championed a boundless confidence in human reason, its new practitioners also probed a universe whose dimensions were unknown and whose immensity Kepler called a "secret hidden horror."[26] All in all, educated men increasingly doubted the validity or even the existence of the boundaries that had given meaning to their traditional cultural experience.

In the sixteenth century, the search for meaning and security was rooted, as Foucault has pointed out, in a fundamental assumption that "each particular similitude was . . . lodged within [an] overall relation," in "a total system of correspondence."[27] This epistemological edifice, however, began to crack under the weight of the lists and compilations that, in the face of the threat to traditional means of ascertaining proof, were expanding interminably. This way of knowing was gradually supplanted in the seventeenth century by an epistemology that emphasized differentiation within an overarching order. But if identity was now defined in terms of difference rather than resemblance, each differentiated unit was still assumed to have its prescribed place in the order of things.[28]

This new epistemology of order mirrored thinking about the social order. The emphasis on difference within a structured order applied as equally to ideas as to "dissociated" individuals. Emerging from a century where the traditional verities—be they social or intellectual—were being challenged, men were confronted with the task of reordering existence, and part of the result was an authoritarian mind set galvanizing a new morality of order and a new order of morality.

Disciplining the Passions, From Stoicism to Civility

Systems of order possess their own suppositions of justification, of rectitude, and thus are inextricably linked with systems of morality and power. Because such systems are cultural constructions, the definition of moralities of order and orders of morality have historical dimensions. Indeed, from the mid-sixteenth to the early eighteenth century, they were defined and deployed within a constellation of power that found church and state (abstractions populated and energized by society's dominant classes) attempting to "purify the city of God on earth," in the name, of course, of right order.[29]

From the sixteenth to the seventeenth century, France witnessed a gradual transition from one system of order to another, the latter exhibiting profoundly authoritarian characteristics. Discipline was a byword of the renewed morality of order, and fundamentally, the passions and by association women were deemed most in need of discipline. Moralists, whose writings cut a broad swath through the literature of early modern France, never tired of reducing the disparate ills of the grand siècle to the uncontrolled passions of men incited by women. Indeed, most of the moralists were men who often singled out women in need of "reform."

This gender distinction and the pervasiveness of the moralists' lexicon of discipline, hierarchy, and purity suggest a growing concern for boundary marking and boundary transgression. They testify to Bouwsma's observations about the sense of confusion that attended the collapse of traditional cultural boundaries and the attempt to shore them up. As Mary Douglas has noted,

> Ideas about separating, purifying, demarcating and punishing transgressions have as their main function to impose system on an inherently untidy experience. It is only by exaggerating the difference between within and without, above and below, male and female, with and against, that a semblance of order is created. . . . The only way in which pollution ideas make sense is in reference to a total structure of thought whose keystone, boundaries, margins and internal lines are held in relation by rituals of separation.[30]

Indeed, the polarities of high and low, male and female, pure and impure, were essential to the masculine morality of order, because the fiction of a fixed social hierarchy was predicated upon assumptions held by early modern men about unequal gender relations.[31] This is why human passions were of such concern to moralists: they were the wellspring of disorder.

In their association of passions with women, moralists assumed that the passions were concupiscent.[32] If this was the primary meaning moralists ascribed to the word in the seventeenth century, however, it had not always been so. In fact, one searches in vain among sixteenth-century texts for an amorous connotation of the term. Sentiment and emotion, yes, but always as sadness, shame, fear, suffering, pain, or affliction.[33] In the early seventeenth century, with the new authoritarian morality of order taking shape, passion continued to refer to sentiment, but now it also included prominent reference to the invariably destructive and disorderly "concupiscent appetite." Later in the seventeenth century and early into the eighteenth century, the semantics of passion may have been nuanced, but with the important concepts of hierarchy, order, and purity were still present. *Belle passion* emerged to describe "faithful, constant, and proper [*honneste*] love," but *passion sale* (filthy) remained in the traditional understanding of the term as "blind, brutal, [and] unregulated [*désreglées*], . . . that which has for its goal bodily pleasures."[34]

If the semantics of passion diversified from 1550 to 1730, so too did ideas concerning what to do *about* the passions, ranging from firm repression by reason, to regulating them to achieve a natural balance between them and reason. As Brulart so clearly reflects for the late seventeenth century, the disciplining of the passions took place on two interrelated fronts that were internal and external to the individual. Even in the sixteenth century, when passions were not associated with amorous sentiment, they were still considered destructive, and Neostoic philosophy counseled disciplining them by reason to attain a "good ordering of the soul [that] . . . provides internal harmony and outward tranquility."[35]

During the seventeenth century moralists like the novelist Madame de La Fayette still assumed that the well-ordered soul mastered the destructive passions, although now she like so many others of her time unmistakably linked passion with amorous sentiment.[36] The Princess of Cleves' mother's response to her daughter's confession of love for the Duke of Nemours illustrates this linkage explicitly, as does the princess's behavior by the end of the novel: "My dear, you are on the brink of a precipice. To keep yourself from going over, great moral constraint is required. Think of what you owe to your husband; think, my sweet, of what you owe to yourself. Reflect on the reputation you stand to lose—a reputation patiently formed and so much desired by me."[37] By the end of the novel, the princess "at last has overwhelmed her enemy—passion" by realizing her love for Nemours will destroy her, and that her "peace of mind depends upon duty."[38]

Moralists of the late seventeenth and early eighteenth century, some of them contemporaries of Brulart and La Fayette, shared these views about the destructive nature of amorous passion. The preacher Vincent Houdry, for instance, asserted that "our passions are the cause of all our disorder because it is from them that comes our unfortunate penchant toward evil."[39]

In the early eighteenth century, as the sermon "The Art of Healing the Passions" by Louis Maimbourg demonstrates, the passions were still deemed destructive, but they were also more openly recognized as a natural phenomenon.[40] In describing the symptoms of the "illness" of passion, Maimbourg sounds the dominant themes of the seventeenth century, but his diagnosis finds greater room for passion in the healthy body than had his predecessors. The affliction sounds bad enough: "See a shameless woman, that brutal and sensual love has enflamed and burned with this fire that concupiscence has ignited and the demon of impurity has fanned with his breath; what horrible ravage has been done to her. This passion? It is an ardent fever that has . . . stripped her of . . . reason and pushed her by a thousand extravagances to the furthest extremities, with the loss of her honor, her goods, her body, her soul, and her salvation." Indeed, in employing a medical metaphor Maimbourg preached that uncontrolled passion is a malady of the soul, akin to fever that afflicts the body: "What heat is to the body, love is to our soul"; but he also asserts that balance is the key to health in both. Consequently, Maimbourg, like many other moralists of the early eighteenth century, more readily accepted the view that the passions had a place in a universal order. The passions were less vilified than before, although they continued to be ruled by a sovereign intelligence, granted "a sort of conditional freedom [*une sorte de liberté surveillé*]."[41]

In the late French Renaissance, in the face of the violence and chaos unleashed by the Wars of Religion, stoicism emerged as the dominant intellectual stance of educated men, especially the officeholding groups.[42] Neostoicism, as Oestreich has observed, was an authoritarian political and social ethic, advocating the use of force in the maintenance of order while simultaneously promoting a moral education demanding obedience from the ruled and self-discipline and dutifulness from ruler and ruled alike.[43] The stoic thus yearned to attain constancy in the internal and external dimensions of his life, and so distanced himself from the passions he believed had engendered discord and sedition. By employing the art of prudence, the stoic sage harnessed his passions to reason and self-control.

For authoritarian moralists intent upon shoring up a system of order with an ethnic of discipline, one solution was the stoic appeal to reason to regulate the passions by means of self-control. Such stoic assumptions were alive and well in the second half of the seventeenth century. Jacques-Bénigne Bossuet, in his *Traité de la concupiscence*, was most fearful of the destructive consequences of lust, which he believed always lurked in the passions,[44] and he continued to champion the power of reason over them. God made man a reasonable creature, he argued, and even after original sin had "unleashed the passions and rendered necessary the establishment of positive laws," these laws had no other role than to restore reason to its full effectiveness: "All laws are based on the first of all laws, which is that of nature, that is to say on right reason."[45]

Stoicism inspired moralistic condemnation of the passions; it also contributed to the formation of the courtier and the doctrine of *honnêteté*. Indeed, as Brulart so clearly illustrates, ideas about disciplining the passions and *honnêteté*—and, indeed, the emergent code of civility—were closely related. The "civilizing process" was marked by a sharpening perception of the difference between the elite and the vulgar (its essential function was to validate social hierarchy), a difference that had as its characteristic mark the repression of man's animality.[46]

Reminiscent of Brulart's harangues on justice, hierarchy, and self-control, this code of civility simultaneously legislated interior and exterior surveillance. It demanded self-restraint of the emotions and scorned uncontrolled passion and unbridled comportment of the body by the individual. It likewise enlisted society's elites to adhere to the code that proclaimed their social distinction. The *savoir-vivre* of civility was embodied in the social ethic of *honnêteté* which, though it underwent some changes, was at bottom throughout the grand siècle consistently predicated upon the control of self, demanding discipline by which the interior being, the conscience, was balanced by the social self.

Honnêteté spread from the court to the town via civility manuals and treatises which assumed unprecedented popularity and importance in seventeenth-century France. As the century progressed, these works prescribed with increasing precision the acceptable modes of dress, actions, and language for men and women in high society (*du monde*). These manuals persistently associated erect posture and cleanliness with decency, purity, and honor, consigning poor posture and uncleanliness to the world of animality, indecency, and impurity.[47] Such binary categorization rendered the presumed necessary task of making social distinction (inclusion and exclusion) straightforward, and Saint-Evremond could succinctly write that the *honnête homme* is the man who cultivates "true honor that regulates the conduct of reasonable persons."[48] Because civility manuals highlight boundary transgression by stipulating gestures of separation, classifying, and cleansing,[49] however, they also permit us to interpret them as rulebooks marking the cultural boundaries of a new moral system.

The ethic of *honnêteté* and the attendant code of civility radiated from the court to the cities and châteaux of the realm.[50] There can be little doubt that court, city, and château were in constant communication—witness the letters of Madame de Sévigné, Roger de Bussy-Rabutin, or Brulart, to take prominent Burgundian examples—with the court having an educative function.[51]

The ethic of *honnêteté* and the *civilisation des moeurs* may have been propelled by developments at court, but its strictures became deeply implanted in the French system of education and, as such, influenced the world view of the highly educated legal community.[52] By 1690, Furétière could write in his *Dictionnaire universel* that "the badly taught youth is the one who is crude, rustic, and uncivil; well taught when he has *honnêteté*, when he knows how to live well."[53] Clearly, civility was a central part of good education, and good education was imparted via simplified variants of civility manuals.

Two such books used in Burgundy in the late seventeenth century, probably in the *colleges* and primary schools, were the *Roti-Cochon, ou méthode très-facile pour bien apprendre les enfans* and *Civilité puérile et morale, pour instruire les enfans à se bien comporter.*[54] As their titles make clear, the moral lessons in these tracts were inseparable from the practical intention of offering reading and writing instruction. Boys were expected to internalize the ethic of *honnêteté*, and stoically inspired counsel about restraining the concupiscent appetite was, as the *Civilité puérile* illustrates, prominent and fundamental. In the interest of "guarding [their] reputations," boys were instructed to "with prudence restrain your concupiscent impulses."[55]

The new order of morality and the morality of order that took shape in the late sixteenth and seventeenth centuries fundamentally concerned an authoritarian ethic of discipline of the passions. Guided by an intense distrust of concupiscence, moralists defined an ethic of *honnêteté* that demanded self-control, that was codified by social comportment, and that affirmed an increasingly hierarchical society. The "tasteful" behavior of *honnêtes hommes* and *femmes* visibly demonstrated the emergent society of "dissociation and difference" while proclaiming the exclusionary and superior status of a self-defined privileged class.[56]

Women and Patriarchy

The concepts of discipline of the passions and hierarchy so crucial to the new morality of order were central to ideas about civility. The hierarchical and authoritarian patriarchal family, sacralized by the Tridentine church and enhanced by royal authority, was the crucible of this revolution in behavior.[57] Indeed, from 1550 to 1730 it was commonly argued in the prescriptive literature—from political theory to moralistic tracts, to theological, medical, and legal treatises inspired by Roman law—that the patriarchal family unit was the microcosm of the well-ordered commonwealth.

The justification for male domination within the family and thus in the commonwealth offered by male writers echoes many of the topics I have already discussed. As mentioned, most of the moralists singled out women of unbridled passions as the primary culprits for a fundamental disorder plaguing contemporary society. Consequently, most of these moralists, and they certainly were not alone, concluded that it was above all women who needed to be disciplined. These men regarded gender as one of the elemental signs of hierarchical distinction that formed the bedrock of the new hierarchical, dissociated society.[58] Joan Scott has suggested that "conceptual languages employ differentiation to establish meaning and that sexual difference is a primary way of signifying differentiation." Consequently, "gender is a primary way of signifying relationships of power." However, in order to legitimize a given distribution of power, the reference of gender relations to power "must seem sure and fixed, part of the natural or divine order. In that way, the binary opposition and the social process of gender relationships both become part of the meaning of power itself; to question or alter any aspect threatens the entire system."[59]

The fiction of a fixed and sharply differentiated social hierarchy was predicated upon assumptions held by early modern men about unequal gender relations. Furthermore, the human (frequently female) body often served as the medium for translating the all-important hierarchical concepts (high and low, pure and indecent) among social, political, and religious ideologies, thus knitting them all together in a mutually supportive moralistic system. That moralists assumed a hierarchical gender differentiation and employed a vocabulary of purity, discipline, and hierarchy in their works, then, is highly significant.

Women, it hardly needs to be said, were denied formal access to power, and were usually portrayed as "unruly" in the patriarchal prescriptive literature of the period. As Natalie Davis has observed, "as a member of the less worthy sex in a hierarchical society, as a member of the disorderly sex, whose wet bodily humors and wandering womb would weaken her will and her mind (so physicians and theologians said), she was required to undertake no actions without her spouse's permission."[60]

Medical and theological as well as moralistic discourse voiced suspicion about female unruliness. This suspicion had it roots in a longstanding struggle in Western philosophy between the passions and reason. Because the irrationality of the sexual act fundamentally threatens a system of order predicated upon rational self-control, asceticism was one time-honored solution to the disorder of passion in Christian society, and so it continued to be in the seventeenth century, not without good cause sometimes called "the century of saints." Since all humans obviously cannot pursue a fully ascetic life, organized monogamy was an attenuated and alternative solution to controlling the primal urges of the body.[61] Beginning in the second half of the sixteenth century and continuing for more than a hundred years, both religious asceticism and an emphasis upon the importance of marriage (and fidelity within it) were enhanced and found a central place in the new morality of order.

As will be seen in chapter 4, the institution of marriage assumed greater importance in the increasingly stratified hierarchical order fashioned by the privileged classes. Marriage perpetuated status by bequeathing to offspring recognizable rank, thereby enabling a clear stratification of society, arguably the most pressing concern of society's privileged groups.[62] Furthermore, marriages were the centerpieces of familial strategies designed to protect and expand the all-important patrimony. Consequently, as Sarah Hanley has convincingly argued, "the most pressing business [for privileged families] was the maintenance and extension of family networks, which were agencies of both social reproduction and economic production; and the negotiation of proper marriage alliances, crucial to that endeavor, depended on effective [paternal] authority."[63]

Thus we return to patriarchy: imperatives of social order demanded that marriage formation be controlled by the father and that fidelity within the union be respected. The supposed passionate and disorderly nature of the female threatened to disrupt this order by interfering with the process of hereditary status and the devolution of property, and so the hierarchical patriarchal family that disciplined the unruly members was quite literally sanctioned. "Marriage engaged the future of society and of the family; in it the divine mixed with the human, the civil with the religious; the union of the spouses was sacralized by rites, their choice ordered by the social milieu, their behavior imposed by moral rules or religious beliefs."[64]

A tract published in 1667 called *Dialogue de l'amour et de la raison* encapsulates this conflict between reason and passion within the context of marital formation. The argument that Reason presents in the dialogue embodies the "structural demands" of privileged society.[65] Reason has two issues to defend: a father's control over the marriage of his offspring, and the prevention of misalliances (inter-class unions). Love, in contrast, argues that choice should rest with the future partners even if the resulting unions obliterate social differences. To Reason, Love's grounds for marriage are an open invitation to violence and disorder, and the tract abruptly ends with Reason's indignant dismissal of Love's position.[66]

Much patriarchal prescriptive literature demanding the disciplining of women was disseminated during the grand siècle. Yet simultaneously and seemingly paradoxically, salons championed a public role for women as arbiters of taste. By finding a place in society for women outside of the home and even marriage, salons ostensibly undermined the patriarchal order, or at least exposed an ambivalence in it, a point I will return to shortly.[67] The salonnières openly advocated social advancement,[68] and they might have had something to do with the genesis of feminism in a later century.[69] It is equally true, however, that, within the context of the seventeenth century, the feminine position in the *querelle des femmes* did not challenge the essential principle of the patriarchal order, that of social stratification. Indeed, as arbiters of taste, salonnières affirmed the emerging moral order based on discipline of the passions and self-control. As MacLean has pointed out, "the salon's members were a self-confessed elite, separated from the *vulgaire* by a bastion of purified language and by a barrier of allusions . . . fiercely intent on the preservation of their self-created world of refinement, taste, and sensibility."[70]

A Dominant Burgundian Elite, The Landed Robins

A dominant privileged elite emerged in the second half of the sixteenth century and, in the midst of a perceived collapse of the traditional way of life, embarked on a search for a more meaningful and satisfying understanding of the world. A new morality of order and order of morality resulted, systems of thought and behavior whose contours became quite distinct by the second half of the seventeenth century (and would last for about another century). A sharply stratified social and gender hierarchy, dissociation and difference, discipline of the lustful passions, self-control, and an enhanced patriarchy marked this new world view.

But who constituted this privileged elite? Generally speaking, it was legal professionals, merchants, financiers, seigneurial and court aristocrats, officeholders, and members of the high clergy. Although it may be misleading to imply that these groups were rigorously or categorically distinct,[71] the role of the legal community deserves to be highlighted. As many historians have asserted, this social group assumed increasing importance in fashioning the social and political prescriptive universe of early modern France.

For Burgundy, Gaston Roupnel convincingly demonstrated years ago that a class of "gentlemen administrators" emerged in the late sixteenth and seventeenth centuries.[72] This group was partly comprised of upwardly mobile families from throughout the province. It also included some families from the rural nobility, however, that had lost social prestige and fortune in the turbulent fifteenth and early sixteenth centuries, only to regain status in the late sixteenth or seventeenth century by way of holding office, eventually for some in the prestigious Parlement or the Chambre des Comptes. This class was concentrated in the towns, notably Dijon, but as we will see, this core of the dominant elite in Burgundy was an officeholding class that had many of the traditional characteristics of the French nobility, specifically possession of land.

The transfer of enfeoffed property (acquisition of a seigneurie may not have guaranteed nobility but it did guarantee familial ascension) began in the fifteenth century (before then, opportunities for acquiring land were rare) and continued through the seventeenth. It was during the second half of the sixteenth century, however, that transfers were most advantageous and numerous. It was then that the *robins* of urban Burgundy, especially the Dijonnais, began a "conquest" of the countryside that would profoundly alter how people conceived of order and power in the province.[73]

Dijonnais citizens (mostly *robins* but some merchants and well-off artisans) became the owners of almost all of the land in the bailliage of Dijon, but the parlementaires also purchased property in all parts of the province and even made acquisitions in Champagne and Imperial Franche-Comté.[74] Not accidentally, the largest landholders were also the dominant parlementary families of the seventeenth century—Brulart, Bouhier, Desbarres, Maillard, Fremyot, Baillet, Joly, Gagne, Sayve, Berbisey. These leading families may have led the way, but all the great *robin* families had a substantial investment in the countryside. In 1666, for example, of the 74 members of the Parlement of Dijon, only 6 had no land in the Dijonnais, but these 6 owned substantial domains elsewhere in Burgundy.[75]

Large landholdings were sources of financial gain and political power, but no family stood alone.[76] Through networks of alliances, power and wealth were immeasurably enhanced. Marriages, of course, united families and patrimonies, and patronage and clientage secured more or less dependable loyalties. Financial relations also contributed to the networks of power and wealth. Loans, gifts, *rentes*, and land purchases and sales bound families in reciprocal fashion.[77]

Furthermore, the colonization of religious establishments secured familial networks that paid handsome financial dividends. For example, at the prestigious Sainte-Chapelle and the Benedictine monastery of Saint Bénigne in Dijon, each clerical "seat" carried a special benefice that continued to be handed down within the invariably *robin* family that had first received it.[78]

Many of Dijon's and Burgundy's abbeys and monasteries, like Saint Etienne in Dijon, Notre-Dame in Beaune, Saint Georges in Chalon-sur-Saône, and Saint Pierre in Mâcon, as well as, of course, Cîteaux and Cluny, had been large landholders since the Middle Ages. Like *robin* families, they also seized the opportunity to acquire more land in the early modern period and, in addition, they received foundations from leading *robin* families. Religious inspiration might have been the source of these donations, but as gifts there also must have been an expectation of reciprocity, which might well have come in the form of reserving a place for a son or daughter, or the provision of credit. Many of these religious houses served as rudimentary banks, providing *rentes constituées* to *robins* and thus facilitating the flow of capital.[79] Religious houses, therefore, were intricately connected to the networks, fundamentally familial, that knitted the *robins* into a dominant class of land- and officeholders.

The *robins*, as mentioned previously, accelerated their pace of land acquisition in the late sixteenth century. Rural impoverishment, peasant and communal indebtedness resulting from population growth, and the Wars of Religion catalyzed this opportunity, and the crisis in Burgundy that resulted from the invasions and pillaging that wracked the province from 1632 to 1655 prolonged the conditions of misery and economic opportunism.[80] A massive transfer of property resulted. In the first half of the seventeenth century, Burgundy—like Languedoc—witnessed a "triumph of rent" as wealth was channeled from the countryside to the town.[81] The flow continued throughout the century, but with the cessation of disorder in the 1650s an agricultural restoration was promoted by the urban-based *robin* landholders, by which the countryside was repopulated, vine cultivation extended, and livestock increased.[82]

The restoration was really a refeudalization of the countryside, and a more efficient feudalism at that. The new seigneurs embarked on a more efficient extraction of traditional dues (*droits*). As *robins*, they knew the law much better than their dues-paying subordinates and so enforced their demands mercilessly in court. For families like the Bouhier, then, the seigneurial domain became a major source of revenue. For many families, the acquisition of the fief was a steppingstone to the acquisition of office.

Dijon had long been a magnet for aspiring provincial families, but its attraction was dramatically enhanced in the sixteenth century because of the plenitude of offices for sale there, from presidencies and above all councillorships in the Parlement or Chambre des Comptes to the office of bailiff (*huissier*) and simple solicitor (*procureur*). Venality might have been considered a bane to many (of the complaints drawn up by the members of the Estates General at Blois in 1588, nearly 100 articles from all three estates complained of the useless multiplicity of offices),[83] but for families on the make it was certainly a blessing. Most aspirants, many of whom were local officeholders, especially in the bailliages, came from smaller towns in Burgundy—Beaune, Vitteaux, Chalon-sur-Saône, Mâcon, Seurre, Nuits Saint-Georges, Saulieu, Châtillon-sur-Seine—indeed, most of the province's wealthy families eventually were attracted to the capital city.[84] Most provincial families could not afford the price of the most prestigious offices (a *Président à Mortier* at the Parlement officially fetched 120,000 *livres* in 1665,[85] but they could at least establish themselves in Dijon by purchasing a lesser office, say a simple solicitorship (the number of *procureurs* practicing in Dijon quintupled between 1500 and 1587),[86] and then begin an ascent that might take generations to complete. Over time, veritable dynasties among the men of the law were established, as sons, nephews, and grandsons populated its ranks.

The legal community in Dijon was tightly knit by familial interest accomplished first by venality and then by marital and hereditary practices.[87] Ralph Giesey has suggested that its male members also experienced a similar education that further validated this group's feeling as a dominant force in society.[88] Sons of parlementaires, for example, destined to inherit their father's office, were often brought up and educated with this career trajectory in mind.[89] Once their formal education was completed, these men often continued to hone their intellectual stance in salons, like the one hosted by the royal councillor and advocate (*avocat*) Lantin in the seventeenth century or by the nationally renowned President Bouhier in the eighteenth. Other councillors at the Parlement, *maîtres* from the Chambre des Comptes, *avocats-généraux*, and *trésoriers*, would gather and discuss philosophical, theological, scientific, political, and of course legal issues of the day.[90] With such cultural reinforcement, it is no wonder that many *robins* displayed a sense of identity that was vocationally and familially based but that also placed men of law in an exalted position in society.[91]

It is hardly surprising that this sense of self-exaltation would be expressed in a world view that was authoritarian and that placed the *robins* in a prominent position in the new order. As stated earlier, Nicolas Brulart, the First President of Burgundy's Parlement for most of the reign of Louis XIV, had much to say about the nature of authority in a hierarchical world, and the logic of his legal paradigm was absolutist. But what exactly he and his fellow *robins* meant by absolutism, and what role they saw themselves as playing, warrants brief discussion.

Given what I have said about his views on hierarchical order and authority, it may be surprising to find that in 1658 Brulart, First President for only a year then, delivered a harangue (as was customary) to the king as Louis presided at a *lit de justice* forcing the Parlement to register several edicts that created new offices in Burgundy (even within the Parlement).[92] In his harangue, Brulart boldly opposed the royal will and earned an exile from his own court for incurring the wrath of the "sun king."

Brulart's resistance, of course, was prompted specifically by his and his fellow officeholders' opposition to the expansion of venality, because it depressed the monetary value of existing offices. More generally, however, he objected to a violation of corporate prerogatives and privileges, and in this he was typical of provincial parlementaires throughout the realm. As Beik has noted for Languedoc, "parlementaires thought of themselves as defenders of provincial liberties and monitors of local life in the name of the king . . . [but sovereign courts were] concentrations of individuals who combined personal authority, manifested through client ties and the control of seigneuries or investments, with corporate power expressed through the companies' vast influence."[93] Such was also the case in Burgundy.

But if this was so, how do we account for Brulart's reinstatement by Louis, and further, by the growing esteem the king had for him? Brulart's harangues do preach the values of obedience to authority, and they incorporate a system of delegation of power from the king.[94] One perhaps too simple answer is that the Parlement of Burgundy was vanquished by the juggernaut of centralist absolutism. After all, the Parlement of Paris and that of Languedoc moved in a similar direction in their relations with the monarchy, from opposition to apparent submission around 1660.[95] Such a reading, however, as both Beik and Hamscher caution us, would badly misinterpret the nature of political culture in the Old Regime. As Beik puts it,

> Louis XIV's great "contagion of obedience" was the result, not of repression, but of a more successful defense of ruling class interests, through collaboration and improved direction. . . . Both the king and his landed aristocracy were exploring ways of defending their interests in a changing world without, at the same time, undermining them. . . . Out of the multitude of proclamations, deliberations, acts, petitions, and denunciations issued by all the major authorities . . . emerges a sort of unwritten

program, or at least a set of aspirations. Let the king symbolize magnifi-
cently the unity of this patriotic, Catholic, hierarchically ordered polity
. . . and even more important, let the legitimate provincial authorities
participate in this glory, applying it, transmitting it, enjoying it. . . . Privileges and liberties, in the sense of customary procedures which allowed
the traditional authorities to have a respectable, if not dominant, place
in the ruling process, should be maintained. . . . Their violation would
be met with a counterreaction of consternation, appeal, protest, which
usually would be followed . . . by some sort of acquiescence.[96]

Indeed, Burgundy's magistrates thought similarly, negotiating power
with their monarch in a way that would benefit both. This practice led not
just to an extension of royal authority in the realm, but also to a judicial
magistracy that laid claim to a share of sovereignty.[97]

In the construction of authority (and ultimately of the meaning of sexuality), the ideology and the practice of law were fundamentally important.
The ideology of authority and legal practice was intertwined in the relationship between "absolutist" kings and a persistently independent-minded
judiciary from the turbulent sixteenth century to the dawn of the Enlightenment. King and magistrate were frequently at odds over how this system
should be constructed, and although *robins* abandoned their outright re-
bellious stance of the late sixteenth century, they continued to negotiate a
system of power-sharing with their king rather than capitulate to an absolutist regime under him. Authority was exercised in a context of power-
sharing and negotiation rather than one of royal autonomy and imposition.

An important element of this occasionally contentious negotiation
between king and magistrate was the construction of the meaning of sovereignty. Kings, of course, claimed complete sovereignty, justified it by
divine-right theory, and asserted its practice in legislation. The unified royal
will was further advocated in the increasing codification of law, guided by
the principle of *reductio in unum*.[98] Magistrates, for their part and much
to the disapproval of the crown, laid claim to a share of sovereignty, point-
ing to the sanctity of the law and their constitutional and divine right to
interpret it while applying it. Parlementary jurisprudence therefore indirectly
challenged royal legislative sovereignty. The king might frown on this, but
the system of power-sharing worked out over the early modern era precluded
him from doing much about it. There may have been a drift toward codification, but there was still plenty of room for magisterial interpretation,
and thus for "legislating" from the bench, as the existence of the *arrêtistes*—
Burgundian jurists in the eighteenth century who continued to claim law-
making authority for parlementary *arrêts*—attests.[99]

The ideology of authority that emerged in this context of magisterial
and royal power-sharing entailed the sacralization of lay authorities, which
in turn enhanced the sanctity of authority. It also led to jurisidictional conflicts between church and state. Gallicanism enshrined lay supremacy, but
if the king gained theoretical victory over the Church, parlements trumped
the ecclesiastical courts through the invocation of the *appel comme d'abus*

(an appeal from ecclesiastical to royal tribunals occurring when the church courts are deemed to have violated jurisdictional boundaries) and emerged by the eighteenth century as the supreme judicial authority in Burgundy and France.

We should not construe from this lay victory, however, that the juridical apparatus of France witnessed the secularization of justice. In fact, as will be seen in the next chapter, many *robins* shared the same goal as the churchmen of the "century of saints" and viewed the law as a means to attain not the secularization of society, but its sacralization.

Conclusion

From the mid-sixteenth to the early eighteenth century, a new order of morality and morality of order emerged. Within this edifice a new epistemology of order mirrored thinking about social order. The emphasis on "difference" within a structured order applied equally to ideas as to "dissociated" individuals. Emerging from a century in which the traditional verities, whether social or intellectual, were being challenged and were thought to be breaking down, seventeenth-century men confronted the task of re-ordering existence. Part of the result was a new morality of order and a new order of morality.

The new moral order that took shape in the late sixteenth and seventeenth centuries centered on an authoritarian ethic of discipline, focusing sharply on the passions. Guided by an intense distrust of concupiscence that emerged in the definition of the passions at precisely this time, moralists defined the widely influential ethic of *honnêteté* that demanded self-control, was codified by social comportment, and affirmed an increasingly hierarchical and sharply stratified society. The "tasteful" behavior of *honnêtes hommes* and *femmes* visibly demonstrated the emergent society of "dissociation and difference" while proclaiming the exclusionary and superior status of a self-defined privileged class.

This hierarchical stratification of society rested upon elemental assumptions about gender relations. Men assumed that males were naturally superior to females, and furthermore that women, given their passionate and irrational nature, were a fundamental source of disorder in the world. Increasingly in the seventeenth century, concupiscence crowded into the definition of the passions, and uncontrolled females were perceived as culpable for this disorder. Thus, integral to male thinking about discipline, hierarchy, and order were male assumptions about females; and if authoritarian control was perceived as the means to eliminating disorder in the world, it was because the same was expected within gender relations. The idea of patriarchy, then, was fundamental to male thinking about the new moral order.

Nicolas Brulart, the First President of Burgundy's Parlement during much of the second half of the seventeenth century, embodies in his extensive writings all of the essential elements of the new moral order. An exemplar of the powerful social group of landed officeholders that coalesced in the late sixteenth and early seventeenth centuries, he profoundly distrusted the passions as "disorderly" and assumed that they could only be mitigated by the ethic of *honnêteté* within an order guided by "justice" dispensed by the rightful rulers of society, the dominant privileged elite of which he was so prominent a member.

2

From the Cloister to the Street

To bring the cloister to the street, to sacralize society, was the goal of devout lay men and women (significantly, many drawn from lay officialdom) no less than clerical reformers. The sacralization of society was an integral part of the new moral vision of a reordered world, and it shared many of the characteristics of this authoritarian morality, whose social, political, and legal views were analyzed in the opening chapter. Like philosophers and jurists, godly reformers and moralists believed that the path to the new moral order must follow the road of self-discipline and social control. Tellingly, the emphasis upon interiorized discipline of the individual and the control of the presentation and representation of the body were characteristics of both the Catholic Reformation and the civilizing process. Many moralists were preoccupied with behavior and rank, and they embodied equally within their understanding of the ethic of *honnêteté* the notions of Christian piety and courtly civility.

Surprisingly, the initiative and impetus for sacralization can be traced to the laity in the sixteenth century. By the seventeenth century, the laity and clergy had agreed that sacralization should be mediated through the justice of the king. Furthermore, because justice was viewed as sacred, one important result of the sacralization of society was the criminalization of sin.

The moral order that rested upon self-discipline and social control was deeply informed by a sexual ethics and the confessionalism that supported it. Unregulated female sexuality was abhorred by reformers and moralists, and as a result concupiscence had to be regulated on two interdependent

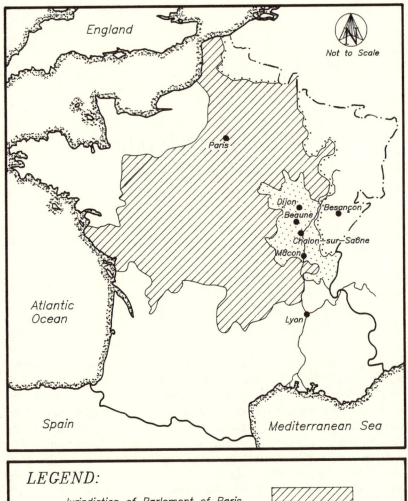

Territorial jurisdictions of the Parlements of Burgundy and Paris, sixteenth and eighteenth centuries.

fronts: in the individual's conscience by means of confession, and in society by the deployment of "justice" and by episcopal control of priests and parishioners. Confessors urging sexual restraint *before* confession, preachers and moralists vituperating against disorderly and lascivious women, bishops publishing synodal statutes and inspecting parishes as well as joining *dévots* (many of whom were *robins* and their wives) in the confinement of wayward individuals (mostly women), all of these groups formed a broad coalition to accomplish the goal deemed necessary to reorder society—its sacralization.

The Sacralization of Society

In an article exploring the "modernizing" elements in reformed Catholicism, Wolfgang Reinhard included "the promoting of discipline among the masses, the development of a new educational curriculum, the reform of the church's administration, an internalization of values, and an emphasis on activism."[1] These characteristics, leaving aside the argument about modernization, were central to the Catholic Reform in France and in Burgundy. We must not lose sight of the fact, however, that these innovations were means to the all-important end, the sacralization of society. Moral reformers like Jean-Jacques Duguet, writing around 1700, believed that "religion is everything, enters everywhere, has control over everything; it is religion that should rule everything, sacrifice everything, ennoble everything. Salvation is not only the most important business, but the only one."[2]

To be sure, the elements Reinhard isolated as characteristic of reformed Catholicism can be traced to the late Middle Ages. As historians like John Bossy and Robin Briggs have argued, however, it was during the second half of the sixteenth century that they coalesced into a system, in Bossy's words, "the institution of Christian religion."[3] The transformation was not so much one of kind but of scale, a product of "a steady pressure for the extension of Christian morality and the religious life into new areas, extending throughout lay society." In this reformed society, the sacred was to be preeminent, ideally "to permeate every level of experience, giving all aspects of life a religious dimension."[4]

One should not assume that the reformed Catholic Church formed a theological bloc, for indeed there was a diversity of doctrines, liturgies, catechisms, synods, and seminaries, and a multitude of religious orders competed with one another for the ears and hearts of the faithful. Nonetheless, beneath this diversity lay a common ideal, the sacralization of society and thereby the salvation of its souls. Even Jansenism, the most well-known theological divergence from Tridentine Catholicism in the seventeenth-century, embraced the essentials of the moralistic reform. Jansenist opposition to lax ethics and its steadfast advocacy of individual self-discipline and improvement in the quality of the clergy brought it close to *dévot* idealism and moralistic activism.[5] Such activism for Jansenists or orthodox

Catholics was to be accomplished by bringing the earthly order into alignment with divine order.

Moralistic activists were far from being a fringe minority by the seventeenth century; in fact, they led a reforming drive of historically unprecedented vigor. The Society of Jesus, for example, the spearhead of the orthodox Catholic and Counter-Reformation, rejected the medieval stance of *contemptus mundi* for a simple detachment from the world, precisely because the latter permitted the all-important apostolic activism that Jesuits in turn viewed as a means to seek and find God in all things.[6]

Sacralizing the Political

Moralists tended to be clergymen, but we would misunderstand the vigor of the reforming drive if we did not appreciate the role played by the laity, men and women alike. Many *robins* in particular justified their social status, authority, and morality in deeply held religious terms; it should thus come as no surprise that recent scholarship has increasingly appreciated the profound impetus, even initiative, that lay people took in pushing for an extension of the sacred in society, a process Bossy has accurately called a "migration of the holy."[7]

With the sacralization of monarchical and magisterial authority, this extension of the sacred to society was effected by an alliance between church and state, especially through the medium of justice.[8] Even in the full flush of the Enlightenment in the mid-eighteenth century, the Burgundian jurist François Serpillon could write that "the Church and religion are under the protection of kings and consequently of royal justice; nothing is more important to the tranquility of the state than the maintenance of religion."[9] In his influential *Traité de la police*, Nicolas Delamare wrote essentially the same thing earlier in the century, and the leading jurist of the late seventeenth century, Jean Domat, took as his first principle of public law the "love of God and one's neighbor." Furthermore, he asserted that "one should regard religion as the most natural foundation of order in society . . . [thus everyone] should be content to remain in his station in accordance with divine will. . . . Religion and the polity have the same common principle in divine order and should cooperate and give each other mutual aid. . . . Religion and good polity are always united."[10]

A century earlier than Domat, during the Wars of Religion and the Holy League, we find laymen from the *robin* class expressing the same sentiments. Jean Bégat, royal councillor at Dijon's Parlement and *élu* for Burgundy's provincial estates, challenged a royal edict of toleration in 1563 for religious and political reasons simultaneously. Good polity, he boldly asserted, must have only one law, one faith, and one king; plurality in any of these— especially, for Bégat, the law and faith—destroys the others.[11]

The League has been called the realization of "an act of sacral unity,"[12] and Leaguers like Etienne Bernard, mayor of Dijon and representative to the Leaguer Estates General of 1593, justified on religious grounds their political opposition to the accession to the throne by the "heretic" Henri of Navarre. Bernard attended the Estates, in his words, "in the service of religion and the general welfare of the kingdom" and professed that all his pains, indeed his life, were dedicated "without any other ambition than to the glory of God."[13]

Politicizing the Sacred

If laymen were sacralizing the political from the mid-sixteenth to the mid-eighteenth century, clergymen, especially during the seventeenth century, were politicizing the sacred. Cardinal Richelieu embodies this trend; according to Jean Orcibal, he felt strongly that the state shared equally in the "participation in divine power" with the church and refused to make either subordinate to the other one.[14]

As a man of state, Richelieu might have been expected to espouse such views, but the politicizing of the sacred was also embedded in manifold sermons of the period.[15] The Jesuit priest Vincent Houdry, for example, who wrote and preached for 24 years during the second half of the seventeenth century and saw his sermons published between 1696 and 1702, explained in his homily "On the Duties of Inferiors to Their Superiors" that "dependency and submission" are divine qualities and everyone is therefore compelled by God to obey his anointed king.[16] This same point was made by his contemporary Nicolas de Dijon in another sermon.[17] Both Houdry and Nicolas were careful to point out that all authority comes from God, and so kings also have a master.

In 1683, Jean Soanen, Oratorian and future Bishop of Senez, in his sermon "On Love of the Fatherland" offered a variation on the theme that united the political and the sacred. "God is order . . . and order wishes that we regard the kingdom in which we were born as a whole of which we are the parts. . . . Our primary existence is that of citizen, and if the Lord wished that religion was in the state, it is to teach us to serve the state."[18] In the early eighteenth century, François Baillet was sounding the same notes when he preached in Paris and at Versailles. In one sermon on "The Duties of Society," he advanced that religion ordered the duties of society and religion sanctified them. Ultimately for Baillet, the linchpin in the system of an obedient society was obedience to the king. He logically concluded that the good subject and the good Christian were inseparable.[19]

Each of these preachers, among the most renowned of the seventeenth and early eighteenth centuries, assumed that hierarchy was sanctioned in society, and each was explicit about the position of the king. The theme of divine and earthly hierarchy occurred in many sermons of other preachers, some sliding slightly down the scale from the royal apex to the "grands," presumably the court aristocracy.

Nicolas de La Volipière, a doctor in theology and a very popular preacher in many towns in the late seventeenth and early eighteenth centuries, exclaimed in a sermon "The Alliance of Piety with Grandeur,"

> Piety is not incompatible with grandeur, [but] the great must be the most
> pious. . . . Since [the great] . . . rule for God and are his lieutenants on
> earth, they must be . . . animated by his spirit . . . in order to govern the
> people according to [God's] intentions and conforming to his orders. . . .
> They must continually hold before themselves this divine model as the
> rule of their conduct. . . . Since they are images of God, they must be
> exemplars of men. Their conduct serves ordinarily as an example and men
> have naturally this inclination to conform to their *chefs*.

Such exemplary behavior, La Volipière concluded, in the end does more
for maintaining "the people in their duties" than any number of edicts and
ordinances.[20]

La Volipière's emphasis on exemplary behavior is echoed by his near
contemporary, Jean-Baptiste Massillon. This Oratorian, professor of theology, and ultimately Bishop of Clermont in 1717, preached in the royal
presence at times. In one sermon "Des Exemples des grands" addressed to
Louis XV, he asserted that the king and the "grands" have a direct role in
the salvation of their inferiors by being good role models. Because the
"crowd" is primarily moved by envy and vanity, it will mimic the behavior
of its betters; "they have no other law than the examples of those who com-
mand them"; logically, the salvation of the people is in the hands of the
great, and it thus is incumbent upon them to be paragons and fair dispensers of justice.[21]

The sacred character of justice referred to by Massillon was something
that parlementaires had already come to assume, as Nicolas Brulart's ideas
illustrate. Clerics like the widely influential Dijonnais Jacques-Bénigne
Bossuet reinforced such associations. This royal advisor and staunch defender
of divine right political theory was born to a family of the Burgundian *noblesse
de robe* and became a doctor of the Sorbonne at the age of 25 in 1652,
Bishop of Condom in 1666, and tutor to the Dauphin in 1670. He was
also a prolific preacher, and his sermons articulating his vision of politicizing the sacred found a central place for justice. They must have resounded
very favorably in *robin* ears. In his sermon "On Justice," Bossuet preached,

> When I mention justice, I mention at the same time the sacred bond of
> human society, the necessary brake on license, the unique foundation of
> tranquility, the equitable temperment of authority, and the gentle bridle
> of subjection. When justice reigns, faith is found in treaties, security in
> commerce . . . order in police. . . . Justice is the principle virtue and the
> common ornament of public . . . persons. . . . It affirms not only princes
> over their subjects, but also . . . reason over the passions.[22]

Crime and Sin

Recently Heinz Schilling endorsed Geoffrey Elton's demand that the history of crime and the history of sin be rigorously separated, at least in re-
gions where autonomous church discipline existed.[23] However, where "legal
circumstances within an established church" encouraged the state to use

religion "to meet the civil moral discipline of the state," and the church "working for reform advanced far into the secular state sphere in order to christianize it," we would likely find a criminalization of sin, that is, no meaningful distinction between crime and sin.[24] Such was the case of early modern France.

But how did sin become criminalized, and how did crimes become sins? John Bossy has noted that from 1400 to 1700 a transition occurred within the history of sin in which, after an individual sinned, the emphasis shifted from reconciliation of the sinner, God, and the Christian community to obedience by the sinner to the sovereign will of God. In the transition, sin ultimately was equated with disobedience.[25]

The pervasiveness of Augustinian ethics in the seventeenth century, and not just in Jansenism, is an ample reflection that this transition occurred. Jean-François Senault, a classic representative of Augustinianism within the orthodox Catholic Church, wrote a treatise in 1644 entitled *L'Homme criminel*.[26] This chaplain to Cardinal Bérulle (one of the leading figures of the French Catholic Reformation) and later Father Superior of the Oratory, brought to his work the Augustinian assumption that through the disobedience of original sin (in which the passions played an instrumental role), "criminal man" offended God. Senault is a fine example of how sin and crime became associated with one another and with the passions by the mid-seventeenth century.[27]

Expansive Augustinianism certainly contributed to the criminalization of sin, but a further clue to how sin became criminal and crime sinful may lie in the transformation of the ideas of Christian charity and community. In the 1400s, according to Bossy, charity in practice, if not in scholastic theory, meant social integration, "enlarged sociability," and occupied a central place in the scheme of salvation. Indeed, it was "the principal end of Christian life."[28] Charity was rooted in personal relations with one's neighbor, and those relations (and reconciliations) were mediated by the church in the person of the priest.

By the 1600s, Bossy continues, the meaning of charity had become more abstract and impersonal. For Jesuits, it meant "efficiently managed and heroically executed works directed to saving the soul, improving the mind, and relieving the corporal needs of a rather abstract and rather passive neighbor." Likewise, for Oratorians, charity meant abstract benevolence, a "generalized [and impersonal] concept of philanthropy." The shift in the meaning of charity from personal to impersonal, for Bossy, spelled the demise of community so important to traditional Christianity, and signaled the transformation of Christianity from a "body of people" to a "body of beliefs."[29]

But should we consign the Christian community to the dustbin of history? Perhaps the small, face-to-face community Bossy assumes characterized traditional Christianity, if there ever had been such a thing, came to an end. But we might well ask what community—and charity—meant to people in the sixteenth, seventeenth and eighteenth centuries as a result of the intrusions of secular authority into the realm of the sacred. King and magistrate, of course, had long claimed to be the protectors of civil peace, and during the early modern period civil peace, as Bossy points out, was increasingly defined as sacred.[30] The maintenance of peace might no longer have been aimed at social integration or effected solely by the church, but it did still have religious purposes, which now in the hands of the sacralized "state" were to maintain peaceful relations within a *dissociated* Christian (and indeed, in Gallican France) French "community." This community might no longer have been the highly personalized entity that Bossy posits for the Middle Ages, but as an abstract collectivity it was a community nonetheless and, furthermore, an essential component of the new moral order. Charity was no longer mediated horizontally solely through the parish priest, but vertically, not only through a thoroughly hierarchical church but equally through God and his earthly representatives, king and magistrate.

Many preachers testified to this important transformation, but none describe it better than Louis Bourdaloue: "Religion is nothing other than a bond that . . . subjects us to God. . . . [This bond] . . . subsumes . . . all the duties and all the obligations which hold men together [in a civil society]. It is impossible to be bound to God . . . without having at the same time with one's neighbor . . . the links of charity and justice."[31] Any violation of the sacred civil peace was a sin against God (as a violation of charity) and likewise a crime against the state.[32] In the new order of morality, crime was sinful and sin criminal.

Self-Discipline and Social Control

To many Frenchmen, lay as well as clerical, Jansenist as well as orthodox, the Catholic Reformation was a religious process with profound political and social stakes, and its moralistic writings cut broadly through the literature of early modern France. In these works the lexicon of purity, discipline, propriety, and hierarchy found prominent expression.

Concepts such as these suggest a concern for boundary marking and boundary transgression, a precoccupation shared, as seen in chapter 1, by so many of society's privileged elites. Mary Douglas's ideas on the fashioning of an orderly system by ritualized relations of separation that purify, demarcate, and punish are suggestive because they seem to apply directly to the increasingly dissociated social world of the seventeenth century, a world in which a hierarchical, authoritarian, and moralistic vision was embedded in the writings of so many Frenchmen.[33]

This authoritarian moral vision insisted on two interrelated premises, both tacitly directed at harnessing the passions: an internal discipline of the individual, and an external control of the presentation and representation of the body.[34] The new ideas on civility as well as the teachings of the Catholic Reformation converged to reinforce these premises, which in turn informed assumptions about proper thought and behavior.

From the Council of Trent (1545–63) emerged decrees that directed the Christian to strive systematically for self-control by meditative prayer and regular examination of the conscience.[35] Nowhere is this emphasis on mental self-discipline, contemplation, and self-analysis more evident than in Ignatian sprirituality[36] or, in the seventeenth century, in the teachings of Saint François de Sales.

The goal of such a system of self-control (called *disciplina*) was deliverance from sin, especially of the concupiscent sort, and the difference between it and traditional penance was that penance was something one did and self-discipline was something one learned.[37] The mechanism that the church used to propagate this transformation for discipline was an insistence upon frequent and regular confession, so that the sinner would have an incentive for "systematic interior monitoring" that would prevent the inclination toward sin.[38]

The Catholic Church was concerned for the salvation of souls and deemed this internalization of religious values conducive to that salutary objective. However, the institutional church was equally a sacrally justified agent of social control, and increasingly it locked arms with secular authorities to accomplish this related goal as well.

Purity and impurity, words which recall Douglas's observations about pollution and boundary construction, appear frequently in moralistic literature and sermons and suggest a deep concern for order. Impurity, which Bourdaloue called "the great disorder of the world," always carried concupiscent assumptions in its meaning. Moreover, the multitude of preachers' dichotomous sermonizing about the dangers of impurity in thought and behavior, and the rewards of "internal purity," reflected a commitment by the church to guide the individual firmly away from venting the sexual passions and toward self-control.[39]

Programs of hierarchical reformism complemented the haranguing of moralists and preachers. Reinforced at Trent and spread to France by reformers like Pierre de Bérulle—cardinal, moralist, and leader of a domestic missionary movement in the early seventeenth century—hierarchical reformism was explicitly suited for the social control that was so important to the Gallican Church. For Bérulle, the visible church was "a divine emanation in which light and power descended through a hierarchy of orders identified in particular with the episcopate and the priesthood. In this system the proper attitude of the human creature was reverence, servitude, adoration. . . . The extent to which this hierarchy . . . paralleled, assumed and indeed incorporated the social and political hierarchies of seventeenth-century France . . . is . . . explicit in Bérulle himself."[40]

Piety and Civility

Exterior and interior surveillance—social control and self-restraint—was characteristic of the Catholic Reformation, but it also increasingly marked the notion of civility over the same chronological period.[41] Civility manuals, an historically long-standing genre that assumed unprecedented importance and popularity in the early modern period, prescribed for men and women of seventeenth-century courtly and aristocratic circles modes of dress, actions, and language, with the purpose of signaling social distinction. Early modern society saw increasing attention to social differentiation and dissociation, and the civility manuals (along with a chronologically coincidental avalanche of sumptuary legislation)[42] reflected the growing concern of society's upper classes in the seventeenth century to set themselves apart, to erect visible boundaries, by articulating "rules for conduct in a specific social milieu."[43]

Civility manuals may have been concerned with hierarchy, but they were also inseparably intertwined with piety. Many authors of these manuals from the mid-sixteenth to the early eighteenth centuries explicitly associated proper courtly behavior with Christian morality.

Pierre Broë, for instance, in a 1555 tract immediately followed his advice to be courteous, gentle, and affable with lines that encouraged his readers to love God and pray to Him, the Virgin, and the saints.[44] Likewise, the Jesuit Antoine de Balinghem in 1618 wrote about the importance of Christian charity in civil behavior, stressing that one's good name is necessary for the edification of one's neighbor and the "true means of acquiring honor is by obeying God."[45]

The layman Antoine de Nervèze, Balinghem's contemporary, considered "working for one's salvation" synonymous with working for one's reputation, since honor and salvation had "a common interest."[46] Melchior de Marmet de Valcroissant, a layman, and Abbé Jean Pic also blended Christian morality into their definitions of civility, Marmet making reference to values of cleanliness and purity throughout his treatise.[47] The immensely popularly Antoine de Courtin assumed that "good disposition within," or modesty, was a state that "fills our minds with Christian humility."[48]

Like other writers of civility manuals, Jean-Baptiste de La Salle, in his *Les Règles de la bienséance et de la civilité chrétienne* first published in 1703, was keenly concerned with keeping the socially inferior classes distinct from their superiors, and he united the social ideology of disciplined hierarchy with the moralistic concerns of Christianity. In this often reprinted book, aimed at a broad audience, he instructed his readers to "pay attention to the social rank" of those with whom they interacted. Readers were advised to treat their superiors "in such a way as their status demands," that is, by obedience and submission. He simultaneously prescribed a Christian mode of behavior, which was "guided by the spirit of God" but which also was "a wise and regulated conduct that one makes evident in one's discourse and in one's exterior actions by . . . modesty." For La Salle, as for so many other moralists, the body was "the living temple of God," and both the body and the clothing covering it must be kept clean as "exterior and palpable mark[s] of the purity of the soul." It logically followed that the place where "one must be very clean because of the respect that one has for God" was in church.[49]

Not only authors of civility manuals blended civility with piety; in the early seventeenth century, Anne de Xainctonge, the daughter of a royal councilor at Dijon's Parlement and former Leaguer, established a religious order dedicated to the education of girls. In a curriculum "saturated with religiosity," the order taught "lessons of civility" that were simultaneously "lessons of Christian modesty." Furthermore, pupils were expected to adhere to a discipline in prayer that, in Xainctonge's words, "taught . . . [a] resolve to bridle the license of [the] imagination . . . and of its passions."[50]

Later in the seventeenth century, the lay moralist Chevalier de Méré claimed that "devotion and honnêteté follow almost exactly the same routes, and mutually aid one another. . . . Honnêteté is far from useless to salvation, and even contributes to it."[51] Likewise, the late-seventeenth-century Jesuit Guillaume de Ségaud preached that "all true Christians are indispensably obliged in conscience to satisfy without exception all the duties of society and of the *honnête homme* . . . and only true Christians can fulfill and acquit these as they must be done."[52]

Clearly, many lay and clerical people associated civility (and thus hierarchical distinction and obedience) with piety, further confirming how social control and self-restraint converged in an authoritarian social and religious order.

Sexual Ethics and Confessionalism

Jean Delumeau has asserted that the medieval Christian motif of *contemptus mundi* continued to dominate European minds in the early modern age, a time when this monastic ethic became a norm for an entire civilization. This "mistrust of the world" was expressed in a hostility to the senses and the flesh, especially to the sensations of sexual pleasure. Multitudes of moralists in the late sixteenth and seventeenth centuries, under the influence of the enormously influential Saint Augustine, increasingly came to view the natural sex drive as a punishment for man's original disobedience or "fall" and so linked sexual activity (except between legitimate husband and wife, which also must be free of any sense of lust) with disobedience and sin.[53] Furthermore, illicit sexual activity, or concupiscence, lowered men to the level of brutes, because it manifested the irrational side of their nature. In an age that believed the loss of reason was a primary threat to sacred order, illicit sexual activity could only be viewed with deep alarm.

Let us consider a few of the countless examples of this ascetic attitude. In his *Oraison funèbre* for the deceased Bishop of Chalon-sur-Saône Jean de Maupeou, Abbé Jacques Thésut-Niquevard in 1677 deemed Maupeou's most laudatory quality his "disinterestedness," his detachment from the world, which underscored his innocence, purity, and modesty and which in turn rendered his chastity inseparable from his faith.[54]

Another Burgundian, the Oratorian Edme Bernard Bourrée, delivered a sermon "On the Adulterous Love of the World," in which he stated that love of the world and for any creature in it for itself, a love not mediated by the Holy Spirit, was adulterous and a crime that the Gospel does not permit to go unpunished.[55] Henri-Marie Boudon, Grand Archdiacre d'Evreux and renowned in the seventeenth century for his asceticism, expressed the sentiment in a sermon entitled "The Misfortune of the World," that "all that is found in the world is either concupiscence of the flesh, concupiscence of the eyes, or pride." Heeding concupiscent inclinations corrupts body and soul and leads to disorder. These urges do not come from God; it is sin that causes these, and the first of the sources of sin is the "voluptuous pleasure of the senses."[56]

Since the thirteenth century, a preoccupation with sins of the flesh had been evident in confessors' manuals, and the fact that after 1450 *summas* and manuals for confessors became extraordinarily popular points to the conclusion that sacramental confession and the sins of concupiscence were brought together in a system of discipline and, more broadly, of attempted social control that rested on the cornerstone of regulation of sexual behavior.[57]

The reformed Catholic church might not have initiated the concern for sexual morality, but it did incorporate that concern systemically, not just in confessors' manuals but also in moralistic prescriptive literature of all types. Confessors' manuals, to be sure, treated far more than sexual transgressions alone, and some were even more preoccupied with financial issues than sexual ones.[58] It does appear, however, that after 1550 attention to the Sixth Commandment and *luxure* (lustfulness) in general continued to attract the attention that they had in the *summas* and compendiums for confessors of the late Middle Ages. In addition, however, a trend that would supplant "a penance of shame and expiation" with "a penance of guilt and remorse" was accelerated and systematized. Indeed, by the second half of the sixteenth century, problems of conscience dominated moral and pastoral theology.[59] The confessor manuals from the late sixteenth century demanded that the penitent examine his or her conscience *before* coming to confession. The detailed investigations that then occurred during confession were intended to plumb the innermost reaches of the soul. The "pastoral of fear" and guilt thus came fully into its own at a time when the Church (and the rest of privileged society) was engaged in a combat against the terrors of cosmic and earthly disorder, a disorder in which concupiscence occupied a prominent place.[60]

Attention to *cas de conscience* and interior purification of the soul can be found in numerous confessors' manuals from the late sixteenth to the early eighteenth centuries. In fact, orthodox Catholics and Jansenists found common ground in a rigorous penitential ethic. The sixteenth-century orthodox Polanco's advice on confessing sins against the Sixth Commandment, for instance, urged the confessor to explore a penitent's lascivious thoughts that were related to a catalogue of words and actions deemed *deshonnestes* or *impudiques* (immodest).[61]

Early in the next century, Saint François de Sales instructed confessors, under the heading "Of what it is necessary that the penitents accuse themselves [*s'accuse*]," that "it is necessary to penetrate *plus avant*, and examine the penitent [about] purely interior desires and urges [*volontez*]." De Sales, as his manual to confessors (as well as most of his spiritual writings) makes abundantly clear, was preoccupied with the impurity of sexuality, and in this case the probing of the conscience was to purge the mind of impure lustful thoughts. If one took pleasure from "thoughts and imaginations of carnal desire," de Sales maintained, then it was a sin committed in the conscience against chastity and charity.[62] Similarly, the Jansenist Arnauld argued against frequent communion unless one was fully prepared in an interior way.

In the early eighteenth century Antoine Blanchard was still probing the conscience of penitents for concupiscent thoughts. In his popular *Examen de conscience . . . pour aider . . . à faire une confession générale* where he treats of "sins against the Sixth and Ninth Commandments," that is, those dealing with lust, Blanchard's first of 55 forthright questions asked penitents whether they had ever had "thoughts contrary to purity" that they had voluntarily entertained.[63]

The pastoral of fear and guilt about lustful passion comes together explicitly in Saint Charles Borromeo's widely used *Instructions aux Confesseurs*, first published in the late sixteenth century, later adopted in 1657 by the French Assembly of the Clergy, and distributed widely thereafter in Burgundy and throughout France.[64] With its emphasis upon mandatory interior preparation for confession by the penitent, this book systematized the tradition of the Church on penitence after the Council of Trent. It repeatedly focused on a key point: the refusal of absolution to unprepared penitents.[65] To even hope for priestly absolution, penitents should have first examined their conscience: "Confessors must not admit to confession those who do not present themselves with the necessary exterior and interior preparation."[66] Borromeo makes it clear that part of this preparation must include banishing lust from one's conscience.

Moralists and Godly Reformers

Confessors' manuals dealt essentially with matters of conscience and were only implicitly concerned with problems of social order. The writings of moralists were equally preoccupied with matters of conscience, but this genre more explicitly addressed the matter of social order, and it furthermore tightly linked human (especially female) sexuality with social disorder.

In his influential tract on political theory, *Les Six livres de la republique*, Jean Bodin associated man's head and his ability to reason with supreme power. By acknowledging a specifically sexual potency in another lower part of the body that the head must control, he foreshadowed the war of reason against the passions that would dominate so much of the moralistic literature of the seventeenth century.[67]

Both Bodin and the moralists and godly reformers developed the organic analogy of reasoned order and control battling disorder from an intellectual beginning to a sexual and social conclusion. For Bodin, the liver was the source of "sensual lust and desire [that] betokeneth the common people." For later reformers and moralists, as well as *dévots* and missionaries, the passions (especially sexual) needed to be bridled for one to lead a Christian life, and it was the task of the godly to instill this message in the faithful. Reason served an all-inclusive order that demanded hierarchy and obedience and, consequently, power asymmetrically distributed to upper-class males and embedded in discursive norms and formal institutions.

If Bodin's ideology is only implicitly gendered, that of the seventeenth-century moralists is explicitly so. From the late sixteenth to the early eighteenth centuries, lay and clerical French moralists carried the themes of hierarchy, sexual purity, discipline, and honor into the realm of pious exhortation and publication, and many pointedly focused on the culpability of female sexuality.[68] In one way or another, all agreed that the passion of erotic love was a destructive force and were concerned with its control.[69] All viewed the passions, usually specifying their sexual element, as dangerous to the individual and to the social order and stability of France. Unbridled, lustful passion not only led one away from God but conquered reason; and by urging one to "luxuriousness," lustful passion simultaneously broke down the social hierarchy and invited concupiscence.

In the late sixteenth century, Pierre de La Primaudaye succinctly connected sexual and social disorder with a threatened hierarchy. He raged that it was "a signe of great . . . baseness of mind for a man to subiect himselfe to carnall concupiscences, which are disordered desires contrarie to reason. . . . He that seeketh by all means to fulfill his untamed desires of pleasure and lust, hath no more use of reason than beasts have."[70] He lamented that the unreasoning disorder of lust might afflict males, "throwing them down headlong into the gulfe of confusion, which is luxuriousness and whoredom," but the cause of the disorder was "unruly" women. It was through the female "that men abase themselves so lowe, as to submit both their bodies and soules to the inconstant will and unrulie desire of a foolish woman."[71] A century later, Thimotée Philalethe and the Jansenist Jacques Esprit, to name two examples, completely agreed with La Primaudaye.[72]

A generation after Esprit, Jean Du Pradel echoed the earlier moralists' position denouncing unregulated luxurious consumption and uncontrolled sexuality and associated them explicitly with the collapse of hierarchical social distinction. Uncontrolled luxurious consumption reflected that "all conditions [i.e., social strata] are confused. . . . The artisan wishes to appear as the merchant, the bourgeois is raised above the gentleman, the latter wishes to equal the marquis." And like La Primaudaye, Philalethe, Esprit, and nearly every other moralist of the last century and a half, he blamed women: "Most women have given an even greater vent [than men] to their ambition and their vanity. . . . All is thus perverted by *le luxe*; neither shame nor laws restrain anymore, the old modesty is banished, vice triumphs, virtue cries plaintively, [but] debauchery and lust reign with impunity."[73]

As we have seen, the fiction of a fixed social hierarchy was predicated upon assumptions held by early modern men about unequal gender relations. Furthermore, the human (frequently female) body was the most common image for representing the all-important hierarchical concepts (high and low, pure and impure, decent and indecent) across political, social, and religious ideologies, thus knitting them all together in a mutually supportive moralistic system.[74]

Women at this time lacked formal access to power and were usually portrayed as "unruly" in the patriarchal prescriptive literature of the period.[75] The moralistic literature of the seventeenth century focused singular attention on women, and the binary and unequal relationship between male and female was assumed as the only possible and proper one.

Moralists from La Primaudaye in the late sixteenth century to Du Pradel in the early eighteenth perceived unregulated female sexuality as boundary transgression. Given the prominence of the ideas of degradation and lack of cleanliness and impurity in their vocabulary (impurity was also a very common theme of sermons)[76] when they wrote about female sexuality, one may justifiably speak of perceived threats to the hierarchy in terms of boundary "pollution," both social and physical. La Primaudaye vituperated against "filthy" lechery, and Louis Habert, author of a confessor's manual popular in the late seventeenth and early eighteenth centuries, counseled the confessor, when dealing with transgressions to the Sixth Commandment, to maintain an especially "angelic chastity in order not to be soiled by dealing with a matter so dirty." He added that because "the sin that God forbids here is shameful, the penitents have great difficulty in accusing themselves of it; several do not explain themselves sufficiently on this matter" and, continuing the theme of impurity, wrote that they thus "rot in filth."[77]

Boileau railed against the "superfluous ornaments" women wore that "engender[ed] lust and impurity" in men and which, if the anonymous author of *La Courtisane déchiffrée* is to be believed, could by ostentatious and vain expenditure bring financial ruin and thus social dishonor to their husbands.[78] Whereas this anonymous author was thinking in terms of social boundaries, Philalethe was concerned with the threat of impure female sexuality to physical boundaries. He clearly associated sacred space with purity and perceived female sexuality as a threat to its integrity. In a book on female modesty, which he continually associated with the purity of chastity, he asserted that "no one can doubt that salvation . . . depends principally on purity. . . . Priests . . . must never permit the entry of anything impure or of the world [into the temples of God], for fear that the God of purity who abides there, finding his dwelling soiled, will abandon it with indignation." This moralist subsequently clarified what sorts of impurity he had in mind, namely, indecently clad women.[79]

A generation earlier than Philalethe, Pierre Juvernay had been mightily offended on God's behalf by "improperly" attired women participating in religious processions, because the pure sacred space marked out by such a ritual was thus defiled by these impudent and sacrilegious women.[80] Predictably, he conflated exterior and interior desecration, first by finding it unacceptable that women presented themselves in the confessional for the rite of inner purification similarly dressed (Borromeo denounced the same thing in his *Instructions aux confesseurs*),[81] and then by railing against the fashion of wearing a cross on a chain around the neck in close proximity to a partially exposed breast. Instead of a cross, which represented the mortification of the flesh (and these women were showing it off!), Juvernay, associating the impure with the impious, suggested that it would be more appropriate for women indulging in this style of adornment to wear an image of a "toad, or of a crow, because these animals live in filth, and their soul is reputed to be like excrement."[82]

Burgundian moralists and reformers reiterated the same themes. Synodal statutes published in 1659 binding the diocese of Mâcon enjoined women "to present themselves to the holy table [for communion] with modesty . . . with a veil over the face, breasts covered, without makeup . . . and in clothes and in countenance so modest that their exterior witnesses their interior preparation."[83] Slightly later, the preacher Nicolas de Dijon published three different sermons "Against Luxurious Clothing" (*Contre le luxe des habits*), an extremely popular subject for sermons at that time.[84] He equated facial makeup and hair dye with "the sin of prostitution because [all] soil the body"; furthermore, "lascivious styles . . . corrupt the spirit by evil thoughts, the heart by impure affections, and the body by an entire prostitution."[85] The Dijonnais preacher Bourrée, also in a sermon entitled "Contre le luxe," asked the women in his audience, "Tell me, worldy women (because it is among you that this vice particularly reigns), how do you accord all of this proud apparel with Christian humility . . . ? And you dare to display it even in our churches[?] . . . It is not by necessity that you dress [in such a way], nor by modesty, but to prostitute yourself!"[86] The disorder of such sartorial behavior, Vincent Houdry informed his audience, was "against modesty and *honnêteté*" and rendered those who dressed so shamefully "infinitely criminal" in the eyes of God.[87]

A similar concern for sacred space and the integrity of its boundaries, as well as the threat of women defiling it, was evident in a custom apparently continuing into the seventeenth century, whereby women who had recently given birth presented themselves at church to be "purified."[88] This was a necessary ritual because, as an "old proverb" put it, humans were "conceived with filth and uncleanliness."[89] A widely published author of a confessor's manual, Mathieu Beuvelet, cautioned his clerical readers that although this custom was fully legitimate in the eyes of the Church, the parish priest who performed the rite "must not admit any concubines or public adulteresses to this benediction."[90]

Similar assumptions about female impurity defiling sacred space apparently guided an episcopal prohibition in 1698 in the diocese of Autun against "women and girls entering the sacristy . . . on Sundays and holy days."[91] One need not dig deeply into seventeenth-century documents to find an association between sacred space and cleanliness and purity,[92] or to find references that associated women with dirt and impurity.

In Salesian spirituality the struggle against the sexual passions held a central place, and although Saint François's tone was milder than that of most moralists, his vocabulary was also drawn from the lexicon of discipline, obedience, and purity.[93] He stressed the power of reason and the importance of the will. In order to avoid the pitfall of self-love and thus damning vanity that an emphasis on reason and will might bring about, however, Saint François taught that the will disciplined by reason must be guided toward the love of God. Following this path, the *dévot* avoided self-love and, significantly, purified himself or herself of any sexual content that the love for another human being might have. For de Sales, the "Doctor of Love," the *dévot* was master or mistress of the self by "dominating the passions and all of the disordered stirrings of the senses."[94]

This inward turn toward asexual self-disciplined purification, so prominent in the widely influential Salesian spirituality, reflected once again the new incentive for the systematic interior monitoring by the individual that was a hallmark of the Catholic Reformation in general. The disciplined body, sexually purified by the examination of conscience, thus became the appropriate sacred space for the holy, as the temple of the Holy Ghost.

Not surprisingly, themes of self-discipline and sexual purity characterized much of the moralistic literature of the seventeenth century. Antoine Godeau, the widely published Bishop of Vence and one-time *dévot*, was so concerned with what he perceived to be the deplorable moral state of France at mid-century that he wrote a book on penitence intended for high society (*gens du monde*). He wanted the message of his illustrated book, which repeatedly dwelt on the dangers of lust, to be "buried in the sinner's conscience" and hoped to convince his audience to expiate "the disorders of their past life."[95]

Like de Sales and Godeau, Boileau urged self-discipline (and recalled its association with purity) in his tract against female nudity. "Make use ... of your reason," he exhorted women, "and it will teach you that you ought to avoid nakedness. ... Hearken to the instructions of your conscience, and it will make you understand that you cannot, without a kind of crime, affect to be seen so naked as you nowadays go, since that nature itself inspires you with fear, aversion, and even also of nakedness." Boileau was appealing to the glimmer of innocence he believed to still exist in these worldly women, reminding them that the first thing that Adam and Eve did when they gained knowledge of good and evil was to cover themselves, being ashamed of their nakedness.[96]

Esprit no less than de Sales and Boileau demanded that women control themselves from within. Like the author of the renowned civility manual Antoine de Courtin who was his contemporary, Esprit believed that motives were inextricably, linearly, and reciprocally linked to actions by way of thoughts and words; chastened and purified language could act favorably upon one's motives, just as motives dictated action. Esprit, a Jansenist, was in agreement with most moralists and authors of civility manuals of his century in the belief that language could be an active force in the suppression of passion and the ordering of society by disciplining the self.[97]

Du Pradel, writing a century after de Sales, echoed the same moralistic concerns as the "Doctor of Love" and invoked a vocabulary of rules and boundaries that marked the entire seventeenth century. Nothing, he asserted, was more opposed to the "rules and spirit of religion" than, to return to a favorite theme of moralists and preachers, the unruliness (*dérèglement*) of self-love and the immodesty of luxurious dress. The unregulated love of pleasure and the unbridling of morality (*débordement des moeurs*) that followed were the shame of du Pradel's century, and only modesty, the greatest and most necessary virtue of women and girls, "represses in the soul the passions that agitate it . . . and regulates interior and exterior comportment."[98] In the moralistic literature from de Sales to Du Pradel, women thus symbolized the chaos of lust that needed to be controlled by self-discipline.

Self-discipline was to be won through the tutelage of pious exhortation and the confessional. Women were theoretically subordinated not only in this fashion, but also by being placed under the constant surveillance of their father or husband within the patriarchal family.[99] Women were the gates of entry to the male-dominated domain of the family—socially by marriage, physiologically by sexual relations—and so the patriarchal family and the institution of marriage that was its linchpin, like perceptions of the social hierarchy and of sacred space (bodily and topographical), were defined, protected, and reinforced by boundaries and portrayed by bodily metaphors.[100] In Renaissance literature, for example, the patriarchal "normative 'woman' . . . is rigidly 'finished': her signs are the enclosed body, the closed mouth, the locked house."[101] Similarly, in 1617 the layman Sieur de Vigoureux argued succinctly that the ideal marital situation would find "women . . . shut up in their homes."[102] Anne de Xainctonge sounded the same note of enclosure in her advice to the women who joined in the order she established in the early seventeenth century: "'When you are out of the house, guard well your senses; these are the gates by which materiality enters the soul and wreaks havoc; virtue escapes by these same gates, if one does not keep them closed.'"[103]

In tracts by moralists, this image of enclosure, of sealing off by visible boundaries, is closely associated with sexual purity as the model for moral female behavior channeled ultimately, for most women, through marriage. Marriage was important, it is worth recalling, because it expressed social stratification and functioned to perpetuate hereditary status and the transmission of patrimonies.[104] Consequently, patriarchy demanded female chastity and fidelity unconditionally, and female purity was carefully guarded, hedged about with boundaries of honor and shame and locked within the institution of marriage, even to the literal extent of the house or the bedroom.

In a key scene in the novel *La Comtesse de Tende*, for example, the classical moralist Madame de La Fayette portrays a symbolic violation of space, female body, and marriage (and thus hierarchy) when the Chevalier de Navarre surreptitiously enters the married Countess's bedchamber. The scene, like the entire novel, revolves around the idea of sexual and bodily transgression. The encounter between the chevalier and countess in a socially unacceptable place is a violation that the countess is keenly aware of, and she fears a direct threat to her person and her reputation. The subsequent fate of the countess is ruin: her adultery leads inexorably to pregnancy and illegitimate birth, and her punishment is simultaneously interior and social: a "breaking apart of the self" from guilt, and dishonor.[105]

Marriage was a social and economic institution, of course, but in the seventeenth century the moralistic program was broadly based, and reformers perceived marriage as the centerpiece of purified Christian society. Furthermore, the new pastoral of the Catholic Reformation and that of the patriarchal family shared an assumption that obedience, discipline, and purity were needed for reform, and associated these qualities with honor. Boileau, for example, wrote of the sanctity of the patriarchal family in terms of its desecration. He began by stating that virgins were the spouses of Christ, so that any who went about with partially exposed breasts and necks, thereby enticing evil thoughts in and actions from men, were "unfaithful to God." He then shifted from God to husband smoothly, and added, "a husband is not less jealous of the purity of his wife, than of his own honor; and as, if he be prudent, he does never indanger himself to lose his honour, so there is not any likelyhood that he should desire his wife to rune the risque of losing her innocence. A husband is always interested in the reputation of his wife."[106] Bishop Godeau gave an explanation why husbands must feel this way, and in the process he reveals how closely intertwined political, social, and religious ideologies had become. He asserted in his book on penitence that the sin of adultery is abhorred by nature because it ruins the basis of natural society which is marriage; and it was condemned by *la politique* because it disrupted the order of legitimate succession by "putting in families those who have dishonored them" and by giving the fruit of the labor of fathers to those to whom it does not belong.[107]

Consequently, husbands needed to be mindful of their wives' reputation, and likewise fathers of their daughters' honor. A woman's honor was a form of property, worth a great deal in the marriage market, and so *rapt* (seduction and abduction of minors for the purposes of clandestine marriage) and adultery were, in a sense, forms of theft. La Primaudaye specifically assailed the adulterer for seeking "against all dutie of nature to take away another mans [*sic*] honor and reputation" and the adulteress for "loosing hir soule."[108] Olivier, no less than Godeau and Boileau after him and La Primaudaye before, blended the social with the religious, arguing that luxurious dress (yet again) was necessary to advance men's reputation and standing at court and thereby "establish and increase their fortunes," but must be condemned on women, because it enticed men to adultery and thereby destroyed family fortunes by endangering the patrimony.[109] It is thus commonplace in moralistic literature from the late sixteenth through the early eighteenth centuries to find the ideal woman portrayed in terms of chastity, with disciplined humility and fidelity serving as props to a certain hierarchical order.[110]

Boileau, refuting the defense that women were unaware that their partial nudity engendered the sin of lust, pointed out that clergymen "continually preach [about it] in their pulpits . . . the learned doctors do teach [it] in their books . . . and the confessors say [it] in their tribunals."[111] This statement suggests that the moral program was being propagated across a broad front. Furthermore, especially during the second half of the seventeenth century, evangelizing missionaries were carrying the program to the countryside and the cities across France.

Evangelists like Saint Vincent de Paul and his Lazarists, and Père Honoré and the Capuchins, attracted large crowds as they traversed France, stopping for up to two weeks at a time in a region or town.[112] The common program of the missionaries began with instruction of the faithful so they could knowledgeably examine their conscience. Preaching, catechizing, singing canticles, meditating on religious works of art, and participating in processions were all geared toward instruction. The sermons of Père Honoré, for example, who came to several towns of Burgundy including Dijon in the late 1670s and 1680s, were impassioned and histrionic affairs.[113] Contrasting the suffering of Christ with the perseverence in vice by the sinner, Honoré echoed the abhorrence of luxury and nudity of women and the concern of many a moralist for trespassing sacred boundaries and polluting sacred space. He was known to focus a large part of his sermons on the sexual disorder of women, railing against their "libertine and evil conduct." Partially exposed breasts and luxurious dress in holy places, for example, were anathema to him, and he turned his rhetoric to the task of correcting such comportment.[114]

Along with emotional preaching that deliberately tried to stimulate the conscience of the faithful, the evangelists catechized (i.e., instructed in humility and obedience to God)[115] and, in a rite of purification before communion, confessed the faithful. Indeed, confession was deemed the primary task of the seventeenth-century missionary.[116] As a self-disciplined act of purification, confession prepared one for communion, and, specifically in the case of Honoré's missions, a general procession afterward.[117] The latter, given Honoré's sensitivity to sacred space, was likely a ritual demarcating sacred space by a purified body of the faithful.

Bishops and Dévots

The religious revival in France, a key part of a reordered society and the new morality that was to infuse it, was carried on numerous backs, both lay and clerical, and much of its intended dissemination was the work of individuals outside the traditional structure of the Church. Authors of civility manuals, educators, moralists, and missionaries from newly established orders, all pushed for the reform of morals. Thus far, very little has been said of bishops and priests, monks and nuns, but many of these representatives of the traditional structure of the Church were also active in reform.

One practical result of Gallicanism and the lack of formal acceptance of the decrees of the Council of Trent in France was that authority within the French church was contested by pope, king, and the Assembly of the French clergy, a group dominated by bishops. Consequently, the Gallican church never developed a consistent theological or pastoral policy,[118] although in many respects, like those pertaining to moral reform, it adhered to the spirit of many of the Tridentine decrees. This contest for authority and the resulting theological inconsistency left great latitude to individual bishops, the enhancement of whose power the Council of Trent had in any event decreed. Their power was further expanded after the Wars of Religion by the alliance with a monarch who appointed them.[119] This alliance found its ultimate expression in a royal *règlement* in 1695, when in exchange for episcopal support for his desperately needed fiscal exactions, Louis XIV tightened the bishops' authority over the parish clergy.[120]

In 1695, even after a century of religious revival and attempts at institutional reform, however, episcopal control of parish priests was still far from complete. One reason was that bishops like those of Langres, Mâcon, and Autun did not control the appointments to even a majority of the benefices in their dioceses, a situation that had not changed significantly since the sixteenth century. At the time, of 600 cures in his jurisdiction, the bishop of Langres directly administered only 132, while his counterpart in Mâcon named only a third of the benefices. Powerful abbeys like Saint Etienne and Saint Bénigne in Dijon, which controlled 30 and 40 benefices respectively, guaranteed formidable impediments to the exercise of episcopal power.[121]

Reforming bishops like Sébastien Zamet of Langres in the early seventeenth century and Gabriel Roquette, Bishop of Autun in the second half of the century, to take two Burgundian examples, therefore had sizable challenges before them. The methods of reform of both bishops (whose dioceses together covered most of Burgundy) centered on systematic surveillance and correction of their parishes. Zamet was keen on combating Protestantism and irreligious "superstition" in the countryside. To accomplish this, he attracted to his diocese zealous preachers from a variety of orders such as Oratorians, Jesuits, and Capuchins.

Zamet also believed that exemplary priests fired the souls of the laity toward devotion[122] and found an ignorant and disorderly, that is, sexually active, priesthood to be intolerable. As he stated in the preamble of his third edition of synodal statutes in 1629, "having discovered several . . . disorders during the course of our visitations" (which were prescribed by Trent and the French Estates General in 1560, 1579, and 1614 and which Zamet recommenced after a long hiatus), it was necessary once again to notify ecclesiastics of their duties.[123] With Zamet, the episcopal visitation took on "a character of spiritual accusation."[124] From 1616 to 1620 he travelled about his huge diocese and was struck by the "disorder and ignorance" of his curés. In order to correct this situation, he established one of the earliest seminaries in France.[125] He also convened numerous synods (which all parish priests were required to attend) like the ones in Langres in 1616, 1622, and 1628, and in Dijon in 1617, publishing the statutes that issued from them.

A spirit of surveillance and episcopal control pervaded these statutes. As a duke and peer of the realm, Bishop Zamet could not devote much time to pastoral visitations; but what he could not do in person, he insisted be performed by individuals directly responsible to him. When in 1628 he found that archdeacons and rural deans were subdelegating visitations and that these visitations were not being performed with proper diligence, he stated in the synodal statute of the next year that "to return ecclesiastical discipline to its former splendor"—and this phrase subsumed clerical chastity—archdeacons and rural deans had to perform the visitations in person and file written reports with the bishop's *official* immediately thereafter.[126]

To further the cause of spiritual regeneration, Zamet steadfastly supported the establishment of numerous religious orders, especially for women. He was also firmly supported by an influential and wealthy laity in these ventures. The Ursulines, an order committed to the pious education of girls in which the values of modesty and chastity were emphasized, were established in Dijon in 1608 by Françoise de Xainctonge, cousin of Anne and daughter of an influential *avocat*. The convent was first situated in a house in Saint-Médard parish, the heart of the quarter where much of the legal community resided, where four years earlier François de Sales had received many devout upper class Dijonnaise women and introduced them to his teachings.[127] When the foundation began to run short of funds, a fresh infusion of capital came from another family from the legal community, this time the widow of a *maître des requêtes* at the Parlement, Catherine de Montholon.[128] Xainctonge, for her part, continued to work closely with Zamet in establishing new congregations of Ursulines, so that by 1650 the congregation of Dijon could count 37 ancillary houses.[129]

Zamet worked closely with other women from the legal community in establishing religious foundations. The Visitation was established in Dijon in 1622 by the subsequently canonized Jeanne-Françoise Fremyot, Baronne de Chantal, daughter of a president of the Parlement.[130] Louise Morel, a widow from a family of magistrates of the Chambre des Comptes, and Marguerite Esmonin, the daughter of a councilor at the Parlement, formed the Sisters of Sainte-Marthe in Dijon, an order whose members, according to the foundation charter, were committed to being "charitable, modest, chaste, faithful, and devout."[131]

Charity, like sexual purity, was an important spiritual quality in the religious reformation, and it took its awkward place beside more mundane motivations in the establishment of hospitals. Taking care of the poor through alms-giving had always been the responsibility of good Christians, and the Catholic Reformation embraced that theological principle fully. However, devout lay and clerical individuals from the privileged classes also were concerned about the apparent and alarming increase in the ranks of beggars that threatened the public order of many a town.

In the 1630s, the existing hospital in Dijon, Saint-Esprit, was inundated by victims of misfortune in that terrible war-torn decade, and Pierre Odebert, a councilor at the Parlement and president in the Requêtes du Palais, with his wife came forward with funds ultimately exceeding 80,000£ to establish a new hospital, Notre-Dame de la Charité. Zamet enthusiastically endorsed the plan, even going so far as "to order his curés to discreetly exhort the faithful" to bequeath charitable legacies to the hospital, and then circulating a pastoral letter to be read after the sermon on the fourth Sunday of Lent once again urging charitable donations.[132]

Charity might have been the spiritual motivation, but ridding the streets of beggars was the more mundane one. Intendants of the Poor were instructed by the town council of Dijon to sweep the streets clean of beggars and incarcerate them in La Charité. Henceforth, street begging was not permitted under pain of flogging and expulsion, nor were citizens permitted to give alms directly to beggars. The hospital itself was to be administered by the Chambre des Pauvres, staffed by a phalanx of *robins*: The First President and two councillors at the Parlement, Dijon's mayor, two aldermen, two officials from the Chambres des Comptes, and a *trésorier général* from the Bureau des Finances.[133]

The efforts of systematic reformers like Zamet met with mixed results, which was not surprising given the magnitude of the task. Furthermore, not all bishops, especially in the early seventeenth century, were as committed as Zamet to the effort. Such might be said of the predecessors of Gabriel de Roquette, Bishop of Autun from 1667 to 1704, but it certainly cannot be said of Roquette. He was cut from the same cloth (and exalted social stratum) as Zamet, and he pursued even more methodically Zamet's program of thoroughly implementing a system of moral surveillance (based largely on the disciplinary decrees of the Council of Trent) that would bring a "proper order" to the priesthood and laity, and guarantee obedience to the increasingly well-defined and widely disseminated articles of the faith.

Like Zamet a half century earlier, Roquette was struck by the ignorance and "disorder"—a term that subsumed sexual license in its meaning—in which the diocesan clergy lived.[134] Until the parish clergy could be brought up to standard (and he held Saint François de Sales up as a model because of his emphasis on interior discipline), he engaged the service of domestic missionaries—Jesuits, Oratorians, Minims, Recollets, and above all, Capuchins—to spread the proper faith and, equally important, to display to the people the proper clerical model, which by now included chastity.[135]

Roquette had become aware of the state of the clergy almost immediately after assuming his espiscopate. In 1668, informally subscribing to the decrees of Trent, he visited the diocese's parishes in order to inspect the physical conditions of the parish churches and the moral state of clerics and laity alike. Given the bishop's involvement in wide-ranging projects for reform, not to mention the necessity of his frequent presence in Paris, the demands on Roquette's time did not permit regular parish visitations in subsequent years. He had no intention of abandoning this arm of episcopal surveillance, however, and so he instructed the 28 archpriests in the diocese to carry out annual visitations with the express intention of gathering information about the morality of curés and vicars. Roquette also instructed them to make surprise visits, no doubt hoping to catch suspect priests with their guard, if not their pants, down. Finally, the archpriests were to provide written reports to him of their parish visits every three months.[136]

Visitations were one way to attempt to correct a wayward clergy, and education was another. Like Zamet before him, Roquette, following Louis XIV's ordinance of 1666 enjoining all bishops to establish a seminary in their diocese, resolved to establish one in Autun. Graduates would become, in Roquette's words, a cadre of "ministers of the altar capable of serving the church and spreading everywhere the science, piety and Christian and ecclesiastical discipline."[137] Begun in 1675, subsequent enlargements to the seminary were in part financed by a broad coalition of the most powerful people in the province and, indeed, the realm: the king, Madame de Maintenon, the Duchess of Guise, Henri de Bourbon (the Prince de Condé), and in 1696, the *élus* of the Estates of Burgundy. In keeping with the lay–clerical coalition, the first superior was the wealthy Abbé Rigoley, a doctor in theology from a Burgundian parlementaire family.[138]

Roquette's systematic assault on clerical disorder also included the annual convening of synods (again informally following the dictates of Trent) and subsequent publication of synodal ordinances. Roquette's statutes reveal the seriousness with which he viewed this task, and the texts, continually employing the language of purity and sanctity, are replete with references to the necessity of sacralizing the world if reform was to be successful. In the preamble of the first ordinance, he informed his clergy that "the sanctification and the salvation of one's neighbor" was dependent upon the priest first sanctifying himself.[139] Considerable space was devoted to the exemplary behavior of the priests; "their bearing, their gestures, their words [all] must inspire veneration and piety" from the flock. "Nothing degrades the sacerdotal ministry more and renders the person of the priest more contemptible and more odious than impurity," by which he specifically meant sexual relations with women.[140]

If Roquette inherited a parish clergy still living in woeful disorder, his episcopal predecessors had successfully encouraged the establishment of new religious communities for both men and women. These orders may have been models of chastity and beacons of a purified world, but neither these new monastic houses nor the existing hospitals could cope with the rising tide of beggars. The establishment of a *hôpital général* in the diocese appeared to be an increasingly pressing matter. In 1660 in the town of Moulins in Roquette's diocese, royal letters patent authorized the founding of one. Like the enormous system of the Hôpital Général of Paris established in 1656 (deemed a "great success" in the letters patent for Moulins), that of Moulins and later Autun were intended to be places of confinement where inmates would be taught self-discipline via "the mysteries of religion" and a trade.[141] The curbing of sexual license, it was assumed by the authorities, would follow.

Before Roquette became bishop, plans existed for the building of a hospital in Autun, but the letters patent from the king were only received in 1668, one year after the diligent bishop took office. Building began immediately, and as had been the case in Dijon several decades before, the hospital was administered by a coalition of clerics and influential *robins*. Begging was declared illegal, beggars were to be cleared from the streets, and citizens were to be fined if they distributed alms to anyone.[142]

During this "age of confinement," one of the purposes of hospitals was to remedy "the scandalous life and [sexual] libertinage of most of the poor beggars."[143] Hospitals were not the only type of buildings erected to confine those suffering from the disorders of libertinage. Notre Dame du Refuge and the Maison du Bon Pasteur in Dijon were two other such establishments. Spearheaded by *dévots* of the confraternity of the Company of the Holy Sacrament and Jean-Baptiste Bernard Gontier, the Grand Vicar of three successive bishops of Langres (including Zamet), these convents which doubled as houses of confinement for penitent females were designed to help remedy, in Gontier's words, the "impurity that reigns presently so licentiously in this kingdom."[144] After the Parlement of Dijon issued an *arrêt* authorizing its establishment in 1655, Notre Dame du Refuge was situated deliberately in a neighborhood of Dijon notorious for promiscuity and prostitution. Said the reverend mother of a sister monastery in Avignon about the site in Dijon, "God wished to make serve his glory a place that had served disorder and sin." Given that parlementary presidents, councilors, and masters of requests and their wives and widows were members of the Company of the Holy Sacrament, it is hardly surprising that Gontier received both moral and financial support from them for the venture. Indeed, the royal councilor Berbis was named the "temporal father" of the convent, while Gontier became its "spiritual father."[145]

By 1675 Gontier and his parlementaire friends were intent on transforming the convent into a house of correction and to confine by force if necessary "debauched girls and women." The objection by the sisters of Notre Dame du Refuge that this policy would violate the necessary willingness for effective penitence led to the foundation in the same neighborhood of the Maison du Bon Pasteur.[146] Bénigne Joly, canon in the abbey of Saint Etienne and son of a *secrétaire* in the Parlement, led this effort which culminated in approval by the Bishop of Langres in 1682, the mayor of Dijon in 1684, and royal letters patent that were immediately registered by Parlement in 1687.[147]

Conclusion

Many devout lay people from the *robin* class resolved to bring the cloister to the street during the early modern era. Initiating the drive to sacralize society in the sixteenth century, these lay people were joined by the French clergy in the seventeenth century. Drawn from the ranks of the legal community, which at this time was asserting its role in the "restoration" of moral order, it is not surprising that these *robins* (and indeed the churchmen, many of whom were drawn from the same social milieu) would assume that sacralization should be mediated through royal justice, or that their vision of a sacralized society would criminalize sin.

Just as the social, political, and legal aspects of this vision rested upon authoritarianism, so, too, did its religious aspects. Godly reformers and moralists were just as convinced as philosophers and jurists that the new moral order could be established only if people embraced self-discipline and submitted to systems of social control. As a result, piety and civility were linked, and the Catholic Reformation found a constitutive place in the civilizing process.

The authoritarian moral order that the devout *robins* and clergymen strove to "restore" was incorporated in their sexual ethics and ideas about the confessionalism that supported these ethics. Suspicion about the destructive capacity of the passions prepared the godly to abhor "unregulated" female sexuality, that is, outside the control of men. Concupiscence consequently had to be controlled, through disciplining of the individual's conscience of lustful urges; episcopal control of priests and parishioners; and controlling bodies, through the law. How this third way was attempted, and what it meant to the people being disciplined, is the subject of the remainder of this book.

II

The Disposition
of Bodies

3

The Power of the Holy:
Reformers, Priests,
and Parishioners

The privileged classes of France—both lay and clerical—envisioned a refashioned moral order in which political, social, and religious ideologies
were in concord and in which a sexual ethic held a constitutive place. This
restructured order entailed a new type of community, no longer one
cemented primarily by horizontal ties, but one constituted over the course
of the seventeenth century of increasingly dissociated and hierarchically
organized individuals held together by the overarching authoritarian ap-
paratuses of a reformed church, a monarchical state, and a dominant and
patriarchally inclined social group. Furthermore, cleric, king, and magistrate came to share a belief that the law of the state had a sacred and central
role to play in the fashioning of this reformulated order of sexual morality,
and so clergy and elite laity locked arms and strode resolutely into the seventeenth century, bent on reform.

Community and Holiness

The religious reformation that was spearheaded in the late sixteenth century by the laity and then embraced by many churchmen in the seventeenth
was arguably the most critical component of this revised moral order, not
least because of the importance that the reinvigorated orthodoxy, especially
in sacramental matters, held for the new hierarchical community. Specifically, for Tridentine orthodoxy (though not for Jansenism) not only did
confession and communion have to be more frequent,[1] but as rituals they
were increasingly detached from the horizontal and corporate function of

61

social reconciliation and attached to a vertical relationship between the individual and God by way of the priest.[2] No longer collective and public as they had been in the Middle Ages, confession and absolution became confidential and individualized in the confessional, and the "socially integrative powers of the host" were transferred from the Mass to the feast of Corpus Christi, the latter a ritual whereby the body of the faithful was dissociated, explicitly hierarchized, and monarchized.[3]

For confession and communion to play the part in the new moral order envisioned by the reformers, systemic changes in the manner of dispensing and receiving these all-important sacraments had to be made. The pre-Tridentine church was not essentially parish-based, and Catholic reformers throughout Europe came to believe that the success of a reform built upon sacramentalism (which, in turn rested upon an individual internalization of the function of guilt and responsibility in salvation), especially in its pastoral dimension, depended upon a parochially grounded church.[4] Of course, the effectiveness of such a church would be dependent in turn upon the parish clergy, the legitimate dispensers of the sacraments. The parish priest, therefore, assumed pivotal importance to the entire reform.

Traditional orthodoxy had long held that the effectiveness of the sacrament was not dependent upon the holiness of the priest. But post-Tridentine reformers became convinced that if priests were the agents of a systematic discipline that was to be the backbone of a restored moral order, then the priests themselves had to be models of holiness. The pre-Tridentine priesthood was not so much corrupt as insufficient for this task. For the priest to be effective, he had to be dissociated from and spiritually superior to the community; and his body had to be pure and sacred, not soiled by sexual contact with women.[5]

Most sixteenth- and even early seventeenth-century priests, even by pre-Tridentine orthodox standards neither approached holiness nor were elevated above their communities. As many studies have amply shown,[6] concubinage was widespread, and priests were deeply integrated in the social life of their villages and parishes.[7] They were usually local men, at best the central participant in rituals of social reconciliation that bound the community, at worst, taking sides in familial disputes that constantly threatened the social peace of the parish. In any case, they did not, nor were they expected to, transcend the traditional social community of their parish.

The Catholic Reformation changed all that. Godly reformers were intent on sacralizing society, and the first step toward this goal was a rigorous separation of the sacred from the profane. The reformed priest was to embody the sacred, and so the reformers insisted that he be separate and distinct from the world around him. This meant that the priest must be distinguished sharply from the laity. In an effort to raise the priest above the village community, new curés were granted benefices far from their native localities.[8]

If the new priest was now an outsider, he also had to be distinguished from his parishioners in both appearance and behavior. As chapter 14, session 23, of the Council of Trent put it forthrightly, the priests must be "so conspicuous for piety and purity of morals that a shining example of good works and a guidance for good living may be expected from them."[9] Seminary education was intended to produce a priesthood that had cut its worldly ties. Instilled with the virtues of modesty, celibacy, self-control, and obedience to hierarchy—values reinforced by episcopal synodal statutes, guides for confessors, and parish visitations—the new priest was a holy agent of discipline.

In synodal statutes, for example, priests were ordered to keep their hair short and remain celibate. What brings these two seemingly disparate "virtues"—short hair and celibacy—together is their relationship to innocence, purity, and hierarchy,[10] concepts that run through seventeenth- and early eighteenth-century statutes like those of Bishop of Langres Sébastein Zamet or Archbishop of Besançon François-Joseph de Grammont.[11] Zamet demanded that priests keep their hair short and their cassocks clean. He railed against the "dirtiness of concubinage" and praised the "purity of conscience" the curé must possess to celebrate satisfactorily "the holy sacrifice of the Mass." Indeed, for Zamet "innocence and purity are the principal interior ornaments of the soul."[12]

Given the connections among sexual purity, separation, boundary articulation, and hierarchy that were explored earlier, we need not be surprised that the language of purity was used so commonly in the reform of the clergy. Antoine Godeau, Bishop of Vence, was far from alone when he wrote "On the Chastity of Priests" in the second half of the seventeenth century, in which he echoed Zamet and many other reformers by asserting that "the nature of the functions of the priest demand continence," and that the sacrifice at the altar demanded purity, specifically virginity.[13] Sexual relations with women were not only a crime against the altar, but also one against the community of the faithful. Debauched priests, according to seventeenth-century clerics like Vincent Houdry or Louis Bourdaloue, created a scandal in the parish, and *scandale* was a sin against Christian charity because it irrevocably robbed others of innocence and incited them to sin.[14]

To function effectively as an agent of the refashioned moral order, the priest had to be pure in thought and deed. In a sense, the priest—his body and mind—was the first human being to be subdued and sacralized in the massive transformation of society that godly reformers, lay and clerical alike, envisioned. The Burgundian Jean de Lesme, called "de l'Hôpital," chaplain of Saint-Mayeul, for instance, could stand as their ideal. This unambitious cleric's entire life was dedicated to a renunciation of worldliness. He was the model of holiness: he catechized the young, tended the poor and sick, styled his life after the saints, feared God, obeyed hierarchy, guarded his celibacy by avoiding eye contact with women and continually mortifying his body with an iron-studded undergarment, and died in "an odor of sanctity" in 1695.[15] Priests like de Lesme were unusual if not singular,[16] but most of the godly reformers would have agreed with the Abbé Le Lorrain de Vallemont that reformed priests and laity should strive to replicate the original Christians: "all were holy then. . . . The minsters of the mysteries were holy. The people were holy."[17]

Libidinous Clerics

By the seventeenth century, then, priests were central to the new moral vision shared by the clergy and elite laity, notably the *robins,* that sought to reinforce hierarchy by imposing discipline. The demand for discipline and order was prompted in no small measure by an anxiety that stemmed from the successes of the Protestant Reformation. Thus, because sacerdotalism had to be reaffirmed to challenge the Protestants effectively, the first bodies to be controlled were priests' bodies. Historians generally contend that the majority of priests were "reformed" by 1700, and that the Catholic Reformation succeeded at that level. This is probably true, but it is also true that a minority continued to resist the demands of celibacy, however, and this minority can illuminate the shifting attitudes concerning the sexual behavior of ordained men. The demand for clerical celibacy is not simply a story about institutional repression, but also about what villagers, city dwellers, lay and clerical authorities, and finally the priests themselves thought and did about sexual behavior.

For nearly the entire sixteenth century, clerical concupiscence was a matter of common knowledge. In the stories of Dijonnais Etienne Tabourot, licentious clergymen are stock characters.[18] Fiction mirrored reality, because evidence depicts the popular clergy—Carmelites, Jacobins, Cordeliers—as often given to sexual license. Prostitution was legal throughout Burgundy until 1561, and one finds ample references to priests as clients of prostitutes.[19] Quite frequent as well were reported instances of churchmen deflowering virgins,[20] but most commonplace of all were clergymen keeping concubines.[21] Canonically, the Church had for centuries prohibited clerical marriage and, somewhat less frequently, clerical concubinage.[22] But if it had been relatively successful in eliminating the first, the latter was still prevalent well into the sixteenth century.

Still, it was during this century that sentiments began to change, and it was not just the church authorities that literally tightened the noose around the neck of some sexually active churchmen. True, the Council of Trent in 1563 proclaimed that any ecclesiastic guilty of keeping a concubine was, on first offense, to be admonished; continued transgression would lead to deprivation of a third of his revenue. For a third violation priests were to be suspended from clerical functions and their benefice, and a fourth violation would make the suspension permanent.[23] Dogmatic decrees such as these were far from new, however, and in terms of severity of prosecution, the Church may have lagged behind pious lay judicial officers and judges.

Since the Middle Ages the Church had claimed jurisdiction over sexual matters among cleric and noncleric alike,[24] but in the sixteenth century powerful *laymen* came to feel it was too lax in enforcing clerical celibacy. Indeed, many must have wondered how serious the Church was, when the synodal statutes promulgated by the bishop of Autun in 1557 and 1558 made no mention whatsoever of clerical sexual behavior.[25] A similar indifference was evident in sixteenth-century pastoral visitations, when the bishop or his representatives were overwhelmingly concerned with the material aspects of the parish and neglected any inquest into the morals of the parish priests.[26]

Because no documentation of first-instance trial proceedings from ecclesiastical courts exists in Burgundy's archives before the eighteenth century,[27] it is impossible to know whether the local church was prosecuting sexually active clergymen. Such records, however, are abundantly preserved (into the 1530s) from Burgundy's neighboring province to the north, Champagne. An incomparably rich collection from the bishop of Troyes's court confirms Roger Doucet's observation that although the *officialité* courts were quite busy prosecuting immoral clergymen during the sixteenth century, it "was in general very moderate in repression; it preferred good counsel to chastisement."[28]

During the first third of the sixteenth century, proceedings at Troyes against churchmen for illicit sexual activity were far from rare, but the punishments of the ecclesiastical courts, compared to what the lay courts meted out at the end of the century, were relatively mild. Often proceedings never reached sentencing,[29] and if they did, fines (never more than six *écus*, and usually much less), verbal or written admonishments, and occasional prison sentences (never more than a month) were the extent of punishment.

For example, in 1515 Eudes and Adam Milot, priests from Troyes, were found by neighbors in Adam's room with two women of "evil ways" (*mauvaise vie*). But even though this event caused a "great scandal," they were only given a verbal admonishment and a fine of one *écu* and a pound of wax each.[30] In 1529, Sanson Caignon, chaplain of Neuvy, was found guilty of sexual relations with eight of his female parishioners and, even though he also toted about the parish an arquebus and a crossbow (highly inappropriate for a man of the cloth), was only fined four *écus* and four pounds of wax.[31] Similarly, Jean de Tours, a priest from Plancy, was sentenced for having a concubine as well as for drunkenness in public taverns and blasphemy, but he was treated much more leniently by the bishop's court in 1530 than if he had been had tried for the same crimes at the end of the century in secular courts. Despite the fact that he had already been admonished to lead a sober and chaste life following an earlier transgression and was still carrying on with the same woman, he was simply warned again (albeit in writing) and fined four *écus* and four pounds of wax.[32]

Not even an outright admission of guilt necessarily prompted a stern reprimand. In 1522, Vautherin Ladvocat, curé of Fresnay, was accused of concubinage. He readily confessed, adding, as if to partially exonerate himself, that his lover had been his servant and was over forty years of age (Canon Law required that female servants of priests be at least that age). As a result, he was verbally admonished to live chastely and was fined two *livres* and two pounds of wax.[33] Similarly, when Jean Baudin, curé of Courcemain, admitted to charges of carnal relations with and impregnating one of his parishioners in 1529, his sentence carried a verbal admonition and a fine of three *écus* and three pounds of wax.[34] More severe by church standards, but still relatively lax compared to what the future held, was the sentence handed down a few years earlier to three priests who, following their confession, were each found guilty of carnal relations with a woman. They were sentenced to prison terms of two weeks, one month, and fifteen days and fined six, one, and two *écus* respectively.[35]

Jurisdiction, Priests, and Women

Granting that several *écus* were of substantial value and wax was a valuable commodity in the early sixteenth century, and judging from the response of lay authorities to ecclesiastical prosecution and sentencing, the penalties were lenient and ineffectual. King Francis I certainly felt this way when in 1516 he goaded church authorities in the Concordat of Bologna to control the sexuality of their clerics, even asserting that the secular arm by way of the criminal justice system could intervene. This royal challenge was not an attempt to secularize the criminal justice system; rather, it was a step toward the sacralizing of society. According to the concordat, not only would offending priests be deprived of their benefices (a self-serving demand on the part of the king, given the provisions of the concordat concerning royal appointment to benefices), but clerical superiors who for "the hope of gain" permitted such abominable behavior would be "eternally cursed" by the "Most Christian King."[36]

In 1539, this king took another step toward reforming the French clergy. In the influential ordinance of Villers-Cotterets, in order to provide his courts with greater scope of action,[37] he attempted to clarify the boundaries between ecclesiastical and secular jurisdiction. Although the king's ordinance perhaps clarified what existed before, jurisdictional ambiguity would mark practical jurisprudence and provide ample material for legal scholars trying to sort it out, until the end of the ancien régime.[38] Of great significance, in fact because of its vagueness, was the king's claim that his courts had supreme jurisdiction over crimes involving "public scandal," even if they involved clerics. One year later he further encroached on traditional ecclesiastical jurisdiction by prohibiting church judges from trying criminal cases without first notifying the nearest *procureur du roi*.[39]

After Francis's reign, church courts could still hear cases of *délit commun* (that is, crimes without public scandal) in which a clergyman was the defendant. Henceforth, however, all cases involving lay persons as defendants could only be heard in secular courts unless the offense were of a purely spiritual or sacramental nature.[40] What constituted "purely spiritual" offenses, the king, in typically ambiguous fashion, did not specify, again allowing his judges to interpret the law as they saw fit. Furthermore, after Francis's reign, if parlementaire judges determined that church courts were overstepping their jurisdictional boundaries (as intimated by the king), the king reserved the right of secular courts to intervene. It was part of the *avocat* or *procureur du roi*'s responsibility to make this distinction in the interest of the public,[41] and the royal judges at Parlement would then hear an *appel comme d'abus*, their subsequent judgment being final. This happened, for example, in 1565 when the Parlement heard an appeal from a disgruntled individual who claimed that the *officialité* (bishop's court) of Autun had overstepped its jurisdiction and encroached on that of the local bailliage. The Parlement ruled in the lower royal court's favor and prohibited "*officials* and other ecclesiastical judges . . . from taking jurisdiction in lay matters under penalty of nullification of the proceedings and payment of all expenses, damages and interests in their own and private names," as well as a fine. These royal judges also ordered the *official* of Autun to appear before the Parlement personally to respond to any questions the parlementaires had concerning his conduct.[42]

One probable result of Villers-Cotterets, beyond generating frequent complaints by ecclesiastics,[43] was a reduction in the caseload that came before the *officialités*.[44] In any case, as subsequent trials amply demonstrate, the king's courts were increasingly inclined to exploit the changes set in motion by Francis I.[45] Secular judges believed that they, no less than their ecclesiastical counterparts, had been entrusted with the spiritual reform of society;[46] and if the church courts were lax in performing their duty, then the secular courts would take over adjudication and reserve the right to circumscribe the church courts' subsequent authority. Francis had provided the opportunity for his judges to interpret the meaning of the ambiguous term "public scandal." In cases of sexual misconduct specifically, secular jurisdiction became greatly extended, first over concubines and, eventually, over wayward clerics themselves.

First to be hauled into secular courts for sexual offenses implicating churchmen were the women involved. This fact is hardly surprising given male ideas about the culpability of women, especially in sexual matters in which it was assumed the man had been victimized. Even before Villers-Cotterets, in 1532 the Parlement of Burgundy had issued an *arrêt* responding to "la plainte, clameur et doléance" made to the court by the *procureur du roi* at the royal bailliage of Dijon concerning "public and scandalous" concubines. The *robins* sitting on the court ordered all of the offending women to be banished from their court's jurisdiction. Reflecting the Neoplatonist mind set so pervasive at the time, the judges feared that macrocosmic disorder—"plagues, famines, and other punishments and flagellations"—that the "Blessed Creator had let loose on His people"—was directly related to the microcosmic disorder of the concubines' bold sexual behavior. In the minds of the parlementaires, the women clearly were culpable (and under lay jurisdiction) but, anticipating future jurisprudential changes, the court also "exhorted . . . all bishops, prelates, and others having power . . . and authority over ecclesiastics within the jurisdiction of this court" to enforce entirely the provision dealing with concubinage in the Concordat of 1516.[47]

The Concordat and the Burgundian *arrêt* that echoed it threatened to strip offending clerics of their benefices, but the subsequent surviving court records over the next half century or so (admittedly urban and appellate) demonstrate that it was women, and not yet churchmen, who were embroiled in criminal trials within the secular courts. For example, in 1560 the 35-year-old Jehanne Menevault was arrested by the procureur syndic of Dijon and charged with concubinage.[48] An immigrant from Aignay-le-duc in the service of Laurent Huguenot, an inaptly named (for a Catholic in 1560) chaplain at Saint Pierre church in Dijon, Menevault did not find her case enhanced by the fact that she was estranged from her husband. The sentence that the moralistic syndic recommended to Dijon's town council was for Menevault to be publicly whipped and sent back to her husband to live "as an honest wife" (*comme femme de bien*). He wrote not a word about the chaplain. The syndic could have charged Huguenot with spiritual incest or adultery, "scandalous" crimes and thus *cas privilégiés* under secular jurisdiction, but apparently he considered the cleric's offense a *délit commun* that was under the jurisdiction of the *officialité*.

We have no record of whether Menevault was whipped, but scarcely three months later a merchant saddler named Nicolas Giroult filed a complaint with the same court alleging that Menevault had for four years lived with Huguenot and was still with him.[49] The concerned saddler complained that the scandalous behavior of these two, as well as of another concubine and priest living in a room above Huguenot's, was setting a bad example for Giroult's children. The indignant saddler knew that Huguenot's superiors had ordered him to send his concubine back to her husband, but apparently to no avail; "for the honor of God," Giroult requested that the banishment of the concubine be enforced. Even though with Giroult's allegation the court could have claimed jurisdiction over the chaplain because the case was now publicly scandalous, it still opted not to prosecute him.

One finds the same tone in a different trial in June of the same year.[50] The offending priests were known by name, both of whom were caught in flagrante delicto by the night watch. It was the five concubines, however, who were arrested. Not that the court lacked curiosity about priestly behavior (the syndic pointedly asked one of the women if she knew any other women "serving" the priests), but until 1560, even though it had the legal authority, the court apparently lacked the confidence to move against scandalous priests. This would change shortly.

An *arrêt* issued by the Parlement in 1563, at the request of the syndic of Dijon, reiterated the secular jurisdictional claims over scandalous clergymen but also ordered a firmer treatment of clerics. Ideas about culpability were beginning to shift; as the reforming ethos of discipline gathered steam, the elite laity increasingly expected clerics to master their lustful passions, and if they could not, they could and would be held responsible. The parlementaires wrote that despite several *arrêts* ordering severe punishment for concubinage, many churchmen continued to keep women. With the Wars of Religion now raging and chaos unleashed upon the land, the judges believed that, "By such acts [of sexual licentiousness] are demonstrated the will to follow their evil and voluptuous affections without having regard for the troubles [the Wars of Religion] that presently are so widespread in the kingdom." And Burgundy's parlementaires were certain about what had caused the "troubles": "principally . . . the corrupt . . . morals of ecclesi-astics."[51]

Up to this point, the *arrêt* of 1563 noted, Dijon's mayor and aldermen had simply urged the churchmen by "gentle means" to behave as their profession and ecclesiastical status required. It appears, however, that the lay authorities were losing patience. When Philiberte Huguenin's conviction for "lewdness and immodest behavior" [*paillardise et vie impudique*] with churchmen was appealed to Parlement from the municipal court of Autun in October 1566, the judges not only ordered Philiberte, the self-styled "Queen of Hungary," whipped, fined, and banished, but it also followed the recommendations of the *Procureur Général* concerning the ecclesias-tics named in the trial, who were to be tried for *crimes privilégiés*. Further-more, the court exhorted "the Bishop of Autun and all other bishops, their vicars, officials and chapters . . . within the jurisdiction of this court . . . to carefully and diligently survey the clergymen within their charge . . . to be informed of their ways and morals, to proceed against the scandalous, and from all of this to be led toward the reformation required by the holy councils and decrees." If the church did not take this action promptly, then Parlement "enjoined municipal officers to proceed with the arrest of ecclesiastics con-versing with lascivious women and girls . . . draw up reports . . . and deliver them to the [Parlement] within fifteen days."[52]

The royal court was as jealous of its jurisdictional privileges as it was earnest about the reform of the clergy; in fact, it viewed its privileges and clerical reform as two sides of the same coin. Two months after the Huguenin appeal, Parlement heard an *appel comme d'abus* against Antoine de Chaumont, vicar of Dessigny. Chaumont had been sentenced by the *of-ficial* of Chalon-sur-Saône for "immodesty and lewdness" with a certain Claudine, one of the vicar's married parishioners. Because such behavior "greatly scandalized the inhabitants" of the parish, Parlement ruled that the case was "privileged" and so within royal jurisdiction, and it annulled the *official*'s sentence. Chaumont was not off the hook, however, because Parlement immediately arrested and imprisoned him, and commenced a criminal trial against him.[53]

Lay judges continued to denounce sexually promiscuous churchmen. In February 1573, a 22-year-old newcomer to Dijon under suspicion of prostitution, Pierrette Faison, was asked pointedly by the syndic if she had slept with any priests since she arrived in town.[54] She said no, but the syndic could have been dubious, given the ample testimony he had from previous unrelated cases. Scarcely a fortnight before Faison's interrogation, for ex-ample, Marie Panon, another immigrant from Burgundy's countryside being tried for concubinage, had freely admitted to carnal relations with priests, selling her favors to Claude Gascon, a priest at Dijon's Saint Jean church.

In addition to Gascon, she had lived with a canon in Gray as well as with a priest affiliated with Saint Michel church in Dijon, bearing the canon a child and on the verge of doing the same for the priest from Dijon.[55]

Clerical concubinage was an offense the lay authorities were apparently becoming quite concerned about. They showed no hesitation in prosecuting women for it, and were beginning to prosecute the men. Simultaneous to Panon's case, proceedings transpired against Anne Marmillot, 25, and Perrenette Marpault, 60, the former for concubinage and prostitution, the latter for procuring.[56] Marmillot's testimony reflected a hardened individual who had had scrapes with the law before. When asked if she had been instructed in a previous sentence for sexual waywardness "to live modestly and chastely," she responded "I don't remember," and when she was asked for what she had been arrested a second time, she retorted, "You know full well and I have nothing else to say."[57] She had been sent home to her mother by an earlier sentence,[58] but depositions by neighbors showed clearly that her mother knew little of her daughter's whereabouts, or where she was sleeping.

It turned out she was living with a certain Chasot, a priest at the royal church of Sainte Chapelle, a liaison that had been arranged by the priest's servant, Marpault. The unsympathetic syndic had had enough of the unrepentant recidivist Marmillot and recommended that she be sentenced to execution by hanging. For Marpault, convicted of procuring as well as aiding and abetting concubinage, the syndic asked for flogging and banishment. The town council was slightly more merciful than the syndic had wished, opting to flog Marmillot and banish her for life. Marpault, because of her age, was spared the whip but also was banished for life. Marmillot promptly appealed to the Parlement (the whole trial from arrest to final sentence took only nine days), which ordered that she be flogged. The stipulated site for the whipping, however, was not the traditional Place du Morimont, but rather the square next to Saint Chapelle, where her former lover was still affiliated. The court may not yet have been ready to bring sexually active churchmen before the bar (especially those affiliated with a church like Sainte Chapelle, whose clerics had close familial ties with many *robins*), but it was taking an increasingly intolerant stance toward them, including this gesture of condemnation, even warning.

Two years later, Dijon's syndic actually interrogated Jean Remonquet, a priest at the parish church of Saint Nicolas. For his criminal misconduct, Remonquet was ordered by the town council to provide 80 sous to his former servant whom he had impregnated, half for the costs of childbirth and half for repatriating her to her native village. This particular temptation was thereby removed from the priest, but he also was admonished to leave "immodest girls and women" (*les filles et femmes impudiques*) alone, "under pain of being punished and chastized in an exemplary manner."[59]

Incrementally, lay courts prosecuted deviant priests, but the authorities took hesitant steps, and jurisdictional boundaries continued to be imprecise. When Jeanne Laurens was purportedly assaulted by a rural vicar, a lower secular court found the priest guilty and not only fined him two *écus* but awarded the young woman's father (who, with the *procureur du roi*, had filed suit) twenty *écus* in *intérêts* to serve as her future dowry. On the moral plane, however, the court wavered. It warned the priest that further scandal would result in another fine, but added that such a case would be taken before the archbishop of Besançon's court at Auxonne. The lower secular court's decision was upheld in an appeal to the Parlement of Burgundy, along with the dowry, but perhaps in order to send a message to wayward churchmen, the fine was increased to a hefty ten *écus*, and the priest was imprisoned until payment was made.[60]

The secular courts, though increasingly assuming the task of disciplining the clergy, apparently were not committed to taking over entirely the caseload of the *officialités*, even of "scandalous" crimes. They preferred that lay and ecclesiastical authorities work jointly toward a sacralized society, with the church more effectively doing its duty in this partnership. Consequently, secular judges continued to exhort the ecclesiastical courts to prosecute wayward churchmen, and they were bold enough to demand that the *officiaux* report to the Parlement that they had done so. In 1588, for example, Parlement appended an *arrêt* sentencing a concubine with an order to publish all previous *arrêts* "given against *les ecclésiastiques concubinaires*" and an order to the *official* of the diocese of Chalon-sur-Saône to proceed against them and to certify before Parlement in one month that he had done so.[61]

Sometimes, secular court officials arrested offending clerics but remanded them to the church court for prosecution. For example, in 1582 this happened to a vicar of the village of Bart named Jean Damas. The *procureur du roi* at the royal bailliage of Auxois accused him of "lustful and scandalous ways" (*vie lubrique et scandaleuse*), but in spite of the alleged scandal, Damas was turned over to the bishop's court for prosecution.[62]

Even though the lay courts only slowly put into practice what they had been empowered to do by the various ordinances of Francis I and those decreed at Orléans in 1561, Moulins in 1566, and Blois in 1579, clerics in the latter part of the sixteenth century (though not yet as much as the women they were involved with) were increasingly at risk of criminal prosecution in secular courts for "scandalous" sexual transgressions of their putative celibate state. In 1588, Dijon's syndic thought he had uncovered a nest of "lustful and scandalous" monks and nuns at the Saint-Esprit Hospital in Dijon, but could only win a sentence against the unfortunate Magdeleyne Richon and convinced the town council to hang her, again selecting a site that would make a clear statement, in front of the hospital. If the other nun and the three monks were released for insufficient evidence, however, the syndic made sure that they could be rearrested if new evidence could be gathered, and he doggedly pursued his quarry by initiating further investigation. Capital sentences like Richon's were automatically appealed to the Parlement, and these eminent jurists, after commuting the execution of Richon to a just slightly less brutal punishment of life imprisonment in solitary confinement at the hospital, pointedly encouraged the syndic to continue his investigation of the other ecclesiastics.[63]

Concubines, not surprisingly, continued to receive their share of trouble from the law,[64] but in the 1580s and 1590s—when many of Burgundy's *robins* were embracing the sacred designs of the Holy League—sexually immoral clergymen also were being hunted down. This trend appeared to be especially true of churchmen without institutional or familial protection.[65] In 1592, for example, a priest apparently unaffiliated with any church was convicted of concubinage by Dijon's town council, ordered out of town, and fined a substantial twenty *écus*. The sentence, crippling for a non-beneficed priest, was upheld in full by the Parlement.[66]

Three years later, when Jean Chardon, a priest from Gevrey, was caught sleeping with his servant Nicole Morisot and, after having been warned to cease such behavior, was caught again four months later, both the man and the woman were arrested by Dijon's syndic. Chardon protested that it was commonplace for servants to sleep with their masters (ignoring the fact that Morisot was married), and Morisot asserted that she thought it was acceptable because she was too old to have children and she kept her son between herself and the priest. All to no avail, at least for Morisot. She predictably was banished, and although we have no record of what happened to Chardon, it is nonetheless significant that he was arrested.[67]

Churchmen like Perrault, a canon from Chalon-sur-Saône, who in 1615 passed a young woman around among several other clerics and, when she became pregnant by one of them, provided her with three *livres* and a place in the suburbs to give birth to the child, may have eluded the grasp of lay prosecutors,[68] but as the seventeenth century progressed, more clerics felt the wrath of secular law for moral crimes. Prosecution was a matter of formulating charges that would justify lay jurisdiction, and moral crimes provided ample ambiguity. Simple concubinage may have remained a *délit commun*, but it was not difficult for a dedicated lay prosecutor to uncover "scandalous" circumstances that would bring the crime under lay jurisdiction as a *délit privilégié*. Any scandal (i.e., threat to public order) surrounding the crime would suffice, as would classifying the offense as "spiritual incest" or "spiritual adultery." Any sexual activity with a woman by a priest could be defined as either of the latter two, since the priest was considered to be either father of his parishioners or married to Mother Church.

In the seventeenth century, it appears that the number of charges against women of concubinage had tapered off in the lay courts but that clerical transgressions were being redefined from *délits communs* to the more severely punishable *délits privilégiés* and consequently brought increasingly under lay jurisdiction. Trials in the early sixteenth century for spiritual adultery in Champagne, for example, demonstrate that the church did not punish offending priests as severely as lay judges in Burgundy did a century later. In 1516 Nicolas Filleul, the curé of Ville-sur-Terre, admitted that he had had carnal relations with one of his married parishioners and did not deny the allegation that he "supported her publicly in the curial house," but for this offense the bishop's court sentenced him only to three *écus* and three pounds of wax in fines and admonished him to send his lover away and never to see her alone again.[69]

Similarly, Louis Lebon, a monk from a local priory, admitted to seeking out a married woman in the nearby village because of her bad reputation. He confessed to carnal relations with her, but claimed that he left her for two reasons, neither of which were spiritually motivated: people had started to talk about his liaison and he hoped to avoid scandal, and he discovered that she had venereal disease (here called the *mal de Naples*, but everywhere outside of France, the "French disease"). The bishop's court did not fine him, but sent him to prison for a month.[70]

Contrast these relatively lenient sentences with that of a vicar from Beaune and his lover, the wife of a royal sergeant, at the hands of lay judges in 1620. Given the lowly status of the lovers, it is unlikely that either was connected to the world of power closely enough to forestall the judgment of Burgundy's Parlement. They were sentenced to be hanged for adultery, and the priest was also fined 1,000 *livres* in damages payable to the cuckolded husband who, after his marriage contract was declared null, also was handed his wife's dowry.[71]

This is the first documented execution of an adulterous cleric in Burgundy's archives (although the records only go back to 1582), but certainly not the last. In 1627 Claude Rossignol, a curé from Cormos, was hanged with his lover,[72] a fate that two years later befell (albeit in effigy) the fugitive curé of the parish of Tavenay, Jean Catheau, and his pregnant lover Anatole Chaussin.[73]

In the early seventeenth century, the Church courts not only began to join lay judges in meting out harsh punishment for crimes like Catheau's and Chaussin's, but they also actively supported one another in prosecution. In 1602 the Bishop of Mâcon, Gaspard Dinet, in synodal statutes exhorted royal officials and others of secular justice to arrest priests suspected or caught in the act of sexual relations with women, though he stipulated that the offending cleric be handed over to the bishop's tribunal for prosecution.[74] Eight years later a royal decree ordered royal judicial officials to provide *mainforte* for the execution of sentences from ecclesiastical judges,[75] and in 1639 Louis XIII assigned an *avocat* and a *procureur du roi* to each ecclesiastical jurisdiction in the realm.[76] In the case of Catheau and Chaussin, the adulterous couple had been charged by the *procureur d'office* of the bishop's court at Saint Martin-les-Autun and then were to be handed over to the secular justice system to be hanged. In upholding the sentence in full, the Parlement not only was satisfied with the lower court's judgment but also was scarcely troubled by the fuzziness of jurisdictional boundaries so long as ecclesiastical discipline and the attendant reforming of society were being implemented.[77]

One finds similar circumstances in another case from 1649,[78] where the *promoteur* in the *officialité* of Autun was joined by a *procureur du roi* in prosecuting Jean Cadioux, a fugitive curé from Alize, and prisoner Anne

Travelet, the wife of a carpenter from Alize. Cadioux was sentenced by the Parlement to hang, as was Travelet, but the latter was spared when her husband agreed to take her "to the country."

One still finds stern jurisprudence handed down by lay and clerical judges for moral laxity among clerics in the second half of the seventeenth century, but there are some noticeable changes. First, churchmen tend to receive harsher judgments than the women with whom they were involved; and second, recourse to capital punishment, at least by the Parlement, appears to have subsided. Death was still decreed, as in 1676 when Jacques Melenet, a curé from St Jean-de-Losne, was prosecuted for "spiritual incest" committed with a nun at the hospital there; however, this case was apparently of some significance and quite unusual, since it was begun in the *officialité* of Dijon but then was quickly taken over by a royal councilor at the request of the *procureur général* at the Parlement. The unfortunate cleric was condemned to be burned alive, a much stiffer punishment, than that reserved for the nun.[79]

A more common (though still severe) sentence for serious moral crimes than capital punishment, at least from the Parlement, was banishment or forced service in the king's galleys.[80] In 1694 Louis Marchant, curé of Pontalier, was charged in the *officialité* of Auxonne with spiritual incest, public adultery, rape, impiety, and sacrilege. He was convicted and turned over to the secular court for punishment, and the royal bailliage, a lower court, then condemned him to be hanged and his body burned to ashes. On appeal to the Parlement, however, the sentence was commuted to service in the king's galleys for life. Claire Mathieu, his sexual partner, was convicted of concubinage, adultery, and lewd and scandalous ways, but unlike women before her who were executed for such behavior, the Parlement only banished her from Burgundy for three years.[81]

The retreat from the taking of life at Burgundy's highest court as well as moderating of sentences against women can be seen in other cases in the second half of the seventeenth and the first half of the eighteenth centuries.[82] In 1662, the curé of St Agnan was banished from Burgundy for six years and fined 300 *livres* by the Parlement for spiritual incest with two sisters who were his parishioners.[83] Six years later, the high court banished a rural curé from the kingdom for life, again for spiritual incest (a crime punished by hanging earlier in the century), for having had sexual relations with a married woman who, for reasons not explained in the decision, was acquitted.[84] In 1670 a priest who confessed to impregnating his lover, in a case of spiritual incest that was initiated by the *officialité* of Dijon but was taken over by the *procureur général* of the Parlement, was ordered to pay child support, assessed a thirty *livres* fine, and banished from Burgundy for life. No formal action was taken against the woman, although she was left with the unlikely prospect of collecting child support from a banished vagrant.[85]

Little had changed by the early eighteenth century, except that first-instance trial records now exist from various *officialités* in Burgundy. In 1717, the *promoteur* of the archbishop's court in Besançon initiated an inquest into, and even requested a *monitoire*[86] against, the behavior of Gaillot, a priest at Macornay. Gaillot's violations of the diocesan statutes were extensive, though we have no record of any punishment. The *promoteur* alleged that he kept young women as servants and was seen with women, especially one young woman of ill-repute, in public. He was so undisciplined (*débordé*) and sexually active that he was totally insensitive to sacred space and time, qualities the Catholic Reformation greatly stressed. Not only did he roam the streets of the village with other young men looking for women, but he also was seen without any *marque de religion* walking in a garden with a young woman of ill-repute during, of all times, Mass. Gaillot's transgression of sacred time was matched by his disregard for the holiness of the night before the festival of Saint Laurent, when he was found sleeping with a young woman.[87]

If we can only wonder what punishment Gaillot received, more is known about the fate of Simon Humbelot, tried for similar crimes. In 1720, this curé of Magny Saint Médard was charged in the *officialité* of Langres with corrupting several of his female parishioners, the seduction actually beginning in the confessional. The lay prosecutor (this time the *lieutenant criminel* at the bailliage) joined the *promoteur* of the *official* in prosecution (evidence that church and state were still working together toward the goal of a sacralized society); but as in Gaillot's case, charges were confined to the priest and excluded any mention of the women involved. The case finally was appealed to the Parlement, which condemned Humbelot to 130 *livres* in fines and nine years in the king's galleys.[88]

The point is not that these were lenient sentences, but rather that the court simultaneously retreated from invoking capital punishments for moral crimes by churchmen and prosecuting the women involved with these priests. The state, however, was keenly interested in regulating the morals of the French clergy; it was commonplace for lay prosecutors to jointly initiate cases with the *officialité* or entirely take them over.

To this point I have examined the role of the priest in the program of the sacralization of society, which was initiated by the lay authorities and was joined in the seventeenth century by the upper clerical establishment. The new moral vision championed sacerdotalism both as an effective challenge to the Protestant heresy and as the necessary bedrock of a reinvigorated hierarchical social and political arrangement. Discipline was the key to a return to both cosmic and mundane "order," and regulating priests was the logical starting point. The demand for clerical celibacy was especially important because of prevailing attitudes toward sexuality which, as seen in chapter 2, were so closely tied to ideas about disorder.

Holiness, Sexuality, Power, and the Law

Historians have generally accepted the argument that the French priesthood had been reformed by 1700,[89] a position I have not tried to contradict. The incomplete nature of the kinds of evidence in Burgundy that historians have used to demonstrate the impact of reformed Catholicism (church court records, parish visitations) on the behavior of priests would make this an impossible task. Wayward priests did, nonetheless, continue in evidence into the eighteenth century. Although perhaps a deviant minority, their existence illustrates, in a qualitative fashion, two important issues: first, by continuing to come in for their share of judicial reprimand, they demonstrate that the authorities continued in their program of sacralization even into the century of Enlightenment; and second, they provide glimpses of ideas about holiness, sexuality, and the exercise of power at the level of the village or city street. If, to this point, the focus has been on institutional developments and perceptions of the authorities, I turn now to the everyday world.

By making the priest the embodiment of holiness, the Catholic Reformation empowered him to an unprecedented degree. By insisting on asceticism, that "solemn ritual of dissociation,"[90] the godly not only affirmed the increasingly rigid hierarchy, but they also hoped to free the priest from sexuality and its consequent ties to disorder, not to mention to family and economic interest. Beyond that, the reformers emphasized the priest's mediation between his flock and God, and granted him powers over demons and of healing body (through the laying on of hands) and soul (through confession, penance, and absolution).

As the locus of spiritual power, the priest was a man to be reckoned with in the village or parish, and he had numerous ways to make his influence felt. Why and how he exercized his power, and what the laity felt about it, are the subjects of the remainder of this chapter.

From 1550 to 1730 there appeared to be a growing intolerance by the laity, and not just among the institutional powers, for clerical sexual transgressions. This trend may show a reformed populace increasingly impatient with the curés' failure to fulfill their expected role in the village or parish as mediator between God and the community. It may also indicate, however, a growing awareness on the part of the laity that the new sexual ethic preached by the reformers and a corresponding responsiveness by reform-minded jurists in court might be powerful tools to advance the laity's interests against curés who, as Hoffman and Tackett have recently demonstrated, as a result of the Catholic Reformation found their social position elevated and themselves increasingly embroiled in worldly matters.[91] Sacralization could have very worldly results.

In Dijon in the late fifteenth and early sixteenth centuries, it was not uncommon for the laity, even groups of female neighbors, to file complaints with the civil authorities about the disorderly behavior of women who consorted with priests. A pious vocabulary may or may not have been used, but the churchmen themselves, though mentioned as keepers of these women, as yet came in for no blame. It was the actions of the wayward women that were reprehensible. These women of "dissolute ways" were likely, as the self-styled "most pious of the bourgeois notables" put it in 1486, to incur the wrath of God for the rest of the community.[92] A generation later the "good wives [*femmes de bien*] of Saint Pierre street" may have been no less worried about God's displeasure, but in their complaint to the town council they stated a more worldly concern about the disorder to their neighborhood when rowdy young men were attracted there by the concubines of priests, whom they requested be kicked off the street.[93]

Throughout the sixteenth century and into the early seventeenth century, churchmen were singled out in the lay discourse of the courts as well as of the streets, but not always for direct opprobrium. Rather, they frequently served as foils for the condemnation of female behavior. It was common in slander directed at women, for instance, to allege sexual relations with priests,[94] just as it was important to note in depositions of criminal cases of prostitution or procuring that among the clientele were clergymen.[95] However, about the time that the civil authorities were willing to prosecute sexually active priests (the late sixteenth century), we find depositions of ordinary people reflecting the same view. Perhaps the laity now felt the confidence to accuse clerics of whom they had long since morally disapproved, or perhaps their attitudes had changed along with those of the civil authorities; in any case, witnesses in criminal cases were more inclined to incriminate clergymen in the last quarter of the sixteenth century than before.

For example, in 1573 the 50-year-old widow Jeanne Pouffict gave testimony in a case of procuring and concubinage. Upon hearing from a group of winegrowers after Mass that a woman nicknamed "la Vinaigrière" (the accused) was staying in a priest's house, Pouffict testified that she, accompanied by a female neighbor, went to the priest's house to ask him (using the formal *vous* form) why la Vinaigrière was there. While confronting the priest Pouffict informed him that the dissolute woman would have to move out immediately because she, Pouffict, could not endure such behavior.[96]

A similarly bold statement against clerical sexual behavior came in 1584, when two artisan boys, leaning from a second-story window, threw a cat onto the head of a churchman leading a solemn procession through a narrow street of Dijon. The priest's head was bared by the screeching animal as his hat was knocked to the ground and soiled. Given the symbolic meaning attached to cats (female sexuality) and bared heads (shame), the boys' gesture said more about clerical morality than words.[97]

Historians note that the purification of the French clergy along the lines demanded at the Council of Trent was ultimately successful, and this might well have been the case, but it is also true that reform proceeded more slowly in some places than in others. For example, in the diocese of Langres, one of the largest in France, pastoral visitations (a key institution aimed at confirming clerical rectitude) were especially difficult to accomplish, given geographic and climatic impediments.[98] Resistance there frequently was, specifically against the demands by the godly for clerical celibacy. Evidence of clergymen continuing their immoral ways throughout the "century of saints" can be easily gathered. Synodal statutes spanning the seventeenth century promulgated by bishops of Mâcon and the Archbishop of Besançon, for instance, reiterated the demands for sexual abstinence among the clergy.[99]

Laymen had their complaints, too. In 1671, for example, François Joly, a *procureur* at the Parlement, bemoaned the "general libertinage of certain clergymen" in Dijon who were constantly trying to entice more people to their libertine ways.[100] Likewise, but for different reasons, at about the same time the poet and future member of the *Académie française* Bernard de La Monnoye ridiculed the clergy and alleged sexual activity by them:

> Le prêtre vit de l'autel
> et la putain du bordel
> mais notre ami Bodeau
> vit de l'un comme de l'autre
> mais notre ami Bodeau
> est chanoine et maquereau.[101]

An example of the clergymen Joly decried and La Monnoye pilloried was the priest who[102] Dijon's syndic was informed about (by a concerned citizen), and whose alleged behavior instigated a request for an inquest in 1680. This cleric reputedly came "night and day" to a young woman and had "so frequent relations with her" that she was pregnant.[103] More discrete but no less sexually motivated, according to a concealed male eyewitness, was a velvet-cloaked canon who came to a widow and her daughter repeatedly at night. The canon reportedly would wait until the street was deserted, glance furtively about to make sure no one was coming, and then slip into the widow's house and spend the night.[104]

Parlementaires were equally disturbed by the apparent libertinage of clerics. In March 1681, Parlement issued an *arrêt* ordering *promoteurs* (prosecutors) at the *officialités* of its jurisdiction to pursue ecclesiastics suspected of concubinage. Five months later, First President Brulart, when asked by the king's secretary Châteauneuf about the *arrêt*, responded that "these days everyone is talking about the libertinage of ecclesiastics," indeed, that the Tournelle had recently heard "six or seven" cases pertaining to it.[105]

The countryside no less than the city harbored occasional wayward priests. Pastoral visitations, though not entirely reliable sources for uncovering clerical misconduct,[106] nonetheless open sporadic insight into such behavior. Visitation records from the diocese of Autun catalogued frequent priestly license during the 1650s, 1660s, and 1670s, after which there was a noticeable falling off. The records are especially extensive for the archdeaconry of Avalon, and in 10 of the 39 parishes concupiscent priests (not to mention two additional collegiate canons) were reported from 1656 to 1671.[107]

Fiacre Grasset, vicar of Pontaubert, received an interdict from his bishop in 1656 for "frequenting taverns, where he drinks to excess, and for keeping a suspect woman in his house with whom he has had children."[108] 1667 was an active year for dissolute clerics, especially in this archdeaconry. The curé of Duns-les-Places was said to frequent both taverns and "suspicious incontinent women," rendering scant surprise that he was noted to be a great gambler and to have a 3-year-old child by one of his parishioners.[109] Similarly, the curé of Saint-Germain-les-Champs "led a scandalous life" with a female tavernkeeper with whom he had a child that he openly claimed and lavished affection upon. His parishioners had other cause to be outraged by their priest, for besides revealing confessions, he was reported to have assaulted one of his flock with a sword and threatened others with a rifle, cursing all the while.[110] The tavern-haunting curé of Empury purportedly had shared a hearth with a woman for 30 years, bringing six children into the world by her, three of whom were still living.[111] And finally, the curé of Vauxclaix reportedly frequented a suspect woman, while the curé of Mhère, an often-inebriated denizen of taverns, was "quite debauched" as well.[112]

When the Bishop of Autun, Gabriel Roquette, visited the parish of Saint-Branché in the same archdeaconry of Avalon in 1668, he discovered that the priest, Charles Lavery, was probably guilty of a broad range of violations. He was admittedly lax in instructing his parishioners in the catechism (saying they never asked for it), but his parishioners accused him of more serious offenses. He allegedly often botched the ritual of the Mass and even witheld the sacraments of baptism and extreme unction. In addition to professional malpractice, Lavery was accused of soliciting women with money, divulging confessions while drunk in the local tavern, suborning witnesses in legal cases, and, most horrifying of all, shoving a hot poker under the skirt of a young girl who had the audacity to resist his sexual advances.[113]

About the time Lavery was tried and incarcerated in the bishop's prison for his offenses,[114] the parishioners of Montigny, once again in the archdeaconry of Avalon, complained that their curé was frequently absent from the parish for long stretches of time. His absenteeism meant that sermons were not preached, Masses were not heard, the children were not catechized, and on one occasion a newborn child died without baptism due to the absence of the parish priest. The parishioners must have had mixed feelings about the curé's absenteeism, however, because while he was in residence he quarreled frequently with them, even cursing and threatening them with a pistol and musket. To top off his scandalous behavior, he also had kept in his house for "seven or eight days two girls suspected of bad conduct."[115]

Of course, the archdeaconry of Avalon had no monopoly on licentious clerics. A generation later Alexis Verdot, curé of Talemay and Châtillon, was accused of concubinage and "scandalous ways" in the *officialité* of Besançon. In the incomplete dossier of his trial one finds several anonymous incriminating letters addressed to the *official*, presumably from an informant, as well as a complaint from a peasant of the parish. From these documents Verdot was alleged to have kept a young servant girl and was also notorious in the parish for drunkenness during divine services and for seducing women.[116]

We do not know what became of Verdot, but found equally guilty as Lavery was Pierre Poitevin, curé of Süin, accused and convicted in 1686 in the royal bailliage of Charolles of, among other offenses, sodomy.[117] Over 40 laymen and women testified, and their allegations ranged from severe crimes to pecadilloes, ultimately winning Poitevin a pierced tongue and life in the galleys. Purportedly inadequate in teaching the catechism (the children knew more than he did), he also wandered about the parish in improper dress, frequently drunk. If his inebriation to the point of stupefaction during Vespers and Mass prompted some parishioners to laugh, however, they were not amused by his reputed attempts to lift skirts or to philander with married parishioners, his divulging confessions, his blaspheming (notably during catechism instruction), and of course, his sodomizing.

Both Lavery and Poitevin appear to have been guilty, but their trials are revealing in other ways. They inform us about the role of the priest in village and parish, as well as how the villagers informally policed the sexual misconduct of their priests. In Lavery's case, for example, there is evidence that he wielded considerable influence over his parishioners in the form of witheld sacraments and suborned witnesses in litigation in which he was engaged. As mediator between the laity and God, he controlled the dispensing of the sacraments and if, as Peter Brown has observed, "above everything, the holy man is a man of power," then this control is, according to Timothy Tackett, the ultimate exercise of his power.[118]

Lavery's morals may not have been typical of seventeeth- and early eighteenth-century priests, but other priests were known to use their status of office for temporal, often sexual gain. In 1670 Claude Chassenay, curé of Molinet in the diocese of Autun, was alleged to have denied last rites to a parishioner. The accuser, a fellow priest sent by the bishop to assist Chassenay after complaints from parishioners about Chassenay's theological ignorance and scandalous behavior, reported that Chassenay's denial of the sacrament was a final act of vengeance against a bitter enemy.[119]

In 1720 Simon Humbelot, curé from Magny-Saint-Médard, was tried in the *officialité* of Langres and then in Dijon's bailliage for seducing women in the confessional, surely an instance of abusing the status of office and the monopoly of spiritual mediation.[120] Equally coercive was Humbelot's practice of suborning witnesses; he tried to force one to retract a deposition against him by threatening, and in fact later carrying through his threat, to deny the mortally ill man a final confession.

In 1711 Jean Guyot, vicar in the parish of Talmay in the diocese of Langres, was alleged to be the father of a child born to Jeanne Rougeot, also of Talmay.[121] Rougeot was solicited by Guyot immediately upon his arrival in the parish, and after an unsuccessful initial seduction he succeeded and continued to have sexual relations with her until she became pregnant. Guyot purportedly used his spiritual influence to seduce the young woman, suggesting first that what they were doing was simply a *bagatelle* (for which he confessed and absolved her), and then, when she became pregnant, trying as a "marriage broker" to arrange a match between her and the *garde de la poste* in Talmay. In 1726 Pierre Morin, curé of Grandvaux, was charged with "scandalous commerce" with one of his female parishioners and with fabricating a *monitoire* and publicizing it against another one of his parishioners.[122] In each of the previous examples, priests used their privileged status to advance their own interests, which often was sexual. Priests who engaged in sexual relations and fathered children obviously had a worldly involvement that they were supposed to have renounced. This attachment to worldly pleasures was likely to be all the more galling to parishioners when priests kept a concubine or "suspect woman" as a servant, because the parish was required to provide for the priest's livelihood by way of tithe and *casuel* (offerings to the priest for his services). Seeing concubines, adulterous women, and illegitimate children supported by their contributions might have been responsible for the many conflicts parishioners had with their priests over the payment of tithes.[123]

Of course, one must bear in mind that allegations do not constitute guilt, and lay people who knew that they might have a chance of winning a court case might well have fabricated charges of sexual activity against a curé who they might have wished to eliminate. In Poitevin's case, the fact that so many parishioners were willing to testify suggests that they were anxious to remove him. This willingness may have been for spiritual reasons if they perceived that he had violated his expected role in the community, which, as the Church had made manifest, was for the priest to be detached from the family ties and economic concerns of his parishioners. Cases appealed before the Parlement as well as first-instance cases at various *officialités*, however, suggest that there was more to the laity's disapproval of its priests than spiritual dissatisfaction. In a way, by placing the priest in a paradoxical position, as dissociated from the world and yet in a powerful position within it, the Reformation may have encouraged the discrepancy between parishioners' expectations and the reality of their priests' behavior.

Determining motivation from records of criminal cases is notoriously difficult for the historian, just as it was for the judges of the time. Increasingly in the seventeenth century, one has the impression that people bringing court cases against priests were seeking vengeance for a worldly grievance as much as wishing to see the clerics punished for immorality. In 1629, for example, Claude Guenebault, curé of Champeaulx, was tried for "lustful and scandalous ways" and, at the same time, for assault committed against a master surgeon from the same village. The surgeon brought charges but was joined by the royal *procureur général*, and the case was heard before the Tournelle of the Parlement. The priest was found guilty and fined 200 *livres* plus 30 *livres* in damages to the surgeon.[124] Clearly, the court was willing to hear such cases (though, given other sentences handed down by this court, the serious crime here was the moral one), and it is small wonder the laity responded.

In 1668 Emillan Pugeot, a peasant from the village of Grandmont, went directly to the *procureur général* and convinced him to initiate criminal proceedings against Pierre Jouan, curé of the parish of Pierre, and Jeanne

Bernard. The priest was charged with attempted rape (in the curial house) of Pugeot's daughter, but one cannot help but wonder if Pugeot tacked on the charge of spiritual incest and adultery with Bernard in an attempt to ensure that the case would be heard. If such were his motivations, they succeeded, because the priest was convicted.[125]

Not all plaintiffs were so fortunate, although previous examples of success encouraged them to try. When Vivant Patureau, a servant of two peasants from Champfergueil brought suit against his curé Louis Berthot, the plaintiff not only charged the priest with shooting his rifle at him while slandering and threatening him, but also with seducing and committing spiritual incest with parishioners, both married and unmarried.[126] The *official* of the diocese of Chalon-sur-Saône, apparently more concerned with the sexual indiscretions and with the priest's penchant for carrying a musket than with his taking a shot at Patureau, condemned Berthot to return to the seminary for six months but awarded Patureau no damages. Patureau found this sentence unsatisfactory and appealed to Parlement. Berthot, not to be outdone, filed a countersuit demanding that Patureau "make reparations to his honor in the presence of such persons that he [Berthot] would wish to call and [that Patureau] declare with bare head and on his knees" that he was wrong and beg forgiveness. The Parlement ended the grudge match by finding for neither party.

Similarly frustrated by the courts was Jean Bonnard. In 1720, this peasant from Pellerey was joined by the *procureur du roi* at the bailliage of Dijon in filing suit at the *officialité* of Langres against Benoist Gamay, curé of Pellerey, for spiritual incest with Bonnard's niece. When the *official* simply condemned the priest to fifteen days in the seminary to regain "the ecclesiastical spirit," Bonnard appealed the sentence to the Tournelle. Here it was learned that Bonnard had suborned witnesses to testify against the curé, and instead of Gamay it was Bonnard who felt the weight of justice and was arrested.[127]

One must not discount as disingenuous the spiritual purity that parishioners demanded from their curés, but at the same time the function of the clergy in the daily life of the village or town must be considered. The sacred and profane were not easily separated. The majority of the clergy may have been "purified" by the eighteenth century, but the trials of a purported libidinous minority tell us a great deal about the expected and actual role of the clergy in Burgundy's cities and countryside, as well as of the tactics of consumption of the powerful resource of the law that the laity could pursue. The Catholic Reformation championed the sacred character of the priest, and thereby greatly empowered him in a world where access to the sacred was of prime importance. As Julia points out, "post-Tridentine ritual attached . . . a capital importance to ecclesiastical mediation represented on earth by the clerics who presided over the ceremonies," and by thus manipulating the sacred, the priest manifested a power that was perceived immediately by the laity.[128] Given such empowerment and sacralization, in a world where the sacred and the profane had been traditionally mixed, the role of the "new" priest could be explosive, especially if the priest's worldly status threatened the influence of the local seigneur. One crucial place where this explosion could occur concerned the power over local patronage.

The following cases demonstrate divided villages, where the priest and the seigneur represented opposite poles.[129] The villagers, for their part, arrayed themselves somewhere in between, depending on ties of dependency or a calculation of what the priest or the lord could offer to advance their interests. In this power struggle between village notables,[130] both priest and lord had "capital" at their disposal and spent it in an economy where sin and sexuality played a large part.

Traditionally, the local lay elite played a powerful role in the religious life of their communities. Confraternities, hospitals, vestries, and even schools had been under their influence and control; however, the church began a program in the seventeenth century to place these institutions under ecclesiastical authority.[131] As the priests gradually gained control of these institutions, local seigneurs who were resentful of their displacement from positions of power and spiritual influence resisted.

Lords also resented changes that the Church, by way of the newly empowered priest, made in "honorific privileges" [*droits honorifiques*]. In 1741, for instance, a local lord in the diocese of Autun filed suit in the bishop's court claiming that the parish priest had violated the traditional manner in which *pain bénit* was distributed.[132] At issue was the priest's decision to distribute it first to the clerics of the parish rather than to the local lord and his family, as was customary.

A similar dispute over honor, precedence, and deference—and, implicitly, over the status of the seigneur in the religious and spiritual life in the community—occurred in 1697 and again in 1734, also in the diocese of Autun.[133] On both occasions seigneurs complained that the parish priest had violated traditional practice by no longer specifically swinging the burning incense over the lord and his family during various religious ceremonies such as High Mass or Vespers. Burning incense was a rite of purification, and because purity and hierarchy were closely associated, denying the ritual individually to the lord was perceived by him as an affront, a refusal to defer to his power and influence by the very individual—the priest—who had been encroaching on the seigneur's position in the community for decades.

Not infrequently or surprisingly, lords wished to have adversarial curés removed from their benefices and found allegations of sexual impropriety, often filed by an unnamed plaintiff or "secret party," to bring to court. Although lords rarely had direct control of appointments to benefices (and there is no way of knowing if such was the case in the examples that follow), and the conditions for obtaining a benefice were procedurally complex,[134] lords could certainly bring their influence to bear upon appointments.[135] In some cases they nominated candidates directly to the bishop, canons, monastic houses, or whoever had control over a particular benefice.

More commonly, lords exerted an informal influence by writing letters in support of given candidates, correspondence that had to be taken into account because, as Tackett points out, "if a curé were to perform his functions effectively, it was important to have the support of the local nobility."[136]

The relations between lord and curé were sometimes far from cordial. For example, in 1700 Thibault Guenard, curé of Jasney, found himself called before the *officialité* of Besançon for sexual impropriety. As the case unfolded, however, it appeared that control over appointment to the important village office of schoolmaster was very much at issue.[137] Education was the primary vehicle for conveying religious, political, and social messages to the young, and the schoolmaster was the conduit for the ethos of discipline and hierarchy. By the terms of the royal edict of 1695, parish priests had control over appointments to and dismissals from this influential position. But as the Guenard case illustrates, local seigneurs were not always willing to accept the king's word.

After charges of sexual misconduct were brought against Guenard, depositions poured in that the priest had tried constantly to seduce young and married women (one allegedly as many as 30 times in one year). Witnesses took great care to specify what the priest had done to them or what they had seen him do to others. Guenard was accused of continually lifting skirts and pinching bottoms. Two young women claimed he had ejaculated on them without penetration, and the 20-year-old servant Jean LeSire observed that Guenard was so brazen in fondling breasts and "shameful parts" (*parties honteuses*), that he and his lover of the moment would appear "as man and wife." All witnesses, predictably, claimed to be scandalized.

The first round of depositions was incriminating, but the *promoteur* felt that further testimony was needed and ordered a *monitoire*. More incriminating depositions flowed in, some contending that Guenard had fathered several children in the parish, one with Gogo Bazard in spite of promising her that she need not worry about getting pregnant because he had some herbs that could prevent it. Only one witness, Claudinette Richard, intimated support for the curé when she testified that when she and Jeanne Constant (from a neighboring village) were coming to give testimony, they were attacked "by a dozen or so women and girls" who shouted that Constant deserved to be hanged because she had slept with the curé.

Guenard counterattacked when he was permitted to confront the witnesses, and it is at this point that one gets the impression that the trial may have been about more than sexual impropriety. The curé was sure that the "secret party" was Madame de Jasney, widow of the late Baron de Pouilly, seigneur de Jasney, and that she was paying the costs of this litigation. He discredited witnesses for being suborned or otherwise coerced by Madame de Jasney to give incriminating testimony. Some were her debtors, some her *mainmortables*, some her employees, but all of their testimony was tainted, as the priest tried to show, because of their dependency on her.

Guenard continued his defense by calling several witnesses of his own. Symon Maquette, a valet of the Countess of Conflans, reported that he had indirectly heard that Madame de Jasney said the curé was a "rogue" (*coquin*) and wished to get rid of him. He added that Jean Jandel, the former schoolmaster in Jasney, had been dismissed from office by the curé, against the wishes of Madame de Jasney, and Jandel had subsequently gone repeatedly to the château of Madame de Jasney to conspire with her against Guenard. Another dozen witnesses confirmed this testimony and the priest's contentions generally. These witnesses included Jean Hommenaux, a 50-year-old peasant from Jasney, who also pointed out that Madame de Jasney was currently engaged in other litigation against the accused and carried a "spirit of contrariness" against him. Concerning the gist of the conflict—control of the schoolmaster position—Dominique Accard, the new schoolmaster, asserted that although most of the village had been unhappy with Jandel Madame de Jasney wanted to keep him anyway. He added that "only those dependent on her" wished to keep Jandel, while 60 to 70 villagers favored his dismissal. Symon Fleury, a day laborer but alderman of the village at the time of Jandel's sacking, claimed that he and the "community" wanted to go against the will of Madame de Jasney concerning Jandel.

Capping his counterattack, Guenard filed a complaint with the court accusing Madame de Jasney of conspiring to injure his reputation, and he not only asked for dismissal of the charges but also that the identity of the anonymous accuser be disclosed and he (or she) be forced to pay "damages and interest" [*dommages et intérêts*]. Madame de Jasney, for her part, was not through with Guenard. No doubt disgruntled that three previous hearings concerning the curé in the *officialité* had not rid her village of this obnoxious priest, she openly filed a request with the Parlement to hear the case as an *appel comme d'abus*, which it agreed to do. She professed to be so outraged by the public sexual scandals perpetrated by the priest (she says nothing of the schoolmaster position) that she felt compelled as "first parishioner" to appeal to Parlement "as protector of the laws and defender of the authority of the canons and of ecclesiastical discipline." Whether or not the priest was guilty of sexual impropriety, however, enough testimony emerged in this case to indicate that mundane issues of patronage, power, and influence in the village could just as easily have been the key issue and allegations of sexual impropriety simply a convenient way to eliminate a local rival.

The trial of Jean-Baptiste Lurot, vicar of Tromarey, commencing in 1704 also in the *officialité* of Besançon, was very similar to that of Guenard.[138] The opening depositions alleged sexual promiscuity by Lurot that reflected more generally an abuse of his position and influence in the village. In order to elicit sexual favors from a married woman, for example, he threatened to denounce her from his pulpit (surely an abuse of spiritual status) as an adulteress if she refused. He was not very discreet about his blackmail, apparently, because more than one witness mentioned it. Many witnesses testified that Lurot was a hot-tempered, proud, and vain man who carried grudges against his parishioners. If his seemingly indiscriminate groping at corsets and skirts vexed his parishioners, and many testified that it did, worse was when he was called to give succor [*secours*] to a young woman as she lay in her sickbed. His "laying on of hands" was far from being spiritually intended, however, when as she herself testified, he instead seized the opportunity to "touch [the woman] dishonestly." So extensive was the incriminating evidence of sexual irregularities against Lurot (and, unlike for Guenard, there was no countervailing testimony) that the *promoteur* ordered his arrest, by force if necessary, and in the subsequent interrogation the vicar was grilled concerning his sexual activities.

Whether Lurot was sexually active is only part of the interest of this case, however. During the confrontation of witnesses, Lurot, like Guenard before him, tried to uncover the "secret party," and again like Guenard, he suspected the local seigneur. Lurot discredited some witnesses by alleging their dependency on "Monsieur le Comte de Vaudrey . . . his enemy." The count, however, was not Lurot's only enemy in the village. In fact, of 23 witnesses, Lurot claimed 8 were his "enemies," another 3 wished him evil, and 6 had reason to falsely testify against him because of involvement in litigation with him. Lurot clearly was a contentious man who used his worldly position (enhanced by the Catholic Reformation) to bend parishioners to his will. The charges of sexual blackmail and high-handed sexual aggression were entirely consistent with his character, but whether or not he was guilty, it is significant that the parishioners, and quite plausibly the local lord, concentrated on Lurot's sexual transgressions in the hope of getting the court to remove him from the parish.

As in the previous cases, the one involving Jean Quirot, curé of Ternant, concerns allegations of sexual promiscuity that mask a desire of the local lord, in this case the Seigneur de Ternant, to rid the parish of the established curé. The litigation began on 14 September 1726 when Anne Sigault, the twenty-five year-old governess of Monsieur de Ternant, filed a declaration of pregnancy in Dijon naming Quirot as the father.[139] Within three weeks Quirot had responded with a petition before the mayor of Dijon's court at the bailliage against Sigault, asking for reparation for what he considered such an atrocious calumny that, if unredressed, would damage his honorable "reputation and character."

From the ensuing depositions it appears that Sigault might have been using allegations of sexual activity with Quirot to gain his expulsion from his curate, and it quickly came out that she was being compelled to do so by Monsieur de Ternant. Jeanne Vaincaut, the 20-year-old daughter of a local peasant, testified that Sigault had told her that she was pregnant, but not by Quirot. Vaincaut added that she had accused the priest of paternity only to force the "bugger" (*bougre*) to leave Ternant, "because he displeases the Seigneur de Ternant." Louis Vienne, a merchant from Ternant, along with a half dozen other witnesses, seconded Vaincaut's testimony implicating the lord, several of them also adding that Sigault had admitted that the Seigneur de Ternant was the father. Why de Ternant wanted to be rid of the curé is unclear, but nearly everyone testifying in this case, including the curé (who claimed that de Ternant was trying "to expose him to the censure of his superiors"), appeared sure that he did. Several witnesses pointedly stated that de Ternant threatened Sigault "with his fist" to incriminate Quirot in the pregnancy declaration and even offered "to make her fortune" if she did.

In a final case dating from the first quarter of the eighteenth century, the local curé and the local lord are again adversaries polarizing the village, and although the motivations for why the lord wished the priest expelled from the parish remain vague, it is clear that patronage was an issue and that sexual impropriety was again the dominant charge against the priest.[140] Hugue-Bonaventure Abbey had been curé of Vadans-les-Pesmes for 33 years before he was accused in 1727 by Barthelemy Legué, a local peasant. Legué was supported by a host of "secret parties" in alleging that Abbey was guilty of a range of misdeeds, from denying sacraments to his parishioners to public drunkeness, suborning witnesses in the many court cases he filed against his flock, and sexual misconduct with several of his married female parishioners. The gist of these allegations is that a priest is using his religious power and influence to advance his personal interests. Whether Abbey was in fact guilty of these crimes (and it seems that he probably was), we can glimpse a view of the priest's worldly position in his community.

Abbey had passed his fiftieth year before he veered from the path of spiritual purity, but according to many witnesses, from that time his behavior was scandalous. He purportedly contracted syphilis from the once beautiful Anatolia Baud, which left the priest's face ravaged and took her life. Undeterred, the curé took up with Christine Cuenot, the wife of a local peasant, and apparently was not terribly discreet in his private encounters with her. She was continually in the curé's house, and several witnesses testified that they had actually seen Abbey and Cuenot engaged in the sexual act. The witnesses testifying against the curé made it appear as if everyone in the parish were opposed to this curé and wished him removed, and it does seem as if the priest had almost gone out of his way to make enemies among his flock. He reputedly boasted from the pulpit that he had won more than fifteen court cases against his parishioners, and in court proceedings he admitted that he was presently litigating against several of the witnesses (and hence their reason for lying in their testimony against him). Furthermore, many of his parishioners were financially indebted to him and had testified dishonestly, Abbey claimed, because one of the "secret parties" had said that if the priest were convicted all debts would be cancelled.

Before the procedural confrontations between witnesses and the accused of this case, the outlines of a polarized community could be seen: one witness said in passing that "quite often when he [Abbey] gave his sermon a part [of the congregation] left the church." During the confrontations, however, when the priest had his chance to speak out, it became clear that there might be, as in all litigation, two sides to the case. The priest seemed certain of who the "secret parties" were (several of whom had testified against him), and who led them. Behind a half dozen local peasants, merchants, and even the surgeon who testified that he had operated on the priest for syphilis, was the local lord, the noble Jean-Baptiste de Montreux de Rossière, seigneur de Vadans et Chevigney.

It appears that part of the reason for wanting to rid the parish of its litigious priest was again the schoolmaster position. According to the accused priest, the former schoolmaster Estienne Chauncelot, who had been dismissed by Abbey, had been bribed by the conspiring "secret parties" to testify against him. He suspected the same of Jean-François Butod, a nonbeneficed priest living in Vadans, whom Abbey felt sure hoped to get his benefice if he were ousted. Abbey's suspicions could have been well-founded, because a proletariat of nonbeneficed clerics had emerged by then, the product of a benefice system comprised of immobile churchmen who were very difficult to dislodge.[141] Butod may have gotten his wish, because the *official* found Abbey guilty and, besides sentencing him to two months in the seminary of Besançon, gave the condemned curé the far more severe penalty of resigning his benefice within six months.

Conclusion

Lay and clerical reformers were intent upon reformulating an order in society, the result of which was a new type of community, linking members vertically rather than horizontally. This community was comprised of dissociated individuals held together hierarchically by an increasingly authoritarian church, monarchical state, and dominant social group.

Confession and communion played an important part in the Reform, and because these activities were parochially based, the parish clergy became essential to the reordering of society, as agents of discipline to reinforce hierarchy and authority. In order to accomplish this task, the clergy had to be pure in thought and deed. Consequently, clerical conscupiscence, given the central identification of passion (especially sexual) with disorder, was categorically intolerable.

The administering of justice in general came to be viewed as a sacred obligation by secular judges, an assumption that underscored their growing exasperation not just with licentious clergymen but also with a derelict ecclesiastical court system all too recalcitrant in the prosecution of sexually criminal clerics. Church court officials in the sixteenth century were repeatedly urged by the king and especially by parlementary magistrates to prosecute their own. By the late sixteenth century, the patience of the secular courts was running out, and in the seventeenth century it ended. By invoking the *appel comme d'abus*, secular courts encroached upon ecclesiastical jurisdiction, claiming a sacred obligation to do so. Priests were increasingly prosecuted by the secular courts, and a few were even executed for their sexual crimes in the early seventeenth century. The priests' female companions had long been feeling the wrath of the law for their sexual crimes with clergymen. As the secular courts backed away from capital punishment in the second half of the century, however, they also attenuated their prosecution and ameliorated the punishment of these women. Whether this change was a result of the "success" of the Catholic Reformation in Burgundy is difficult to say, given the incomplete state of the surviving evidence.

The prosecution patterns of priests nonetheless demonstrate quite clearly the *attempted* regularization or the fixing of an ideology, as well as "situational adjustment" or the attempted application of that ideology. When the relationships between holiness, sexuality, power, and the law in the villages of Burgundy are examined, we can see not just further instances of situational adjustment, but also the indeterminacy inherent in the fluid situations of everyday experience.

The reform insisted that the priest be an embodiment of the holy and, ironically, in so doing greatly empowered the priest in the world. How a priest exercised his influence was of paramount importance to the village community, not least to the local lord. If a priest were perceived as overweening or a threat to the seigneur's influence, attempts to remove the priest might be mounted. How to get rid of a rival? Allege licentious behavior that touched the essence of disorder as enshrined in the new morality, and bring the weight of the reformers' sacred law upon the priest's head. Such a use of the law may have had other purposes than the reformulation of an ordered society, but as we will see in the following two chapters, the uses of the law quite frequently escaped the intentions of the reformers who envisioned it as the essential tool of the new order of morality.

4

Marriage and the Uses of the Law: Legislation, Adjudication, and Litigation

During the early modern period, authority and sexuality were defined in a moral order constituted by intersecting and reciprocally supportive ideologies of authoritarian politics, hierarchical social relations, reformed religion, and the law. The ediface of power and authority was patriarchal, and so a marital ethic was perhaps the fundamental mortar holding the structure together. This ethic was clearly embodied in royal legislation, and it just as clearly guided the jurisprudence of the courts of the realm. But if honorable marriage was the goal of nearly all French men and women, regardless of social rank, how people (especially women) used the laws pertaining to marriage in marital strategies and what impact this had upon practical jurisprudence (if not legislation) reveals that the meaning of the ethic was much more complex than prescriptive literature or legislation might suggest.

Because the cornerstone of the ethic was honorable marriage sanctioned by the parents (more specifically, the father), it may be fruitful to devote attention to its antithesis, clandestine marriage and *rapt*. These criminal offenses are not to be confused with rape (forceful fornication without marital intention), although forced fornication was an element of them at times.[1] Rather, they were characterized by forceful abduction or seduction with the intention to marry without parental approval.

The marital ethic embodied in royal legislation from 1579 (the royal ordinance of Blois) to 1730 (a royal declaration against *rapt de séduction*) reflected the concord between religious, political, and social ideologies worked out during that period.[2] The sixteenth-century Catholic doctrine reaffirmed at the Council of Trent simply required consent of the partners for a marriage to be valid. The kings of France, on the other hand, demanded parental (especially paternal) consent for validity. This conflict between church and state was resolved by the creation of a legal fiction, *rapt de séduction*. The courts of the realm were left with the task of enforcing the legislation embodying this ethic.

On the one hand, Burgundy's judges, in their adjuducation of *rapt* cases, championed the paternalism that was the bedrock of royal political theories and of the social ideology (social stratification) of society's dominant classes.[3] On the other hand, they found too severe the royal legislation and its unswerving demands for the death penalty for *rapt*, be it violent or seductive. By the middle of the seventeenth century, two significant trends emerged, illustrating an increasingly tolerant position taken by the *parlementaires*. First, the involvement of public prosecutors in *rapt* cases tapered off (see Table 4.1). Second, the magistrates began to lighten their sentences, shifting from corporal punishment to remuneration of the wronged parties (*dommages et intérêts*), and eventually to a reduction of the amounts of remuneration.

The judges, especially those at the Parlement, certainly believed that stiff capital penalties were counterproductive, for two reasons. First, they believed that the institution of marriage and the social stability it guarenteed, in which men of their station firmly believed, could best be protected by, depending upon the circumstances, either encouraging marriage between the litigants, or, more commonly, returning the plaintiff (almost invariably a woman) to the father by blocking marriage. Second, even though the plaintiff was usually a woman and the defendant a man, the judges came to suspect that culpability was not as clear-cut as royal legislation would have

Table 4.1. Instigation of Prosecution in Rapt Cases Appealed to Parlement, Selected Years, 1583–1727

Dates	Public prosecutor alone	Pub. prosecutor joined by civil party	Civil party alone	Rapt *cases* appealed to Parlement
1583–1622	7	17	0	24
1627–1664	8	18	0	26
1583–1664	15	35	0	50
1668–1674	1	7	7	15
1681–1727	1	7	15	23
1668–1727	2	14	22	38
Total	17	49	22	88

Sources: Dates and figures reflect a sample of *arrêts définitifs criminels* and *arrêts à l'audience criminelle* from the Parlamentary chambers of the Tournelle, the Enquêtes, and the Grand' Chambre (B II 45 and 46), and of copies of original parlementary *arrêts*, since lost, compiled by seventeenth- and eighteenth-century jurists (BMD, Ms. 1110).

it. "Seduction," they came to believe, was bound up with marital strategies. Blind to the disturbing outright force if not the deceit of false promises for marriage many men appear to have used to gain sexual favors, the judges were more concerned about how women appeared to be using the law to pursue marriage. They seem to have become convinced that guilt in many *rapt* cases was shared by the man and the woman, and their sentences reflected this outlook. In the application of the law, then, the supposed aims of female litigants were influential in altering the jurisprudential application of an unbending royal legislation.

Law and the Formation of the Marital Ethic

When lay and clerical reformers set out to control the institution of marriage, they were confronted with the overridng question of determining what constituted a legitimate union. Issues of legitimacy, of course, presuppose norms, and if legal, doctrinal, or social (or, more accurately, cultural) standards vary, then the issue of legitimacy becomes contentious. This is the situation we find in the sixteenth century, but steadily as we traverse the epoch of the Catholic Reformation, there is an increasing solidarity in the legal, religious, and social ideologies of men of power and influence. A pastoral reform, indeed a sacralization, of the laity was an avowed intention of church *and* state during this period.

Since the Gregorian Reform and the codification of canon law in the High Middle Ages, the Church had concerned itself with the question of legitimate marital union. Even within the Church there was disagreement, but by the late Middle Ages canon law was widely interpreted as stipulating that simple consent between the two parties over the minimum age (7, 12, or 14, depending on gender and circumstance) was necessary for a valid marriage. Such a position could, and did, undermine parental authority. It validated clandestine marriage as well as intercourse following a promise of future marriage, because such a promise presumed consent.[4]

Under such a system, control of marriage was largely in the hands of the prospective partners, but already in the late Middle Ages a parental counteroffensive was in motion against such independence.[5] In the late Middle Ages, French church courts were beginning to bend to parental pressure; and by the sixteenth century, synodal statutes expressed concern for too widespread clandestine marriages, indirectly supporting parental anxieties. In order to avoid such "abuses," in 1544 and 1553, for example, two successive bishops of Autun, Jacques Hurault de Cheverny and Philibert Dugny de Courgengouch, prohibited priests from celebrating marriages between people not from their parish.[6] The French delegation to the Council of Trent was instructed by its king to press for a decree that would make parental consent a doctrinal precondition for valid marriage. This effort was in vain, as it turned out, and the decree "Tametsi" reaffirmed the primacy of consent of the future partners.

ˈf church doctrine endorsing free consent of the betrothed was ush-
ι through the front door at Trent, however, church teaching more
ᴐle to parental control was brought in through the back, at least in
. The Fourth Commandment, "Thou shalt honor thy father and
ːr," received increased emphasis throughout the era of the French
ᵗⁱc Reformation, and conducive to parental control of their children's
ᴇs, the motivation behind the child's choice was scrutinized.[7] In
ː Maillard's widely popular *Confession* published in the late fifteenth
ry, the confessor is told to inquire of the woman "with what intention she married," adding that marrying for "pleasures of the body" was
sinful.[8] A later confessor's manual more openly sought to sever the link
between premarital intercourse and marital consent by advising confessors
to obtain a general confession from the betrothed seven to eight days before marriage, the time when "temptations are the most frequent and stron-
gest."[9]

For much the same reason, the synodal statutes of Gaspard Dinet,
Bishop of Mâcon, in 1602 prohibited priests from marrying anyone who
had not already confessed and communicated at least three days before the
marriage. This stipulation was reiterated in 1659 by one of Dinet's succes-
sors, Jean de Lingendes, who added that those betrothed who were not
sufficiently instructed in the necessary points of faith of the "true" religion
(among which he specified the Commandments) should be denied the
marital sacrament.[10]

Finally, the connection between parental authority over children and
the circumscribing of free choice by church tutelage (if not doctrine) is clear
in popular preaching. On a first sunday after Epiphany in the late seventeenth century, for example, Louis Reguis preached a sermon on obedience of children to their parents, poignantly addressing premarital sexual
relations. He asserted that as God saves the child's soul, so the parents save
their bodies. With obedience hopefully fresh in his youthful parishioners
minds, he followed one week later with a sermon "On Marriage." If in the
earlier sermon he railed against libertine sons and daughters, in this one he
admonished that "the purpose of marriage is not at all to satisfy shameful
passions, but to place a brake on them and contain them within prescribed
limits." Certainly parents could only surmise that he was supporting their
influence in marital choice and concur when he concluded that if such pre-
scriptions were followed, then God would not permit bad choices in marriage.[11]

If the Gallican church was ambivalent about free choice and parental
influence in the marital ethic, the position of the king and his jurists was
much less so. We have already encountered the "sacralizing state" in the
reform of clerical morals, and in the formation of the marital ethic we encounter it again. There is no reason to assume that early modern monarchs
(or, more accurately, their jurists) were implicitly secular when they championed the power of parents over children and so directly challenged the

Tridentine Church's doctrinal position on consent. Indeed, the vocabulary invoked by kings blends sacred and temporal concerns, suggesting no clear or antagonistic difference between the two. It even gives primacy to the sacred. In the preamble of the famous edict against clandestine marriages of 1556, for instance, Henri II juxtaposed filial disobedience in clandestine marriage with a violation of the Fourth Commandment: "the complaint [has been] made to us of marriages that are contracted in our kingdom daily by a carnal, indiscreet, and disordered will by the children of respectable familes [*enfans de famille*] to the disappointment and against the will and consent of their fathers and mothers, not at all having before their eyes the fear of God, the honor, reverence and obedience that they owe in everything and everywhere to their said parent." Later in the preamble, he joins the temporal and the sacred again when he justifies the royal position as "executing the will and commandment of God."[12]

In reading this edict against clandestine marriages, one is struck by the sacred authority the king assumes. Disobedience to the will and consent of parents is "irreverence" because it transgresses "the law and commandment of God," a serious offense worthy of disinheritance of the offending child.[13] As in the correction of clerical abuses, it appears that royal authority was expanding for sacred as much as for temporal reasons—indeed, it makes little sense to separate the sacred from the temporal. Clandestine marriages, according to Henri, simultaneously violated sacred and royal law, the former "inseparable from [the defense of the] public utility" required of the latter.

Doing God's work was serious business for French kings, and with such a self-appointed mandate they increasingly extended their control over the French clergy to effect their goals. In the preamble to the ordinance of Blois in 1579, Henri III assumed as a fundamental charge that "the clergymen be returned to good *estat* by the reestablishment of ecclesiastical discipline, according to the decrees of which the defense and protection belongs to us [the monarchy]."[14] This charge was important to the marital ethic espoused by the crown because an obedient clergy, as stated in article 40 of the same ordinance, was needed for extended royal control over marriages, especially concerning the "respectable" social classes. Henri "enjoin[ed] the curés, vicars, or others to inquire carefully about the *qualité* of those who would wish to be married, and if they [were] children of respectable families [*enfans de famille*], [he] order[ed] them [the clerics] expressly to forego the celebration of the said marriages if the consent of fathers, mothers, or guardians [was] not apparent, under pain of being punished as accomplices to the crime of *rapt*."

Henri's association of clandestine marriage with *rapt* was a momentous step, because unlike the edict of 1556 against clandestine marriages that only called for disinheritance, a conviction of *rapt* carried, as Henri III specified in the ordinance of Blois, the sentence of death. Because capital crimes were indisputably within secular jurisdiction, the association of *rapt* and clandestine marriage aggressively challenged ecclesiastical jurisidiction over marital issues. Lay judges were quick to seize the opportunity.[15] There were social considerations here, but it would be a mistake to assume that the social (or temporal) could be dissociated from sacred considerations, at least before the eighteenth century. In the royal declaration of 1639, Louis XIII reaffirmed in totality the stipulations of Blois, and if anything, the language of sacred authority used by the king is even more pronounced. In the preamble to this declaration, Louis expressly stated that royal legislation concerning clandestine marriage had been "based on the first commandment of the second tablet [that is, the Fourth Commandment], containing the honor and reverence that is owed parents." Illustrating the intersection of social, political, and religious ideologies, he also added that this reverence was "the bond of legitimate obedience of subjects to their sovereign" and justified such "holy and salutary" legislation as protection from "unworthy profanation" of "the sanctity of so great a sacrament [marriage] that is the mystical sign of the conjunction of Jesus Christ with his church."[16]

In a royal *règlement* in 1697, Louis XIV sounded the same religious emphasis in condemning still all-too-frequent clandestine marriages, and the entire decree was aimed at priests wayward in their duty. Priests who were "obliged to inspire respect by their example even more than their words," instead "prostitute their ministry as well as their faith" by grossly violating "the holy councils [which have] prescribed as one of the essential solemnities of the sacrament of marriage the presence of the proper curé," meaning the priest from the parish of the betrothed.[17]

Scarcely three months later, Louis issued another declaration on the same matter, having been informed by some bishops and archbishops that marriages were continuing to be solemnized by priests other than the betrothed's own, and even by notaries. The involvement of notaries greatly vexed the king because it "tended to reduce the sacrament of marriage to the status that it was among the pagans," anathema to a monarch who pronounced that "all the powers that it pleased God to establish in the world ought not have any object but to converge for His glory and in His service."[18]

Legal and Gallican theological opinion had held long before Louis's declarations that marriage was equally a sacrament and a civil contract.[19] Already in the sixteenth century, jurists fueled this Gallican position by arguing that marriage was *not* essentially a sacrament with only civil effects, as the Ultramontane and Tridentine churchmen would have had it, but rather *simultaneously* a civil contract and a sacrament, the first forming the "substance" of the second.[20] Such an ambiguous position played into the hands of kings and magistrates intent on sacralizing their authority and extending their jurisdiction, for now they could legitimately regulate the formation of marriage and judge the validity of marital unions, even though such matters clearly involved the sacrament of marriage and had traditionally fallen under the jurisdiction of ecclesiastical courts. Such jurisidictional claims staked by magistrates in Burgundy and elsewhere bent on protecting family interests and paternal authority were in part driven by the urgent need to preclude clandestine marriages.[21] Burgundian parlementaires seized upon such jurisdictional claims to assert repeatedly in the late sixteenth and early seventeenth centuries that cases concerning marriage promises made by minors without the consent of the parents, for example, were within the jurisdiction of secular courts.[22]

In the seventeenth century theologians and jurists made subtle distinctions between the sacrament and the contract.[23] Gerbais, doctor of theology at the Sorbonne, summed up the position in 1690 that had been building over the century that marriage existed in nature, was legitimized by civil society in a contract, and then was blessed by Jesus and his subsequent institutional embodiment, the Church.[24]

However, the seventeenth and early eighteenth centuries saw no agreement as to whether the sacrament was conditional upon the contract or vice versa. Gerbais deduced from his premise that the sacrament was primary, and so the church courts should hear cases concerning marriage. Chancellor Pontchartrain a decade later would deduce from the same premise the opposite conclusion, that such a premise suggested that royal judges should hear such cases.[25] Many practicing judges anticipated Gerbais's premise and Pontchartrain's deduction by ruling that magistrates had the legitimate and sanctified authority to rule in cases involving the formation and validity of marriages.

Throughout the late sixteenth and seventeenth centuries many ecclesiastics repeatedly challenged these secular jurisdictional claims, and Gallican jurists and judges and even the king did not yet conclude that marriage was *exclusively* under secular jurisdiction. In 1634 Richelieu attempted to clarify jurisdictional boundaries by offering the following distinction, ultimately to no avail: "There is this difference between the ecclesiastical tribunal and the courts of Parlement, that the former in dissolving a marriage declares and pronounces it null, insofar that it pertains to the sacrament, and the courts [of Parlement] declare it invalidly contracted, insofar as it touches on the contract."[26]

Royal ordinances, edicts, and declarations were no more effective in cutting through the jurisidictional thicket. Kings often stipulated that marriage be under ecclesiastical jurisdiction, but if such pronouncements are read carefully, key passages are fraught with ambiguity. In 1580, for example, Henri III "prohibited royal judges from interfering with the course of ecclesiastical justice in the matter of marriage *without great and apparent reason* [italics added]." Similarly, in 1606 Henri IV responded to complaints from an Assembly of the Clergy by ordering that "the [legal cases] concerning marriage *ought to be* [italics added] within the competence of the Church." Finally, in 1695 Louis XIV directed that "it is prohibited that royal judges and even the parlements take cognizance of affairs [concerning the sacraments, but they shall] . . . hear *appel comme d'abus* for disputes concerning civil effects of the sacraments."[27] In each of these pronouncements, magistrates could and did construe reasons why they should continue to extend their jurisdiction over cases concerning the sacrament of marriage.

From such jurisprudential practice it was but a short step to legal treatises that interpreted the *contract* of marriage primary to its *sacramental* character. This in turn permitted them to deduce that the contract alone validated the marriage, and thus the state had complete and sole jurisdiction over nullification and validity. The royal *avocat général* Denis Talon and the jurist Launoy first voiced this position in the late seventeenth century, an interpretation that was repeated again in 1766 by Pierre Le Ridant in his *Code matrimonial* and by his contemporary Robert-Joseph Pothier in his hugely influential *Traité du contrat de mariage*.[28]

Certainly before the eighteenth century, however, it would be a mistake to assume that judges, jurists, or the king wished to sever the religious from the civil character of marriage, even though the jurisidictional claims laid by them in the sixteenth and seventeenth centuries ultimately led to just that. In the ordinance of Blois in 1579, for instance, Henri III forbade the formation of marriages by the simple exchange of promises even before a notary, demanding that the marriage be celebrated *in facie ecclesiae*.[29] Henri IV and Louis XIII reiterated these demands in 1606 and 1639 respectively, and in 1698 Louis XIV ordered that valid marriages depended not simply upon the presence of a priest at the ceremony, but also upon his active participation in giving the nuptial benediction to the union.[30]

Louis XV's declaration on clandestine marriages in 1730 (specifically *rapt de séduction*) may have understated the religious condemnation for such unions. Only once does the king refer to religion, stating that "we owe it to the sanctity of religion to prevent the abuse of a great sacrament." Thus, his 1730 declaration may have heralded a more secular future, but many philosophers and jurists could still be found in the eighteenth century who continued to view the validity of marriage as still somehow connected to its sacramental nature.[31]

In *jurisdictional* terms, however, the responsibility for determining the validity of marriages had long been moving in a secular direction, and lay judges ruling in cases involving the formation and validity of marriages had long ago agreed with the patriarchal and monarchist position Louis XV held in his declaration of 1730 that "we owe [the defense of valid marriage] . . . to the conservation of our authority . . . [and to] the public welfare and the common interest of families."[32]

The Crime of Rapt

Highlighting the "interest of families" by Louis XV was not new in 1730; in fact, such interest justified royal marital legislation as early as the sixteenth century, and it certainly guided judges in their practical decision-making.

As Sarah Hanley has pointed out, "the most pressing business of early modern times was the maintenance and extension of family networks, which were agencies of both social reproduction and economic production; and the negotiation of proper marriage alliances, crucial to that endeavor, depended on effective parental authority."[33] Because the power and influence of the king depended upon the loyalty of influential families in the provinces, a "family-state compact" was forged that embraced paternalism, an ethic, as we have seen, that also had religious justification. Clearly, the issue of marriage formation was of fundamental concern to families and king alike.

The crime of *rapt* is an excellent context within which to explore how the concerns of church, state, and society's dominant classes intersected. We can begin to trace the paths of this intersection by examining the formulation of royal legislation on *rapt*. The edict of 1556 and the decrees of Trent brought to a head the conflict between royal law and canon law over what constituted valid marriage, the former demanding parental approval, the latter requiring only consent by the partners. Given that both church and state were concerned with a Christian reform of society, such a contradictory situation was unlikely to be tolerated for long. Gallican church teaching and preaching circumvented the Tridentine doctrinal position of free consent, and royal legislation further smoothed the way for a resolution of the contradiction by legally defining *rapt* in a way acceptable to church and crown. The result was the emergence of the legal theory of *rapt de séduction*, a definition of *rapt* that at once "safeguarded the pretentions of the Church and the laws of the state, and gave at the same time satisfaction to the decrees of the one and the ordinances of the other."[34]

Juridical opinion came to presume *rapt* occurred if parental consent to the marriage was lacking, and furthermore, that violence no longer need be assumed to accomplish the act. Rather, *rapt* could be accomplished by a seduction that rendered one of the parties a victim of false promises.[35] This definition of rapt satisfied royal demands for parental consent, but it also satisfied the church decrees of Trent, which held expressly that *rapt* constituted an impediment to valid marriage and any marriage contracted as a result of *rapt* was null.[36] Up to this point, *rapt* had historically assumed violent abduction,[37] but by expanding the definition to include nonviolent seduction, seemingly free consent could now be construed under certain circumstances as seduction under false promises, and therefore *rapt*. The demands of both state and church could now satisfactorily be met. A legal fiction, *rapt de séduction*, was thus created to facilitate the coming together of church and state in a Christian reform of society.

In his edict of 1556, King Henri II expressed concern over the perceived proliferation of clandestine marriages and thus the flouting of parental control. However, he made no direct connection between *rapt de violence* and clandestine marriage. Charles IX's ordinance of Orléans in 1561, however, linked them. Now anyone who had "sequestered any girls and married them against the will and wishes of the fathers, mothers, and kin" shall be prosecuted for the "crime of rapt."[38] Furthermore, in the ordinance of Blois in 1579, a window was opened for *rapt* to be interpreted not simply as violent abduction for marriage, but also as nonviolent seduction. First, articles 40 through 44 recapitulated and expanded upon the ordinance of Orléans's association of *rapt de violence* with clandestine marriage: "We wish that those who are found to have suborned minor sons or daughters . . . under the pretext of marriage . . . without the will, knowledge, wishes or express consent of the fathers, mothers, and guardians be punished by death without the hope of grace or pardon." The same ordinance then added the following clause, however, implying a role for seduction (and thus nonviolence) in the definition of *rapt* as well: clandestine marriage is *rapt* "notwithstanding any consent, given either at the time of the rapt or before, that the said minors might allege [to have given]."[39]

In seventeenth- and eighteenth-century (to 1730) legislation and in eighteenth-century legal dictionaries and handbooks, *rapt*'s definition continued to include violence and seduction, both warranting capital punishment.[40] During the seventeenth and early eighteenth centuries, in fact, *rapt de séduction* came to be considered the predominant type of *rapt*, and the most threatening to property and familial honor. The royal declarations of 1697 and 1730 repeated nearly verbatim the wording of the declaration of 1639, by which successive kings had excoriated clandestine marriages, especially those resulting from seduction rather than violence. Louis XIII claimed that they resulted in "evil and disorder that troubles the repose of so many families and brands their honor from unequal and often shameful and infamous alliances." Nearly a century later Louis XV confirmed that sentiment in nearly the same words and added that such matches "often become the cause of the ruin" of those families.[41]

In royal legislation on *rapt*, then, we can see the coming together of religious, political, and social ideologies rooted deeply in a marital ethic which was assumed, if applied effectively, to guarantee social and moral order pleasing to father, king, and God.

Rapt *in Court*

Given the "family-state compact," the necessity of parental consent in marital legislation, and the religious concerns of a French monarchy committed to an expansion of its authority, how the royal legislation on *rapt* which embodied each of these was applied in the courts of the realm is an important historical question.

From what was seen in an earlier chapter, it should not be surprising that the jurisdiction over *rapt* by ecclesiastical courts was entirely eroded from 1550 to 1730, although church courts did continue to hear cases pertaining to marriage (broken promises, parental opposition, and occasionally premarital pregnancy).[42] In the extensive collection of *arrêts* from the criminal chambers of the Parlement of Burgundy (the Tournelle, and after 1631 the Enquêtes) dating from 1582 to 1730, on the other hand, the incidence of *rapt* cases is not rare. Parlement was the court of final appeal, and in the judicial decision (the *arrêt*) the lower court ruling was recapitulated (often all too laconically) prior to the final decision. From 3,024 of these records, I have been able to compare lower and appellate court decisions, and to gauge some continuities and changes over time.

Although sentences do not invariably reveal a court's jurisprudential intentions,[43] several trends in the sentences are discernible. The most notable characteristic is the relative severity with which the judges dealt with *rapt* cases in the sixteenth century and the distinct shift away from corporal punishment that marked the late seventeenth and eighteenth. It is seldom clear in these records whether the *rapt* was violent or seductive, leading one to suspect that the judges felt little compulsion to make the distinction themselves. What is clear is the drift away from corporal or capital punishment.

This development is likely part of what Langbein has called "a revolution in the law of proof" which occurred during the seventeenth century and applied to all crimes.[44] The new law of proof embraced "a standard of subjective persuasion" that rested upon "free judicial evaluation of the evidence." It did not immediately replace the Roman-Canon law of proof which emphasized "objective certainty" for conviction.[45] Indeed, both systems existed side by side, with the Roman-Canon legal system being embraced by kings in their system of statutory proofs, a system by which monarchs aimed to eliminate judicial discretion by their magistrates. It is in judicial practice, however, that this revolution in the law of proof can be seen most clearly. Whereas the Roman-Canon law of proof rested upon a standard, of "objective certainty," which required either two eyewitnesses or confession for conviction, the new law of proof admitted circumstantial evidence and made it easier to convict the accused of serious crimes, although without invoking the death penalty.[46] Rather than reflecting a leniency toward crime, this trend toward judicial discretion to sentence based on circumstantial evidence arguably gave judges more power to maintain order, because fewer highly suspect individuals who the judges deeply suspected of guilt would escape punishment altogether.

Until 1670 lower court judges regularly handed down punishments for *rapt* calling for hanging, service in the king's galleys, or banishment, and the Parlement judges were equally severe until the late 1640s. As legislation from Blois onward made manifestly clear, such stern jurisprudence aimed at shoring up the edifice of paternalism, and, for a time, Burgundy's judges obediently applied the legislation.

In 1622, for example, the court heard a case in which Palamedes Bourgeois, *sieur de* Molleron, accused Claude Gaspard, *sieur de* Marcilly, of kidnapping (*rapt et enlévement*) Hipolite Bourgeois, his daughter.[47] Unfortunately, as with all *arrêts* of this nature, we possess only a cursory recapitualation of lower court decisions and the sentence. This sentence, however, speaks loudly about the importance of paternalism. Gaspard was found guilty of *rapt* and condemned to be broken on the wheel. The fact that he was a fugitive at the time saved his life, but not his property. After payment of 3,000£ to the king and 6,000£ to the plaintiff, the remainder of his goods (*biens*) were to be confiscated. Meanwhile, Hipolite was to be "apprehended and returned to the power of the said Palamedes," her father. The marriage, "if any had taken place or been contracted," was declared "null and clandestine." Furthermore, any "promises, gifts, conventions, and dispositions . . . made by the said [Hipolite] Bourgeois against the consent, will, and authority of her said father" were "revoked and annulled" by the court.

Such stern measures were in keeping with the demands of royal legislation on *rapt*, but by mid-century they had abated in parlementary sentences. In lieu of corporal or capital punishment (which continued to be demanded for *rapt* by royal law even in 1730), first the appellate court and then the lower courts began to soften their sentences. Paternalistic concerns, however, remained. In 1694, for instance, the *procureur du roi* at the bailliage of Bresse and the *présidial* court of Bourg filed suit against a woman named Bernard (her first name is not given) for seducing for the purposes of marriage the minor François Camus, a bourgeois from Bourg.[48] Burgundy's Parlement upheld the lower court's decision to fine Bernard 30£, and, disregarding her claim that she and Camus were husband and wife, declared the marriage contract established between them "null as contrary to the [royal] ordinances." Camus, of course, was then forbidden to marry Bernard without the permission of his parents. Finally, the court called for an investigation of the notary who had drawn up their marriage contract.

As the Bernard case demonstrates, the judges remained supporters of paternalism, but they came to favor monetary remuneration in the form of *dommages et intérêts*, child support, or dowries instead of corporal or capital punishment. The last sentence of banishment for *rapt* issued by the Parlement occurred in 1669 (which overturned a lower court sentence of hanging in effigy, since the condemned was a fugitive),[49] but the most recent previous sentence calling for death or exile had come in 1646 (life in the galleys).[50] And the last execution for rapt ordered by Parlement had come in 1629.[51]

There were no changes, however, in the criminal *legislation* on rapt between the Ordinance of Blois in 1579 and the Declaration of 1730.[52] Indeed, for much of this period judges were specifically enjoined by the king to obey a law that demanded the death penalty for *rapt* of any kind, violent or seductive. It had not always been that way. In the edict against clandestine marriages in 1556, in fact, Henri II gave his judges latitude: people involved in clandestine marriages were subject to "such punishments that will be advised, according to the demands of the case, by our judges . . . whose honor and conscience we charge."[53] Such magisterial discretion disappeared in the Declaration of 1639, when Louis XIII "specifically enjoined . . . [his] judges to punish the guilty with the penalty of death . . . without the possibility of moderation."[54] Quite possibly the king was seeking to arrest the drift toward leniency by his judges adjudicating *rapt*.[55]

Louis's pronouncement notwithstanding, in Burgundy the royal judges, and slightly later the judges in lower jurisdictions, clearly came to favor monetary remuneration over capital punishment for *rapt*. The Declaration of 1639 intended to enhance royal and, by extension, paternal authority, and the king assumed that *rapt* (either seductive or violent) that was not appropriately punished would destablize the social hierarchy because it left the way open to misalliance. Given the social status of Burgundy's parlementary jurists, they had every reason to be similarly concerned and equally committed to patriarchy. Yet their judicial decisions went directly against the consistently severe royal edicts, ordinances, and declarations. Indeed, at times they even forced the guilty party to marry the victim, thus undermining the notion that rapt per se was an impediment to a valid marriage. How could they justify such jurisprudence which departed so clearly from royal legislation?

If royal legislation continued to classify *rapt* as a capital crime, the Parlement of Burgundy drifted toward a different conclusion. The provincial judges heard *rapt* cases regularly, but eventually abandoned handing down sentences of flogging, time in the galleys, or hanging in favor of *dommages et intérêts* awarded to the wronged party (in Burgundy, nearly always the woman, her father, or lacking him, her closest relatives.) Knowing that the king demanded execution for the crime, Burgundy's judges must have seriously pondered how effectively paternalism was supported by draconian capital punishment. Not much, suggest their decisions after the middle of the seventeenth century.

A primary purpose of the judicial process in cases of *rapt* came to be the rehabilitation of the honor of the woman or, more accurately, her family.[56] The judges were operating according to the rules of a sexual economy. They conceived of a woman's honor as a commodity with a monetary value pegged to her social station and therefore her marketability in marriage. The litigants, for their part, understood the same rules. Women professed

Table 4.2. *Rapt* cases at the Tournelle (*arrêts définitifs criminels* and *arrêts à l'audience criminel* [after 1668]), Selected Years

Date of Appeal	Rapt *cases*	Total extant	
		Criminal cases (*including* rapt)	Percent
1583–1592	20	952	2.1
1628–1631	12	390	3.1
1646–1649	7	158	4.4
1668–1671	10	140	7.1
1687–1700	13	410	3.2
1720–1727	5	171	2.9
Totals	67	2221	3.0

Note: The Court of Enquêtes, established in 1631 ostensibly for "petit criminel" cases, heard only five *rapt* cases·from 1631 to 1727, four of those after 1720; The Grand'Chambre heard only two *rapt* cases from 1583 to 1727. These figures have not been included in this table.

Source: ADCO B II 45 and 46.

that honor "was the dearest thing in the world," and men deemed it legitimate to break a promise for marriage if they discovered that the woman had lost her virginity and thus her honor before their engagement. Hearing that one's betrothed had previously given birth to a child was a common charge of the loss of honor and the breaking of an engagement.[57]

In 1587 the court heard an appeal from the royal chastelleny of Saulle-Duc where Nicolas Barthélemy was convicted of "contraventions to the edicts and *arrêts* concerning clandestine marriages."[58] Pursuing a calculus of honor and money, the Parlement ordered Barthélemy to pay a 20£ fine to the king and 10 *écus* [30£] in damages to the wronged parties (a *lieutenant en la Chastellenie*, his daughter, and a merchant from Ays-sur-Tille). He also was sentenced "to say to the plaintiffs in the presence of six of their kin . . . that the men are *gens de bien* and that the girl is chaste and modest."

Less than a fortnight later Parlement handed down a similar sentence against Claude Perreau, a *praticien* from Chan.[59] Anne Patey, the widow of a notary from Chalon-sur-Saône, filed suit at the local bailliage accusing Perreau of extorting secret promises of marriage (which she called *rapt*) from her daughter Magdelaine. Before a sentence was passed at the lower court, Perreau appealed. His appeal was to no avail, however, because he was ordered to pay a 20 *écu* fine to the king and, in addition to paying 10 *écus* in damages, was required to swear in the presence of the plaintiffs and six of their kin that he held Magdelaine to be "chaste, virtuous and honorable."

More than 130 years later, rehabilitation of honor continued to be a significant issue in *rapt* cases. In 1719, Jeanne-Marie Defforges, the widow of a notary and *procureur* at Luzy, with her daughter Claudine Ballard (who had already reached majority) accused Jean Renardet, the son of the *subdélégué* of the Intendant, of the crime of *rapt et séduction*.[60] In the lower court (the *justice de Toulon*) Defforges asked for 15,000£ damages payable to Claudine and 10,000£ to herself. The court found Defforges's sense of her social worth as inflated as the damages she requested, but it did award 3,000£ to Claudine and 500£ to Defforges for "reparation of the scandal." On appeal, Parlement reduced the damages still further (to 1,500£ and 300£, respectively) although still justifying these payments as reparations to honor.

Cash settlements (*dommages et intérêts*) like these may not have restored virginity, but they did aim to "repair" honor which, in the context of marriage markets and marital strategies, was of estimable consideration to women and parents alike.[61] Attaching cash value to honor in many instances was a way of restoring a woman's marketability in marriage by providing her with a supplement to an existing dowry.

There is reason to believe that the term *intérêts* could imply dowry when used in the context of *rapt* cases,[62] and occasionally in the sentences themselves the courts used precisely the term "dowry" to describe the cash settlement. In 1582, a priest was convicted of "an attempt on the modesty" of an unmarried woman and was fined 20 *écus intérêts* as *dot* [dowry] for the woman.[63] In 1669 Claude Rouget, a peasant from Chaveyriat, was convicted of *rapt* of Marie Dupuys (the illegitimate daughter of the Count of Ferrasière) and as part of his sentence was ordered to pay up to 1,000£ to Dupuys "to dower" her.[64] Similarly, in 1680 a lower court, the mayor's court at Dijon's bailliage, ordered Bénigne Borgne, the son of a *procureur* in the Chambres des Comptes in Dijon, "to dower Marie Gallet [the daughter of one of the king's jewellers] with the sum of 2,000£ . . . if he does not wish to marry her."[65]

In 1667, when recommending the sentence in a *rapt* case, the *procureur fiscal* of the *Juge Mage de Cluny* recalled the royal legislation of 1639 that stipulated the guilty "be condemned . . . to feed and raise the child and to dower the girl or the widow in proportion to what the father or mother could dower her, particularly when the accused is of a condition above the plaintiff." He then suggested that the defendant in the case, who outranked the plaintiff in social status, pay "her damages and interest in proportion to what her mother and father could give her in marriage."[66]

In his late eighteenth-century dictionary of criminal law, Muyart de Vouglans opined that this practice was widespread throughout the kingdom: "the ordinary punishment for those convicted of being the authors of the pregnancy consists not only in being charged to raise and dower the children, but also to dower the person seduced . . . according to the *qualité* and *facultés* of the seducer and in regard to the condition of the woman."[67]

If the court usually wished to repair the honor of the woman and return her to the family, such was not always the case. Sometimes, if the court found the male all-too-willing to seduce a woman but all-too-hesitant to marry her, Burgundy's judges ordered the parties married. Frequently in such cases there were offspring to be considered. In 1643 the Parlement convicted Estienne Gauthereau of the *rapt* of Benoist Creusot and ordered that the imprisoned Gauthereau be "led by two bailiffs from the court with the said Creusot to Saint-Médard church [in Dijon] . . . to be married."[68] The laconic nature of *arrêts* like this one precludes knowing whether the parents had insisted on the union, but some lower court rulings (which preserve more expansive documentation) are more explicit.

In a case heard at the mayor of Dijon's court at the bailliage of Dijon in 1650, the journeyman surgeon Guillaume Bossuet was convicted of *rapt* against Anne Randollé, the daughter of Master cabinetmaker Pierre.[69] The sentence specifically called for a notary and priest, the former to draw up the civil contract of marriage, the latter to solemnize it, but only after Bossuet was led in irons under guard to the nearest church where his bride and the priest awaited him. This trial, however, unlike the parlementary *arrêts*, also documents that the father of Anne, who by the time of the sentence was the mother of Bossuet's two-year-old child, *demanded* a marriage. The court, in this case, was upholding patriarchal authority by its decision.

More common were the proceedings where marriage was presented as an alternative to payment of damages and interest, and in these cases pregnancy and offspring were nearly always at issue. In 1609 a man referred to only as Laton was given a choice: either marry Magdaleine Gauthier, the daughter of a merchant from Chalon-sur-Saône, or pay 2,000£ *intérêts* to Magdaleine, 300£ *intérêts* to her father, and 100£ per year as *pension* for Laton's and Magdaleine's child, Marie.[70] He married her. In 1637 we find a similar *arrêt* issued by the Parlement.[71] Vincent Soucelier, the son of a *procureur* at Burgundy's Parlement, was convicted of *rapt* of Catherine Monnet, the daughter of a Dijonnais merchant. To gain his freedom, the imprisoned lawyer's son could either marry the merchant's daughter or pay her 3,000£ *intérêts* and provide 60£ per year *pension* for the child resulting from the liaison. Like Laton, he chose to marry.

In the 1720s, Parlement was still adjudicating some cases in this fashion. In 1722, it convicted Jean-Baptiste Bailly de Bailleuville, the *receveur au grenier à sel* of Charolles, of having seduced (*rapt par séduction*) Demoiselle Jeanne Caulnier de La Noue, the underage and seven-month pregnant daughter of an *avocat* at Charolles. The sentence of the lower court (the bailliage of the county of Charollais) had ordered Bailly to marry the young woman within three months or pay her father in her name 4,000£ in damages and interest, plus 400£ to cover the costs of childbirth. Parlement upheld the sentence in full.[72] Two years later the ill-named Prudent Quantin, from Veronne-les-Grands, was convicted of seduction of the Dijonnaise Anne Generoin and was sentenced to either marry her or pay her 1,000£ in damages and interest, plus 80£ to cover childbirth expenses, plus unspecified "expenses" (*frais*) for raising the child to the age of fourteen, when he was to learn a trade suitable to his status.[73]

Sentences such as these that encouraged marriage seem to contradict the spirit of ecclesiastical law, which required free consent of the betrothed; royal legislation, which opposed marriages resulting from *rapt* because they were presumed to lack parental consent; and even most of the judgments of the Parlement itself, which settled most cases by simple payment of damages and interest. Unfortunately, *arrêts* are imprecise documents nearly devoid of discussion of extenuating circumstances that could have guided judges to make exceptional decisions. In any case, it is quite difficult to tease the judges' motivations from them.

Each of the cases mentioned above do not seem to be social misalliances, and in all but one the condemned is in fact offered a "choice." If we bear in mind that the judges of Burgundy's highest court were committed to an ideology that sought to secure social stability and social stratification and to protect family interests at all cost, marriage between appropriate partners was a worthy goal and under certain circumstances could be deemed satisfactory outcome for a rapt case. Whether the offense was violent or seductive was not of primary consideration. The judges' jurisprudence, unlike their king's legislation, was pragmatic, even though judge and king were guided by the same social ideology. Both were deeply committed to instituting a new moral order, but unlike their monarch, the magistrates were confronted with daily experiences that forced them to innovate in the pursuit of their ideology.

The Parlement's judges remind us repeatedly in their *arrêts* that they were guided by social utility (the "public interest"), which could lead them in some cases to nullify or invalidate a clandestine marriage resulting from *rapt* or, conversely, to "encourage" a marriage. Social utility also guided the awarding of birth costs and child support if pregnancy resulted from *rapt*. Of the 88 *rapt* cases appealed to Parlement in my sample, 37 involved pregnancy, and the majority of those occurred after the mid-seventeenth century. (See Table 4.3.) Whether such cases reflected violent or seductive rapt unfortunately must remain open to speculation. Certainly, the court was keenly interested in providing for mother and child, and it may have considered corporal punishment of the father to be counter-productive to social stability. Given the already severe growth of pauperization in the sixteenth and seventeenth centuries, by ordering men convicted of *rapt* to provide for the mother and offspring, the judges in some cases probably hoped to avoid contributing to the rising tide of alms-seekers. Of course, they had to attempt to balance the mother's need with the father's ability to pay.

The *arrêts* themselves do not always record the occupation or status of the litigants (and we may surmise that relatively fewer cases involving the lower classes would be appealed owing to the costs involved), but judging from the examples where status or occupation is listed and from the occasional modest amounts of damages and interests awarded, we can confirm that many litigants did come from society's lower though not indigent ranks.[74] These individuals were at risk to fall into penury, even vagrancy, if cash settlements were not provided the abandoned mother and child or, conversely, were too high for the father to afford. Judges keen on maintaining social stability and the avoidance of social unrest might well consider the need to keep this vulnerable social stratum solvent.

Table 4.3. Pregnancies in *Rapt* Cases, Appeals before Parlement

Date of Appeal	Total Cases	Pregnancies (%)
1583–1622	24	5 (20.8)
1627–1664	26	8 (30.8)
1583–1664	50	13 (26.0)
1668–1674	15	10 (66.7)
1681–1727	23	14 (60.9)
1668–1727	38	24 (63.2)
Total	88	37 (42.0)

Note: Dates and figures reflect a sample of *arrêts définitifs criminels* and *arrêts à l'audience criminelle* from the Tournelle, Enquêtes, and Grand' Chambre (B II 45 and 46), and of copies of original parlementary *arrêts,* since lost, compiled by seventeenth- and eighteenth-century jurists (BMD, Ms. 1110).

In 1646 the peasant Antoine Joubet from Pont-de-Pany was convicted of *rapt* against Laurence Laurencin, and though the document lists only her father's name and residence, the village of Boz, we can surmise that these were individuals of modest means, because the lower court, the seigneurial justice at Pont-de-Pany, ordered the defendent to pay the young woman just 50£ *intérêts* which was expected to cover birth costs and child support. Parlement raised the amount to 100£, no doubt convinced that the father could afford it and that the mother needed it.[75]

In 1670, however, Parlement lowered from 150£ to 40£ the amount of *intérêts* that Jacques Remond, the son of a royal notary at Sautigny, had been ordered by the bailliage of Avalon to pay Madeleine Picard, the pregnant daughter of a peasant from the same place.[76] Four years later, in a case involving a peasant and the daughter of a day laborer, both from the village of Villebichot, the convicted man was ordered by Parlement to pay the woman 100£ for child support and *intérêts*, a slight reduction from the 120£ ordered by the lower seigneurial court of Villebichot.[77] In 1690, once again dealing with parties of modest means, Parlement lowered the fine. When Catherine Jacquet won a decision by the lower court for *rapt* against the Dijonnais Pierre Renault, the latter was required to pay 50£ for *intérêts* and to "nourish and support" the child from the union, although no cash amount was stipulated for the latter. On appeal, Parlement lowered the amount of *intérêts* to a mere 15£.[78]

If my sample holds some examples of adjudication between litigants of quite modest station (especially after the mid-seventeeth century), it in fact holds many others from all ranks of society. Artisans (both rural and urban), well-to-do peasants, village notables, petty urban officers, *procureurs*, merchants, *avocats*, seigneurs, and even royal councilors found themselves or their children implicated in *rapt* cases. Few of the kidnappings or seductions in my sample could be considered misalliances, however, and so the reasons for lower courts and Parlement finding the defendents guilty of *rapt* and demanding payment of damages and child support reflect, for the most part, an upholding of the ideology of paternalism. For whatever reasons, less obvious when misalliance was not an issue, the parents in most of the *rapt* cases were opposed to the unions in question, and the law (if not always the judges) demanded that the courts uphold the integrity of parental consent to marriage.

The Parlement, it is worth recalling, was guided by a practical jurisprudence in which it sought to balance the dictates of an uncompromising royal legal code with an everyday world defined by contingencies and singular situations. It kept the public welfare continually before its eyes, and social stability was its unswerving goal. As many demographic studies have demonstrated, it became increasingly difficult for single women to marry as the seventeenth century unfolded,[79] and unmarried women with children were especially at a disadvantage in the marriage market. At least the court could stipulate the payment of at times substantial sums in damages to the woman or her family, and funds to guarantee an appropriate upbringing of the offspring.

This concern for illegitimate offspring reveals how far Burgundy's high judges went to attenuate what they must have thought to be a counter-productive royal law, for they often restored what the law took away. Ostensibly to protect inheritances, French kings had ordered at Blois in 1579 and confirmed throughout the seventeenth century that children born of *rapt* were barred from legitimate inheritance. The Parlement of Burgundy's response demonstrates a practical jurisprudence at work.

In 1616, Jacques de Simiannes, *sieur* de Vennes, was convicted of *rapt* against Demoiselle Margueritte de Minstrat, the daughter of the twice-widowed Dame Silvie de Brancas (whose second husband had been a president at the Parlement of Aix). He was ordered to pay 1,000£ in damages to Margueritte and to provide each of the two girls he fathered 300£ per year *pension* plus a 3,000£ dowry upon her marriage.[80] The daughters had no claim to Simiannes's inheritance by royal law, but Parlement saw to it that they were not left without means.

In 1649, the court demonstrated a similar judgment, this time concerning litigants further down the social scale. It convicted Claude Beuchot, a peasant from Villy-en-Auxois, of *rapt* against Jeanne Lachot and ordered support for their offspring. Beuchot was required to pay 40£ annually in child support and 500£ to Lachot, in part, as the court explicitly pointed out, as a dowry for the child.[81]

The court was similarly guided, if more creative, in 1681. It ordered Jacques de Vallette, the son of a royal councilor at the Parlement of Toulouse, to pay Margueritte de Lesfacque, the daughter of an *avocat de conseil* and mother of de Vallette's child, 4,000£ cash for the support of their child. It further stipulated that de Vallette must invest an equal amount in *rentes*, the interest of which was to go to the mother for child support and the principal of which was to be turned over to the child when he or she reached the age of 25.[82]

The Parlement judges were committed to a social ideology that prized social stability and hierarchical structure, and they pursued pragmatic jurisprudence to secure that goal. Their judicial decisions in *rapt* cases changed between 1580 and 1730 while the law did not. Looking at the chronology of these decisions, we can see that generally the mid-seventeenth century is a watershed: a retreat from capital sentences in favor of remuneration (for restoration of honor, birth costs, child support), accompanied by a decrease in the amounts of remuneration; and a shift in provenance of litigation from the public prosecutor to the civil party (see Table 4.1). These developments reflect a de facto decriminalizing of the offense of *rapt*. That is, although by law it was still a capital criminal offense, jurisprudentially it was increasingly treated as a civil offense, repaired not by corporal punishment but by payment of damages, and increasingly left to the private individual to initiate legal proceedings.[83]

But why the shift? The sharp increase in civil parties initiating litigation without a public prosecutor (from 0:50 before 1664 to 22:38 from 1668 to 1727) may reflect fiscal restraint on the part of public officials;

plaintiffs bore the initial cost of litigation, and the absence of a public prosecutor meant that the civil party shouldered the entire cost. Once the case was in court, however, why did judges drift toward remuneration and away from corporal punishment? Surely this trend was related to the revolution in the law of proof which saw jurisprudence drift away from demands for objective certainty for conviction and toward admission of circumstantial evidence and a corresponding shift from the death penalty to a lesser punishment.

In a way, however, this explanation still begs the question. It is possible (though difficult to prove conclusively from the documents) that fraud replaced violence as the defining characteristic of rapt and thus warranted monetary rather than physical punishment. Perhaps the reason for the shift is also partly related to the shifting demographic situation, especially regarding the female population. The seventeenth century witnessed a postponement of first marriage, notably among females, and a growth in the unmarried and never-to-be married female population. The judges probably perceived a destabilizing threat here, and they pursued a practical jurisprudence aimed at avoiding such instability: repair of honor and return to paternal control; forced marriage; required child support. The king no less than his jurists may have been responding to the same trend. Given the relative overabundance of women in the marriage market, it was necessary to strengthen their attachment to their fathers. Women who were free from male control were a contemporary metaphor for disorder. The fear of unattached women might have guided paternalistic royal legislation as early as 1556, and the growth in the seventeenth century of the population of unmarried women reaching legal majority might have prompted the king in 1639 to declare that even men and women who had reached majority needed the written consent of their parents before they could be married, or they would be guilty of the crime of *rapt*.

Traditionally, *rapt* had meant violent kidnapping, but from the middle of the sixteenth century to the early eighteenth, the implication of seduction without violence came increasingly into play. At one level, this emphasis on seduction represented a compromise between church and state over the issue of consent and paternal authority in the formation of marriage. In popular judicial handbooks, at least from the eighteenth century, *rapt de violence* was distinguished from *rapt de séduction*. As *rapt*, however, both types flouted parental authority over the woman and were punishable by death. *Rapt*, whether of a violent or seductive nature, continued to assume marriage was at issue and thus did not distinguish from rape at one extreme and "illicit commerce" at the other.

King and judges assumed that *rapt* involving violent abduction was perpetrated by males, but despite the allegations of women, they were not inclined to perceive violence or male coercion in *rapt de séduction*, which came to be the predominant terminology in the seventeenth and eighteenth centuries. Indeed, the authorities increasingly blamed the woman as much as the man. The edict of 1730 attests, "As subornation can come equally

from one or the other side, and since the one that comes from the . . . more
feeble gender is often the more dangerous, the ordinances have not made
any distinction in this regard between men and women."[84]

Such suspicion of women and their objectives may well have been shared
by Burgundian judges and guided them in their adjudication of *rapt* cases.
Their drift toward leniency in the prosecution of men may suggest that
judges began to suspect that the women involved—pressure by men notwithstanding—shared some of the "guilt," and a rigid adherence to royal
legislation would have unduly punished only one of the "guilty" parties.[85]
True, the appeals themselves almost always found a male as defendant and
a female as plaintiff, but the dynamics of "seduction" as told in courts of
law commonly found a woman resisting the man's often aggressive advances,
only to grant him her "last favors" after marriage was promised. Frequent
sexual relations and, not surprisingly, pregnancy often resulted. Lower court
as well as appellate trial records imply that the judges presumed a female
marital strategy as much as masculine lust, and thus attenuated the guilt of
the man and implicitly placed some of the blame on the woman.

Marital Strategies and Litigation

Historical documents generated by the legal process can be exceptionally
useful in the interpretation of the past, and they open a window upon a
large sector of the population that most other kinds of sources do not. For
determining marital strategies and the uses of the law they can be helpful,
but by the time an individual became a litigant, he, or most commonly she
in the cases of *rapt*, was already several paces into the strategy. Fortunately,
these records offer considerable opportunities to infer earlier steps.

For the vast majority of unmarried French women living in the sixteenth
to eighteenth centuries, their objective in life was to marry with honor. This
goal did not preclude premarital sexual activity, so long as such activity was
preceded by a promise of marriage and followed by matrimony. And if a
promise was broken, women and men knew that legal recourse was available, either in church courts (*officialités*) or, if *rapt* were alleged, in secular
courts.[86] In either jurisdiction, plaintiffs presented the same kinds of complaints, usually pertaining to defamation of honor, and similar kinds of sentences were handed down—an order of marriage, or "damages" and
"interest."

Premarital sexual activity and promises to marry were nearly always
mentioned in *rapt* cases but, by the time litigation began, the litigant had
exhausted other recourses. If pregnancy resulted from a courtship and the
man balked at marriage, the logical option for many women was to conceal the pregnancy if possible, dispose of the infant in some fashion (place-
ment with a wetnurse, abandonment, infanticide), and then return to the
patrimonial family and the pool of eligible brides without a loss of honor
and reputation. Of course, such a strategy was illegal (in fact, a capital offense
since 1556), and so it only surfaces in the historical record when it failed.

Take, for instance, the case of Estiennette Saunetez. In 1619 this domestic servant of a *procureur* at Burgundy's Parlement named Berthélemy Guillemard was arraigned for failing to declare pregnancy and thus suspected of intention to commit infanticide (as defined by the edict of 1556). She confessed to Dijon's municipal authorities that she was pregnant by her master. While in custody she asserted that Guillemard had counseled her to go to Dijon's suburbs to have the baby, stay there fifteen days, and then "at midnight carry the infant to Saint Esprit," Dijon's foundling hospital. To prevent self-incrimination, however, Saunetez told the interrogating officer that she had no intention of following such advice, but rather had planned on taking the baby to Guillemard's house and leaving it there "in order to make him support [*nourrir*] it."[87]

It is not known how Saunetez was apprehended, but seventeenth-century municipal authorities like those of Dijon were deeply concerned about clandestine pregnancies in general.[88] In 1644, the town's syndic was notified by an unknown informant that several pregnant young women were presently in private homes anticipating giving birth. Hearing this, he immediately set out to investigate, and his sleuthing took him to five different homes in one night. In a weaver's house he found two young women, one eight months pregnant and one three months pregnant. The syndic warned the young women that recently a considerable number of infants had been abandoned at the foundling hospital, and any woman apprehended for such an act would be "exemplarily chastised." The young women assured the officer that they had no intention of taking their babies to Saint Esprit and, like the four others the syndic visited later that night, promised him that they were going to retain custody of their infants.[89]

It was not unusual for the syndic to be notified of unmarried pregnant women hiding in private homes waiting to give birth. When the officer received such information, his response was immediate. One April night in 1669, Dijon's syndic was notified that a young woman had just given birth in the house of a local midwife. He hastened there because, as he put it in his report, he was worried that the expectant mother might "expose her newborn," an all-too-frequent practice, according to the authorities.[90] Upon arrival at the house, he interrogated the young mother, a certain Margueritte Champonions, daughter of a tanner from Chalon-sur-Saône. He discovered that she had come to Dijon to hide her unfortunate pregnancy from her parents. She had been seduced by a young man while she was in service at one of her aunts in Chalon and, because her parents disapproved of a marriage between the two, when she became pregnant she lied to her parents and aunt, saying she wanted to move to Dijon to find work as a servant. Upon arrival in Burgundy's capital, she headed for the neighborhood apparently known for having available midwives with lodgings—near the gate by the river Ouche in Saint Philibert parish—and there she hoped to give birth in anonymity.

Although there is no way to quantify this practice, it appears that the dutiful syndic was simply uncovering the tip of an iceberg, an iceberg of premarital pregnancy that continued to float in the sea of courtship at least into the nineteenth century.[91] His investigations sketch the outlines of a world that appears relatively well organized, advertised by word-of-mouth to pregnant women in desperate need of help and, above all, secrecy. Most of these unfortunates, often lodged with several other young women in a similar condition, had come from beyond the city walls. Dijon appears to have been a magnet with a field encompassing most of Burgundy and even part of Champagne. For young women from as far away as Langres to the north, Besançon to the east, the Morvan to the west, and Mâcon to the south, the province's largest city offered birthing facilities and anonymity. These early modern, clandestine "maternity wards" were clustered geographically in Dijon's neighborhood pocked with tenements and brothels, but squalor might have been an acceptable price to pay for secrecy. Imagine, then, how devastated, indeed, terror-stricken, a woman—perhaps in labor—must have been when the syndic's firm rap sounded on the midwife's door.

For an unmarried pregnant woman whose courtship had come to a bad end by a recalcitrant man, one option, then, was to conceal the pregnancy and birth to preserve the visible manifestation of honor and her future prospects for marriage. For many others who appear in ecclesiastical court records, however, a frank use of litigation was their central tactical component. Even in the late seventeenth century, *officialités* were hearing cases pertaining to marriage, though certainly fewer than had been heard there in the fifteenth and sixteenth centuries,[92] and many of these suits were brought by women demanding "the enforcement of a marriage promise."[93]

Such was the case in 1649, for example, in the *officialité* of Autun when Margueritte Marion demanded that the 35-year-old Adam Bonnard be forced to marry her, since he had promised to do so in writing in her father's house and again verbally, "in front of the church."[94] It is not known how the court ruled in this case, but in the diocese of Troyes in nearby Champagne the ecclesiastical judge did occasionally either order couples in similar suits married[95] or direct the defendent to pay "damages and interest" in lieu of matrimony.[96]

Some pregnant, unmarried women went to church courts to demand fulfillment of a marriage promise,[97] but by the second half of the seventeenth century the secular courts heard many of these cases as well, usually in the form of *rapt* litigation.[98] Filing accusations of *rapt* in courts of law or, in a related juridical action, declaring pregnancy to a municipal official, might have been—given the alternatives of clandestine birth, infanticide, or abandonment of the child—a necessary means of survival for a significant number of women. There is no way of knowing what percentage of courting couples engaged in premarital sexual activity,[99] or how many of those women ultimately wound up in court charging *rapt* or broken marriage promises, or before officials declaring their pregnancies. Demographic evidence suggests that the percentage of extramarital births in the seventeenth century was low (1–3%),[100] although it did increase in the eighteenth

century. That same evidence, however, also tells us that premarital conceptions were far from rare, probably around 10 percent in 1700.[101]

The Burgundian documents seem to suggest that *following* forcefully
persistent and at times deceitful "courting" by men, a not inconsiderable
number of pregnant women *subsequently* pursued a strategy in which their
pregnancy might be turned to their advantage.[102] Social status and demographic pressures had some bearing on the use of this strategy. Many of
the women alleging *rapt* or declaring pregnancy in the records were servants or otherwise relatively independent of parental supervision, and such
women did not have the benefit of following the conventional strategy that
operated within familial networks. Demographic shifts, such as later average age at marriage (upward of 25) and increasing numbers of women who
would never marry (by 1700, 10–15%) affected these women, as well as
those of higher station. Dimmed prospects for marriage were a specter
haunting all classes of women, which may account for the number of *rapt*
cases involving women of high station as well as low. Many of these women,
once "seduced" by a man for whom they might well have felt affection,
might *then* have become pregnant and, to hold the man to his promise of
marriage, admitted the pregnancy frankly to the authorities.

Not surprisingly, some officials and jurists suspected the women litigants of deceit as much as the men, although given the early modern male's
deprecatory attitude toward females, it is difficult to lend much credence
to their suspicions. In 1667, the *procureur fiscal* at the seigneurial court of
the *Juge Mage* of the monastery of Cluny wrote in his concluding statements concerning a trial for a *rapt* resulting in pregnancy that it was commonplace throughout the province for young women to "charm . . . and
[then] make love to those whom they . . . hope to marry."[103] The eighteenth-century jurist Muyart de Vouglans said much the same thing. Pregnant women "most often took advantage of the rigor of this jurisprudence
in order to procure a rich husband," an action which, according to this jurist,
prompted judges to convert the death penalty for *rapt* to payment of damages and interest.[104]

To see how this strategy might unfold, consider the following story
recounted in a pregnancy declaration, a quite typical example. In 1698
Louise Simon, the 23-year-old daughter of a *charbonnier* from Fontaine-
en-duemois, became pregnant while in the service of a *maître* at the
Chambres des Comptes in Dijon.[105] The alleged father, named Pierre
Peultert, was a lackey in the same household. Simon declared that Peultert
"pursued her [for two months] with caresses and solicitations to make her
succumb to his desires" until one evening when the owners of the house
were out, he slipped into her bed and "under the promises that he would
make her his wife he knew her carnally two times." Eight days later he had
sex with her two more times, and then during the rest of the month they
had sexual relations "in the attic . . . where she did the wash . . . in the
cellar . . . where she fetched wood . . . and . . . once during High Mass on
the mistress's bed." Not surprisingly, Simon was soon pregnant and, be-

cause of Peultert's marriage promises, fully expected to meet him at the altar—with the help of the law, if necessary.

Declarations of pregnancy only tell the woman's side of the story, and these narratives are formulaic and self-serving;[106] still, they reflect assumptions on the part of the woman of what had the possibility of being a successful course of action. Once overcome by the man and made pregnant, some women were aware that the law could be a useful tool in attaining the promised marriage.

Most declarations, like that of Louise Simon, attest that before the woman succumbed to the man's wishes to have sexual relations, she resisted his sometimes violent solicitations and only softened when she received from him a promise of marriage. Such promises often were accompanied by a ring or gift. In this sexual economy, in exchange for rings or gifts the woman would offer her "last favors," but clearly under conditions she assumed to be a binding contract. She must have known promises of marriage were enforceable in courts of law, and that a judge would look even more favorably upon her case if a child were involved.

In 1659 Marie Michea, the daughter of a peasant from Seure and servant of a royal councillor in Dijon, was made pregnant by one of her master's coachmen. She claimed to have resisted his advances for three months, but gave in when he promised marriage, something he had confirmed before witnesses. Once Michea was pregnant, however, he reneged on his promise. To force his hand, Michea declared her pregnancy to the municipal authorities of Dijon.[107]

This sort of story was not uncommon. In 1721, Jeanne LaPlace, a *fille majeure* (that is, over age 25) and servant of a brigadier of the guards of the governor of Burgundy, reported to the authorities that a journeyman harnessmaker named Massot had courted her, saying "he had no other intention than marriage." He had "contracted with her" by giving her a silver ring, and when she accepted it, he followed with a promise of marriage. He continued to make only "proper caresses" (*caresses honestes*), until abruptly one night "he knew her carnally by force," nevertheless assuring her that he intended to marry her. When he learned that she was pregnant, however, he reputedly made plans to leave town. She confronted him with the rumor, but he still assured her that "they needed to set a date for their marriage." Perhaps for added assurance she went to the syndic and filed her declaration of pregnancy.[108]

Some women's strategy in their negotiations for marriage was thus to line up as many guarantees as possible: recourse to law, rings, love letters,[109] and promises of marriage (sometimes verbal, sometimes written).[110] The law was especially pertinent if the woman was victimized by a deceitful and aggressive man and made pregnant.

In 1723 Margueritte Fadin, a 25-year-old servant, claimed to be pregnant by Pierre Marie, a lackey of the First President of Burgundy's Parlement. He had promised marriage and gave her a golden ring with some gems mounted on silver. But it turned out that he expected something in return; one day he surprised her doing the wash and violently "knew her carnally." When she became pregnant and he reneged on his promise to marry her, she reported to the syndic; she used her declaration of pregnancy "to file suit against the said Marie."[111] A declaration two years later by Jeanne Jaquin concluded with the same request of the syndic: a copy of the declaration to be used in the "pursuits that she intends to make against" the alleged father.[112]

Declarations of pregnancy are formulaic documents and do not necessarily reflect what actually transpired. Indeed, lower court criminal trials for seduction and *rapt* (for which some records have been preserved) were far from formulaic. They give a more detailed picture of the negotiations and exchanges that marked some courtships than do declarations of pregnancies. Significantly, they square in many important ways with what women were saying in the self-serving declarations.

In 1634 Dame Estiennette Duchassain, the widow of a butcher from Mâcon, filed suit in the presidial court in Mâcon for a *rapt* committed against her 18-year-old daughter, Jeanne Galaud.[113] The alleged perpetrator was Philippe Noblet, brother of Damoiselle Anne Noblet in whose service Jeanne had been placed. Duchassain alleged that Noblet had used "flattery," solicitations, and promise of marriage to persuade Jeanne to "let him [Noblet] deflower her." With her daughter six months pregnant with Noblet's child, Duchassain was in court claiming *rapt*, a crime, as she correctly threatened in her petition, "that merits exemplary and capital punishment."

Depositions taken in the consequent investigation revealed that a sexual relationship had likely developed between the two. Several witnesses testified that the couple had been seen kissing and fondling on more than one occasion, and rumor had it that Philippe's sister, Anne, had surprised her brother and Jeanne *à la ruelle du lict* (beside the bed), the well-known site for sexual encounters, as Jeanne herself admitted later. When a neighbor confronted Anne and asked why she did not do something about her brother's relationship with her servant, she said she did not want "a scandal."

The fear of misalliance must have also weighed heavily on Anne. We can imagine her consternation when Philippe bestowed upon Jeanne domestic gifts (a pair of scissors and some pins), surely taken by Jeanne (as she intimated in a response during her interrogation) as part of a reciprocal negotiation leading toward marriage. The witness relating this information made the same assumption, no doubt, because she deemed it significant enough to mention in her deposition while she was discussing Noblet's courting of Galaud. The authorities were concerned enough about reciprocal obligations to ask Noblet about the gifts when they questioned him. During the interrogation, Noblet denied any sexual relationship with Jeanne, indeed, calling her a foul-mouthed libertine and charging that her claims were a ruse to get him to support her.

When Galaud was interrogated, she refuted all of Noblet's denials. She was seduced by him, she said, promised marriage, and given gifts. When he broke his promises, she turned to her mother and then to court. The court believed Galaud and ordered Noblet to pay Galaud and her mother 2,000£.

In 1648 a case of *rapt* briefly noted already came before the mayor's court at the bailliage of Dijon.[114] Pierre Randollé, a master cabinetmaker in Dijon, filed suit on behalf of his daughter Anne, 21 years old and pregnant. Anne supposedly had been "sollicited to dishonor" by a 30-year-old journeyman surgeon, Guillaume Bossuet. Anne, according to her father, had every reason to assume a marriage was in sight; Guillaume had so promised, and the betrothed couple had exchanged golden rings to seal the agreement. As in the Noblet-Galaud case, depositions reported affectionate actions that were interpreted by witnesses as part of courtship (kissing, hugging, fondling, delousing). Anne herself confirmed all of this, adding that she had had repeated sexual relations with Guillaume, always following promises of marriage. When she became pregnant, Bossuet balked at marriage, although he did attempt to arrange the childbirth in Troyes and service for Anne in a household in Paris. She claims to have initially objected to his plan, but when he threatened to kill her, she sagely reconsidered. He persuaded her to sell some of her belongings to finance the trip to Troyes and then Paris, and, hoping to keep the affair secret from her father, she slipped out of town. We do not know when or why she returned to Dijon or why or how her father could have remained so ignorant of his daughter's plight. Following the last of the depositions of witnesses taken about a week after the suit commenced, an order to arrest Bossuet was issued. It took until June 1650 to collar him (we do not know why the delay). When questioned about the allegations of marital promises, caresses, rings, and so on, Bossuet declined to respond, one time adding that "he only wanted to answer to My Lords of Parlement." Perhaps he had heard that Parlement was coming to view *rapt* with a more lenient eye than were lower courts or even than royal legislation dictated, and he may have calculated that a hearing there would be to his advantage. If this were the case, he was right about the trend in Parlement's jurisprudence, but he miscalculated how the royal judges would rule in his case.

While Parlement was deliberating, Bossuet peremptorily agreed to marry Randollé. Parlement held documents alleging that Bossuet had made similar promises before and suspected that he might be making a spurious one again to gain release from prison. To preclude such a possibility, it issued an *arrêt* stipulating that a notary would draw up a marriage contract; then Bossuet would be released from prison and escorted under guard across the street to the nearest church, where a priest would be waiting with Anne to solemnize the union.

Early in the next century, similar outlines of courtship negotiations can be glimpsed in yet another *rapt* case.[115] In 1720 Jacques Rousselet, an *avocat* at Parlement, filed a suit alleging *rapt* of his daughter Guillemette-Therèze by Antoine Fromageot, the 22-year-old son of a deceased *procureur* at the same court. Fromageot's mother (and wife of a royal councilor at the

Présidial court) opposed the marriage and filed a countersuit alleging that Guillemette-Thérèze had in fact seduced her son.

The depositions that were taken leave little doubt that the couple was amorously involved. Guillemette-Thérèze declared that Antoine was an ardent pursuer. He had made promises of marriage, and she believed that it would be safe to meet him in a room in a small inn in the village of Vougeot, south of Dijon. There, one day in October, he locked the door. She resisted for three hours, but finally, taking advantage of the "weakness of her gender," he obtained from her "the last favors and knew her carnally." Subsequently, they had sexual relations regularly, always, she carefully pointed out, accompanied by "renewed promises of marriage, verbally and also in letters." When she told him that she was pregnant, he assured her not to be troubled, that he was a "man of honor." She continued to trust him because "he swore more than ever his promise to marry," and so "she regarded him as her husband."

The reference to the inn at Vougeot was the break the authorities needed in the case. The wife of the innkeeper where Rousselet and Fromageot had met reported that the couple had been there a dozen times during the autumn, spending two to three hours together, often behind closed doors. The innkeeper's daughter added that she had peeped through the keyhole and seen the couple embrace, and, as chambermaid, she could attest that every time they checked out the bed was messed up (*derangé et foullé*).

The sentence from the lower court is missing (if there was one), but the case was appealed to Parlement. Before any sentence was rendered, however, Fromageot admitted to his intentions to marry Rousselet and to the paternity, and the families agreed to a marriage.

In 1723 Margueritte Patron, a servant of the chief clerk (*Greffier en Chef*) at the Court of Requêtes at Parlement, filed suit at the mayor's court in Dijon alleging *rapt*.[116] The suspect was 20-year-old Jean-Baptiste Guilleminot, the *précepteur* in the same household. Margueritte claimed that Guilleminot had courted her, promising marriage. One night he surprised her, and after resistance by her, Guilleminot "enjoyed her and knew her carnally." Eventually she became pregnant, and Guilleminot balked at fulfilling his promises. Depositions testify to an amorous courtship. Patron followed up with another petition demanding that Guilleminot support the child and pay her 2,000£ "for damages and interest that resulted from him having ravished her and taken her honor." Guilleminot was then interrogated. Asked if he had known Patron carnally, was father of the child, and was willing to "repair Patron's honor by taking her as his wife," to all queries he replied simply, and, we might imagine, meekly, "yes."

Many studies have established that most of the women declaring pregnancy were the notoriously vulnerable domestic servants, and my sample confirms that sociological profile.[117] Of the 87 declarations sampled between 1619 and 1730 (nearly three-quarters of which date from the eighteenth century), at least 52 were made by servants.[118] Furthermore, 80 percent of those declaring were from out of town, and the entire sample had an average age of 25. These indicators point to a population of marriageable age and cut loose from parental protection, but also one less likely to attain marriage through conventional channels.

Once a vulnerable women became pregnant, often in the most unfortunate circumstances, she necessarily embarked on a course of action in which she had everything to lose if she could not bring the man (and father) to the altar. Honor, as the pregnant litigant Françoise Coutot frankly asserted, was at stake.[119] This servant and daughter of a Dijonnais *tripier* believed (like countless others) that "her honor . . . [could be] recovered by marriage," and she went to court to accomplish just that. If she lost the case, her honor was squandered and, in all likelihood, so was her chance of ever marrying. She would be left with a baby and a destroyed reputation.

The courts did not always require marriage, but the law could at least be used to exact monetary damages. Margueritte Febvre, the 21-year-old daughter of a master surgeon from Dijon, used the threat of litigation to settle out of court.[120] Perhaps to encourage the alleged father, another master surgeon named Dechaux, Febvre reported to the syndic that she was pregnant. She gave her declaration five days before a settlement was reached and recounts the familiar actions of courting (her initial resistence to his advances, then being overcome by the aggression of the man, and then having regular sexual relations, resulting in pregnancy). These allegations convinced her lover to pay Febvre and her father 370£ in damages. Dechaux demanded in return, however, that they agree to discharge him "from all inquiries, actions, and claims, and promise not to trouble him again with the subject of the said pregnancy."

If declarations of pregnancy and, indeed, seductive *rapt* cases illustrate that some women were using the law to attempt to control their own honor or material destiny, for others they reveal the woman's desperation. In 1716 24-year-old Jeanne Gagé, daughter of a coachman, reported her pregnancy to the syndic,[121] revealing that she was pregnant by a certain Sieur Dechargère from Arcenay near Saulieu. He allegedly had taken advantage of her "weakness" by using demonstrations of love, tenderness, and promise of marriage to convince her to have sexual relations with him. She had become pregnant, but that pregnancy was not the one she was declaring now. It seems that Dechargère had made her pregnant a second time, again with promises of marriage (made even to the unfortunate woman's father) and still had not fulfilled his promise. Worse, he had left town, and the ingenuous Gagé confessed to the syndic that she was afraid that she had been "deceived like the first time."

As early as 1665 a similar tale of despair had unfolded.[122] Six years a widow, Claudine Brullot declared that she was pregnant by a livestock merchant who had lodged with her during his business trips to Dijon. This pregnancy was not her first by him. Two years before, she had had his child (who had since died), and before both pregnancies, she had received promises of marriage. No doubt hoping she had not been deceived again, Brullot assured the authorities that at this moment her lover was in his native province getting the necessary letter from his curé so that the couple could be married.

Eleven years later, Dijon's syndic received word that a servant named Charlene was causing "a scandal by the cries and noise" she was making in the neighborhood.[123] She apparently was screaming for all to hear that her employer and alleged author of her pregnancy, the master shoemaker François Robert, had betrayed her. She claimed that he was trying to kick her out of the house. Desperate to avoid a shelterless and no doubt penniless existence, she had been hiding under a neighbor's attic staircase, pushing away food and drink, crying day and night (for two days), and refusing to come out. When the syndic arrived and questioned her, she told him that Robert had promised to marry her, and despite his breaking that promise now that she was pregnant, she still did not want to leave his house.

There are other examples of desperation. In 1715 a 26-year-old washerwoman from Semur-en-Auxois, Catherine Berthier, reported to the syndic that she was five months pregnant.[124] Introduced to a man by one of her relatives, she received promises of marriage and in return she "succumbed to his desires . . . and twice knew him carnally." She knew that her lover—she did not know his name—was from Paris, and she believed that he was "well-to-do." If he had not promised marriage, she said, she never would have "granted him the last favors."

In 1705 Anne Guignier, the daughter of a wheelwright from Cessey, declared that she was pregnant by a royal official at the Salt Office in Dijon.[125] There is no mention of marriage in the declaration but Guignier noted that her lover had promised marriage for her with a young man whom he knew. Her trust was misplaced, since at the time of the declaration no such marriage had been arranged, but the young woman must have thought that this was not an opportunity to pass up.[126]

Most women making these declarations spoke of broken promises of marriage and, tragically, marriage eluded many of these unfortunate women. Some women declaring their pregnancy, however, confessed to being "seduced" yet made no mention of marriage promises. Few of those, however, failed to mention promises of material support. Did these women conclude that being an unmarried mother with an out-of-court settlement or court-ordered child support was a more attractive option than being impecunious and unmarried? Many of the women declaring pregnancy were in vulnerable, exploited positions. Perhaps, given the predatory and often brutal approach many men took with women, they saw victimization as a likelihood. With the invariable and deplorable result of such liaisons (loss of shelter and job), might some have felt that they would do well to take any advantage of any situation they could?

Gaining promises of material support could be reason enough for some women to have sexual relations, especially if the pursuer were her master or above her in social status.[127] In 1707, for example, Catherine Burot, the orphan of a peasant from Bèze in the service of another peasant from the same place, reported her pregnancy in Dijon. She alleged that the purported father, Jacques Chevenet, capitalized on his position of authority and the stereotypical "weakness of her gender" and seduced her. Following regular sexual encounters, she became pregnant. She said nothing of promises of marriage—out of the question since Chevenet was married—but she did claim that Chevenet "had promised to take care of her, saying that she would want for nothing" if she allowed him to make love to her.

The declarations of pregnancy do not tell us what happened to the men and women involved, but it was within the legal right of a woman to pursue her seducer into court and accuse him of *rapt*. From the records of *rapt* cases, we can continue the stories, if with different characters. It is no accident that petitions filing suit for *rapt* often sound like pregnancy declarations.

Indeed, in a first-instance *rapt* case begun in November 1730, Françoise Gavinet, a 21-year-old servant from Auxonne, accused Claude-Joseph Martin, an *avocat* at Auxonne, of seducing her and making her pregnant.[128] Her petition was formulated like a declaration of pregnancy; in fact, it reiterated just such a document recorded the previous July before a notary in Auxonne. The case was complicated by the suspected involvement of Gavinet's master, Philippe Fourent, a bourgeois and customs officer in Auxonne. It seems that Gavinet rescinded the first declaration of pregnancy that implicated Martin, replaced it with a second naming Fourent the father, and then rescinded that one with a third that reaffirmed the initial charges. If Gavinet's inconstancy undermined her case we cannot know from the extant records, but depositions in the case suggest that Gavinet's relationship with Fourent was suspicious. Rumor had it that Gavinet's presence in the Fourent household was causing discord between husband and wife, and that while Fourent was insistent on keeping Gavinet in his service, his wife (so she told a surgeon while he was pulling one of her teeth) was trying to throw her out.

Martin openly asserted that Fourent was the father; everyone knew that Gavinet and Fourent were engaged sexually, and Fourent had promised Gavinet that he would not abandon her, pledging to give her great sums of money, including some to accuse Martin of paternity. Fourent urged this, Martin said, because he hated Martin for litigation currently in process between them. Whether Martin's allegations are true we will never know, but that is almost beside the point. The assumptions, motivations, and negotiations that are suggested in this case reflect, no doubt, a common situation.

Pregnancy declarations were often prelimary salvos that could escalate into *rapt* cases. In a case of *rapt* in 1716 filed by Louise Du Garreau, the daughter of the *procureur d'office* in the seigneurial jurisdiction of Chailly, the first document in the dossier is Du Garreau's declaration of pregnancy, dated the day before she filed suit for *rapt*. The opening petition, furthermore, repeated the pregnancy declaration. Du Garreau, in the service of a *procureur* in Dijon, alleged that she had become pregnant by a local law clerk, Claude Villot. Although initially she had resisted, Villot had his way with her, and from repeated sexual relations Du Garreau became pregnant. She never mentioned promises of marriage, though witnesses attest that they had heard Villot admit to paternity and promise to take care of her.

Under interrogation, Villot confessed to Dijon's syndic that he was the father, but he denied making any promises to support or to marry Du Garreau in order to win her "last favors." Promises or no, the syndic recommended that Villot be required to "take care of the child, . . . to feed and support him until the age of twenty, and during the said time to have him learn a trade." He was also to pay Du Garreau 100£ damages.

In 1726 Margueritte Pasquier, the daughter of a bailiff at the Chambres des Comptes at Dôle, recounted how Sieur Gagnet, a bourgeois from Beaune, had made her pregnant.[129] The preferred but not exclusive location for the tryst was a private garden in Beaune, and before their first sexual encounter, Gagnet had assured Pasquier that "if she got pregnant she would lack nothing." When she in fact became pregnant and informed him, however, he laughed at her. Such an indignity, which she reported in her pregnancy declaration some months later, prompted her "to carry her complaint to the mayor of Beaune." The mayor ordered Gagnet to pay Pasquier 16£ to support the infant.

Eight and one-half months pregnant and still without the cash, Pasquier, now in Dijon for the birth, declared her pregnancy to the local syndic. The declaration was enough to squeeze the 16£ from Gagnet, but for Pasquier it was not sufficient. In another declaration, this time during labor, Pasquier asserted that Gagnet had not provided her "the help he had promised," and immediately after giving birth she asked the syndic for a copy of her declaration, presumably to serve as a basis for a subsequent lawsuit.[130]

There was no mention of marriage promises in Pasquier's declaration, nor was there any in one given two years later by Philiberte Garchey.[131] While this 19-year-old daughter of a blacksmith from Montcénis was a chambermaid at an inn in Chalon-sur-Saône, she met Louis Lesage, an itinerant journeyman wheelright from Normandy. She matter-of-factly recalled how (on three different occasions) he had slipped into her room "where she slept, placed himself next to her and knew her . . . carnally." The syndic sought further information, probably assuming that any young woman declaring pregnancy was seeking marriage or financial support. He asked Garchey, "if as a means to these last favors the said Lesage promised to marry her." Garchey responded negatively but added that Lesage had assured her that he would care for her.

After male pressure for sex resulted in pregnancy of vulnerable females, these women often pursued a strategy to attain marriage or material support following promises of such from their seducers, with the likely prospect that the courts would rule favorably for the women. Of course, not all courtships were adversarial, but within the social world of the people appearing in the court records, many were.

As the *rapt* trials and the declarations of pregnancy make abundantly clear, many men fraudulently promised marriage or material support to seduce women; they had no intention of marrying their sexual partners (otherwise, they would not appear in court).

Additional evidence to support this conclusion comes from Antoine Blanchard's queries in his confessor's manual of the early eighteenth century. Blanchard instructed confessors to ask their male parishioners, "Have you ever employed promises or threats to conquer more easily [a woman's] resistance? Have you given presents for this purpose? . . . Have you ever seduced some girl under the promise of marrying her? Did you keep your promise? Not having kept your promise, have you at least repaired the damages that you have caused? Have you caused her to be defamed so that she cannot be placed in a family [by marriage] suitable to her conditon?"[132]

Rapt cases confirm Blanchard's suspicions. Witnesses often testified that the men believed it was better to pay the women "damages and interest" than marry them if their affair came to litigation. This is precisely what the *procureur* Jean Dumois and the merchant Claude Dantremille, both from Cluny, told the local seigneurial court in 1657 that a defendent in such a *rapt* case had said to them.[133]

Nearly verbatim testimony was heard in Dijon's lower court in 1681, this time by witnesses Pierrette Lallebatrier, the 50-year-old wife of a weaver, and Margueritte Barbier, the similarly aged widow of a tailor.[134] Lallebatrier recounted how she had admonished the accused, the coachman Jacques Lebon: "'Jacques, you are the father of the daughter [born of his liaison with Anne Vincent, a servant in the same household]. You have to marry [Vincent] since you have abused her,' to which he responded that he would rather marry the rope, and that he was promised to another, to which [the deponent] answered 'then you must support the unfortunate baby.' On that, he said, 'for sure, I would rather support *it* than marry *her*!'" Barbier (and a third witness) reported that he was at least good to his word, because he reputedly gave Vincent the not insignificant sum of 20 *écus*.

Lebon may have been good to his word, but many other men, upon hearing that their lover had become pregnant, sought ways to discredit the allegations of their paternity. As one might expect, allegations of and even countersuits charging sexual license (*vie libertine*) or prostitution (a man could not be tried for *rapt* or even rape if a prostitute were the person "ravished")[135] abound in these records.[136] True or not, it was the males' best defense and could lead not only to an acquittal in the *rapt* case but condemnation of the woman.[137]

Conclusion

During the early modern period, a marital ethic that combined religious, political, and social ideologies was embodied in royal legislation, designed to control social reality by ideological regulation. This was only partly successful, undercut by how the law was used by litigants and judges alike.

Female litigants used the laws pertaining to marriage (notably concerning clandestine marriage, *rapt*, and declaration of pregnancy) in their strategies to achieve honorable marriage, or at least material well-being, and, they were largely successful. Judges, for their part, sought to support honorable marriage, for they saw it as the bedrock of patriarchy and, ultimately, social order, but they came to realize that a rigorous application of unbending royal legislation was counterproductive to their goal. The clash of interests in the courtroom caused them to alter the application of legislation in the process of litigation. In their adjudication of *rapt* cases, Burgundy's judges championed the paternalism that was the foundation of royal political theories, the social ideology (based upon social stratification) of society's dominant classes, and the new moral order sought by the authorities. But, they found the royal legislation and its inflexible demands for the death penalty for *rapt* too severe and by the middle of the seventeenth century had begun to lighten their sentences, shifting from corporal punishment to remuneration of the wronged parties. Over the course of the second half of the seventeenth century, a trend toward reducing the amounts of this remuneration is also discernible.

In the cases appealed to Parlement after 1668, the initiative for litigation shifted dramatically and ultimately almost exclusively from the public prosecutor to private litigants. This change-over certainly exhibits a drift toward a de facto decriminalization of *rapt* and an informal civil definition, perhaps reflecting a hesitancy on the part of public officials to assume the costs of litigation but also a decision to leave the initiative to the women (or their families) who believed themselves wronged. Significantly, in nearly two-thirds of the cases heard on appeal after 1668, the female plaintiff was pregnant, whereas barely one-fourth had been between 1583 and 1664. This jurisprudential trend was not entirely favorable to women, to whom payment of "damages and interest" became ever smaller.

The judges, especially those at the Parlement, believed that harsh capital penalties were counterproductive, for two reasons. First, they believed that marriage and the attendant social stability could best be protected by encouraging marriage between the litigants, or, more commonly, returning the plaintiff (almost invariably a woman) to the father by blocking marriage. Second, the judges came to suspect that culpability was not as clearcut as royal legislation would have it; rather, they presumed, seduction was bound up with female marital strategies as much as with male aggression and fraudulence. This supposition seems to have convinced them that men were not entirely culpable in many *rapt* cases and that lighter sentences were fair. In the application of the law, then, the aims of female litigants contested in court were influential in altering the application of an unyielding royal legislation, and, as such, were part of the judicial revolution transpiring during the seventeenth century.

5

Bartered Bodies: Infanticide, Lasciviousness, and Prostitution

In 1671 an informant notified the *procureur syndic* of Dijon that Estiennette Dumeney was reaching term in her pregnancy and was staying at the home of a master tailor.[1] The informant added that Dumeney "had the intention of concealing the birth." Because Dumeney had not yet declared her pregnancy, the syndic assumed that she also intended to dispose of the child, by suffocation or abandonment.

To prevent such an occurrence, the syndic hastened to the tailor's house and interrogated Dumeney. At first she denied that she was pregnant, speciously protesting that she was there on business. The syndic reminded her that she was under oath, but in spite of appearing pregnant (as the syndic noted in his report), she still denied her condition. Only when he informed her that he could arrest her, take her to prison, and have midwives examine her did she break down. She fled to a closet, then, in tears, returned and answered some of the syndic's questions.

She was the 23-year-old daughter of a local and now deceased bourgeois, and yes, she was pregnant. When asked who the father was, she said she would rather die than disclose his name (something she had not even told her "father confessor"). Asked who was paying for the birth costs, she responded, her mother. Had the father "advised her to conceal her pregnancy, and . . . did he want to make her take some potions [*breuvages*] to prevent [birth] or to make her deliver [prematurely]?" All of this she denied. The syndic continued his questioning: With what wetnurse was she going to leave the child, or did she intend to abandon it? Predictably, Dumeney said she had arranged for a wetnurse in the nearby village of Rouvres. The

124

syndic concluded his interrogation by asking Dumeney whether she knew that her failure to declare her pregnancy if followed by the death of her child, by accident or otherwise, would cost Dumeney her life? Dumeney replied that she did not know that, an implausible response because earlier in the interrogation she had demonstrated an apparent awareness of the law of 1556 to which the syndic was referring. At that time she had retorted to the syndic's query about the identity of the father that "she was not obliged to declare that or anything else" about her pregnancy. She was legally correct.

This dense document reveals many of the concerns of the authorities when confronted with the pressing social problem of illicit sexual relations and pregnancy outside marriage. Public authorities suspected that the couples in question would turn to contraception or abortion (taking "potions"), or, failing the availability or effectiveness of those avenues, to infanticide or abandonment. Dumeney, of course, only admitted to the safest, and legal, route of putting a child out to nurse, but the direction of the syndic's questioning suggests that the other options were common considerations of women in such circumstances. Although there is no way to quantify precisely the frequency of any of these alternatives to marriage before the eighteenth century (and even then only abandonment to foundling hospitals can be charted), a significant quantity of documentation is available to permit the sketching of the strategies women (and sometimes their lovers) employed when confronted with pregnancy and no possibility of marriage. Even more evidence is available concerning the prescriptive attitudes of the legal, political, and religious authorities concerning abortion, infanticide, or abandonment, as well as the adjudication of such "strategies."

We do not know what became of Dumeney, but other records of women in similar straits left a trail from failed courtship to lay concubinage, "lasciviousness" (the term often employed by the authorities), or prostitution. Although these alternatives were far from attractive, given the dire circumstances pregnant women or unmarried mothers found themselves in when courtship failed, it is apparent that some women pursued them as logical trajectories of their strategies for survival that began in premarital sexual relations but did not end in marriage.

Abandonment, Infanticide, and Abortion

When saddled with a child but without marriage,[2] many women (increasingly from the second half of the seventeenth century) abandoned the child, sometimes on the doorstep of the father[3] or, more commonly, at foundling hospitals. We have no way of knowing what percentage of premarital pregnancies abandonment represented, but at the foundling hospitals in Paris between 1640 and 1649, only an annual average of 305 were abandoned. Between 1710 and 1719 the annual average had risen to 1,675.[4] No figures exist for Burgundy, but indirect evidence suggests a similar trend. In 1675, Dijon's syndic complained of the rising tide of abandonments.

Abandonment was not without risk for the mother or father. It required concealing the pregnancy and birth, and if the child perished—and most did—the mother could be apprehended, with a court sentence of death likely.[5] If the child survived and the parents could be located, the court could order payment of support to the foundling hospital.[6]

In the eyes of the authorities, with abandonment on the rise and the high mortality rates related to such a practice, associating abandonment with the intention to commit infanticide was a logical connection. This is precisely what the *procureur d'office* of the seigneurial court of the county of Beaumont assumed in 1700. He filed charges against the widow Claudine Chenevière, accusing her of "having abandoned and wishing to let die the child of which she had given birth." The wording of the charge suggests that the child did not perish, but the *procureur d'office* clearly was convinced of an intention to commit infanticide, an offense warranting the death penalty since the royal edict of 1556.[7]

Chenevière's child did not perish, but many other infants did. Some of their mothers were apprehended for the crime and ultimately tried before the Parlement of Burgundy. Concealing pregnancy and infanticide were extraordinarily difficult crimes to discover and to prove (since *corpus delicti* was required), so the number of cases tried represents only an unknown fraction of the actual incidence of the crime. Nevertheless, it is clear that an increasing percentage of the criminal caseload before the Tournelle dealt with this crime, with a notable escalation during the second half of the seventeenth century (Table 5.1). Whether this increase represents more fre-

Table 5.1. Cases of Infanticide or Concealed Pregnancy
Appealed to the Parlement of Dijon, Selected Years,
1582–1726

Date	N^1	N^2	% of Criminal Cases
1582–1593	5	1037	0.5
1628–1631	8	411	1.9
1646–1649	10	223	4.4
1668–1671	12	205	5.9
1687–1700	31	382	8.1
1720–1726	10	221	4.5
Totals	76	2479	3.1

Source: *Arrêts définitifs criminels* and *arrêts à l'audience criminel* (from 1668) (ADCO, BII 46 and 45).

Note: Nearly all such cases were heard in the Tournelle, although *Vacations* and the Grand' Chambre heard a few. The court of *Enquêtes*, on the other hand, never heard these criminal cases. Consequently, N^1 = cases of infanticide or concealed pregnancy and N^2 = criminal cases heard before all courts of Parlement except the *Enquêtes*. The crime of 74 of these cases was infanticide; of 2, concealed pregnancy.

quent prosecution or a greater incidence of the crime is unknown, but from the mid-seventeenth century, the authorities certainly appear to have become more concerned about the prevalence of the crime. Gabriel Roquette, Bishop of Autun during the second half of the seventeenth century, demanded closer surveillance of midwives by church officials, requiring licensing by the bishop, and regular interrogation about their activities by parish priests.[8]

Judges no less than bishops appear to have been concerned about infanticide. For the first time since Henri II's edict of 1556, in 1649 a parlementary *arrêt* appears in the 3,024 *arrêts* between 1582 and 1730 that I examined, which ordered the edict to be read from the pulpit of all parish churches in Parlement's jurisdiction so no one could claim ignorance of the law.[9] For the rest of the seventeenth century and especially in the early eighteenth century, such addenda to *arrêts* became common. In 1708 Louis XIV reissued Henri II's edict, but both before and after this date reiterations of that edict of 1556 were appended to several *arrêts* sentencing women for concealing pregnancy and infanticide.[10]

In 1726, for example, following a flurry of trials for the crime, Parlement's judges enjoined "all the curés or their vicars [to read the edict] every three months during the sermons of the parish masses . . . [and] to send a certificate [verifying such publication] signed by them to the . . . *procureurs du roi* of the bailliages of this jurisdiction."[11] The *arrêt* also demanded that the *procureurs du roi* send copies of the edict to all *procureurs du roi* of the royal *prévôtés* and *châtellenies* as well as to all of the *procureurs d'office* of the seigneurial jurisdictions in Burgundy. Finally, it ordered each of these royal officials to certify to the Parlement every six months that publication of the edict had been made and authorized those officials to seize the temporal goods of the curés and vicars who had not complied.

The authorities may have become more alarmed by the apparent increase in the incidence of infanticide in the second half of the seventeenth century, but killing one's child had always been considered a serious crime, by the law as well as by the perpetrator. One can well imagine that disposing of ones's infant indicated despair. And it was not rare to find women in such a plight. Concealing pregnancy was the first step in this tragic strategy; hiding the birth was the second; taking the child's life, the final step, must have been the most difficult and an indicator of the mother's despair.

In 1595 Anne Gueniotte, an 18-year-old unemployed domestic servant living in Dijon, was arrested for infanticide.[12] Dijon's syndic had been notified by an innkeeper that a young and apparently pregnant servant had checked into her inn and within three days had given birth. The innkeeper had spotted a dead infant in the privy. Accompanied by the innkeeper and a midwife, the syndic went immediately to the inn. Inspecting first the blood-spattered privy and ordering the retrieval of the body from it, the syndic confronted Gueniotte. In this and in a subsequent interrogation, Gueniotte contended that she had not known that she was pregnant when she had checked into the inn. She claimed that she had fallen and when on the privy had felt a pain. Only when the syndic presented the infant's body and informed Gueniotte that it had been found in the privy did she admit that the child was hers. This was sufficient evidence (*corpus delicti*) to warrant conviction and a sentence of hanging, which is what the syndic requested and probably got.[13]

If one can sense the desperation, and then the resignation of Gueniotte in the preceding trial, such sentiments are just as palpable in the pathetic and bizarre case of Hélène Gillet.[14] This daughter of the noble *châtellain* of the town of Bourg-en-Bresse was seduced and impregnated by a curé from a neighboring village in 1625. Terrified of her father's reaction, she concealed the pregnancy and then suffocated the newborn. Apprehended, she was tried and ultimately condemned to death by the Grand' Chambre of Dijon's Parlement. Her noble blood saved her from the ignominy of hanging, to be beheaded instead. Her executioner's first blow, however, was wide of the mark and struck Gillet's shoulder, prompting the crowd to grow restive. His second blow also missed the neck, striking Gillet in the back of the head. The crowd exploded in anger, pelting the headsman with stones. The executioner's wife now came to her husband's aid, attempting to garrot Gillet, and failing in that, stabbing her in the throat repeatedly with a pair of scissors. The crowd now sensed a miracle was transpiring because Gillet was still alive. They stormed the scaffold, drove the executioner and his wife to the sanctuary of the chapel beneath the gallows, rescued the bloodied Gillet, and rushed her to a nearby surgeon. Astonishingly, considering the extent of the wounds cataloged in the surgeon's report, Gillet survived. Parlement was prepared to continue to demand her death, but Louis XIII intervened with a pardon. Convinced that God had saved her life, Gillet dedicated the remainder of it to the Church by retiring to a convent in her native Bresse.

Desperation and resignation must have been common sentiments shared by women driven to infanticide. The plight of the widow Claudine Tâtevin of Cluny was similar to that of Gueniotte and Gillet, and no doubt many others.[15] In 1668 the Seigneur de Trades, the *lieutenant particulier* of the seigneurial jurisdiction of the Abbey of Cluny, was informed that Tâtevin had been made pregnant by François Ducroux, a local locksmith. De Trades was told that she had concealed her condition; fifteen days before, she had given birth and left town. De Trades shared the suspicion of the informant that the child had been killed and buried in the cemetery of Saint Marcel Church in Cluny.

Following the request for an inquest (because this crime "merits an exemplary punishment"), de Trades received depositions from several people who knew Tâtevin and Ducroux well. Jeanne Audiner, Tâtevin's neighbor, for example, reported that a fortnight previous she had observed blood running down Tâtevin's leg as she climbed the stairs, something that "ordinarily happened to women at the time of birth." She did not know whether Tâtevin in fact had delivered a child but believed the rumor that she was pregnant by her neighbor Ducroux with whom she had shared table, drink, and bed for more than a year.

The deposition of Dame Jeanne Du Cerf, the 27-year-old wife of a nailmaker, suggests that she was more Tâtevin's confidant than Audiner. Du Cerf recounted how on the previous Thursday Tâtevin had come into Du Cerf's house and had immediately broken into tears. "'My poor friend,'" Tâtevin reportedly sobbed, "'I am so miserable and so pitiable[!] I must confess to you that not fifteen days ago I had a baby by . . . Ducroux[!]'" Du Cerf continued that Tâtevin had told her that, to save her honor, Ducroux had privately baptized the infant (she claimed to have seen the foot move, thus assuming it was alive). When the infant died (no cause was reported), Tâtevin had asked Ducroux to bury it in a field by a nearby chapel. She then left town.

Another witness, the surgeon Claude Fournier, recalled that on the previous Thursday, upon hearing the rumor that Tâtevin had given birth, he had gone to Ducroux's house and had asked him if it were true. Ducroux had admitted that it was. Fifteen days previous, so Ducroux had recounted to Fournier, the locksmith had come into Tâtevin's house and had found her crying "in despair." When he asked the subject of "her torment," she said that she had given birth and that the child was dead. Ducroux saw the little linen-wrapped corpse in a chest, and, at the request of Tâtevin, had carried it to a cemetery for burial.

Such testimonies were sufficient to warrant the arrest of both Tâtevin and Ducroux, but because they were fugitives, no more evidence was marshaled in the case. Convinced that violation of the edict of 1556 was demonstrated (he considered their flight as tantamount to a confession of guilt), de Trades requested, and received, a sentence of hanging (in effigy).

Examples of infanticide (or suspicion thereof) could be multiplied, each with its own tragic story. Even before the actual act of killing one's child, however, the sense of despair already could be well in evidence. Attempted abortions, for instance, may reflect the same sentiment, but at an earlier stage. If infanticide was difficult to prove in courts of law, however, abortions were nearly impossible.[16] Rare to the point of near singularity are trials like one held in 1671 when Damoiselle Marie Potot was tried for, along with spiritual incest and infanticide, "use of abortifacients" [*usage de rémèdes abortifs*].[17]

There were few trials for abortion, though the practice may have been fairly widespread.[18] The authorities certainly thought so. In 1677 Dijon's mayor requested a *monitoire* on the subject, suggesting that the populace knew a great deal more about this practice than they were telling the authorities. It read, in part, that women "of libertine and debauched ways . . . in order to cover their fault and their pregnancy . . . [use] remedies and potions . . . to make them lose their fruit." Such actions constituted "an enormous crime which nevertheless [is] quite often practiced . . . in order to cover the honor of the young woman."[19] The mayor's concluding supposition suggests that abortion was not confined to "libertine and debauched" women but may have been a recourse of other women whose honor was threatened.

Most people believed that ingesting certain drugs could cause abortion. It was not unusual for a man bent on seduction to assure the woman not to worry about pregnancy because he had certain "herbs" or other unspecified abortifacients.[20] Some women, like Catherine Charmin, employed more radical measures.[21] In 1616 this 30-year-old domestic servant was tried before the bailliage of Mâcon for the attempted abortion of a seven- or eight-month fetus by drinking rat poison. The documentation is not sufficient to determine the motivation, but one plausible interpretation is this: By Charmin's own admission, the young man from her village who, she alleged, had made her pregnant had been away in the army and did not know that she was pregnant. When he was interrogated by the authorities, he was still ignorant of the fact, but he admitted that he had promised to marry Charmin. Tellingly, *before* he was told that she had been pregnant and attempted abortion, he had denied that he had ever had carnal relations with her. So why did she attempt abortion apparently just before his return from the army? Perhaps to terminate a pregnancy (by another man) that was likely to end her prospect for marriage with her betrothed.

Obtaining drugs to use as abortifacients presented an obstacle that required an intricate strategy to overcome. In a well-documented first-instance trial from the bailliage of Mâcon in 1634, Jeanne Archigny, a 40-year-old domestic servant, feigned illness to hide her pregnancy (she knew if her condition was discovered, she would be dismissed, a gloomy prospect for an unmarried woman of her age) and to obtain drugs she hoped would produce a miscarriage.[22] Archigny had claimed that she had dropsy (*hydropsie*), which accounted for her physical enlargement. In order to cure the condition, she obtained certain medicines from a local apothecary, and, supplementing the effectiveness of medical science, she also turned to religion and undertook a pilgrimage to the monastery of Cluny. Both methods failed: Archigny gave birth shortly after her return from Cluny, and her strategy crumbled.

In the subsequent trial for concealment of pregnancy and infanticide, Archigny followed the advice of her alleged seducer, her master the royal councillor to the bailli, Claude Verjus (who was never prosecuted), and denied that she knew that she was pregnant. She added that she had been examined by a doctor, diagnosed to have dropsy, and had received the medicines to treat the condition from her master's apothecary. The doctor who had examined her in her seventh month of pregnancy admitted in his deposition that he thought dropsy was the problem, although, he added, he was not entirely certain because Archigny had breathed loudly during the examination, perhaps, he offered, to obscure the sound of fetal movement. Archigny did not reveal that she had been examined by a surgeon and a midwife in her eighth month, and neither had any doubt that she was pregnant. It was at this point that Archigny, realizing the ineffectiveness of the apothecary's drugs, had opted for a pilgrimage, which she hoped would coincide with her delivery date. If her timing had been more accurate, she might well have been able to deliver the infant out of town, return to Mâcon, and plausibly explain her "cure" by divine intervention. As it was, the child delayed its entry into the world, and its mother was arrested on a capital charge.

Seventy years to the day later, another domestic servant feigned illness to obtain the unwitting help of medical professionals in the termination of an unwanted pregnancy.[23] Antoinette Marechale was accused by the *procureur du roi* of the bailliage of the Charolais of having "procured a premature birth." The child in question, subsequent depositions in the trial confirmed, was stillborn at five months, shortly after Marechale had convinced a surgeon that she had a stomach ailment requiring bleeding. Four bleedings (at least one by a woman innkeeper), in the mind of the prosecutor, were sufficient to induce premature labor, which he charged was infanticide. Marechale's case certainly was not helped by her reputation for sexual libertinage, and because, rumor had it, she had been pregnant twice before, the prosecutor did not believe her story that she had not known she was pregnant when she was bled.

The surgeon, too, was questioned. He claimed that her fever and "oppression of the chest . . . had made such a corruption in the mass of the blood that it was impossible to know," apparently a not entirely satisfactory response, as far as the prosecutor was concerned. The surgeon was "convicted of having imprudently and carelessly bled . . . the said Marechale . . . [and] for punishment . . . [was] condemned to a five *livres* fine to the king and prohibitted from bleeding . . . any other young woman without first inquiring and examining her carefully if there is any suspicion of pregnancy." Marechale was not so fortunate. She was convicted of concealed pregnancy and infanticide and, following the edict of 1556, condemned to death by hanging.

The law of the realm and that of the Catholic religion condemned infanticide and abortion. Abandonment, however, was not a capital offense; in fact, it was not an offense at all in the eyes of the Church and was rarely tried in the Burgundian courts of law, probably because it was virtually impossible to track down the parents.[24] Abandonment with the intent to allow the child to perish, however, was a very different matter, as Claudine Chenevière found out.

Similar assumptions regarding intent seem to guide abortion trials. There is no clear indication in the *arrêts* themselves as to why a death sentence might be warranted, but if a judicial decision handed down in 1691 is indicative, the fetus had to be more than two and a half months in development.[25] In that year Pierrette Morisot, the daughter of a day laborer from a village near Langres, was convicted of having thrown into a well a fetus of that age, "which she had just aborted."[26] A lower court decision condemned her not to death, however, but to be beaten bloody, branded, and banished for life. On appeal, Parlement called only for banishment for three years. Clearly, in the eyes of the law, this was not infanticide.[27] Marechale's case, in contrast, ended in hanging, the stillborn fetus having been five months old.[28] Apparently, if fetal movement were detected, a death sentence was warranted; otherwise, Burgundy's courts consistently refrained from the death penalty.[29]

Abortion of a quickened fetus was infanticide, and the crime the authorities were keenly concerned about.[30] Henri II's edict of 1556 made it clear that failure to declare a pregnancy was prima facie evidence of the intent to commit infanticide, and so any woman who did not declare and could be linked to a dead child or an aborted fetus that had quickened would be tried for that capital offense.

Unlike its jurisprudence in *rapt* cases, Burgundy's Parlement applied this royal legislation diligently. Of 58 death sentences Burgundy's lower courts handed down for infanticide between 1582 and 1730, the Parlement upheld 47 (but it augmented 3 noncapital lower court decisions to execution). Of the 11 it overturned, 8 came after 1668.[31] Only 1 of those 8 was a practical acquittal (*hors de cour*); 5 of them released the accused with the proviso that rearrest and continuation of the trial would occur if more evidence were found (*renvoyer à rappel*).

In cases of this nature, women were always considered the primary culprit, but on many occasions men (usually the father of the infant but occasionally members of the woman's family) were also arraigned. High conviction and execution rates paint the gloomy picture for women, but what about the men? Infanticide, the trials leave no doubt, was a female crime. Of the 23 cases in which men were arraigned as accomplices, not one was executed (although one was hanged in effigy in 1694). The most severe sentence Parlement handed down was for nine years in the king's galleys in 1726, and the only other instances in which any punishment at all was administered occurred twice in 1671 (a nine-year banishment and a 200£ fine), and once in each of the years 1674, 1700, and 1723 (fines of 20£, 12£, and 50£, respectively). In other words, 16 of 23 men involved received no punishment whatsoever.

Moreover, on seven occasions, Parlement reduced penalties decreed by lower courts against the men while maintaining the sentences against the women.[32] In 1692, for instance, the seigneurial court of the Marquisate of Lage convicted the weaver Claude Collet of "having participated" in the infanticide of the child born of his union with Benoiste Bardin. He was condemned to accompany Bardin to the gibbet with a rope around *his* neck and to stand at her feet while *she* was hanged. On appeal, Parlement threw the sentence against Collet out of court but upheld the execution of Bardin.[33]

Aside from the emotional anguish Collet was likely to have experienced in watching his former lover hang, this lower court sentence was not as severe as the one handed down seven years later against Antoine Pallordet by the court of the county of Pondenelle. Pallordet, an innkeeper at the village of Ronat, was convicted of the same crime as Collet but was condemned to three years in the king's galleys and a 60£ fine. Margueritte Rabuet, the woman in question, was to be hanged, a sentence with which Parlement agreed on appeal. But while the woman swung from the gallows, her lover walked away a free man, having seen the charges against him dropped.[34]

Nearly as fortunate as Pallordet was François Nicoux, a man convicted in 1723 in the seigneurial court of La Cuillie of impregnating his servant Benoîte Rossan and then aiding her in the subsequent homicide of the infant. Nicoux was sentenced in La Caillie to ten years in the galleys and a 500£ fine, a penalty overturned by Parlement in favor of only a 50£ fine. Rossan was hanged.[35]

Infanticide, then, was prosecuted as an overwhelmingly female crime. From the perspective of the women, this was a crime of desperation. Many of these women lived perilously close to the margin of subsistence. Of the 76 women in my sample accused of concealing their pregnancy and thus of intending or committing infanticide, at least 11 were domestic servants. In 24 cases, the fathers' occupations were given: 7 peasants, 6 winegrowers, 6 rural artisans, and 5 day laborers. Women who worked in domestic service or had grown up in a household headed by a father who was a peasant, artisan, or laborer were, in all likelihood, at the margin of subsistence. And when we consider that in at least 19 cases the father of the woman was deceased and as many as 68 were unmarried (8 were widows), the connection between infanticide and an extremely vulnerable situation in life is clear.

Concubinage and "Lascivious Ways"

In 1781 Jean Fournel authored a treatise on seduction in order to clarify the muddle of legal terminology that continued to surround illicit sexual behavior.[36] His aim was to define once and for all the meaning of *rapt de séduction*, but in the process he was forced to distinguish seduction, fornication, and prostitution. The distinctions were far from clear-cut.

Muyart de Vouglans wrote in his mid-eighteenth-century treatise on criminal law that fornication, being "evil commerce with a debauched person," was a crime punishable at law.[37] Only women, however, were liable for prosecution, and this feature of the laws of the kingdom led Muyart to associate fornication with prostitution. He had nothing to say about "lascivious ways" (*vie lubricque*) or their association with concubinage. Actual cases from the sixteenth, seventeenth, and early eighteenth centuries, however, show that *vie lubricque* often subsumed concubinage, which was a crime punishable at law. What kind of behavior does this term *vie lubricque* reflect, and why were the eighteenth-century codifiers confused about its meaning?

In the trials and appeals for the crime of *vie lubricque et scandaleuse*, the alleged behavior appears to encompass two possible, if not always distinguishable, forms of sexual behavior: lay or clerical concubinage and occasional prostitution (that is, in the explicit absence of procuresses, which was a different category of crime).

Prosecution of clerical concubinage was not rare, nor was its incidence.[38]

The prosecution of lay concubinage, on the other hand, was almost non-existent in Burgundy unless it was accompanied by "scandal," a signpost term suggesting the authorities perceived a disruption of the social, and hence moral, order. When concubinage was defined as scandalous, however, it became difficult to separate from the not-infrequent charge of *vie lubricque et scandaleuse*. In some trials, concubinage, or cohabitation outside marriage, was clearly the transgression; in others, suspicion of occasional prostitution was the offense. In both cases, however, a perceived disruption of the moral and social order prompted the authorities to prosecute.

In a case tried before the mayor's court of Dijon in 1572, lay concubinage was clearly the offense, and the prosecution revolved around the notion of scandal.[39] In this case scandal meant two things, both linked to notions of public order. Margueritte Millan, a 30-year-old widow and seamstress, was accused of *train lubricque et scandaleux*, an imprecise charge that nevertheless meant *concubinage*. The scandal arose from suspicions of several of her neighbors that she was prostituting herself to "several young men" and by other neighbors that she lived in an unmarried state with a man nicknamed "La Chappelle" (a twenty-six-year-old tailor named Jean Galimard) with their illegitimate child.

Certainly the neighbors made it clear that Millan and La Chappelle should marry, but their indignation came largely from the apparent hesitancy of La Chappelle to provide support for Millan and her child. One witness, a 59-year-old widow named Jannette, scolded La Chappelle for "not having done his duty for a long time by not supporting Margueritte." The direction of the prosecution suggests that the authorities defined scandal in the same way: a disruption of order. Millan protested that she had received a marriage promise from La Chappelle, an allegation the syndic took seriously enough to arrest and incarcerate him.

In 1582, the authorities again overtly linked a disruption of social and moral order with scandalous lay concubinage. Isabeau Domino and her lover, Nicolas de La Tour, were charged with an "unregulated and lascivious lifestyle" (*vie lubricque et débordée*) and "debauchery" or "lustful behavior" (*paillardise*).[40] The syndic of Beaune's municipal court where Domino and de La Tour were first tried gained a sentence condemning Domino to be placed on the large rock in front of the town hall with a mitre on her head bearing the words *paillarte et concubine*, a public sentence for a scandalous transgression. The documents from this trial are unclear about what was scandalous about Domino's behavior, but it likely had to do with the two children Domino and de La Tour had had outside of marriage. Beaune's syndic, like his counterpart in Dijon who had tried Millan and La Chappelle for the same crime, was deeply concerned about the welfare of these children, who had resulted from their mother's "debauchery," and so, in addition to public humiliation, he sentenced Domino to "nourish, feed, and raise" them.

Surprisingly, there was no specific or formal legislation associating concubinage with criminality. Indeed, perhaps it is owing to the lack of any formal laws against concubinage that the authorities prosecuted it in conjunction with other punishable transgressions, most notably sexually scandalous behavior. Of course, lay and clerical concubinage had been condemned in the Concordat of Bologna and definitively at the Council of Trent, and it was enshrined in canon law and enforced in synodal statutes.[41] Furthermore, it violated the ethic of marriage that was undergirded by the religious, social, and political ideologies of France's dominant families, not to mention its crown. So the prosecution of concubinage was a logical development, if the law is meant to serve as an instrument of enforcement of dominant ideologies.

Royal law since 1639 had nullified the validity of *donations* or proprietary gifts made to concubines (in an effort to ensure the devolution of the patrimony only through marriage),[42] and by the eighteenth century, jurists were able to sum up in their dictionaries what the syndics and judges had been moving toward in their jurisprudence. Guyot wrote in 1784, "In France, concubinage is regarded as a debauch contrary to the purity of religion and to good morals. It is a misdemeanor (*délit*) that the laws punish, not only when it is committed by clerics, but also when laymen are proved guilty. We regard it as contrary to the welfare of the state, and from this point of view, it is the object of the severity of our laws. However, when it is not accompanied by scandal, the ordinances of the realm have not pronounced any punishment against the laymen."[43]

Concubinage per se was rarely charged in Burgundy's courts of law (table 5.2) unless it attained "scandalous" proportions; then it was likely to be associated with the rather imprecise but certainly far more common charges of *vie lubricque et scandaleuse, vie impudique,* or, by the late seventeenth century, *vie libertine.* In any case, the association between sexual disorder and moral and social disorder is manifest and marks the entire period of the Catholic Reformation.

In 1553, the town council of Dijon issued a proclamation illustrating how the authorities perceived social and sexual disorder to intersect.[44] It began by outlining the threat to the physical security of law-abiding inhabitants that was "to the detriment and scandal of the public welfare [and] . . . the ruin and detriment of [Dijon]." The culprits were "people of various estates and trades" who were not employed in their appropriate occupations and instead engaged in "scandals" like "larcenies, thefts . . . and *debaucheries [paillardises]* [italics added]." In order to remedy such a social ailment, Dijon's authorities expelled all workers not employed in their trades, as well as all *gens de mestier concubinaires* who kept "lascivious women" (*femmes lubricques*).

In 1695 similar associations were still being made in the minds of the authorities. In a case charging "blasphemy, concubinage, and lascivious ways," the same association of violation of social order and illicit sexuality (here still called concubinage) is manifest.[45] The *procureur du roi* at the bailliage of Avalon arrested a "troop of vagabonds" and won convictions against all six of them. It is not surprising that vagabonds would be arrested

Table 5.2.   Concubinage, *Vie lubricque*, Procuring, and Prostitution

Date	Concubinage	Vie Lubricique	Procuring and/or Prostitution	Extant Criminal Case[h]	Percent
1582–1592	3[a]	12[b]	8[c]	1,037	2.2
1628–1631	0	3	2[d]	411	1.2
1646–1649	0	2	4	223	2.7
1668–1671	0	2[e]	6	205	3.9
1687–1700	1[f]	8[g]	11	382	5.2
1720–1726	0	3	2	221	2.3
	4	30	33	2,479	2.7

Source: ADCO B II 45, 46.

[a] All three cases had the associated charge of *paillardise*.

[b] One case was *paillardise* associated with theft; one case with adultery; the others bore charges of *paillardise*, *vie lubricque* or *vie impudicque*.

[c] One case with adultery.

[d] One case with adultery.

[e] One case with theft.

[f] Associated charge of *libertinage*.

[g] One case with *rapt*, three with theft.

[h] Extant cases heard before Tournelle and Vacations (Grand' Chambre and Enquêtes never heard appeals pertaining to these crimes), selected years.

as threats to social tranquility, but that concubinage and licentiousness would be related charges is telling.

Margueritte Jaquenet was the leader of the troop, which included her son, Jean, and daughter, Jeanne, plus two other unrelated men and an unrelated woman, none married but all living together. Because they had no home, their living arrangements were by definition public, and therefore scandalous—hence, the charge of concubinage. For the offenses, Margueritte Jaquenet was condemned to hang; Jean was to spend the rest of his days in the king's galleys; one of the other men was sent to the galleys for five years; the remaining man and two women were to be present at the execution of their leader and then banished from the bailliage forever. On appeal before the Parlement in Dijon, Jaquenet's sentence was reduced to branding and banishment from the kingdom for life; her son, Jean, was whipped and banished from Burgundy for nine years; and the other three were released from prison.

Other cases drawn from the late seventeenth and early eighteenth centuries point to the connection between sexual licentiousness and other antisocial forms of behavior. By now, the term *vie libertine* was often used, and trials of women in which the charges of sexual libertinage and theft were filed simultaneously were not uncommon.[46] In the 1703 trial of a young woman, identified only as "one named Minot," promiscuous sexual behavior was linked with incitement to theft.[47] This daughter of a municipal sergeant from Saulieu, prosecutor and witnesses concurred, scandalized her neighborhood. She was given to "scandalously and continually receiving men and boys"—even having sex in the relative open of the fish market—and she had incited the lackey of a royal councilor's wife to rob his employer. This behavior was clear evidence of a *vie libertine, publique et scandaleuse* that caused "great disorder in the town" and could not be tolerated.

The records do more than reflect the attitudes of the authorities concerning the scandalous nature of concubinage and *vie lubricque* and their perceived social and moral threat; they also reveal the situation of these unfortunate women. Most fell into their state out of sheer necessity, for survival or some material security.[48] The authorities, nevertheless, were not sympathetic to this "choice."

If infanticide was an extreme consequence of a failed courtship and unwanted pregnancy, some "seduced" and impregnated women had other, though extremely gloomy and degrading, options. Concubinage was one. At a time when women were marrying later or not at all, and perhaps facing dire circumstances, gaining material sustenance from a man (especially one of higher station, or even a priest) in exchange for sex may not have been entirely repugnant. It entailed risks, however. It might be against the law (if scandal were demonstrated) and the increasingly rigorous morality of the Catholic Reformation, and if a stable relationship could not be established, it could be a fateful step down the road to prostitution.

For many poor and uprooted young women, finding a priest, or, indeed, any other man, as protector may have been a common initial strategy. The authorities, at any rate, appear to have suspected this practice. In mid-January 1573, for example, 18-year-old Jehanne Loran drifted from her home in Chalon-sur-Saône to Dijon in search of work.[49] Before she was in town a fortnight, she was arrested for "lasciviousness" (*lubricité*). The syndic clearly suspected concubinage or prostitution. He thought it highly likely that Loran was having sex with "priests or married men" and that she had made such arrangements through acquaintance with other *filles lubricques* and *maquerelles* (procuresses). Subsequent depositions confirmed his suspicions about priests, and, following a sentence of whipping, banishment, and fine, a second arrest of Loran barely a month later seems to confirm the syndic's hunches about prostitution.[50] In the first sentence, handed down on 11 February, Loran had been banished, but she admitted under interrogation in her second trial, beginning on 13 March, that she had departed through one town gate only to reenter promptly through another. The second time, she was caught with a local cordwainer under some stairs, a circumstance sufficient to warrant rearrest for *lubricité* and yet another sentence of whipping and banishment.

A case before the *officialité* of Besançon in 1713 evinced a similar strategy of survival.[51] Jean Foley, the curé of the parishes of Contréglise and Senoncourt, was accused of seducing and impregnating a young woman in his parish named Anne Barisien. Fifteen witnesses, men and women from all social stations, confirmed the common rumor that Foley was the father. They also confirmed that the priest was far from discreet; he had been caught in Anne's bedroom pressed up against the wall trying to extinguish a lamp and openly caressed her publicly and showered her with cheeses, apples, and even the Burgundian delicacy, *pain d'épice*. Anne willingly accepted the attention and the gifts. She must have known, as did many of the villagers, that Foley had connections to take care of an unwanted pregnancy (by abandonment or put out to nurse), so with such largesse coming from a man with a guaranteed income and influence, it is understandable that Anne would succumb to his temptations.

Prostitution

In 1720 the public prosecutor for the city of Dijon, the *procureur syndic*, initiated legal proceedings against two unmarried women for "scandalous ways" (*vie scandaleuse*).[52] He contended that "together [they] enticed men to their house day and night which caused disorder in the families [of the men and the women] and a frightful scandal in the neighborhood where the women live. Of all the crimes of youth, this [is] the most horrible since . . . it gives birth to difficulties in the families that are so grievous that [the families] are soon destroyed."

About the same time, Bernard de La Monnoye, man of letters, lawyer, royal official, and eventual member of the Académie française, jotted down the following poem, "Bordel," in his private notebook:

> Il est vraye monsieur le Syndic
> Le bordel n'est plus si public
> On vous craint comme le tonnerre
> Mais ne faire pas tant le vain
> Ce n'est pas après tout un grand exploit de guerre
> De prendre à force un [sic] putain.[53]

> It's true, Monsieur le syndic
> the brothel is no longer public.
> They fear you like the thunder,
> but don't let that go to your head.
> It's not, after all, a great feat of war,
> to take by force a whore.

The syndic's words appear in stark contrast to La Monnoye's, a contrast that raises important questions about the body, the law, and the prostitute in early modern France. The weight of this book rests on the prescriptive nature of patriarchy, but La Monnoye reveals a fundamental ambivalence within the elite about prostitution in particular and perhaps even about patriarchy in general.[54]

Many scholars—Freud, Elias, Foucault, to name only a prominent few—have identified the social control of the body as a fundamental theme in western history.[55] The insight that bodies are disciplined by "technologies of power" that impose penalties on deviants has proved remarkably fruitful,[56] but the recent appreciation of the role of agency has informed our understanding of these technologies not simply as one-directional mechanisms of repressive social control but as generating forces, which operate in contested fields of human activity.[57]

The law is one such technology, and when deployed in a context like early modern patriarchal society, a central site of contention is the female body since it concerns the reproduction of society. From a prescriptive patriarchal perspective, the female body must be controlled because of the woman's role in reproduction. Her mediation in this process was essential, and in that mediation, men perceived a potential threat to their patriarchal power. Social control rooted in an order of patrimonial descent erected upon property and power—an elemental assumption of rational and order-loving men dedicated to erecting the new moral order—was thus dependent on men restricting women from realizing the potentiality of their power.[58] The attempted enforcement of social control was discursive and physical. Thus arose the sexual dangers of womanhood portrayed so vividly in patriarchal prescriptive literature against the "disorderly" passions, and the flogging, branding, and banishment or later incarceration meted out to "wayward" women.

Mary Douglas suggests that all social systems are vulnerable at their margins and that all margins are accordingly considered dangerous to the constituted order.[59] In patriarchal society, the prostitute was certainly a marginalized character, and by Douglas's interpretation, a threat to order. The prostitute's well-known difficulties with the law may emanate from this perceived threat. But patriarchal attitudes toward prostitution were highly ambivalent, and baroque patriarchy both enabled its practice—because prostitutes were creatures of male erotic desire—and opposed it—because they were deemed a threat to some of society's most cherished ideals: the controlled, orderly woman, the respectable and honorable family, and public tranquility. Consequently, prostitutes were consigned by men to a marginal and degraded existence, and because they remained a disorderly body dangerously independent of male control (husbands or fathers), they had to be regulated. Not surprisingly, baroque men shuttled back and forth between repressive regulation (legal prosecution) and permissive toleration of prostitution.

The history of early modern prostitution is characterized by toleration punctuated by occasional prosecution. Before 1561 prostitution was in fact legal in France, provided it was confined to licensed (often municipal) sites. Responding to demands of the Third Estate at the Estates General in Orléans in 1560, however, the crown banned all brothels in the kingdom.[60] This was the only royal legislation against prostitution of any significance promulgated before 1684, when Louis XIV issued three ordinances, directed specifically at Paris, calling for the incarceration of *les débauchées*.

The article of Charles IX's ordinance of 1561 that prohibited brothels was aimed not specifically at prostitutes but at the disorder that seemed to erupt where they did business. The deputies at the Estates General and Charles were chiefly concerned with ensuring public tranquility and wished to quell several causes of turbulence. Idleness was as much the "crime" as prostitution. Charles decreed: "We prohibit all persons from lodging and receiving in their houses, more than one night, idle and unknown people [*gens sans aveu et incogneu*]. And we enjoin them to denounce them to justice, under pain of prison and arbitrary fine. We also prohibit all brothels, gaming houses, [and] quill and dice games."

This ordinance was the only royal legislation against prostitution applicable to the entire kingdom until the Revolution. The royal declaration of 1713 against prostitution, like the ordinances of 1684, applied only to Paris.[61] Clearly, as far as the kings of France were concerned, the matter of prosecution of prostitution was a local or regional matter.

In Burgundy, prostitutes were prosecuted throughout the early modern period. In 1563, Dijon's town council closed its own municipally run brothel, and subsequently, prostitutes in Burgundy's capital were periodically haled before the municipal court, as were similar unfortunates before similar courts in other towns of the province. Moreover, since sentencing of prostitutes could impose not just banishment but corporal punishment (flogging) or bodily mutilation (branding), which automatically triggered an appeal to Parlement, Burgundy's Tournelle heard its share of cases as well (but only one or two per year). Given the inchoate state of first-instance criminal court records, there is no way of knowing what percentage of the actual incidence of the "crime" these cases, however plentiful, represent. Indirect evidence, however, makes it safe to assume that prostitution was widespread but only occasionally prosecuted. Why was this case? What circumstances triggered prosecution? And what was the "crime"? Answers to these questions rest on baroque men's concept of prostitution.

As late as 1781, the legal terminology that surrounded illicit sexual behavior, including prostitution, remained muddled.[62] Indeed, from the early sixteenth to early eighteenth century, a variety of practices, all apparently punishable at law, were considered illicit sexual behavior: *mauvaise vie, vie impudicque, vie lubricque, vie paillardise, vie libertine* (from the late seventeenth century), and occasionally *prostitution* (a term rare even in the eighteenth century).[63] These practices were considered prostitution, that is, the exchange of sexual services for payment,[64] but also referred to lay or clerical concubinage.[65]

Perhaps, however, to look for precise legal terminology describing prostitution as we understand it is to miss what baroque men were especially troubled about—not prostitution per se but the threat such activity posed to their conception of order. In this sense, they shared Charles IX's concern. True, women engaged in such sexual practices were guilty before the law even before a case was brought against them. Deprived of legal rights, as "unpunished delinquents,"[66] they were thus continually at the mercy of prosecution whenever the authorities decided to initiate it. What initiated prosecution, however, was not the authorities' learning that a certain woman was engaged in prostitution or was even running a brothel, but rather when that activity became too disorderly, or, in the terminology of the day, "scandalous."

Before the 1560s prostitution in public brothels was legal, if not entirely respectable; the authorities, in fact, viewed it as a necessary evil,[67] a cure for the dangers of male lust that shielded the honor of respectable women.[68] Streetwalking, prostitution outside licensed sites, however, was never officially tolerated, nor were procuresses who were reputed to recruit respectable women to prostitution. Indeed, procuring was abhorred into the seventeenth and eighteenth centuries. Bénigne Joly, a moralistic canon of the abbey of Saint Etienne in Dijon and the son of a royal official in the late seventeenth century, dedicated his energies to establishing a religious community for former prostitutes, the Maison du Bon Pasteur in Dijon. His compassion was both spiritually and socially motivated, in that he saw such an establishment as an opportunity for the *filles pénitentes* to gain salvation and for their families to regain their honor.

Joly, and many other men, viewed prostitution as an opportunity for penitence for prostitutes. The Burgundian preacher Edme Bourée, for example, delivered a sermon to the *files du Bon Pasteur* in which he emphasized that Christ was a good shepherd of infinite bounty with eternal love and compassion toward his "wayward sheep." He implored the formerly disorderly women in his audience to follow Christ in "docility" and "fatten themselves on heavenly manna . . . [which] will inspire [them] . . . to hold in disgust the pleasures of the senses."[69]

These moralists, like Joly, held nothing but contempt for procuresses, however, and desired nothing less than their eradication. Their sin was heinous: they deceived innocent young women, enticing them down the path to debachery and perdition.[70]

Legal opinion mirrored the moralistic. In 1554 Joost Damhoudere wrote that "procuresses . . . are in a state of damnation, as vile slaves and diabolical instruments; indeed, [they are] worse than devils, because often many honorable young women and good wives and men of the church . . . are induced by them to choose dishonor." For their diabolical criminality, Damhoudere intoned, these bawds "are grievously punished and always corporally, either by the gibbet, public flogging, pillory, banishment or other punishment according to the . . . discretion of the judge."[71]

In the mid-eighteenth century, jurists like Muyart de Vouglans and Ferrière still concurred with Damhoudere, albeit without reference to diabolism. Procuring was an "enormous and dangerous" crime, according to Muyart, worse than many others because it "foments all the other vices of lust." Appropriate punishments were flogging, mitering, branding, and banishment for women, and for men, the galleys. Damhoudere did not mention prostitution, but Muyart pointedly asserted that procuring was a worse crime than prostitution itself because bawds often lured honorable young women to a life of corruption. When this happened, according to Ferrière, the woman "of honor," married or single, lost her most precious possession, and Muyart and Ferrière agreed that a sentence of death could thus be handed down to the real culprit, the procuress.[72]

Because punishment for procuring depended on the discretion of the judge, the Burgundian court records can be used to determine how close practical jurisprudence hewed to learned legal opinion. In a sizable sample of cases appealed to Parlement between 1571 and 1726, 76 lower court cases charged prostitution or procuring.[73] Of these, 55 charged procuring and 19 prostitution without any mention of procuring. In these 76 cases, 79 people (61 women, 18 men) were tried for procuring; 25 (all women) were arraigned for prostitution only, although another 20 were arraigned in cases in which their bawds were arraigned for procuring.[74]

The most notable characteristic in the sample is the disproportionate representation of procuring over prostitution, a fact that seems to confirm the jurists' opinion about the varying degree of severity between the two offenses.[75] A closer look at the actual adjudication, however, shows that the Burgundian judges, particularly those at Parlement, were more lenient, at least after the mid-seventeenth century, than learned theorists might have wished. In these 76 cases, only 4 death sentences were issued, and each of those had aggravating circumstances. One, in 1586, resulted from a joint arraignment for larceny. Two others, in 1591 and 1629, were complicated by convictions for adultery.[76] In the fourth, in 1672, Nicolas Bourgeois was charged not only with procuring but also with larceny, hiding stolen property, assumption of a false identity, and resisting arrest.[77] In each of these cases, procuring was accompanied by other capital offenses.

More common were less severe sentences. In 1571, for example, the widow Jeanne Le Bon heard Parlement uphold a sentence from the mayor's court of Dijon condemning her to the pillory for an hour at midday wearing a miter on her head inscribed with the words "worthless and detestable procuress." From the pillory she was led with a rope around her neck to the principal squares in town, flogged until bloody, and then banished forever from the town's jurisdiction.[78]

By 1700 little had changed, at least in the lower courts. Claudine Chevenet, the wife of a mason, was convicted in Dijon of procuring and was sentenced to be whipped at the "usual squares . . . of this town, to be branded with a hot iron on the left shoulder . . . to wear a miter [saying] 'public procuress', [and] to be banished for five years" from the town's jurisdiction. But if little had changed in first-instance adjudication between 1571 and 1700, Parlement had come to view the crime more leniently. In an entirely typical appeal, Parlement struck down the decision against Chevenet and condemned her only to a five-year banishment from Burgundy.[79]

Flogging, pillorying, and branding were sentences that Parlement was inclined to uphold on appeal only until the 1640s.[80] The year 1644 marked the last time Parlement permitted corporal punishment of prostitutes or procuresses, although mitering and banishing remained in practice. When lower courts continued to call for flogging or even branding, Parlement always struck down the sentence and specifically deleted the corporal punishment.[81]

Few seventeenth-century Burgundian justices invoked the full rigor of the law against prostitutes and bawds. They certainly prosecuted procuring more forcefully than prostitution, but both practices were deemed serious transgressions only when they crossed the threshold of public scandal. Scandal, however, was ambiguously interpreted and its boundaries variously defined. Some individuals viewed these practices as more heinous than others, and if they were in positions of authority, prosecution could be triggered more readily. This appears to have been the case in Dijon in 1648 and 1649 when Jean Chipporée, the town syndic, brought a flurry of accusations over an eleven-month period for procuring and for prostitution.[82] Once he even appealed the decision of his own court to Parlement, apparently distressed by the overly lenient sentences of the town council.[83]

Zealous public officials like Chipporée might alter the boundary of scandal, but procuring associated with other criminal activity would also put the perpetrator at greater risk of prosecution.[84] So would procuring clients for one's wife, daughter, or other family member.[85] Procuring and prostitution were viewed by many of the authorities as temptation to young men of respectable families, temptation that, if yielded to, would bring ruin upon these families. Protection of the honor of the family, of course, was the bedrock of the social and political ideology of society's dominant classes—patriarchy. Indeed, behind all accusations of procuring and prostitution lay the notion of public scandal, and behind that lay the notion of disruption of the family and even the neighborhood.

Practitioners of everyday jurisprudence, like the syndic of Chalon-sur-Saône, the Bishop of Langres' *official*, the *promoteur* of the archdeaconry of Cluny, or the syndic of Dijon, succinctly associated scandal with deleterious actions to family and neighborhood.[86] In a sentence for procuring against cabinetmaker Jean de Chassagne in 1623 that the syndic of Chalon-sur-Saône recommended, the prosecutor noted that "such actions [were] as scandalous and odious to the public as to [Chassagne's] neighbors" and that a "traffic so vile and so pernicious to a well-policed state" merited capital punishment.

In 1631, the *official* of Langres was alarmed by malefactors who prostituted even their own children. Such illicit and immoral activities "cause[d] great beatings, outrages . . . breaking of windows in the houses of neighbors, [and] execreble blasphemies of the holy name of God." In 1666, Dom Paul Rabusson of the archdeaconry of Cluny echoed these sentiments in an opening statement initiating charges for procuring and prostitution against four women from Cluny. He found their debauchery "an offense to God and a scandal to one's neighbor [which led to] the loss of the youth [of Cluny]." Prosecution (joined by the secular power) and ultimately expulsion, Rabusson continued, would be "the remedy [ensuring] the greatest glory of God, the edification of one's neighbor, and the public welfare."

Finally, recall the case of 1720 when Dijon's syndic initiated legal proceedings against two unmarried women for "entic[ing] men to their house day and night which caused disorder in the families [of the men and the women] and a frightful scandal in the neighborhood where the women live." It was not just the syndic who feared such worrisome outcomes as destruction of the family itself. The father, a cousin, and an uncle of the women petitioned the court to incarcerate the women in a local convent for wayward females, as the father of one of them said, "in order to correct her morals and make her lead a more regulated life." These men were quite typical in defining when the boundary to scandal had been crossed, and it had much to do with the intersection of ideas about physical and moral order—in the family, the street, the neighborhood.

In most trials for prostitution or procuring from the mid-sixteenth to the early eighteenth century, there is some reference to scandalized neighbors. Indeed, often charges were filed because of complaints lodged by neighbors who would no longer tolerate the moral and physical disorder such activity brought to their street. Even when prostitution was legal, "respectable" inhabitants of towns like Dijon were concerned with keeping disreputable activity within the confines of the municipal brothel. In 1486, in the heyday of supposed toleration of prostitution,[87] "several notable personages" of Dijon asked for the expulsion from town of the women who led "so sordid and dissolute a life."[88] They were alarmed by the "evil and sinful" practice of this trade in "good streets," fearing that such proximity to "notable bourgeoises and young women" led to the "seducing, spoiling . . . and selling of . . . married women, young women, and servants."

In the early sixteenth century, similar complaints were lodged, some with more explicit descriptions of the disorder. The inhabitants of Grands Champs street in Dijon complained of "the sale of girls" outside the municipal brothel.[89] Like the respectable folk of 1486, they assumed that bawds would lure the respectable women, daughters, and servants into prostitution. The prostitution that was being carried on in several houses on the street did more than threaten the honor of respectable families and bring disgrace to the neighborhood; it brought physical disorder as well. Dice- and card-playing men "of evil and dishonorable ways" gathered at the brothels day and night, bringing larcenies and burglaries to the neighborhood. Like the "respectable women of Saint Pierre street" in the same town for the same reasons and at about the same time,[90] the Grands Champs street neighbors requested that, "for the love of God . . . and good justice," the illicit activities be confined to the municipal brothel.

The prohibition of brothels after 1561 did not eradicate prostitution or procuring. Neighbors continued to voice complaints to the authorities, and throughout the early modern period they were as concerned with the physical disorder as they were with the moral. In 1571 Laurence *La Chatte* was arrested for procuring and prostitution, and many of her neighbors on Saint Philibert street in Dijon testified against her.[91] Pastrycook Jehan Gosiner knew that she was "an evil-living procuress," an opinion confirmed by the tailor Guillaume de Brasey, who added that La Chatte's behavior was "seditious" because she quarreled with her neighbors. Fowler Nicolas Jacquin, as well as several artisan wives, like Henriette Barthélemi and Thomette Mareschal, echoed Brasey's observation about quarrels, adding that the procuress's activities not only brought discord between neighbors but thefts to the neighborhood—both incompatible with neighborhood order.

In the 1580s, inhabitants of du Four and du Tillot streets, again in Saint Philibert parish in Dijon, complained on two different occasions about the *lubricité* and, invoking the language of pollution and marginality, "dirty comportment" of women on their street involved in the "dishonorable traffic of procuring." Plaintiffs emphasized the danger to the people of the neighborhood as well as threats to respectable women. Indeed, such "licence and immodesty," according to the twenty signatories of one of the complaints, was "against the honor of God, good morals, and police."[92]

Multitudes of examples of concern among neighbors for good morals and good police could be presented.[93] In 1623, for example, a woman from Chalon-sur-Saône castigated a neighbor, allegedly a "procurer and seller of girls," as diabolical,[94] and in 1647 in Dijon a crowd of neighbors assembled shouting their "unanimous complaint" to the syndic when he arrived to arrest a notorious bawd for "immodest and unregulated ways" that were "detrimental to the youth and to the public and scandalous to neighbors."[95]

Little had changed by 1689, or 1716 for that matter.[96] In 1689, Dijon's syndic initiated proceedings against Heleine Jouanne for procuring on Saint Philibert street: "So great were the complaints [he] had received for her scandalous ways" that he "commenced a criminal procedure to stop the complaints from the neighborhood." In 1716, the wife of a carpenter was reported to Dijon's syndic by "virtuous and pious persons" for her "infamous commerce." Her procuring, the neighbors charged, brought young men and thus disruptions to the street; such disorder "scandalized the neighbors."

If complaints lodged with the authorities illustrate attitudes of respectable people toward procuring and prostitution, when it reached scandalous proportions, one could confirm such sentiments by examining the vocabulary of insult deployed in altercations in early modern streets. "Whore" and variations on it were arguably the most common, but *maquerelle* (bawd) was also common. Such slanders stung and prompted wronged parties not only to reciprocate with verbal salvos of their own but to file charges in court. In 1638 in Mâcon, Catherine Bornier, the widow of a *procureur*, charged neighbor Benoiste de Fruie with uttering "atrocious and scandalous slanders against the honor and reputation of not just her but her daughter as well." The slander? That Bornier had prostituted her daughter.[97]

Slanders hurled in public were serious matters because they threatened to strip the victim of honor and reputation, both highly valued. There were other ways to stain reputation, too. In 1670, for example, Margueritte Thenenin, the widow of a master mason from Dijon, found herself accused in court of "procuring and scandalous ways."[98] Whether Thenenin was guilty the inconclusive document does not state or prove, but the widow did file a countersuit alleging that the charge was not only false but "the most sensitive slander that one can make against people who have always lived without any reproach." She alleged that the anonymous original plaintiffs (*parties secrètes*) intended by the very charge that she "lose her honor and reputation."

Neighbors seem to have embraced a central credo of traditional Christianity, the importance of amicable neighborly relations.[99] Respectable citizens repeatedly filed petitions with municipal authorities complaining of the disorder and "scandal" that inevitably came to their street when procuresses and prostitutes set up shop there, and always they concluded with a request to expel the unwanted transients.[100] Expulsion was always the fate of convicted bawds and prostitutes, but many prostitutes must have suffered the same fate as Jeanne Mariche, who was evicted from her rented lodgings by an intolerant landlord even before she was arraigned by the authorities for procuring in 1648.[101] Wayward women seldom stayed in one place very long, and while they were there, they stayed to themselves and engaged in the discourse of the street only in adversarial or contentious terms.

Neighborhoods in early modern cities were tightly knit entities, and disruptive transients were not well integrated into their complex system.[102] Indeed, a partial response by the prostitutes to exclusion was to gather in certain neighborhoods, eventually turning them into "red-light" districts. This appears to have been the case in Dijon near the gate by the river Ouche or on Saint Philibert street,[103] as with the suburbs of Saint Martin-des-Champs and Saint Jean-des-Vignes outside of Chalon-sur-Saône.[104] Fear of such an eventuality underlay many neighborhood complaints.

Neighbors and authorities concerned with community morals and order forced exclusion and marginality upon prostitutes and especially procuresses. In the late seventeenth century, exclusion from respectable society on more occasions than ever before meant confinement. In 1656, the General Hospital system began operation in Paris; it ran La Pitié with the intention of incarcerating beggars, idlers, vagabonds, and generally *gens sans aveu*. Its sister institution for women, the Salpêtrière, also caught in its net prostitutes and procuresses. In Dijon the "great confinement" that aimed to correct transgressors by labor and piety was evidenced by Dijon's creation of Notre Dame du Refuge in 1655 and the Maison du Bon Pasteur in 1681. If litigious neighbors could not purify their neighborhoods, then perhaps *dévots*, religious reformers, and legal authorities (women were sentenced to the Maison du Bon Pasteur as a *maison de force*, or house of correction) could lend a hand.[105] These institutions were deliberately erected in a neighborhood notorious for prostitution in Dijon because, according to the

Reverend Mother from a sister monastery in Avignon commenting on the establishment in Dijon, "God wished to make serve to his glory a place that had served disorder and sin."[106]

Marginality was a fact of the prostitute's and procuress's life. Indeed, it contributed to the formation of an illicit culture defined by its marginal, urban, and fundamentally feminine characteristics.

That prostitution was an urban phenomenon is hardly surprising.[107] (I found no cases of prostitution prosecuted at the village level). More surprising, perhaps, is the only sporadic incidence of men involved in the trade as procurers, and most of these men were the husband of a woman who was a bawd.[108] Such were the cases, for example, of Joseph Pelletier in 1644 and Léonard Liegard in 1700.[109] Pelletier was convicted in Dijon of "having aided and abetted" his wife's procuring, while Liegard was sentenced for "having allowed . . . his wife to procure [*retirer*] debauched young women into their house."

The authorities appear to have assumed that in terms of both incidence and relative culpability, procuring was a feminine crime. Of the 79 people in my sample tried in Burgundian courts as *maquerelles* or *maquereaux*, 61 were women, and of the 18 men, only 5 were seemingly unassociated with a procuress. The husbands who were involved were likely to be less severely punished for the crime than their wives. In 1649, for example, François Hautmonte, a soldier from the garrison at Seurre, was arraigned with his wife, Symonne Julien, for procuring.[110] In the lower court, Julien was condemned to be whipped and banished, but Hautmonte was ordered only to return to his garrison, a sentence the Parlement revised by demanding that, in lieu of corporal punishment for the woman, Hautmonte take his wife with him, never to return to Dijon.

In the absence of males, prostitutes and procuresses were well aware of their relative independence, and on occasion they defiantly defended it, as Jeanne Gavinet did. Along with a 16-year-old orphan named Jeanne Gruchet from Autun, this 25-year-old woman from Châtillon-sur-Seine was arrested for prostitution by Dijon's syndic.[111] Both women boldly and immediately admitted to the practice and readily revealed how long they had been prostitutes, the names of their bawds, and even how many children they had had through illicit encounters. Such frankness makes the depositions of witnesses that follow ring true. Several people testified that, upon being reproached for her scandalous behavior by neighbors, Gavinet had retorted that "she was mistress of her body."[112] She added that "it was legal to be a prostitute provided that she was not public," no doubt meaning scandalous. Consequently, she defiantly concluded, she would do with her body what "seemed good to her." One witness added that Gavinet said that "she would house [*retiroit*] girls when they came to her and that she would make her living from them," an independent sentiment echoed almost verbatim in 1720 by a suspected procuress named Chevenet, the wife of a shoemaker. She reputedly said to her neighbors, many of them male, "that she would house [*retiroit*] whom she wished."[113]

Such statements suggest that procuresses thought of their practices as businesses marketing a commodity. Advertisement might take the form of nicknames—La Juste, La Joyeuse, Dame Bonnefeste, La Chatte, La Petite Jeanne, La Parisienne. Procuring for commercialized sex appears to be the dominant characteristic of bawds, but this conclusion may be distorted by the source that reveals the activity. A focus on court records may well over-look less scandalous activity that was part of the bawd's trade. Sixteenth- and early seventeenth-century French comedy commonly cast procuresses, sometimes in leading roles.[114] They might arrange for abortions or clan-destine births or wetnurses for pregnant or postpartum unmarried women (many, no doubt, prostitutes). Or they might help to coerce a father to provide child support.[115] True, there is Gillette of *Les Tromperies* whom Pierre de Larivey cast as a bawd of a brothel in 1611, but most *maquerelles* of comedy were *entremeteuses* (go-betweens). Their business might entail arranging brief sexual encounters, as Meduse does in Larivey's *La Fidelle*,[116] but it also might involve arranging encounters between young men and women who wanted to court, even against their parents' wishes. Marion of *Les Esbahis*, Guillemette of *La Veuve*, and Françoise of *Les Contens* each arranged marriages. Of course, being "vehicles for desperate lovers"[117] tacks very closely to complicity for *rapt*, a far from infrequent crime. Whether procuresses on the street engaged in the same activities of procuresses on the stage can never be proved, but there seems a strong likelihood.

In French theater, bawds arranged liaisons of short or lasting duration by furtively approaching respectable women under the guise of selling some innocuous and legitimate product. Criminal records suggest that this prac-tice actually occurred.[118] The lifeblood of a procuress's business was recruit-ment, and such surreptitious techniques, and apparent occasional success, greatly alarmed respectable inhabitants and the authorities. Burgundy's Parlement said as much in 1613 when it convicted Claudine Rogier of Châtillon-sur-Seine of "seducing and suborning respectable girls and women . . . luring them into her house and prostituting them."[119]

Procuresses, despite the fears of the respectable folk, seem to have been most successful in recruiting by enticing young women who had already lost their honor or found themselves below the threshold of poverty. Anne Bonnard was reputed to recruit young women recently released from the convent for (supposedly) penitent prostitutes and other wayward women, the Maison du Bon Pasteur.[120]

Successful recruitment might also result from offering attractive sums of money (perhaps initially as loans),[121] clothing, food, shelter (perhaps from an abusive husband),[122] or a steady client of elevated social status. In 1697, for example, a man named Goret and his wife, posing as members of a trav-elling opera troop, promised Margueritte Bossu the huge sum of 800£ per year plus room and board if she would "work" for them, enticement enough for this 22-year old daughter of a notary from Mantoche to be prostituted at least once before the leaders of the troop were arrested.[123]

In 1707 Pierrette Noël, the daughter of a master craftsman from Dijon, was approached by a procuress named Myon (Pierrette apparently never learned or would not divulge her first name) under the pretext of selling scarves. When Myon was certain that Noël's father was not present, she promised Noël that "she would make her fortune in gold and silver and she would want for nothing" if she agreed to be the mistress of "a person of quality," the royal councilor Baillet. She received a gold *louis* (10£)—a substantial sum—for the first encounter in a secluded garden. But after four months of regular liaisons, Noël ended up not with the fortune the bawd had promised but with a child, a battered body resulting from beatings the councillor rained upon her, and no child support.[124]

Ten years earlier, Dijon's syndic was prosecuting a procuress, Pierrette de Lettre, called La Beaunoise, for "seducing and suborning" women into prostitution.[125] He went to the Maison du Bon Pasteur to gather depositions and was told by Marie Remy, a 22-year-old from Metz, that de Lettre "had clothed her and then prostituted her." Philiberte de Losnay, the 23-year-old daughter of a *procureur* from Chalon-sur-Saône, added that de Lettre had prostituted her to a man "of quality" for the remarkable sum of 4 gold *louis* (what it might take a salaried Parisian mason more than a fortnight to earn in peak season or a construction laborer two months),[126] adding that on that day de Losnay ate meat, a rare treat.[127] Similarly in 1660, Claudine Thimonet, the wife of a pastry cook, was alleged to have provided food and drink to young women as enticements to prostitution, and some of Thimonet's prostitutes, quite well dressed according to witnesses, were receiving as much as 3 gold *louis* from their clients for sex.[128] In 1681, Dame Catherine was reputed by witnesses to provide food to *filles libertines*, suggestion enough for the authorities to assume that she was a procuress operating a brothel.[129]

The greatest recruiting device a procuress could offer was a promise of material security. The records do not tell why the prospective prostitutes would turn a receptive ear to such enticements, but one can imagine any number of reasons: failed courtships resulting in pregnancy or dishonor, being one of several daughters inadequately dowered, or economic privation. In 1697, the bogus opera performers Goret and his wife succeeded in recruiting the daughter of a master driller to prostitution, as the father himself admitted, so that she could help him pay the rent.[130] In 1648, a bawd named Barbe approached 20-year-old Catherine Jacquelin who was selling wine in the streets of Dijon. Jacquelin had been a domestic servant but had been unemployed for two months and was a wine peddler (*revendeuse*) out of necessity. Barbe told her that she could do better "abandoning herself" to a man of quality and that she, Barbe, could arrange such a liaison. That began Jacquelin's life of prostitution, which lasted only six weeks in Dijon, until she was apprehended, convicted, whipped, and banished.[131]

Given the straits in which unemployed and unprotected young women could find themselves in the early modern city (most of the women recruited were *du peuple*, as Arlette Farge puts it,[132] from the swollen propertyless underclass) promises of cash, food, clothing, or shelter by a procuress could have been considered fortuitous by women in need, especially if they had already lost their respectability and honor. A bawd telling her that "she could show her how to earn a living without working," as a wife of a master mason said in 1670, could be a siren's call difficult to resist.[133]

Catherine Robin heeded the call, only to find further misfortune in an already miserable existence. This 22-year-old daughter of a shoemaker from Saulieu was arrested by Dijon's authorities in 1647 for streetwalking. She claimed that her brother had returned from war and, upon finding her pregnant, had kicked her out of the house. A failed courtship propelled Robin toward prostitution. Dishonored, she had wandered Burgundy's roads, and when she could not find employment as a servant, she fell in with a gang of women in similar straits led by 21-year-old Guillemette Barbier from Nuits Saint-Georges. One of her new companions, the 25-year-old daughter of a clerk from a village near Lyon named Jeanne Bouchard, had been a camp follower after a courtship had failed and her honor was lost. She had followed the regiment to Burgundy where she, too, met Barbier. When the women were arrested for prostitution, they made no effort to conceal their activities, but they offered as explanation that they did it, as Robin said, "to stay alive."[134]

The promise, perhaps illusory, of immediate material security from selling sex is evident in this example as in so many others. The documents are vivid and tragic portrayals of desperate women trapped in an exploitative and degrading institution. Clients often abused the women they "purchased," and procuresses exploited the prostitutes they marketed.[135] These calculating madams manipulated an exploitative system that was powered by men as consumers.

The urban, marginal, and feminine characteristics of this illicit culture may appear fairly constant over time, but there were some changes. Because we are dependent on court records, we can never be certain whether these changes were in fact occurring or were simply reflecting a shift in prosecution patterns or intensity. It is clear, however, that before the late seventeenth century, streetwalking and working informally out of rented rooms dominated the criminal records. From the late seventeenth century, in contrast, a greater proportion of women prosecuted were working in established bordellos and even as what appear to be courtesans.[136]

By the late seventeenth century, it appears, the male authorities may have become more hesitant to prosecute procuring and prostitution in court.[137] Reality may have been mirrored in literature. In 1670, for example, in *Le Maître d'hostel aux halles* François-César Oudin de Préfontaine wrote of a brothel run by Dame Ragonde that was known by the police but was allowed to continue to operate because it was in a location far from respectable townsfolk.[138] Likewise, court documents display a noticeable indulgence by the authorities coincidental with more lenient sentences. It was not that prosecution became rare, but the authorities would frankly admit in given trials that illicit activity had been going on for some time without punishment.[139]

In 1689, for example, Anne Bonnard was arrested for and convicted of "procuring, prostitution, and lascivious ways [*maquerellage, prostitution, et vie lubricque*]" but only after fifteen years of such activities.[140] Bonnard's social profile certainly raised the eyebrows and the ire of the Dijonnais authorities trying her case, for she was relatively high-born, well-educated (for a woman), and well-connected. She was the daughter of a barrister at Burgundy's Parlement and the widow of the *Procureur du roi* at the Table de Marbre, the royal court in Dijon with jurisdiction over natural resources. Both men were deceased by the time this 35-year-old woman ran afoul of the law.

Bonnard's fall from social respectability to such "vile commerce" began when, while estranged from her husband, she fell in love with a journeyman cabinetmaker who jilted her and apparently left her pregnant. From then on she settled into a life of procuring and prostitution. She was arrested for this activity only when the authorities finally decided it had reached scandalous proportions.

Similar indulgence by the authorities can be seen in a 1703 trial. Dijon's syndic, initiating prosecution of a case of "infamous commerce" against a procuress and her husband, admitted in his own petition that such conduct had been going on "for a long time" and that he had received several complaints from neighbors. He even knew that the suspected parties had moved since the first complaints, and he was aware that their illicit activities continued in their new location. He had asked for an inquest only after physical damage was done to a house on the street where they had set up shop.[141]

Concern for damage to property, which, with rowdy males, prostitution always seemed to bring in its train, was a perennial concern of neighbors and authorities alike. But the indulgence of the authorities evident by the late seventeenth century suggests that some illicit sexual activity was becoming more orderly.[142]

Furthermore, along with what appears to be a more sedentary existence for some women selling sex, it seems that a more pronounced hierarchy emerged among them, mirroring the process of dissociation occurring in society at large.[143] Some prostitutes and bawds were careful to point out that they were not available to everyone, and witnesses in the trials frequently seconded this hierarchical pride by clarifying whether an accused prostitute or madam sold sex to everyone or only to "men of quality."[144] Jeanne Gavinet, for example, promptly admitted her prostitution but was mindful to add that she was socially selective, proudly informing a neighbor that she was not a "public whore" and that she had sex "only . . . with honorable men."[145]

No doubt Gavinet wanted to distinguish herself from the more ordinary prostitutes working the streets, like Pierrette Quenot, the 18-year-old daughter of a day laborer from Auxonne, and Anne Prinstet, the 22-year-old unmarried immigrant from Brassey. In 1675, following a complaint by a citizen alarmed by noise in the street, Quenot was discovered hiding in an attic with a group of lackeys. Under interrogation, she confessed that she had been living with these men for over a week in the guardhouse of the *logis du roi* and had known many of them (she could not say how many) carnally. Prinstet, like an unnamed "abandoned" woman who was caught in a recessed doorway on a Dijon street in the sexual act with a "young debauched man" wanted for murder, was apprehended by the night watch in "indecent and scandalous postures" with two young men near the Ouche gate.[146]

The cases of selective prostitutes or bawds provide glimpses inside the apparently more prevalent bordellos of the late seventeenth and eighteenth centuries and more elaborate settings for sexual encounters. Spying neighbors report tables laid out with food and drink[147] stocked by caterers.[148] Laughter and bawdy singing, witnesses indignantly reported, often roared from the windows of these establishments, as the *filles de joie* entertained their well-heeled clients under the watchful eye of madams like Dame Bonnefeste.

Such a life-style, paradoxically, might be considered simultaneously exploitative and independent. Prostitution was rooted in degradation, the toleration of the practice by the authorities, and the patronizing of bordellos by men encouraging the exploitation of women's bodies. Prostitutes were vulnerable and their lives nasty and brutish. Clients frequently beat them, and venereal disease and pregnancy were constant, life-threatening risks. Nor could prostitutes of whatever status file charges for rape or *rapt* in courts of law.

But some young women selling sex arranged by procuresses attained some material security, perhaps as much as they might have enjoyed had they pursued other occupations available to women of their station—domestic service, spinning, or peddling. The life-style of the prostitute and the procuress must be considered against the living conditions and occupational opportunities otherwise available to women hailing from their walks of life. These women had few options, and a well-laid table, a roof over their heads, and some cash in their strongboxes (even after the procuress had taken her share) may have seemed a worthwhile exchange for engaging in a dangerous trade that respectable society judged dishonorable. This was especially so for vulnerable itinerant women, like Catherine Robin, who had already lost her honor (through a failed courtship) and her home.

Conclusion

Desperation and vulnerability deeply mark the lives of many women who remained outside marriage. Women pressed by lustful and often duplicitous males for sexual relations and made pregnant by them frequently failed to gain honorable marriage from them, and only the fortunate few were able to secure material support from men unwilling or unable to marry them. For the rest, stark and unsavory choices confronted them, none of which found a legitimate place in the new morality of order and order of morality. Aborting the fetus or abandoning or killing the infant produced by failed courtships was a desperate decision, but the presumed necessity of returning to the pool of eligible, honorable brides drove many women to make it nonetheless. Failure to conceal the crime meant death for those caught by the authorities, but, given the nature of these offenses, the disposition of female bodies was only partially within reach of law.

There were other options available to these desperate women. Concubinage and occasional prostitution was one grim possibility. The authorities may have found this behavior unrespectable but they were unsure about the relative criminality of this practice—unless it became "scandalous." Then, such sexual disorder was thought to pose a direct threat to social order and was prosecuted.

Concubines and prostitutes were occasionally prosecuted in the courts of Burgundy, but, in the eyes of the authorities, the most detested culprits were the bawds. Here too the importance of scandal looms large in the authorities' views of procuring, and these predatory women (who were apparently victimizing other vulnerable women) were prosecuted much more severely than concubines or prostitutes.

Prosecution for the female crimes like infanticide, prostituion, and procuring rose steadily in the seventeenth century peaking between 1687 and 1700 and then falling off. This jurisprudential trend probably reflects rising interest in these crimes by public prosecutors (the litigation over these offenses, unlike *rapt*, was always initiated by the public official), but it is not always clear why. This vigilance does not necessarily reflect a rising incidence of these crimes, but it does suggest an increasing vigilance over crimes involving public scandal and thus threatening to public order. Indeed, it is perhaps indicative that infanticide and procuring were offenses against the family unit, the stability of which was fundamental to the patriarchal definition of the new order of morality. After 1700, ordinary police activity resulting in temporary incarceration rather than prosecution probably increasingly dealt with prostituion and procuring, and consequently the courts may have been called upon less often.[149]

Paradoxically, alongside this jurisprudential trend, a notable indulgence on the part of the authorities existed in their treatment of prostitution and procuring. The key to solving the paradox may be that public officials were intolerant of disorderly prostitution and of procuresses' enticing young respectable women into prostitution but more tolerant of the "necessary evil" of prostitution as long as it was not disruptive to public order. Procurers and prostitutes who became "too scandalous" found themselves prosecuted. When the boundary demarcating this line was crossed was not always clear; furthermore, the authorities were tolerant of these practices as long as they remained in the shadows. Cases against prostitution often reveal that the authorities had known, sometimes for years, that the accused had been engaged in the activity but prosecuted only when it became too scandalous. Baroque men evidently were deeply ambivalent about this female activity; they enabled its practice and periodically condemned it.

Male authorities may have prosecuted these women in the name of good order, but other men enabled its practice. Bernard de La Monnoye, a late seventeenth and early eighteenth-century renowned author, eventual member of the French Academy, man of the law, and royal official, not only wrote doggerel implicitly endorsing the practice of prostitution and even procuring but also mocking its prosecution. In a poem entitled *Voleur des choses* (Thief of things) scribbled in an unpublished notebook, he wrote:

> Peintre, combien cette donzelle?
> Un Louis. Eh, se-moques-tu?
> On auroit chez la maquerelle
> L'original pour un écu.[150]

> Painter, how much for [this painting of] this wench?
> One *louis* [10£]. Eh, are you joking?
> One could have from the bawd
> the original for one *écu* [3£].

In one called *Maquerellage* (Procuring) he lightheartedly wrote:

> O que la fille, O que la mère
> En peu de temps feront de fruit!
> Voulez-vous savoir le mystère?
> L'une engendre et l'autre produit![151]

> Oh, the girl, oh the mother
> shortly will bear fruit!
> Do you want to know the mystery?
> The one generates and the other produces!

Not only did La Monnoye mock family values, but, as we have seen in the poem where he belittled the syndic's busting of prostitutes as a less-than-heroic deed, he also made fun of authorities who prosecuted these women.

It is perhaps telling that La Monnoye confined these feelings to poems he never published, and probably never intended to; his published work and his letters were eminently respectable, even esteemed (judging from his admission to the French Academy). Prostitution, like La Monnoye's bawdy notebooks, was best kept in the shadows; bringing it into the light would be scandalous.

This ambivalence deep in the ethic of patriarchy resulted in an increasing incidence of litigation against female "crimes" and the emerging outlines of an increasingly orderly culture of illicit but tolerated sexuality. Indeed, by the late seventeenth century, the world of illicit sexuality was increasingly dissociated and stratified, a mirror-image of respectable society.

The experience of women like Anne Bonnard, despite her social background that makes her an unusual historical example in some respects, embodies many of the dilemmas, constraints, and opportunities (however limited and degrading) confronting unmarried women in Old Regime France. They lived in a patriarchal world, and without male protectors (fathers or husbands), they faced that world in an independent but vulnerable position. But they were not without options, not entirely powerless. On the one hand, they were victims exploited in a world where the deck was hopelessly stacked against them, but they tried to make the best of a bad lot. Bonnard, for instance, lost her father, her husband, and even her lover, and although the patriarchal culture ultimately would punish her for her actions, for fifteen years she maintained a degrading, marginal, but nevertheless autonomous existence in which she manipulated male sexual gratification for gain. In such a contradictory netherworld of dependency on men (the cash of her clients, the indulgence of the authorities) and independence from them (she ran her own business), Bonnard was very much like many other unmarried women, and not just prostitutes, who bartered their bodies.

Once again, legislative attempts to fix social reality—laws against concealment of pregnancy, infanticide, concubinage, prostitution or procuring—were undercut by the dynamics and uncertainties of the processes of everyday life in which countless individuals pursued strategies of survival, no matter how meager the fruits or how grim the choices.

Conclusion

Traditional historiography asserts that the Enlightenment dawned in the late seventeenth century and accelerated in an ever more secular direction over the course of the eighteenth century. Concurrently, the energies of the Catholic Reformation were spent as the Age of Reason unfolded and French society was dechristianized. More recent historians have pointed to a decline in the punishment of irreligion and immorality, as well as to evidence of increasing premarital sex, illegitimate births, and abandoned children.

There is much accuracy in this later picture, but it should not blind us to the continuities of the seventeenth and eighteenth centuries. The Catholic Reformation may have peaked in France between 1660 and 1690, but it did not end abruptly thereafter or even in 1730, nor did French people come to think that religion was unimportant to social life. Furthermore, although historians disagree about the relative status of women during the Enlightenment, many would agree that ideas about gender difference were still predicated on hierarchical difference—an assumption that served as the bedrock of patriarchy. These ideas would change only in the late eighteenth century.[1] Indeed, hierarchy was as essential to thinking about social stability throughout the eighteenth century as it had been in the seventeenth—so much so, in fact, that the doctrine of civility and its attendant behavioral and sartorial display was accentuated as it delimited with increasing precision hierarchical social differentiation.[2]

Nonetheless, there are good reasons for concluding this book around 1730. It has explored the nature and meaning of authority as it related to human sexuality between 1550 and 1730. Consequently, it has focused on morality and the law, including the magistrates who administered the law, and it has emphasized the importance of religion in the new moral order. Between 1550 and 1700, the church and state worked to achieve the sacralization of society. The first deep cracks in the new order appeared in the early eighteenth century.

As Jeffrey Merrick has shown, the papal bull *Unigenitus* (1713) provoked deeply contentious debate about the religious and political order of France—indeed, about the disposition of authority in the kingdom. Parlementaires were the self-appointed watchdogs of Gallicanism, and it was the liberties of the Gallican church that the *robins* believed were attacked by this ultramontane bull that condemned Jansenism. Most of the French clergy and the king, in contrast, supported the bull less because of its ultramontanism than because it struck down Jansenism.

The ensuing storm of controversy surrounding the bull undermined the apparent unity of the moral order constructed over the previous century and a half. Since the sixteenth century, France's privileged elite had been building a public order that identified the kingdom with divinely ordained kingship and that reserved a prominant place for officialdom in it. Beginning with the controversy following *Unigenitus*, however, this apparent unity was shattered. The magistrates squared off against the French clergy in the matter and the king as well. They asserted that the king's support of ultramontanism was not representing the true interests of France. This challenge to the monarchy was reminiscent of the allegations of the sixteenth-century Burgundian parlementaires like Jean Bégat who had asserted that a certain order in the realm transcended the king. But whereas the threat of the League contributed to a conjunction of church and state in the seventeenth century, the parlementary challenge to the king in the eighteenth led to their separation.

By the eighteenth century the magistrates associated order with public interest, and they had long since assumed that the defense of the public interest was their raison d'être. Consequently, in raising the public interest above the king as they did in the *Unigenitus* controversy, they both implicitly challenged divine right absolutism and fractured the reciprocally supportive relationship religion and politics had shared over the previous century or so.[3]

Emerging from the sixteenth century with the traditional verities apparently collapsing, baroque men faced the awesome task of laying a new foundation for a moral order. They developed an epistemology that mirrored their thinking about social order, focusing much of their thought on the destructive nature of the passions—especially the concupiscent—and fashioning an authoritarian ethic of self-discipline and social control, summed up in *honnêteté*, piety, and law. Tasteful behavior demonstrated the emergent hierarchical society of dissociation and difference, with confessionalism, legislation, and jurisprudence attempting to guarentee it.

Lay and clerical reformers aimed to restore the traditional order in society, but the unintended result was the emergence of a new moral order built on a new type of community. Linked vertically rather than horizontally, this community was comprised of dissociated individuals held together hierarchically by an increasingly authoritarian church and state.

The hierarchical stratification of society so dear to men rested on elemental assumptions about gender relations, which were also hierarchical. Men assumed that males were naturally superior to females and that the passionate and irrational nature of women needed to be controlled by reasonable men. Patriarchy, though not new, consequently found a fundamental place in the new moral order.

The ideology and the practice of the law were vitally important to the authoritarianism of the new order. The ideology of authority and legal practice intertwined in the relationship between absolutist kings and a persistently independent-minded judiciary. King and magistrate were frequently at odds over the distribution of authority in the new order, but they did negotiate a mutually beneficial system of power-sharing that maintained the fiction of absolutism while it gave magistrates a share of sovereignty. Kings may have claimed total legislative sovereignty by divine right, but parlementary jurisprudence, with the latitude of magisterial interpretation, indirectly contested the royal monopoly and thus contributed to the judicial revolution in the law of proof in the seventeenth century and planted the seeds of the parlementary challenge to absolutism of the eighteenth.

The ideology of authority that emerged entailed the sacralization of lay authorities, which strengthened the sanctity of authority. This may have led to jurisidictional disputes between church and state, but the Gallicanism that enshrined lay supremacy was not yet about secularization—that would have to wait until the eighteenth century—but rather sacralization.

Indeed, the sacralization of society was the goal of lay people as well as clergymen. Many of the most influential devout laymen and women were from the legal community, and it hardly comes as a surprise to discover that these people assumed that sacralization should be mediated through royal justice administered by them, or that they would be inclined to criminalize sin.

Just as the social, political, and legal aspects of this vision rested on authoritarianism, so, too, did the religious. The moral order that the godly sought was supported by their sexual ethics and their commitment to confessionalism, and their deep suspicion of the concupiscent passions and demand to control "unregulated" female sexuality led to their call to use the law to discipline "unruly" women.

Confession and communion played an important part in the restoration of moral order and the Catholic Reformation. The reform was to be parochially based and the parish clergy agents of discipline. To play this role effectively, reformers concluded, priests had to be pure in thought and deed. Given the identification of sexual passion with disorder in the new ethos, clerical concupiscence was intolerable. Secular judges, who came to view the dispensing of law as a sacred obligation, increasingly brought wayward ecclesiastics into their royal courts. These trials tell us a great deal about the godly intentions of parlementaires, but also about the relationships of holiness, sexuality, power, and the law in general and the uses of the law and litigation in particular.

The requirement that priests be an embodiment of the holy greatly empowered them, and their exercise of this influence was important to the village community, not least to the local lord. A seigneur who perceived a priest as a threat to his influence might attempt to remove the curé, and what better way than to allege behavior that touched the quick of disorder—sexual licentiousness—and bring the weight of the reformers' sacred law upon the priest's head? Such a use of the law and litigation may have had other purposes than the restoring of moral order, but it proved quite useful nonetheless.

These uses of the law and litigation also undermined the royal legislative intentions to impose a marital ethic that combined religious, political, and social ideologies. Female litigants used the laws pertaining to marriage (notably concerning clandestine marriage, *rapt*, and declaration of pregnancy) in their strategies to achieve honorable marriage at best, or material well-being at worst. Judges, too, sought to support honorable marriage, for they viewed it as the foundation of patriarchy and, ultimately, social order. But these judges came to realize that a rigorous application of royal legislation was counterproductive to that goal, and over time, their application of the law became more flexible. In their adjudication of *rapt* cases, Burgundy's judges championed the paternalism that undergirded royal political theories and the social ideology (based upon social stratification) of society's dominant classes, but they came to believe that the royal legislation and its inflexible demands for the death penalty for *rapt* were too severe. By the middle of the seventeenth century they had begun to lighten their sentences, shifting from corporal, even capital punishment to everdiminishing remuneration of the wronged parties.

The judges, especially those at the Parlement, believed that capital penalties were counterproductive to their goal of order, for two reasons. First, they believed that the institution of marriage and the attendant social stability could best be protected by encouraging marriage between the litigants or, more commonly, returning the plaintiff (almost invariably a woman) to the father by blocking marriage. Second, although the plaintiffs were usually women and the defendants men, the judges came to suspect that culpability was not as clear-cut as royal legislation would have it. Rather, they presumed that seduction was bound up with female marital strategies as much as with male fraudulence and therefore the man was not entirely culpable in many *rapt* cases. Their sentences reflect this new belief. In the application of the law, then, the aims of female litigants contested in court were influential in altering the application of an unyielding royal legislation and were part of the judicial revolution transpiring during the seventeenth century.

For many women who remained unmarried, desperation and vulnerability were their constant companions. Women pressed by lustful and often duplicitous males for sexual relations and made pregnant by them frequently failed to gain honorable marriage from them, and only the fortunate few were able to secure material support from men unwilling or unable to marry them. For the rest, grim choices confronted them, none with a legitimate place in the new morality of order and order of morality. Aborting the fetus or abandoning or killing the infant produced by a failed courtship was a desperate step, but the presumed necessity of returning to the pool of eligible, honorable brides drove many women to take it. Those who were caught by the authorities faced a sentence of death. Nevertheless, given the clandestine nature of these offenses, the disposition of female bodies was only partially within reach of law.

Women in these circumstances faced grim possibilities, including concubinage and prostitution. Reflecting an ambivalence rooted deep in the patriarchal ethos, the authorities may have found this behavior unrespectable, but were unsure whether it was criminal and were inclined to tolerate it if practiced in an orderly and nondisruptive fashion. If they viewed it as scandalous, however, such sexual disorder was thought to pose a direct threat to public order and was prosecuted.

Authority and sexuality were inextricably connected in Burgundy between 1550 and 1730. What they had to do with one another comprises the substance of this book and pertains directly to its tacit analytical theme: the dialectical relation between prescription, or, "The Morality of Order and the Order of Morality," and practice, or, "The Disposition of Bodies." Men like Nicolas Brulart might assert that justice has the moral duty to discipline the unruly passions of women, while women like Jeanne Gavinet might declare that they are mistresses of their bodies and will do with them what they see fit. But the Brularts of the world had to reckon with the reality of the bodies of the Gavinets all too often beyond the reaches of authority while they reckoned with the motives of these women to manipulate authority to their advantage. The Gavinets, for their part, had to reckon with the reality of a patriarchal authority that presumed their guilt as well as with the implements of its power if it apprehended them in a crime it defined: courtrooms, whips, and even nooses.

Notes

Abbreviations

ADA	Archives départementales de l'Aube
ADCO	Archives départementales de la Côte-d'Or
ADD	Archives départementales du Doubs
ADSL	Archives départementales de la Saône-et-Loire
ACCS	Archives communales de Chalon-sur-Saône
AMD	Archives municipales de Dijon
BMD	Bibliothèque municipale de Dijon
BN	Bibliothèque Nationale
MSHD	Mémoires de la société pour l'histoire du driot et des institutions des anciens pays bourguignons, comtois, et romands

Introduction

1. Such gendered language evokes the League's willingness to bypass the Salic Law at the 1593 Estates General when the most radical of the Leaguers advocated a female monarch, Isabella of Spain, to replace Henri IV. I thank Mack P. Holt for this information.

2. See Peter Stallybrass and Allon White, *The Politics and Poetics of Transgression* (Ithaca, N.Y., 1986). On the body as metaphor, see Mary Douglas, *Natural Symbols* (New York, 1982), and idem, *Purity and Danger* (London, 1985).

3. Sally Falk Moore, *Law as Process* (Cambridge, Mass., 1977), p. 39.

4. See Victor Turner, *The Anthropology of Performance* (New York, 1988), pp. 97–98; Moore, *Law as Process*, p. 51.

5. Moore, *Law as Process*, p. 41; see also Stephen Greenblatt, *Renaissance Self-Fashioning: From More to Shakespeare* (Chicago, 1980), p. 220.

6. Pierre Bourdieu, *The Logic of Practice*, trans. Richard Nice (Stanford, 1990), p. 88.

7. Ibid., p. 109.

8. In the following discussion about power and economies, I have been influenced by the following theorists: Bourdieu, *Logic of Practice*; Stephen Greenblatt, *Shakespearean Negotiations* (Berkeley, 1988); Michel de Certeau, *The Practice of Everyday Life*, trans. Steven Rendall (Berkeley, 1984); Anthony Giddens, *Central Problems in Social Theory: Action, Structure, and Contradiction in Social Analysis* (Berkeley, 1979); Hans Medick and David Sabean Introduction, to their *Interest and Emotion: Essays on the Study of Family and Kinship* (Cambridge, 1984); and Norbert Elias, *The Civilizing Process* 2 vols., trans. Edmund Jephcott (New York, 1978, 1982).

9. Most notably, see his *Discipline and Punish: The Birth of the Prison*, trans. Alan Sheridan (New York, 1977), and *The History of Sexuality: An Introduction*, trans. Robert Hurley (New York, 1980).

10. Judith Butler, "Foucault and the Paradox of Bodily Inscriptions," *Journal of Philosophy* 86:11 (November, 1989), 601–7. See also Ladelle McWhorter, "Culture or Nature? The Function of the Term 'Body' in the Work of Michel Foucault," *Journal of Philosophy* 86:11 (November, 1989), 608–14.

11. See Judith Butler, *Gender Trouble: Feminism and the Subversion of Identity* (New York, 1990).

12. Caroline Walker Bynum, "Introduction: In Praise of Fragments; History in the Comic Mode," in idem, *Fragmentation and Redemption: Essays on Gender and the Human Body in Medieval Religion* (Cambridge, Mass., 1992), pp. 19–20.

13. Haunani-Kay Trask, *Eros and Power: The Promise of Feminist Theory* (Philadelphia, 1986); Adrienne Rich, *Of Woman Born* (New York, 1976); Robin Morgan, *Going Too Far: The Personal Chronicle of a Feminist* (New York, 1977); Meredith B. McGuire, "Religion and the Body: Rematerializing the Human Body in the Social Sciences of Religion," *Journal for the Scientific Study of Religion* 29:3 (1990), 283–96; and Audre Lorde, *Sister Outsider* (Trumansburg, 1984).

14. John Giles Milhaven, "A Medieval Lesson on Bodily Knowing: Women's Experience and Men's Thought," *Journal of the American Academy of Religion* 57:2 (Summer 1989), 341.

15. Bynum, "The Female Body and Religious Practice in the Later Middle Ages," in *Fragmentation and Redemption*, pp. 220, 223. See also Milhaven, "Medieval Lesson," pp. 353, 358.

16. The interpretation of the meaning of St. Ignatius Loyola's *Spiritual Exercises* illustrates this development. As Michael Barnes, "The Body in the Spiritual Exercizes of Ignatius of Loyola," *Religion* 19 (1989), 263–73, points out, the earliest version of the *Exercises* and the early directories of the Society of Jesus of the middle third of the sixteenth century encouraged "penetrating the truth" with the intellect and "'by the feelings.'" Directories from the following century shed the Aristotelian influence for Platonic; they shifted toward "an overriding emphasis on intellect" and deemphasized the feelings, illustrating a rationalistic interpretation of the *Spiritual Exercises*.

17. See, for example, Roger de Rabutin, Comte de Bussy, *L'Histoire amoureuse des Gaules* (Paris, 1966); idem, *Mémoires secrets de M. le Comte de Bussy-Rabutin, contenant sa vie publique et privée, ses aventures galantes . . .* , 2 vols. (Paris, 1882; 1st ed. 1696); Théophile de Viau, *Le Parnasse satyrique* (Paris, 1855; 1st ed. 1623); and Gedéon Tallemant des Réaux, *Les Historiettes* (Paris, 1929).

18. Bynum, "Introduction," p. 18.

19. J. M. Berthelot, "Sociological Discourse and the Body," in Mike

Featherstone, Mike Hepworth, and Bryan S. Turner, eds., *The Body: Social Process and Cultural Theory* (London, 1991), p. 397. On the order and flux of incorporation, see Pierre Bourdieu, *Outline of a Theory of Practice*, trans. Richard Nice (Cambridge, 1977), and *Logic of Practice*; Douglas, *Natural Symbols*; and Bryan S. Turner, "Recent Developments in the Theory of the Body," in Featherstone, Hepworth, and Turner, eds., *The Body*, pp. 1–35.

20. Butler, "Foucault and the Paradox of Bodily Inscriptions," p. 607.

21. Dorinda Outram, *The Body and the French Revolution: Sex, Class, and Political Culture* (New Haven, 1989), p. 20.

22. My thinking about this issue was stimulated by Theodore Rabb, *The Struggle for Stability in Early Modern Europe* (Oxford, 1975).

23. William J. Bouwsma, "Lawyers and Early Modern Culture," *American Historical Review* 78 (1973), 317.

24. Ralph E. Giesey, "Rules of Inheritance and Strategies of Mobility in Prerevolutionary France," *American Historical Review* 82 (1977), 286.

25. Bouwsma, "Lawyers," p. 324.

26. See Bryan S. Turner, *Religion and Social Theory* (London, 1983), p. 118.

27. A great deal has been written on the Catholic Reformation. Many of these studies have been based on ecclesiastical court records and parish visitation documents, neither of which exists in sufficient quantity in Burgundy to support a convincing claim that the Reformation was a success or a failure.

28. On the relationship between bodies and power, see the formative works by Michel Foucault, especially *History of Sexuality* and *Discipline and Punish*. My thinking has also been influenced by Greenblatt, *Renaissance Self-Fashioning*, pp. 80, 140–41; Certeau, *Practice of Everyday Life*, pp. 139, 149; Bryan S. Turner, *The Body and Society: Explorations in Social Theory* (Oxford, 1984), passim; and Butler, *Gender Trouble*, pp. 33, 129–33.

29. Turner, *Body and Society*, p. 13.

30. June Starr and Jane F. Collier, "Introduction: Dialogues in Legal Anthropology," in idem. eds., *History and Power in the Study of Law: New Directions in Legal Anthropology* (Ithaca, N.Y., 1989), pp. 2, 4. See also Martha Albertson Fineman and Nancy Sweet Thomadsen, eds., *At The Boundaries of Law: Feminism and Legal Theory* (New York, 1991).

31. I have been guided by the critical legal studies movement, which questions the assumption that rules are neutral. Indeed, as John M. Conley and Wiliam M. O'Barr, *Rules Versus Relationships: The Ethnography of Legal Discourse* (Chicago, 1990), pp. 12, 87, 163, have pointed out, the "rule-centered approach gives voice only to the powerful." The critical legal studies movement views law not only as a constraint but also as a resource, and thus as an "enabling mechanism" as well as an "instrument of limitation." I thank Michael Maltz and Marcia Farr for this reference. See also Starr and Collier, "Introduction," pp. 2, 4, 6–9, 12.

Chapter 1

1. Lawrence W. B. Brockliss, *French Higher Education in the Seventeenth and Eighteenth Centuries: A Cultural History* (Oxford, 1987), observes that Stoicist works were most widely read by students in higher education (and thus all *robins*) in seventeenth- and eighteenth-century France.

2. Quoted in E. de La Cuisine, *Le Parlement de Bourgogne depuis son origine jusqu'à sa chute* (Dijon and Paris, 1864), 1:163–4. Many of Brulart's harangues

are quoted extensively in La Cuisine. Unless otherwise stated, all translations are mine.

3. Quoted in ibid., 1:169.

4. Quoted in ibid., 1:169, 165.

5. Quoted in ibid., 1:155–56.

6. Ibid., 1:195, 196, 200.

7. Ibid., 1:262, 266.

8. Quoted in ibid., 1:258.

9. E. de La Cuisine, ed., *Choix des lettres inédites, écrites par Nicolas Brulart* (Dijon, 1859).

10. On the importance of honor among nobles, see Kristin Neuschel, *Word of Honor* (Ithaca, N.Y., 1989), pp. 74, 76.

11. La Cuisine, *Lettres par Brulart*, 18 April 1679, 2:205; 24 April 1679, 2:206–14.

12. Ibid., 24 February 1658, 1:46–49.

13. Ibid., 18 June 1674, 2:179–80; see also 6 January 1668, 2:84–91.

14. La Cuisine, *Parlement*, 1:243–53; see also the harangue of 1683, "De l'Ordre et de la bienséance," in ibid., 1:267–69.

15. José Antonio Maravall, *The Culture of the Baroque: Analysis of a Historical Structure*, trans. Terry Cochran (Minneapolis, 1986), pp. 157–58. Simon Schama, "The Unruly Realm: Appetite and Restraint in Seventeenth-Century Holland," *Daedalus* 108:3 (1979), 103–23, finds uncertainty and anxiety to be fundamental characteristics of seventeenth-century Holland as well.

16. Gaston Roupnel, *La Ville et la campagne au XVIIe siècle: Etude sur les populations du pays Dijonnais* (Paris, 1955), p. 91.

17. C. Lalourcé and F. Duval, eds., *Recueil des cahiers généraux des trois ordres aux Etats-Généraux* (Paris, 1789), 4:366.

18. Roupnel, *La Ville et la campagne*, pp. 97–98.

19. For the sixteenth century, see Emmanual Le Roy Ladurie, *Carnival in Romans*, trans. Mary Feeney (New York, 1979), and most recently, Barbara B. Diefendorf, *Beneath the Cross: Catholics and Huguenots in Sixteenth-Century Paris* (New York, 1991), and Henry Heller, *Iron and Blood: Civil Wars in Sixteenth-Century France* (Montreal, 1991). For the rebellions in the seventeenth century, see Boris Porchnev, *Les Soulèvements populaires en France au XVIIe siècle* (Paris, 1972); Roland Mousnier, *Fureurs paysans: Les Paysans dans les révoltes du XVIIe siècle* (Paris, 1967); Yves-Marie Bercé, *Fête et révolte* (Paris, 1976); and Charles Tilly, *The Contentious French* (Cambridge, Mass., 1986), esp. chaps. 1–5. For useful overviews of rebellions in early modern Europe, see Perez Zagorin, *Rebels and Rulers* (Cambridge, 1982), and Bercé, *Révoltes et révolutions dans l'Europe moderne, XVIe–XVIIIe siècles* (Paris, 1980).

20. See Jan DeVries, *European Urbanization* (Cambridge, Mass., 1984), and Richard Gascon, *Le Grand commerce et la vie urbaine au 16e siècle* (Paris, 1971).

21. See Anthony Levi, *French Moralists: The Theory of the Passions, 1585–1649* (Oxford, 1964); and Paul Bénichou, *Man and Ethics: Studies in French Classicism*, trans. Elizabeth Hughes (New York, 1971).

22. François Bluche, *La Vie quotidienne au temps de Louis XIV* (Paris, 1984), on Paris, p. 85.

23. Nannerl Keohane, *Philosophy and the State in France: The Renaissance to the Enlightenment* (Princeton, 1980), p. 122.

24. William Bouwsma, "Anxiety and the Formation of Early Modern Cul-

ture" in Barbara Malament, ed., *After the Reformation* (Philadelphia, 1980), pp. 237; Bouwsma, "Lawyers and Early Modern Culture," *American Historial Review* 78 (1973), 324.

25. Zachary Schiffman, *On the Threshold of Modernity* (Baltimore, 1992), pp. 6–11. See also Donald Kelley, *The Foundations of Modern Historical Scholarship* (New York, 1970).

26. Michel Baridon, "Science and Literary Criticism," in *Cambridge History of Literary Criticism* (Cambridge, 1991), pp. 3–4. I thank the author for providing me with a copy of this article.

27. Michel Foucault, *The Order of Things: An Archaeology of the Human Sciences* (New York, 1973), pp. 54–55.

28. Ibid., pp. 52, 54–55. See also Stephen L. Collins, *From Divine Cosmos to Sovereign State: An Intellectual History of Consciousness and the Idea of Order in Renaissance England* (New York, 1989), pp. 6–7, 166.

29. Robert Muchembled, *Société et mentalités dans la France Moderne, XVIe–XVIIIe siècle* (Paris, 1990), p. 128.

30. Mary Douglas, *Purity and Danger: An Analysis of the Concepts of Pollution and Taboo* (London, 1985), pp. 4, 41.

31. For a fuller treatment, see James R. Farr, "The Pure and Disciplined Body: Hierarchy, Morality and Symbolism in France during the Catholic Reformation," *Journal of Interdisciplinary History* 21:3 (1991), 391–414. On the notion of polarity in general and "high" and "low" in particular, see Carlo Ginzburg, "High and Low: The Theme of Forbidden Knowledge in the Sixteenth and Seventeenth Centuries," *Past and Present* (1976), 28–41.

32. See Ioan Couliano, "A Corpus for the Body," *Journal of Modern History* 63 (March 1991), 62.

33. E. Huguet, *Dictionnaire de la langue française du seizième siècle*, 7 vols. (Paris, 1925–1966), *passim*.

34. Antoine Furetière, *Dictionnaire universel* (The Hague, 1690; Paris, 1978), *passion*.

35. Nannerl Keohane, *Philosophy and the State in France* (Princeton, 1980), p. 151.

36. See, for example, Madame de Villedieu, *Les Désordres de l'amour* (Washington, D.C., 1982); Villedieu was a contemporary of La Fayette.

37. Madame de La Fayette, *The Princess de Cleves*, trans. Walter J. Cobb (New York, 1989), p. 39.

38. Ibid., pp. 160, 156.

39. Jacques-Paul Migne, ed., *Collection intégrale et universelle des orateurs sacrés du premier ordre* (Paris, 1845–), 36:1143.

40. Ibid, 10:240–42.

41. Jean Ehrard, *L'Idée de nature en France dans la première moitié du XVIIIe siècle* (Paris, 1963), 1:375–76.

42. See J. H. M. Salmon, *Renaissance and Revolt: Essays in the Intellectual and Social History of Early Modern France* (Cambridge, 1987), pp. 13, 27; Keohane, *Philosophy*, p. 131; Gerhard Oestreich, *Neostoicism and the Early Modern State*, trans. David McLintock (Cambridge, 1982).

43. Oestreich, *Neostoicism*, p. 7.

44. Ibid., pp. 21, 138, 185, 183, 153, 255.

45. Ehrard, *L'Idée de nature*, p. 335.

46. Robert Muchembled, *L'Invention de l'homme moderne* (Paris, 1988),

pp. 203, 156, 383, 11. See also Denis Crouzet, *Les Guerriers de dieu* (Seyssel, 1990).

47. See, for example, the immensely popular books by Nicolas Faret, *L'Honneste homme, ou, l'art de plaire à la court* (Geneva, 1970, reprint of 1636 ed.), and Antoine de Courtin, *The Rules of Civility* (London, 1703). On civility manuals and the importance of the idea of civility, see Roger Chartier, "From Text to Manners, A Concept and Its Books: 'Civilité' between Aristocratic Distinction and Popular Appropriation," in idem, *The Cultural Uses of Print*, trans. Lydia G. Cochrane (Princeton, 1987), pp. 71–109; Norbert Elias, *The Civilizing Process* (New York, 1978, 1982). For medieval contrast, see Jonathan Nicholls, *The Matter of Courtesy: Medieval Courtesy Books and the Gawain-Poet* (Woodbridge, 1985). The relationship between cleanliness and civility is already in evidence in Desiderius Erasmus, trans. A. Bonneau, *La Civilité puérile et honnête*.

48. Charles de Saint-Evremond, "Observations sur la maxime," *Oeuvres en prose* (Paris, 1962–69), 2:149.

49. Douglas, *Purity and Danger*, p. 41.

50. Bluche, *La Vie quotidienne*, p. 44.

51. See Norbert Elias, *The Court Society*, trans. Edmund Jephcott (New York, 1978).

52. Marc Fumarolli, *L'Age de l'éloquence: Rhétorique et "res literaria" de la Renaissance au seuil de l'époque classique* (Geneva, 1980), associates the court with Jesuitical theology, a cult of luxury, and the *gloire* of the king, and the parlements, in sharp distinction, with Augustinian, even Jansenist theology, austerity, and self-denial. Thus, he argues, the parlementaire critique of royal absolutism extended to court society. Certainly some parlementaires fit Fumarolli's scheme, but his categories are too oppositional. *Robins* were steeped in a hierarchical world that they had no interest in changing; to this end they, no less than court aristocrats embraced the status consciousness of court society and the concomitant ceremonial display. David A. Bell, "The 'Public Sphere' and the World of the Law in Eighteenth-Century France," *French Historical Studies* 17:4 (Fall 1992), similarly suggests that Fumarolli's dichotomy does not accurately apply to the *robe* experience of eighteenth-century France.

53. Quoted in Bluche, *La Vie quotidienne*, p. 196.

54. *Roti-Cochon, ou méthode très-facile pour bien apprendre les enfans à lire* . . . (Dijon, n.d.), and *Civilité puérile et morale, pour instruire les enfans à se bien comporter* . . . (Dijon, n.d.).

55. *Civilité puérile*, pp. 6–8.

56. See Michael Moriarty, *Taste and Ideology in Seventeenth Century France* (Cambridge, 1988), p. 140. There is no consensus among historians about the extent of the unity among the privileged; specifically at issue is whether a robe-sword dichotomy split their ranks. For various perspectives on this issue, see Donna Bohanon, "The Sword as the Robe in Seventeenth-Century Provence and Brittany," in Mack P. Holt, ed., *Society and Institutions in Early Modern France* (Athens, Ga., 1991), pp. 51–62; Denis Crouzet, *Les Guerriers de Dieu: La Violence au temps des troubles de religion, vers 1525–vers 1610* (Seyssel, 1990); Daniel Dessert, *Argent, pouvoir, et société au Grand Siècle* (Paris, 1984); Jonathan Dewald, *The Formation of a Provincial Nobility: The Magistrates of the Parlement of Rouen, 1499–1610* (Princeton, 1980); Robert J. Harding, *The Anatomy of a Power Elite: Provincial Governors in Early Modern France* (New Haven, 1978); Arlette Jouanna, *Le Devoir de révolte: La Noblesse française et la gestation de l'état moderne*,

1559–1661 (Paris, 1989); Ellery Schalk, *From Valor to Pedigree* (Princeton, 1986), pp. 77, 86, 138, 152; and James B. Wood, *The Nobility of the Election of Bayeux, 1463–1666: Continuity through Change* (Princeton, 1980).

57. Muchembled, *Invention*, pp. 11, 338.

58. Stephen Greenblatt, "Fiction and Friction," in *Reconstructing Individualism: Autonomy, Individuality, and the Self in Western Thought*, ed. Thomas Heller, Morton Sosna, and David Wellbery (Stanford, 1986), p. 35.

59. Joan W. Scott, "Gender: A Useful Category of Historical Analysis," *American Historical Review* 91 (1986), 1069, 1070, 1073.

60. Natalie Z. Davis, "Boundaries and the Sense of Self in Sixteenth-Century France," in *Reconstructing Individualism*, p. 55, and idem, "Women on Top," in idem, *Society and Culture in Early Modern France* (Stanford, 1975), pp. 124–51. On the juridical incapacity of women, see Paul Ourliac, *Histoire du droit privé français de l'an mil au Code Civil* (Paris, 1985), p. 271.

61. Bryan S. Turner, *The Body and Society: Explorations in Social Theory* (Oxford, 1984), pp. 12–13.

62. Carolyn Lougee, *Le Paradis des femmes: Women, Salons, and Social Stratification in Seventeenth-Century France* (Princeton, 1976), p. 92.

63. Sarah Hanley, "Family and State in Early Modern France: The Marriage Pact," in Marilyn J. Boxer and Jean H. Quataert, eds., *Connecting Spheres: Women in the Western World, 1500 to the Present* (New York, 1987), p. 54.

64. Ourliac, *Histoire*, p. 285.

65. Niklaus Luhmann, *Love as Passion: The Codification of Intimacy* (Cambridge, Mass., 1986), p. 94.

66. Ibid., pp. 94–95. Luhmann asserts that the author's intention was equivocal; he was suggesting that love and reason each had defensible (however incompatible) positions. (Love voiced the argument of the future when love will penetrate marriage as "family ties and solidarity are no longer systematically needed as a pillar of the social system.") One need not accept Luhmann's evolutionary thesis to conclude, however, that when read within the context of most moralistic prescriptive literature of the time, the tract must have been unequivocal to most readers; to them the position of reason had to seem the proper one and that of love irrational and downright dangerous.

67. Lougee, *Paradis*, pp. 6, 52; Joan B. Landes, *Women and the Public Sphere in the Age of the French Revolution* (Ithaca, N.Y., 1988), chap. 1; and Ian MacLean, *Woman Triumphant: Feminism in French Literature, 1610–1652* (Oxford, 1977), p. 142. Indeed, there is also a growing literature demonstrating that women lower on the social scale also expanded their public roles, especially during the sixteenth century. See, for example, Natalie Z. Davis, "Women in the Crafts in Sixteenth-Century Lyon," in Barbara B. Hanawalt, ed., *Women and Work in Preindustrial Europe* (Bloomington, Ind., 1986), pp. 167–97, Judith C. Brown, "Women's Place Was in the Home: Women's Work in Renaissance Tuscany," in Margaret W. Ferguson et al., eds., *Rewriting the Renaissance: The Discourses of Sexual Difference in Early Modern Europe* (Chicago, 1986), pp. 206–24; Merry E. Wiesner, *Working Women in Renaissance Germany* (New Brunswick, N.J., 1986); and James B. Collins, "The Economic Role of Women in Seventeenth-Century France," *French Historical Studies* 16:2 (Fall 1989), 436–70.

68. Lougee, *Paradis*, p. 45.

69. Landes, *Women and the Public Sphere*, p. 1.

70. MacLean, *Woman Triumphant*, p. 152.

71. See William Beik, *Absolutism and Society in Seventeenth-Century France: State Power and Provincial Aristocracy in Languedoc* (Cambridge, 1985), introduction. Jonathan Powis, "Order, Religion, and the Magistrates of a Provincial Parlement in Sixteenth-Century France," *Archiv fur reformationsgeschichte* 71 (1980), 192, has demonstrated that Bordeaux's parlementaires were no "isolated bureaucratic caste" but rather were linked with ecclesiastical institutions of the province as well as with landowning nobility of the region. See also Powis, "Officiers and Gentilhommes: A Parlementaire Class in Sixteenth-Century Bordeaux?" in *Bordeaux et les Iles Britanniques* (Bordeaux, 1973), pp. 27–36; and M. L. Bush, ed., *Social Orders and Social Classes in Europe since 1500: Studies in Social Stratification* (London, 1992).

72. Roupnel, *La Ville et la campagne*, pp. 168–69, 174, 176. On the emergence of a gentry in sixteenth-century France, including Burgundy, see George Huppert, *Les Bourgeois Gentilhommes* (Urbana, Ill., 1977).

73. Roupnel, *La Ville et la campagne*, p. 235; Henri Drouot, *Mayenne et la Bourgogne: Etude sur la Ligue (1587–1596)* (Dijon, 1937), 1:45. On the accelerated transfer of land in the late sixteenth century, see also Pierre de Saint-Jacob, "Mutations économiques et sociales à la fin du XVIe siècle," *Etudes rurales* 1 (1961), 34–49.

74. Roupnel, *La Ville et la campagne*, pp. 209, 211. Archives départementales de la Côte-d'Or, Notaires, hold thousands of *acquets* and *ventes* contracts that record these transactions during this period.

75. Roupnel, *La Ville et la campagne*, pp. 223–24.

76. On the importance of family interest to officialdom, see Ralph E. Giesey, "State-Building in Early Modern France: The Role of Royal Officialdom," *Journal of Modern History* 55 (June 1983), 191–207.

77. Kristin B. Neuschel, *Word of Honor: Interpreting Noble Culture in Sixteenth-Century France* (Ithaca, N.Y., 1989), p. 158. See also Sharon Kettering, "Patronage in Early Modern France," *French Historical Studies* 17:4 (Fall 1992).

78. Roupnel, *La Ville et la campagne*, p. 217. Powis, "Order, Religion, and the Magistrates," 190–91, explores similar links between orthodox religious institutions and parlementaire families in the Bordelais.

79. Roupnel, *La Ville et la campagne*, pp. 66, 213, 215.

80. Ibid., pp. xix, 242, 244.

81. On Languedoc, see Emmanuel Le Roy Ladurie, *The Peasants of Languedoc*, trans. John Day (Urbana, Ill., 1974).

82. Ibid., p. 300.

83. Georges Picot, *Histoire des états généraux* (Paris, 1872), 4:30.

84. On the sixteenth century, see Drouot, *Mayenne*, 1:47, n.1; seventeenth century, Roupnel, *La Ville et la campagne*, p. 188. The number of officials, both high and low, recorded on the tax rolls in Dijon expanded dramatically between 1464 and 1750. Despite appearing on these rolls many of these officials paid no taxes, and most were venal officeholders. In 1464, 33 appeared on the rolls; in 1556, 105 did; in 1643, 250; and in 1750, 313. See James R. Farr, "Consumers, Commerce, and the Craftsmen of Dijon: The Changing Social and Economic Structure of a Provincial Capital, 1450–1750," in Philip Benedict, ed., *Cities and Social Change in Early Modern France* (London, 1989), pp. 136, 138–39.

85. Antoine Joly de Blasy, *Souvenirs d'un Président au Grand Conseil sous Louis XIV*, ed. Ernest Petit (Paris and Dijon, 1899), p. 76.

86. Drouot, *Mayenne*, 1:49.

87. On how this was accomplished by officialdom, see the important article by Ralph E. Giesey, "Rules of Inheritance and Strategies of Mobility in Prerevolutionary France," *American Historical Review* 82 (1977), 271–89.

88. Ibid., p. 286.

89. La Cuisine, *Parlement*, 1:92.

90. Marcel Bouchard, *De l'Humanisme à l'Encyclopédie: L'Esprit public en Bourgogne sous l'Ancien Régime* (Paris, 1930), pp. 430, 495. See also Robert Mandrou, *From Humanism to Science, 1480–1700*, trans. Brian Pearce (Harmondsworth, 1978).

91. See Jeffrey K. Sawyer, "Judicial Corruption and Legal Reform in Early Seventeenth-Century France," *Law and History Review* 6:1 (1988), 95–117. I thank Professor Sawyer for providing me with an offprint of this article.

92. La Cuisine, *Parlement*, 3:80–85.

93. Beik, *Absolutism*, pp 46–47, 77.

94. See, for example, "L'Action," given in 1672, La Cuisine, *Parlement*, 1:231–43; "L'Union des vertus dans les devoirs," 1689, ibid., 1:275–78; and, in harangues to the provincial estates, "L'Autorité et l'obéissance," in 1679, ibid., 1:278–82; and "Le Génie du prince," in 1691, ibid., 1:297–99.

95. Albert N. Hamscher, *The Parlement of Paris after the Fronde, 1653–1673* (Pittsburgh, 1976), p. xxi.; Beik, *Absolutism*, p. 97.

96. Beik, *Absolutism*, pp. 31, 176.

97. See James R. Farr, "King, Parlement, and the Nature of Sovereignty in Early Modern Burgundy" (forthcoming).

98. See Donald R. Kelley, *The Human Measure: Social Thought in the Legal Tradition* (Cambridge, Mass., 1990); p. 217; and John A. Carey, *Judicial Reform in France before the Revolution of 1789* (Cambridge, Mass., 1981), chap. 1.

99. See Jean Bart, "Coutume et droit romain dans la doctrine bourguignonne du XVIIIe siècle," *Mémoires de la société pour l'histoire du droit et des institutions des anciens pays bourguignons, comtois et romands* 28 (1967), 145.

Chapter 2

1. Cited by A. Lynn Martin, *The Jesuit Mind: The Mentality of an Elite in Early Modern France* (Ithaca, N.Y., 1988), p. 229. See Wolfgang Reinhard, "Gegenreformation als Modernisierung?" *Archiv für Reformationsgeschichte* 68 (1977): 226–52.

2. Jean-Jacques Duguet, *Conduite d'une dame chrétienne pour vivre saintement dans le monde* (Paris, 1724), pp. 316–17. This text, according to Robin Briggs, *Communities of Belief: Cultural and Social Tension in Early Modern France* (Oxford, 1989), p. 238, was probably written around 1700.

3. John Bossy, *Christianity in the West, 1400–1700* (Oxford, 1985), esp. chap. 7; Robin Briggs, "Idées and Mentalités: The Case of the Catholic Reform Movement in France," *History of European Ideas* 7:1 (1986), 11; Thomas N. Tentler, *Sin and Confession on the Eve of the Reformation* (Princeton, 1977), p. 52. See also Ioan Couliano, "A Corpus for the Body," *Journal of Modern History* 63 (March 1991), 63.

4. Robin Briggs, "Idées and Mentalités, 12, 13.

5. See Alexander Sedgwick, *Jansenism in Seventeenth-Century France: Voices from the Wilderness* (Charlottesville, 1977), esp. chap. 8.

6. Martin, *Jesuit Mind*, pp. 28, 231.

7. Bossy, *Christianity in the West*, chap. 8. See also Philip Hoffman, *Church and Community in the Diocese of Lyon, 1500–1789* (New Haven, 1984); Kathryn Norberg, *Rich and Poor in Grenoble, 1600–1814* (Berkeley, 1985); Robert Sauzet, "Le Milieu dévot tourangeau et les débuts de la réforme catholique," *Revue d'histoire de l'église de France* (1989), 159–66; Keith Luria, *Territories of Grace: Cultural Change in the Seventeenth-Century Diocese of Grenoble* (Berkeley, 1990), p. 45; and Emanuel Chill, "Religion and Mendicity in Seventeenth-Century France," *International Review of Social History* 7:3 (1962), 400–25.

8. See Robert Muchembled, *Société et mentalités dans la France Moderne, XVIe–XVIIIe siècle* (Paris, 1990), pp. 130–33.

9. François Serpillon, *Code criminelle ou commentaire de l'ordonnance de 1670* (Lyon, 1767).

10. Cited by William Farr Church, *Richelieu and Reason of State* (Princeton, 1972), p. 17; Nicolas Delamare, *Traité de la police* (Paris, 1722).

11. Jean Bégat, *Remonstrances faictes au roy de France* (Anvers, 1564), esp. 6r. See also John Bossy, "Leagues and Associations in Sixteenth-Century French Catholicism," *Studies in Church History* 23 (1986), 171–89.

12. Denis Crouzet, "La Ligue (1588–1589); un enracinement panique?" in *La Guerra del sale*, ed. Giorgio Lombardi (Milan, 1986), p. 62. I thank the author for generously providing me with a copy of this article.

13. Joseph Garnier, ed., *Lettres d'Etienne Bernard, maire de Dijon, sur l'assemblée des Etats Généraux de la Ligue en 1593* (Paris, 1860), p. 12, letter dated 31 March 1593, from Paris.

14. Jean Orcibal, "Richelieu, homme d'église, homme d'état," *Revue d'histoire de l'église de France* 34 (1948), 100. See also Church, *Richelieu and Reason of State*.

15. See Peter Bayley, *French Pulpit Oratory, 1598–1650* (Cambridge, 1980).

16. Jacques-Paul Migne, ed., *Collection intégrale et universelle des orateurs sacré du premier ordre* (Paris, 1845–), 36:11; 37:218.

17. Ibid., 17:685.

18. Ibid., 40:1282.

19. Ibid., 49:1412.

20. Ibid., 9:636.

21. Ibid., 42:17–19, 49, 52.

22. Ibid., 24:1092–93.

23. Heinz Schilling, "'History of Crime' or 'History of Sin'? Some Reflections on the Social History of Early Modern Church Discipline," in E. I. Kouri and Tom Scott, eds., *Politics and Society in Reformation Europe* (New York, 1987), pp. 289–90, 303.

24. Ibid., pp. 303, 304. See also Bruce Lenman and Geoffrey Parker, "The State, the Community, and Criminal Law in Early Modern Europe," in V. A. C. Gatrell, Bruce Lenman, and Geoffrey Parker, eds., *Crime and the Law: The Social History of Crime in Western Europe since 1500* (London, 1980).

25. Bossy, *Christianity in the West*, p. 135.

26. Jean-François Senault, *L'Homme criminel* (Paris, 1644).

27. Jean Delumeau, *Sin and Fear: The Emergence of a Western Guilt Culture, 13th–18th Centuries*, trans. Eric Nicholson (New York, 1990), p. 288.

28. John Bossy, "The Social History of Confession in the Age of the Reformation," *Transactions of the Royal Historical Society* 5th ser., 25 (1975), 22, points out that Scholastic theology interiorized the notions of sin and repentance and

the "change was institutionalized with the universal imposition of private confession by the Lateran Council of 1215." Bossy, *Christianity in the West*, pp. 143, 57. On the importance of charity as a theological virtue in the sixteenth century, see A. N. Galpern, *The Religions of the People in Sixteenth-Century Champagne* (Cambridge, Mass., 1976).

29. Bossy, *Christianity in the West*, pp. 146, 144–45, 171.

30. Ibid., pp. 155, 161.

31. Migne, *Collection*, 14:626.

32. The word *scandale*, in fact, carried meanings of violation of charity and civil peace. *Scandale* harmed the innocence of others and so, according to preachers like Bourdaloue and Houdry (see ibid., 14:80 and 36:188, respectively), was an attack on Christian charity since it offended God and neighbor; it also meant violation of public tranquility and was one criterion the crown used to justify bringing perpetrators of "public scandal" before secular courts.

33. Mary Douglas, *Purity and Danger: An Analysis of the Concepts of Pollution and Taboo*, (London, 1985), pp. 4, 41.

34. See Muchembled, *Société et mentalités*, p. 166.

35. H. Outram Evennett, *The Spirit of the Counter-Reformation* (Cambridge, 1968), pp. 31, 36.

36. Martin, *Jesuit Mind*, p. 79.

37. Bossy, *Christianity in the West*, p. 126.

38. Ibid., p. 127. Tentler, *Sin and Confession*, has shown that by the late Middle Ages, sacramental confession and penance functioned as means of discipline and social control; not until the second half of the sixteenth century would problems of the culpability of conscience dominate moral and pastoral theology. See also Delumeau, *Sin and Fear*, chap. 17.

39. See, for example, Migne, *Collection*, 39:461, "De la pureté intérieure" by the Dijonnais Edme Bourrée; 14:566, "Sur l'impureté," by Bourdaloue; and 28:713, "Sur l'impureté" by François de Salignac de La Mothe-Fénelon. See also Muchembled, *Société et mentalités*, p. 160.

40. John Bossy, "Postcript," in Evennett, *Spirit*, p. 140.

41. See Robert Muchembled, *L'Invention de l'homme moderne: Sensibilités, moeurs et comportements collectifs sous l'Ancien Regime* (Paris, 1988), pp. 288, 357, 367.

42. Louis XIV planned but never established *un grand conseil de modes* which would have procureurs, auditeurs, correcteurs, and judges who would have been charged with enforcing rules about dress (length of sleeves, for example, or quality of materials) to insure that they were commensurate with the approprtiate social station of the wearer. See Bluche, *La Vie quotidienne au temps de Louis XIV* (Paris, 1985), p. 72. On sumptuary legislation, see Louise Godard de Donville, *Signification de la mode sous Louis XIII* (Aix-en-Provence, 1978).

43. Roger Chartier, "From Texts to Manners, a Concept and its Books," in idem, *The Cultural uses of Print*, trans. Lydia Cochrane (Princeton, 1988), p. 80.

44. Pierre Broë, *Des Bonnes moeurs et honnestes contenances* (Lyon, 1555), p. 16.

45. Antoine de Balinghem, *La Vraye point d'honneur . . .* (Saint Omer, 1618), chap. 10, p. 491.

46. Antoine de Nervèze, "La Guide des courtisans," in idem, *Les Oeuvres morales* (Paris, 1610), 66r.–67v.

47. Melchior de Marmet de Valcroissant, *Maximes pour vivre heureusement dans le monde et pour former l'honneste homme* (Paris, 1662), and Abbé Jean Pic, *Discours sur la bienséance . . .* (Paris, 1688).

48. Antoine de Courtin, *The Rules of Civility* (London, 1703), 1, 2, 5. Courtin's book went through fifteen editions between 1671 and 1730.

49. Saint Jean-Baptiste de La Salle, *Les Règles de la bienséance et de la civilité Chrétienne* (Rouen, 1760; orig. ed. 1703), pp. ivr., iiir., 5, 7.

50. Gaston Bernoville, *Une Fondatrice d'ordre: Anne de Xainctonge* (Paris, 1956), pp. 171, 176–77, 227.

51. Cited by Nannerl Keohane, *Philosophy and the State in France: The Renaissance to the Enlightenment* (Princeton, 1980), p. 287.

52. Migne, *Collection*, 47:502. See also ibid., 21:1209. (Nicolas La Pesse, a Jesuit from Lyon and one of the most distinguished preachers of the Louis XIV era, saw his sermons published in 1708. He invoked this theme often. See, for example, ibid., 21:889.)

53. Delumeau, *Sin and Fear*, chaps. 1, 8 passim. See also Jean-Louis Flandrin, *Le Sexe et l'occident: Evolution des attitudes et des comportements* (Paris, 1981), esp. pt. II; Jacques Solé, *L'Amour en occident à l'époque moderne* (Paris, 1976), esp. chap. 3. In a book review of *Sin and Fear*, *Journal of Modern History* 26:2 (Winter 1992), 435–38, Keith Luria has rightly criticized Delumeau for equating the clerical mind set he describes with a *mentalité* of a civilization. Rather than identify the "contempt for the world" as part of a prescriptive attempt to reorder the world, Delumeau very questionably assumes that "what the clergy preached" was "what the people believed" (p. 437).

54. Jacques de Thésut-Niquevard, abbé, *Oraison funèbre de messire Jean de Maupeou* (Chalon-sur-Saône, 1677), pp. 17–18.

55. Migne, *Collection*, 39:504; Bourrée (1652–1722) was born and died in Dijon but also preached in Chalon-sur-Saône and Langres. He published over 40 volumes of sermons, with most of them appearing in the first decade of the eighteenth century.

56. Henri-Marie Boudon, *Oeuvres complètes* (Paris, 1856), 2:230–31.

57. Tentler, *Sin and Confession*, pp. 28, 220, xix; see also Hervé Martin, "Confession et contrôle social à la fin du Moyen Age," in *Pratiques de la confession des pères du désert à Vatican II* (Paris, 1983), p. 125, and Delumeau, *Sin and Fear*, chap. 6.

58. Marcel Bernos, "Les Manuels de confession: Peuvent-ils servir à l'histoire des mentalités?" in *Histoire sociale, sensibilités collectives, et mentalités: Melanges Robert Mandrou* (Paris, 1985), p. 94. See Robert Sauzet, "Dieu et mammon: Les Réformes et la richesse," *History of European Ideas* 9:4 (1988), 443–50, addressing the general issue of the perceived needed reform of the entire beneficial system.

59. Tentler, *Sin and Confession*, pp. 52, 165.

60. Nicolas Lemaître, "Confession privé et confession publique dans les paroisses du XVIe siècle," *Revue d'histoire de l'église de France* 69 (July–December 1983), 196.

61. Juan Polanco, *Directoire des confesseurs* (Anvers, 1556), reprinted in Pierre Milhard, *La Vraye guide des curez . . .* (Lyon, 1604), pp. 628–29.

62. Saint François de Sales, "Advertissement aux confesseurs," in *Les Oeuvres du bienheureux François de Sales* (Paris, 1647), p. 883.

63. Antoine Blanchard, *Essay d'exhortation pour les états différents . . . on y a*

joint un Examen général sur tous les commandements et sur les péchés de plusieurs états (Paris, 1713), p. 234.

64. See, for example, *Instructions pour les confesseurs du diocèse de Chalon-sur-Saône tirée du avis de St Charles* (Lyon, 1682). This text notes (pp. ii–iii) that St. Charles's text, as well as Saint François de Sales's "Avertissement," were assigned at an earlier synod to the curés of the diocese.

65. Marcel Bernos, "Saint Charles Borromée et ses 'Instructions aux confesseurs': Une Lecture rigoriste par le clergé français (XVIe–XIXe siècle)," in *Pratiques de la confession*, pp. 185, 189–90.

66. Saint Charles Borromeo, *Instructions aux confesseurs* (Lyon, 1672), p. 20.

67. See Anthony Levi, *French Moralists: The Theory of the Passions, 1585 to 1649* (Oxford, 1964).

68. See, for example, Pierre de La Primaudaye, *Academie françoise, en laquelle il est traitté de l'institution des moeurs . . .* (Paris, 1580) (subsequent references will be to the English translation of 1586); Jacques Olivier, *L'Alphabet de l'imperfection et malice des femmes* (Rouen, 1634); Pierre Juvernay, *Discours particulier contre les femmes debraillées de ce temps* (Geneva, 1867; orig. pub. Paris, 1637) and *Le Foudre foudroyant et ravageant contre les péchés mortels* (Paris, 1635); Marie Madeleine Pioche de La Vergne, Madame de La Fayette, *Histoire de la princesse de Montpensier. Histoire de la Comtesse de Tende* (Geneva, 1979); Chevalier de Méré, *Oeuvres complètes* (Paris, 1930); Jacques Boileau, *De l'abus des nuditez de gorge* (Paris, 1675); Jacques Esprit, *Le Fausseté des vertus humaines* (Paris, 1678); Timothée Philalethe, *De la modestie des femmes et des filles chrétiennes dans leurs habits* (Lyon, 1686); and Jean Du Pradel, *Traité contre le luxe des hommes et des femmes* (Paris, 1705). p. 234.

69. Louise Horowitz, *Love and Language: A Study of the Classical French Moralist Writers* (Columbus, Ohio, 1977), pp. 4–5.

70. La Primaudaye, *The French Academy* (London, 1586), pp. 238–39.

71. Ibid., pp. 234, 239.

72. Philalethe, *De la modestie des femmes*, p. 75; Horowitz, *Love and Language*, p. 118.

73. Du Pradel, *Traité*, pp. 7, 8, 5.

74. Peter Stallybrass and Alton White, *The Politics and Poetics of Transgression* (Ithaca, N.Y., 1982), p. 192. Georges Vigarello, *Le Corps redressé: Histoire d'un pouvoir pédagogique* (Paris, 1978), p. 52, notes that during the seventeenth and eighteenth centuries, the body was like a picture and how it was viewed was of paramount importance. On the importance of the body as a metaphor for proper ordering of society, see Ted Polhemus, "Social Bodies," in Jonathan Benthall and Ted Polhemus, eds., *The Body as a Medium of Expression* (New York, 1975), pp. 11–35; and Natalie Z. Davis, "The Sacred and the Body Social in Sixteenth-Century Lyon," *Past and Present* 90 (1980), 40–70.

75. See Natalie Z. Davis, "Women on Top," in *Society and Culture in Early Modern France* (Stanford, 1975); Sarah Hanley, "Engendering the State: Family Formation and State Building in Early Modern France," *French Historical Studies* 16:1 (Spring 1989). Hanley, p. 15, discusses the formation of a "Family-State compact [which] outlined a family model of socioeconomic authority under patriarchal hegemony." This is not to suggest that there was no voice extolling the virtues of woman, but, as Ian MacLean, *Woman Triumphant: Feminism in French Literature, 1610–1652* (Oxford, 1977), p. viii, suggests, "feminist" works tended

to advocate "some relaxation of the marital and social oppression of women . . . [but] no far-reaching reforms." See also Marc Angenot, *Les Champions des femmes: Examen du discours sur la supériorité des femmes, 1400–1800* (Montreal, 1977).

76. In Migne's collection of sermons of clergymen preaching before the mid-eighteenth century, impurity was the most popular topic relating to sexual morality.

77. Louis Habert, *Pratique du sacrement de pénitence* (Rouen, 1711), pp. 291–92. In contrast, neither cleric Olivier Maillard, *La Confession* (Bourges, n.d. [c. 1495]) nor layman Jean Bouchet, *Les Triumphes de la noble et amoureuse dame et l'art de honnestement aimer* (Paris, 1539), pp. xciii–cxvii v, employed the vocabulary of filth in their discussions of transgressions of the Sixth Commandment.

78. *La Courtisane déchiffrée* (Paris, [1637]), p. 96.

79. Philalethe, *De la modestie des femmes*, pp. 53–54, 63, 68, 74.

80. Juvernay, *Discours*, p. 41.

81. Borromeo, *Instructions*, pp. 20–21.

82. Juvernay, *Discours*, p. 41.

83. Jean de Lingendes, Bishop of Mâcon, *Ordonnances synodales . . .* (Mâcon, 1659), p. 59. See also Gaspard Dinet, Bishop of Mâcon, *Ordonnances générales . . .* (Lyon, 1602), p. 60.

84. In Migne's collection of sermons of clergymen preaching before the mid-eighteenth century, *contre le luxe* was the second most popular topic relating to sexual morality.

85. Ibid., 17:350, 354.

86. Ibid., 39:69.

87. Ibid., 37:583, 584 ("Sur le luxe et l'immodestie des habits").

88. Mathieu Beuvelet, *Instructions sur le manuel . . .* (Paris, 1659), 1:91–93.

89. Pierre Boiastuau, *Le Théâtre du monde, où il est faict un ample discours des misères humaines* (Antwerp, 1580), p. 51.

90. Beuvelet, *Instructions*, 1:93.

91. ADSL, G922 fol. 116, 1698.

92. See, for another example, *Instructions pour les confesseurs du diocèse de Chalon-sur-Saône* (Lyon, 1682).

93. On women influenced by Salesian spirituality, see M.-C. Gueudre, "La Femme et la vie spirituelle," *XVIIe siècle* 62–63 (1964), 47–77.

94. René Bady, "François DeSales, maître d'honnêteté," *XVIIe siècle* 78 (1968), 7.

95. Antoine Godeau, *Les Tableaux de la pénitence* (Paris, 1656), 2d ed., preface.

96. Boileau, *De l'abus*, pp. 41–43.

97. Horowitz, *Love and Language*, p. 121.

98. Du Pradel, *Traité*, p. 278. Houdry, in a sermon "On modesty," says essentially the same thing; Migne, *Collection*, 37:1076. Indeed, modesty in women was a common theme in sermon literature.

99. Davis, "Women on Top," pp. 124, 126. Confessors' manuals like that by Antoine Blanchard, *Essay d'exortation pour les états différents . . .* (Paris, 1713), p. 223, reinforced this gender hierarchy in teachings on the Fourth Commandment. On the concept of patriarchy, see Margaret W. Ferguson et al., eds., *Rewriting the Renaissance: The Discourses of Sexual Difference in Early Modern Europe*

(Chicago, 1986); and Sheila Rowbotham, "The Trouble with 'Patriarchy,'" and Sally Alexander and Barbara Taylor, "In Defence of 'Patriarchy,'" both in Raphael Samuel, ed., *People's History and Socialist Theory* (London, 1981), pp. 364–69, 370–73.

100. Davis, "Women on Top," p. 125

101. Peter Stallybrass, "Patriarchal Territories: The Body Enclosed," in Ferguson et al., eds., *Rewriting the Renaissance*, p. 127.

102. Cited by Carolyn Lougee, *Le Paradis des Femmes: Women, Salons, and Social Stratification in Seventeenth-Century France* (Princeton, 1976), p. 85.

103. Quoted in Bernoville, *Anne de Xainctonge*, pp. 237–38.

104. Lougee, *Le Paradis des Femmes*, p. 92

105. Madame de La Fayette, *Histoire de la Princesse de Montpensier. Histoire de la Comtesse de Tende*. See Horowitz, *Love and Language*, p. 57.

106. Boileau, *De l'abus des nuditez*, pp. 135–36, 141–42.

107. Godeau, *Les Tableaux*, p. 363.

108. La Primaudaye, *French Academy*, p. 240.

109. Olivier, *L'Alphabet de l'imperfection*, p. 262. He cites (p. 263) Saint Augustine: "Shameless and lascivious clothes are the marks, signs, and means of an adulterous heart, and a soul entirely lascivious and lewd." In a sermon on *volupté*, (unrestrained passion), Massillon presents nearly the same argument: The betrayal of patrimonies and decadence of families can be traced to *volupté* by both men and women. Migne, *Collection*, 43:1111–12.

110. Not surprisingly, the topic of female chastity was common in sermons; see, for example, Migne, *Collection*, vol. 9 (Nicolas de La Volipière), 31 (Jerome of Paris), and 39 (Bourrée).

111. Boileau, *De l'abus des nuditez*, p. 77. In his manual for confessors, *Pratique*, p. 301, Habert specifically instructed confessors how to confess a woman concerning her *sein découvert*, associating it with a violation of the sixth commandment.

112. Jean-François Soulet, *Traditions et réformes religieuses dans les Pyrénées Centrales au XVIIe siècle* (Pau, 1974), p. 240. According to Maurice Rey, ed., *Histoire des diocèses de Besançon et de Saint-Claude* (Paris, 1977), p. 130, more than 250 missions were held in the dioceses of Besançon and Saint Claude in eastern France between 1682 and 1790.

113. Antoine Beaugendre, *La Vie de Messire Bénigne Joly* (Paris, 1854; orig. ed. 1700), p. 74; François Bluche, *La Vie quotidienne au temps de Louis XIV* (Paris, 1985), p. 189.

114. Soulet, *Traditions*, p. 249.

115. G. Chalumeau, "Saint Vincent de Paul et les missions en France," *XVIIe siècle* 40 (1958), 322, 325.

116. Soulet, *Traditions*, p. 246. See also Bernard Dompnier, "Missions et confession au XVIIe siècle," in *Pratiques de la confession*, pp. 201, 205.

117. Raoul de Sceaux, "Le Père Honoré de Cannes, capucin missionnaire," *XVIIe siècle* 40 (1958), 367.

118. Robin Briggs, *Early Modern France, 1560–1715* (Oxford, 1977), p. 167.

119. The crown often used nominations to bishoprics as patronage to noble families (before 1630, to the great nobility, after that, to the nobility of the *robe*). Increasingly as the seventeenth century progressed, as Joseph Bergin has said, the "French episcopate moved from being a rather loosely related collection of men,

many of whom were . . . individually powerful because drawn from royal, princely or aristocratic families to being a far more self-conscious body of men of increasingly similar background. . . . Taken as individuals, bishops' power and authority might be past its prime and declining, but as a corporate group . . . their collective power was on the increase. Joseph Bergin, "The Making of the French Episcopate in the Age of Henri IV and Louis XIII" (paper presented at the Annual Meeting of the Western Society for French History, 22 October 1992, Orcas Island, Wash.). I thank Dr. Bergin for sharing his paper with me. See also Joseph Bergin, "Richelieu and His Bishops? Ministerial Power and Episcopal Patronage under Louis XIII," in Joseph Bergin and Laurence Brockliss, eds., *Richelieu and His Age* (Oxford, 1992), pp. 175–202.

120. François Isambert et al., eds., *Recueil générale des anciennes lois Françaises* (Paris, 1833), 20:243ff.

121. Henri Drouot, *Mayenne et la Bourgogne: Etude sur la Ligue* (1587–1596) (Dijon, 1937), 1:65.

122. Sébastien Zamet, *Statuts et ordonnances faittes en diverses assemblées synodales tenues par reverendissime père en Dieu Messire Sébastien évesque duc de Langres pair de France* (Langres, 1629), p. 28.

123. Ibid., p. 4.

124. Georges Viard, "Les Visites pastorales dans l'ancien diocèse de Langres: La Réglementation épiscopale et sa mise en oeuvre," *Revue d'histoire de l'église de France* 63 (July–December, 1977), 258.

125. Noel Prunel, *Sébastien Zamet: Evêque-duc de Langres* (Paris, 1912), pp. 96, 102–3.

126. Zamet, *Statuts*, pp. 57–58.

127. Noel Prunel, *Sébastien Zamet: Evêque-duc de Langres* (Paris, 1912), p. 125.

128. Ibid., p. 126.

129. Ibid., p. 135.

130. Ibid., p. 155. See also M. Thomas, *Sainte Chantal* (Paris, 1953).

131. Cited Prunel, *Zamet*, pp. 166, 169.

132. Ibid., p. 303.

133. Ibid., pp. 303, 304, 306.

134. Zamet's successor, Simiane de Gordes, pursued similar goals in the diocese of Langres. See Viard, "Les Visites pastorales," p. 258.

135. J.-Henri Pignot, *Gabriel de Roquette, un évêque reformateur sous Louis XIV* (Paris, 1876), 1:302, 303.

136. Ibid., 1:323.

137. Cited by ibid., 1:256.

138. Ibid., 1:269, 271.

139. Cited by ibid., 1:306.

140. Cited by ibid., 1:311.

141. Ibid., 1:363.

142. Ibid., 1:366.

143. Ibid., 1:363.

144. Noel Prunel, "Deux fondations de la Compagnie du Saint-Sacrement de Dijon: Le Refuge et le Seminaire, 1653–1660," *Revue d'histoire de l'église de France* 25 (1911), 16.

145. Ibid., pp. 5–7, 9, 13.

146. Ibid., pp. 9–10.

147. Beaugendre, *La Vie de Messire Bénigne Joly*, pp. 79–82.

Chapter 3

1. See Philip Hoffman, *Church and Community in the Diocese of Lyon, 1500–1789* (New Haven, 1984), p. 39, and Dominique Julia, "La Réforme posttridentine en France d'après les procès-verbaux de visites pastorales: Ordre et résistances," in *La Società religiosa nell'età moderna* (Naples, 1973), p. 382.

2. Hoffman, *Church and Community*, p. 123.

3. John Bossy, "The Mass as a Social Institution, 1200–1700," *Past and Present* 100 (1983), 58–59.

4. John Bossy, "The Counter Reformation and the People of Catholic Europe," *Past and Present* 47 (1970), 53.

5. On the relationship between the holy, the sacred, and the priest, see Peter Brown, "Society and the Supernatural: A Medieval Change," *Daedalus* 104:2 (1975), 133–49.

6. For the diocese of Autun, for example, see Thérèse-Jean Schmitt, *L'Organisation ecclésiastique et la pratique religieuse dans l'archdiaconé d'Autun de 1650 à 1750* (Autun, 1957), pp. 133–34.

7. For the diocese of Lyon, see Hoffman, *Church and Community*, p. 49. See also Andrew Barnes, "The Social Transformation of the French Parish Clergy, 1500–1800," in Barbara B. Diefendorf and Carla Hesse, eds., *Culture and Identity in Early Modern Europe, 1500–1800: Essays in Honor of Natalie Zemon Davis* (Ann Arbor, 1993).

8. Timothy Tackett, *Priest and Parish in Eighteenth-Century France* (Princeton, 1977), p. 151; Jean Quéniart, *Les Hommes, l'église, et Dieu dans la France du XVIIIe siècle* (Paris, 1978), p. 65.

9. John C. Olin, ed., "Reform Decrees of Trent, 1563," in idem, *Catholic Reform from Cardinal Ximenez to the Council of Trent, 1495–1563* (New York, 1990), p. 97.

10. See James R. Farr, "The Pure and Disciplined Body: Hierarchy, Morality, and Symbolism in France during the Catholic Reformation," *Journal of Interdisciplinary History* 21:3 (1991), 391–414.

11. Sébastien Zamet, *Statuts et ordonnances faittes en diverses assemblés synodales tenves per reverendissime père en Dievu Messire Sébastien évesque duc de Langres pair de France* (Langres, 1629), esp. pp. 28–29; François-Joseph de Grammont, *Statuta seu decreta synodalia Bisuntiae . . .* (Vesoul, 1707), passim.

12. Zamet, *Statuts*, pp. 9, 12, 13.

13. Jacques-Paul Migne, ed., *Collection intégrale et universelle des orateurs sacrés du premier ordre* (Paris, 1849–), 1:344.

14. Ibid., 36:188 (Houdry), 14:80 (Bourdaloue).

15. J.-Henri Pignot, *Gabriel de Roquette, un évêque reformateur sous Louis XIV* (Paris, 1876), 1:203–6.

16. Another Burgundian priest, Adrien Gagnare, curé of Pouilly-en-Auxois, also reportedly died in "an odor of sanctity" in 1688. Ibid., 1:206, n. 1.

17. Abbé Le Lorrain de Vallemont, *Du Secret des mystères ou l'apologie de la rubrique des missels* (Paris, 1710), p. 378.

18. Etienne Tabourot, *Les Bigarrures du Seigneur des Accords, et les escraignes Dijonnaises* (Geneva, 1970, orig. ed. 1583), e.g., story 34.

19. AMD I 142, [no day or month] 1486; AMD I 142, 26 May 1508; ADCO B II 360 file 44, 12 February 1559. See Jacques Rossiaud, *Medieval Prostitution*, trans. Lydia G. Cochrane (Oxford, 1988).

20. ADCO B II 360 file 40, 23 March 1555; 360 file 44, 5 June 1560. Due to the lack of archival documentation from Burgundy's ecclesiastical courts before the eighteenth century, we cannot know if this behavior was prosecuted by the church, but the extensive records from the bishop's court in the nearby province of Champagne, indicate that it was, and frequently. For examples of priests' deflowering virgins there, see Archives Départementales de l'Aube, G 4191, fol. 280 r.-v., 1507–8, summarized in H. D'Arbois de Jubainville and Francisque André, eds., *Inventaire sommaire des archives départementales de l'Aube antérieurs à 1790*, series G, vol. 2 (Paris, 1896), p. 353; G 4192, fols. 21r.–23v., 25r., 52r., 53r.–56r., 80v., 83v.–84r., 1515 (Jubainville and André, pp. 355–56); G 4194, fols. 236r.–240r., 244r., 246r., 248v.–251r., 271r., 282r.-v., 284v., and 394v., 1516–17 (Jubainville and André, pp. 383–84); G 4196, fols. 17v.–18r., 21v., 31r., 4 June–26 June 1522 (Jubainville and André, p. 393); G 4199, fols. 113r.–114v., 121r., 126v., 142r., 1529–30 (Jubainville and André, p. 417); G 4200, fol. 2r., 1530–31 (Jubainville and André, p. 422).

21. ADCO B II 360 file 40, 8 June 1554. Dominique Julia, "Le Prêtre au XVIIIe siècle: La Théologie et les institutions," *Recherches de science religieuse* 58 (1970), 552, states that in the sixteenth century, many clerics in France could scarcely be distinguished from the laity by their labor, appearance, or sexual behavior.

22. Henry Charles Lea, *The History of Sacerdotal Celibacy in the Christian Church* (New York, 1957), esp. chap. 20.

23. Ibid., p. 466.

24. James Brundage, "Sex and the Canon Law: A Statistical Analysis of Samples of Canon and Civil Law," in Vern L. Bullough and James Brundage, eds., *Sexual Practices and the Medieval Church* (Buffalo, N.Y., 1982), p. 87.

25. Bibliothèque nationale, ms. B5530, fols. 5r.–9v., 22 June 1557 (Bishop Philibert Dugny de Courgengouch), and fols. 10r.–12r., 15 November 1558 (Bishop Pierre de Marcilly).

26. Georges Viard, "Les Visites pastorales dans l'ancien diocèse de Langres: La réglementation episcopale et sa mise en oeuvre," *Revue d'histoire de l'église de France* 63 (July–December 1977), 248.

27. ADD, ADCO, ADSL.

28. Roger Doucet, *Les Institutions de la France au XVIe siècle* (Paris, 1948), 2:788.

29. Examples abound; see, for example, ADA G 4192, fols. 27v.–28r., 26 April 1515 (a curé accused of paternity) (Jubainville and André, *Inventaire*, p. 356); fols. 62r.–64r., 1515 (a curé accused of carnal relations) (Jubainville and André, p. 356); G 4194, fols. 236r.–40r., 244r., 246r., 248v.–51r., 271r., 282r.-v., 284v., 394v., 1516–17 (a curé accused of deflowering a virgin and impregnating her) (Jubainville and André, pp. 383–84); G 4197, fol. 89r., 1526–27 (a priest accused of carnal relations) (Jubainville and André, p. 400); G 4199, fols. 113r.–14v., 121r., 126v., 142r., 1529–30 (an abbot of an Augustinian monastery accused of deflowering a virgin) (Jubainville and André, p. 417).

30. ADA, G 4192, fols. 116r.-v., 117v., 118r., 1515 (Jubainville and André, *Inventaire*, p. 357). Other examples of priests' having carnal relations with disreputable women and the fines assessed include: ADA G 4197, 145v., 1526–27 (Jubainville and André, p. 406), (a prior-curé was convicted of such relations; he was verbally admonished and fined 2 *écus* and one pound of wax, the same sentence handed down to a sword-wielding monk who surreptitiously slipped out of

his monastery nightly to have sexual relations with a woman, with whom he has several children); ADA, G 4200, fol. 131r., 1530–31 (Jubainville and André, p. 429).

31. ADA G 4199, fols. 33v., 82v., 88v., 90v., 1529–30 (Jubainville and André, *Inventaire*, pp. 412–13).

32. ADA G 4200, fols. 178v., 179r.–v., 1530-31 (Jubainville and André, *Inventaire*, pp. 429–30).

33. ADA, G 4196, fol. 18r., 22r., 25v., 1522 (Jubainville and André, *Inventaire*, p. 393).

34. ADA G 4199, fol. 191r., 1529–30 (Jubainville and André, *Inventaire*, p. 420).

35. ADA G 4197, fols. 11r., 281v., 19 May 1526 (Jubainville and André, *Inventaire*, pp. 394–95).

36. François Isambert et al., eds., *Recueil générale des anciennes lois Françaises* (Paris, 1833), 12:90–91.

37. Ibid., 12:601–2.

38. For prominent examples of legal texts that addressed jurisdictional matters, see Charles Loyseau, *Traité des seigneuries* (Paris, 1613); Charles Fevret, *Traité de l'abus et du vray sujet des appellations qualitiées de ce nom d'abus* (Dijon, 1654); René Choppin, *Traité de la police ecclésiastique* (Paris, 1662); Louis d'Héricourt du Vatier, *Les Loix ecclésiatiques de France dans leur ordre naturel* ... (Paris, 1714); and Daniel Jousse, *Nouveau commentaire sur lédit du mois d'avril 1695, concernant la jurisidiction ecclésiatique* (Paris, 1757), and *Traité de la jurisdiction volontaire et contentieuse des officiaux* (Paris, 1749).

39. Isambert et al., *Recueil générale*, 12:714.

40. Ibid., 12:601–2; Frederick Baumgartner, *Change and Continuity in the French Episcopate: The Bishops and the Wars of Religion, 1547–1610* (Durham, N.C., 1986), pp. 89–90.

41. Choppin, *Traité*, p. 659.

42. BMD MF 1496, fols. 172 r.–v., 4 June 1565. For an example concerning a case of "immodesty and lustfulness" [*impudicité et paillardise*] of a priest in the bishopric of Chalon-sur-Saône, see BMD MF 1496, fols. 208 r–v., 5 December 1566.

43. Complaints by clergymen about the prevalence of *appels comme d'abus* prompted the first article of the edict of Melun in 1580 and an edict by Henri IV in 1606 that reiterated the stipulations of Villers-Cotterets and added some provisions designed to reduce the frequency of such appeals. See Isambert et al., *Recueil générale*, 15:304.

44. Doucet, *Les Institutions*, 2:789; and Baumgartner, *Change and Continuity*, pp. 89–90.

45. Although many cases of concubinage are noted in the legal records of Burgundy, a quantified presentation of the evidence would be meaningless, for much the same reasons that historians of criminality have turned away from quantification: not only is the actual incidence of the crime missed, but the diverse conditions and motivations for litigation and prosecution (or the lack thereof) cannot be adequately represented. For these reasons, I illustrate trends by presenting the evidence by narrative example. On the inadequacies of quantitative analysis of early modern criminality, see Bruce Lenman and Geoffrey Parker, "The State, the Community, and Criminal Law in Early Modern Europe," in *Crime and the Law*, ed. V. A. C. Gatrel, Bruce Lenman, and Geoffrey Parker (London, 1980).

46. See Etienne Delcambre, "Witchcraft Trials in Lorraine: Psychology of the Judges," in E. William Monter, ed., *European Witchcraft* (New York, 1969), pp. 88–95.

47. BMD MF 1496, fol. 30r., 1 March 1532. In 1551 a similar *arrêt* by the Parlement of Toulouse claiming secular jurisdiction over concubines raised a howl of protest from the church, with the Bishop of Montauban actually complaining to the king. Henri II rescinded the Parlement's ruling but took back what he had given by adding that royal jurisdiction was applicable if the "concubinage is public, notorious, [and] scandalous" and if it appeared that the ecclesiastical judge showed "too great negligence" in prosecuting the crime. See Fevret, *Traité*, 2:223.

48. ADCO B II 360 file 44, 20 April 1560.

49. AMD I 142, 13 August 1560.

50. Ibid., June 1560.

51. Ibid., 11 May 1563.

52. BMD Ms. MF 1496 fol. 204r.–205r., 15 October 1566.

53. Ibid., fol. 208r–v., 5 December 1566.

54. ADCO B II 360 file 50, 1 February 1573.

55. Ibid., 17–25 January 1573.

56. Ibid., 17–28 February 1573. Included in this trial were two municipal ordinances dated 28 April and 26 June 1572 against, among other things, concubinage.

57. Ibid., 6 February 1572.

58. Ibid., 14 April 1571.

59. Ibid., 29 July 1575.

60. Ibid., B II 46 file 1, 5 October 1582.

61. Ibid., file 2, 5 March 1588.

62. Ibid., B II 360 file 1, 10 May 1582. We do not know the outcome of this case.

63. ADCO B II 46 file 2, 8 April 1588.

64. See, for example, ibid., file 1, 18 January 1583, 19 October 1584; file 2, 5 March 1588, 23 December 1591 (two cases on same day). In both cases on 23 December, the women were sentenced to be flogged and banished by the lower courts; the sentences were upheld in full by the Parlement.

65. Although there is no way to correlate systematically the clergymen who were prosecuted with their relative social status or affiliations with powerful lay families, it does appear that few canons of the powerful religious houses of the towns of Burgundy were prosecuted, despite evidence of their sexual activity. Low prosecution of canons appears in sharp contrast to the prosecution of rural curés and vicars.

66. ADCO B II 46 file 2, 8 May 1592.

67. Ibid., B II 360 file 54, 10 December 1594–24 April 1595.

68. Archives Communales de Chalon-sur-Saône, Series FF, file 9, 16–22 August 1615.

69. ADA, G 4193, fol. 274, G4194, fols. 16v.–17r., 18r., 1516 (Jubainville and André, *Inventaire*, pp. 371–72).

70. Ibid., G 4200, fols. 109v., 112v., 1530–31 (Jubainville and André, *Inventaire*, pp. 427–28). For other examples of spiritual adultery between priest and married parishioner and the sentences that were handed down in the bishop's court at Troyes, see ADA G 4192, fols. 97v.–98r., 1515, no sentence (Jubainville and André, *Inventaire*, p. 357); G 4193, fols. 262v.–264r., 1515–16, no sentence

(Jubainville and André, p. 370); G 4197, fols. 90r., 91 v., 1526–27, sentence: eight days in prison, 2 *écus*, and four pounds of wax in fines (Jubainville and André, p. 401); G 4200, fol. 2r., 1530–31, sentence: 60 *sous* and three pounds of wax in fines, admonsishment not to see the woman alone again (Jubainville and André, p. 422).

71. BMD MF 1110, fol. 31, 7 October 1620. Awarding the husband the wife's dowry struck at the woman's blood kin by depriving them any legal claim to the dowry, which by the marriage contract provided the husband only with usufruct. This evidence demonstrates that adultery was a familial, not simply personal, crime.

72. Ibid., fol. 32, 19 October 1627.

73. The *officialité* records for the bishopric of Troyes appear to corroborate this speculation. In the 32 *registres d'audience* from the *officialité* of Troyes covering 1665–1790 (ADA G 4236–68), only one case dealt with what might have been a sexual transgression by a priest, although the charge was never explicit. The reprimand came for employing a female servant under the permitted age of 40: ADA G 4255, fol. 46r., 11 February 1702.

74. Gaspard Dinet, Bishop of Mâcon, *Ordonnances générales faictes par Mgr le Révérendissime evesque de Mascon pour le règlement de son diocèse* (Lyon, 1602), pp. 36–37.

75. Isambert et al., *Recueil générale*, 16:11.

76. Ibid., 16:511.

77. ADCO B II 46 file 6, 17–24 July 1629. This is the first instance of any case from any *officialité* being appealed to the Parlement since adequate records appear in the archives in 1582. Because all crimes of this nature in *officialités* would be appealed to the Parlement, it is unlikely that any examples have escaped the purview of this study.

78. Ibid., file 10, 6 August 1649.

79. BMD MF 1110, fol. 35, 30 January 1676. The nun was confined for five years in a monastery for wayward women in Dijon, the Notre Dame du Refuge.

80. Sentencing to the galleys may have furthered the sacralizing goals of king and magistrate, since the galley corps, which was established in 1665, massively expanded the fleet and, according to Paul Bamford, *Fighting Ships and Prisons: The Mediterranean Galleys in the Age of Louis XIV* (Minneapolis, 1973), p. 6, "epitomized the great Christian tradition of fighting for the faith." Furthermore, "the catholic laity in France and many of the Gallican clergy . . . looked on Louis' galleys as religious tools," since chaplains were assigned to the ships to preach to and reform the condemned. See also André Zysberg, *Les Galériens: vies et destins de 60,000 forçats sur les galères de France, 1680–1748* (Paris, 1987).

81. ADCO B II 46, file 18, 24 March 1694.

82. Compare with witchcraft jurisprudence; Joseph Klaits, *Servants of Satan* (Bloomington, Ind., 1985), and Brian Levack, *The Witch-Hunt in Early Modern Europe* (London, 1987).

83. BMD MF 1110, fol. 37, 10 January 1662.

84. ADCO B II 45 file 2, 13 January 1668. Concerning the relative severity of sentences against women, the records support no meaningful interpretations one might make about correlations between social status and severity of punishment. Women of high rank could be and were punished severely for sexual crimes.

85. Ibid., 17 July 1670. See also 19 September 1674: a priest convicted of incest, adultery, and impiety was fined 50 *livres* and banished from France for life.

86. An injunction made by ecclesiastical authorities, sometimes on the demand of a lay judge, to testify about what one knows on a criminal case, under pain of excommunication. See Marcel Marion, *Dictionnaire des institutions de la France aux XVIIe et XVIIIe siècles* (Paris, 1923, 1979), p. 383.

87. ADD G 609, December 1717. For another example of a village priest's allegedly roaming the streets with youth gangs, see idem, G 785, 23 October 1704.

88. ADCO B II 45 file 11, 30 April 1720. For a similar judgment for *commerce scandaleux* by a priest, see ibid., B II 46 file 23, 13 August 1726.

89. See, for example, Jean Delumeau, *Le Catholicisme entre Luther et Voltaire*, 3d ed. (Paris, 1985); Hoffman, *Church and Community*; and Tackett, *Priest and Parish*.

90. Peter Brown, "The Rise and Function of the Holy Man," *Journal of Roman Studies* 61 (1971), 91.

91. Hoffman, *Church and Community*, p. 105; and Tackett, *Priest and Parish*, p. 167.

92. AMD I 142, [no day or month] 1486.

93. Ibid., 26 May 1508.

94. See, for example, ADCO B II 360 file 48, 23 August 1570; 360 file 51, 9 July 1584; B II 46 file 1, 23 July 1584; Archives Communales de Chalon-sur-Saône FF8, 30 July 1584; ADCO B II 360 file 63, 30 August 1646; B II 360 file 103, 26 July 1680.

95. See, for example, ADCO B II 360 file 44, 12 February 1559; B II 360 file 65, 4 September 1648.

96. Ibid., file 50, 17 February 1573.

97. Ibid., file 51, 22 July 1584.

98. Viard, "Les Visites pastorales," p. 236.

99. Dinet, *Ordonnances générales*, pp. 36–37; Jean de Lingendes, Bishop of Mâcon, *Ordonnances synodales d'illustrissime et reverendissime père en Dieu Jen de Lingendes* (Mâcon, 1659), pp. 33–34; François Joseph de Grammont, *Statuta seu decreta synodalia bisuntiae . . .* (Vesoul, 1707), p. 11.

100. ADCO B II 360 file 91, 11 May 1671.

101. Bernard de La Monnoye, manuscript notebooks, BMD, Ms. 873, M–O. "The priest lives at the altar / the whore at the brothel / but our friend Bodeau / lives at one as well as the other / but our friend Bodeau / is canon and pimp. See also idem, *Oeuvres choisies* (La Haye, 1770), 1:420.

102. See, for example, ibid., file 148, 7 June 1703, where it appears in ample testimony that Marie Gavinet, being tried for "scandalous ways," consorted with priests on many occasions.

103. Ibid., file 103, 2 August 1680.

104. Ibid., file 89, 9 May 1670.

105. E. de La Cuisine, ed., *Choix des lettres inédites* (Dijon, 1859), 2:236–37.

106. Historians including Dominique Julia, "La Réforme posttridentine en France d'apres les procès-verbaux de visites pastorales," in *La Socièta religiosa nell 'èta moderna* (Naples, 1973), pp. 324–28, have noted that parishioners, for whatever reasons, were frequently not forthcoming in complaints about their curé's moral habits, and consequently the records generated by pastoral visitations may not accurately reflect those habits. Indeed, Robert Sauzet, *Les Visites pastorales dans le diocèse de Chartres pendant la première moitié du XVIIe siècle* (Paris, 1970), in comparing records from the *officialité* of Chartres with those of pastoral visita-

tions conducted there, found evidence of clerics prosecuted for serious sexual misconduct in their clerical work who were reported as morally upright.

107. Keith Luria, *Territories of Grace: Cultural Change in the Seventeenth-Century Diocese of Grenoble* (Berkeley, 1990), p. 48–9, records similar results for the diocese of Grenoble in 1672. An episcopal visitation found of 142 priests that only 20 merited "a good mention, and only eight passed inspection without reservation." Among the many miscreants, 85 were cited for sexual misconduct, from concubinage to promiscuity.

108. ADSL G 907, fol. 15v., 1656.

109. Ibid., G 910, fol. 25v., 1667.

110. Ibid., fol. 37v., 1667.

111. Ibid., fol. 52, 1667.

112. Ibid., fols. 97v, 107v., 1667.

113. Ibid., G 911, 5 October 1668.

114. Ibid., G 916, fol. 137v., 1671.

115. Ibid., G 919, fol. 154v–155r., 1671.

116. ADD G 796, 1709–17.

117. ADSL B 622, 27 April–7 December 1686.

118. Brown, "Rise and Function of the Holy Man," p. 87, and Tackett, *Priest and Parish*, p. 152.

119. Schmitt, *L'Organisation écclésiastique*, pp. 138–39. For similar examples elsewhere in France, albeit earlier in the century, See Sauzet, *Les Visites pastorales*, pp. 133–34.

120. ADCO B II 45 file 11, 30 April 1720. In 1623 Pope Gregory XV issued a bull specifically condemning the seduction of women in the confessional. I thank William Monter for this information.

121. Ibid., B II 365 file 1, 9 January 1711. Tackett, *Priest and Parish*, p. 160, suggests that elsewhere in France, it was not uncommon for priests to serve as marriage brokers.

122. Ibid., B II 46 file 23, 13 August 1726.

123. Tackett, *Priest and Parish*, pp. 172, 185, asserts that the "single most common subjects of litigation between laymen and the church were problems involving the tithes. . . . Perhaps the most common sources of conflict between priest and parish were the revenues paid by the parishioners to the curé himself."

124. ADCO B II 46 file 6, 12 January 1629.

125. ADCO B II 45 file 2, 13 January 1668.

126. Ibid., B II 46 file 19, 7 August 1698.

127. Ibid., B II 45 file 11, 19 July 1720.

128. Julia, "La Réforme posttridentine," p. 389.

129. Ibid., p. 352, n.148, suggests that this was far from uncommon.

130. On the rivalry between lay and ecclesiastical notables in the villages of the Dauphiné, see Tackett, *Priest and Parish*, chap. 7.

131. Hoffman, *Church and Community*, p. 143.

132. ADSL B 644 no. 69, 1741. *Pain bénit* was bread blessed by the priest that parishioners shared at mass, a ritual parallel to the taking the Host and symbolizing the unity of the parish community. See Hoffman, *Church and Community*, p. 56.

133. Schmitt, *L'organisation ecclésiastique*, p. lxx, n. 166.

134. See Roland Mousnier, *The Institutions of France under the Absolute Monarchy, 1598–1789*, trans. Brian Pearce and Arthur Goldhammer (Chicago, 1979, 1984), 1:304–11.

135. At the Estates General at Orléans in 1560, the nobility lobbied for election of priests to their curés by seigneurs in the parish or by an assembly of the three orders in the parish (which they likely dominated). M. G. Picot, *Histoire des états généraux* (Paris, 1872), 2:230.

136. Tackett, *Priest and Parish*, p. 104.

137. ADD G 784, 21 April–24 May 1702.

138. Ibid., G 785, 23 October 1704–7.

139. ADCO B II 365 file 1, 14 September 1726.

140. ADD G 805, 10 July 1727–20 February 1728.

141. Julia, "La Reforme posttridentine," pp. 341–42.

Chapter 4

1. Judges were careful to distinguish between *rapt* with the intention to marry and forced fornication. Before 1650 or so, *rapt* could mean rape (forced fornication with no intention to marry) *or* abduction and seduction for the purposes of marriage; after the mid-seventeenth century, *viol* was used instead to mean rape. See BMD Mss. MF1110, fol. 421, 8 April 1568; ADCO B II 360 file 50, 13–20 March 1573; B II 46 file 1, 23 September 1583; file 6, 7 March 1630; BMD Mss MF 1110, fol. 426, 23 March 1643; ADCO B II 360 file 61, 16 July 1644. For rape designated as *viol*, see ADCO B II 360 file 76, 22 July 1660; B II 45 file 2, 14 August 1668; B II 46 file 15, 8 July 1670; B II 45 file 2, 10 October 1673; B II 360 file 104, 29 December 1681; B II 46 file 22, 18 December 1722; B II 45 file 11, 11 May 1724; ADSL B 1814 file 1, 17 June 1732.

2. On the central importance of marriage to social hierarchy, see Carolyn Lougee, *Le Paradis des femmes: Women, Salons, and Social Stratification in Seventeenth-Century France* (Princeton, 1976).

3. See, for example, Georges Pieri, "Les Particularités de la puissance paternelle," *MSHD* 26 (1965), 51–90; and Jean Bouhier, *Commentaire sur la coûtume de Bourgogne* (Dijon, 1742–46), 1:300: "The lack of paternal consent nullifies the marriage, and even though this be a point of controversy among the doctors . . . we have always held [this] in Burgundy . . . as conforming more to the public welfare, to reason, and to the rights of paternal authority."

4. See Charles Donahue, "The Canon Law on the Formation of Marriage and Social Practice in the Later Middle Ages," *Journal of Family History* (Summer 1983), 144; Penny S. Gold, "The Marriage of Mary and Joseph in the Twelfth-Century Ideology of Marriage," and James Brundage, "Concubinage and Marriage in Medieval Canon Law," in Vern L. Bullough and James Brundage, eds. *Sexual Practices and the Medieval Church* (Buffalo, N.Y., 1982).

5. Donahue, "Canon Law," p. 156.

6. BN, ms. B 5530, Philibert Dugny de Courgengouch, *Constitutiones synodales dioceseos Heduensis recentur excusae.*

7. See John Bossy, "Moral Arithmetic: Seven Sins into Ten Commandments," in Edmund Leites, ed., *Conscience and Casuistry in Early Modern Europe* (Cambridge, 1988), pp. 214–34.

8. Olivier Maillard, *La Confession* (Bourges, n.d. [1495]), fol. 10r.

9. *Instructions pour les confesseurs du diocèse de Chalon-sur-Saône* (Lyon, 1682), pp. 39–40.

10. Gaspard Dinet, *Ordonnances générales faict par Mgr le reverendissime*

évesque de Mascon pour le réglement de son diocèse (Lyon, 1602), p. 25; Jean de Lingendes, *Ordonnances synodales* (Macon, 1659), pp. 43–44.

11. L. Reguis, *La Voix du pasteur* (Paris, 1766), 1:90, 92, 96, 107.

12. François Isambert et al., eds., *Recueil générale des anciennes lois Françaises* (Paris, 1833), 13:469–70.

13. Ibid., 13:470.

14. Ibid., 14:381.

15. In his legal handbook Job Bouvot, *Nouveau recueil des arrests de Bourgogne* . . . , (Coligny, 1623; Geneva, 1628), 2:616, wrote that the Parlement of Paris issued *arrêts* in 1584, 1585, 1590, 1594, and two in 1599 prohibiting *officials* from hearing *rapt* cases.

16. "Declaration de Louis XIII, 26 Novembre 1639," in Pierre LeRidant, *Code Matrimonial* (Paris, 1766), pp. 35–38.

17. Isambert et al., *Recueil générale*, 20:287–88.

18. Ibid., 20:292.

19. For a useful overview on the various views on the contractual and sacramental nature of marriage, see James F. Traer, *Marriage and Family in Eighteenth-Century France* (Ithaca, N.Y., 1980), chap. 1.

20. Paul Ourliac and Jean-Louis Gazzaniga, *Histoire du droit privé français de l'an mil au Code civil* (Paris, 1985) p. 298.

21. J. Gaudemet, "Legislation canonique et attitudes séculières à l'égard du lien matrimonial au XVIIe siècle," *XVIIe siècle* 102–3 (1974), 20.

22. Jules Basdevant, *Des Rapports de l'église et de l'état dans la legislation du mariage du Concile de Trent au Code civil* (Paris, 1900), pp. 141–2. Parlement issued *arrêts* to this effect in 1584, 1585, 1595, and 1601. On the protection of family interests and paternalism, see also Ourliac, *Droit privé*, p. 298.

23. Basdevant, *Des Rapports de l'église*, p. 28; Ourliac, *Droit privé*, p. 298.

24. Basdevant, *Des Rapports de l'église*, p. 32.

25. Ibid., pp. 37–38.

26. Cited by Gaudemet, "Legislation canonique," p. 22.

27. Cited by Basdevant, *Des Rapports de l'église*, p. 137.

28. Ibid., pp. 15–16, 58, 45; Gaudemet, "Legislation canonique," pp. 22–23.

29. Gaudemet, "Legislation canonique," p. 25.

30. Basdevant, *Des Rapports de l'église*, pp. 74–75.

31. Gaudemet, "Legislation canonique," p. 23.

32. Isambert et al., *Recueil générale*, 21:339–40.

33. Sarah Hanley, "Family and State in Early Modern France: The Marriage Pact," in Marilyn J. Boxer and Jean H. Quataert, eds., *Connecting Spheres: Women in the Western World, 1500 to the Present* (New York, 1987), p. 54, and, more fully, Hanley, "Engendering the State: Family Formation and State Building in Early Modern France," *French Historical Studies* 16:1 (Spring 1989), 4–27.

34. Léon Duguit, "Etude historique sur le rapt de séduction," *Nouvelle revue historique de droit français et étranger* 10 (1886), 615. See also G. Pacilly, "Contribution à l'histoire de la théorie du rapt de séduction: Etude de jurisprudence," *Tijdschrift voor rechtsgeschiedenis* 13 (1934), 306–18; and Mark Cummings, "Elopement, Family and the Courts: The Crime of *Rapt* in Early Modern France," *Proceedings of the Western Society for French History* 4 (1976), 118–125.

35. Duguit, *Etude historique*, 616.

36. According to Pierre Milhard, *La Vraye guide des curez* (Lyon, 1604), p. 104, *rapt* with violence was a mortal sin.

37. James Brundage, "Rape and Seduction in the Medieval Canon Law," in Bullough and Brundage, *Sexual Practices.*

38. Isambert et al., *Recueil générale*, 14:91.

39. Ibid., 14:392.

40. On legislation, see decrees in 1639, 1697, and 1730, see ibid., 16:520 (1639); 20:287–92 (1697), and 21:338 (1730). On legal dictionaries and handbooks, see, for example, Claude-Joseph de Ferrière, *Dictionnaire de droit et de pratique* (Paris, 1749), 2:671–75; Pierre-François Muyart de Vouglans, *Institutes au droit criminel* (Paris, 1757), pp. 499–505; and Jean-François Fournel, *Traité de la séduction* (Paris, 1781), pp. 303–10.

41. Isambert et al., *Recueil générale*, 21:338.

42. *Officialités* records are quite rare for Burgundy before the eighteenth century, but a substantial holding exists in the Archives départementales de l'Aube in Troyes. From these documents, it is apparent that the caseload before the *officialité* had shrunk considerably between 1550 and 1750, but it is also clear that it continued to hear cases concerning marriage right to 1790. See H. d'Arbois de Jubainville and Francisque André, eds., *Inventaire sommaire des archives départementales antérieures à 1790: Aube* Series G, vol. 2 (Paris, 1896), pp. 268–464, and Francisque André, Jules-Joseph Vernier, and Pierre Piétresson de Saint-Aubin, eds., *Inventaire sommaire des archives départementales antérieures à 1790: Aube* Series G, vol. 3 (Troyes, 1930), pp. 1–95.

43. Deducing jurisprudence from punishments ordered by an appellate court can obscure the following information: that cases dealing with multiple transgressions might have had significant factual differences and circumstances that could result in different penalties; that other ways exist for determining a court's intentions, such as whether cases were prosecuted by the public prosecutor alone or with a *partie civile*, which would reveal the state's relative interest in criminalizing certain behavior; and that appellate *arrêts* did not fully recapitulate all the facts in a case and ignore the filtering of cases heard at lower levels in the judiciary. I deal with each of these issues.

44. John H. Langbein, *Torture and the Law of Proof: Europe and England in the Ancien Régime* (Chicago, 1977). D. Ulrich, "La repression en Bourgogne au XVIIIe siècle," *Revue historique de droit Français et étranger* 50 (1972), 410, has found that death sentences in general leveled off in the first half of the eighteenth century (handed out to 13–14.5% of all accused between 1715 and 1750), but dropped sharply in the second half (to 8.5% between 1758 and 1760 and then below 5% between 1770 and 1779). Alfred Soman, "Criminal Jurisprudence in Ancien-Régime France: The Parlement of Paris in the Sixteenth and Seventeenth Centuries," in Louis Knafla, ed., *Crime and Criminal Justice in Europe and Canada* (Waterloo, 1981), p. 54, argues that judicial repression in the sixteenth was not as severe as has commonly been thought.

45. John Langbein, *Torture and the Law of Proof* (Chicago, 1977), pp. 48, 56–60. See also idem, *Prosecuting Crime in the Renaissance: England, Germany, France* (Cambridge, Mass., 1974).

46. Alfred Soman, "Criminal Jurisprudence in Ancien Regime France, p. 56, points out that "in small villages where everyone knew his neighbors only too well, the chances of finding two *impartial* witnesses to a crime were almost nil."

47. BMD Ms. 1110, p. 424, 9 August 1622.

48. ADCO B II 46 file 18, 2 April 1694.

49. Ibid., file 15, 12 August 1669.

50. Ibid., file 10, 23 January 1646.

51. Ibid., file 6, 26 January 1629.

52. In a text written for law students, Jean Melenet, *Dissertation sur le rapt* (n.d. [eighteenth century], mss. at BMD), sided with Parlement.

53. Isambert, et al., *Recueil générale*, 13:470.

54. Ibid., 16:520.

55. Charles Fevret, *Traité de l'abus et du vray sujet des appellations qualifiées de ce nom d'abus* (Dijon, 1654), 2:87.

56. This was cited as the primary reason for *rapt* laws in the mid-eighteenth century; see ibid., 2:671.

57. On men breaking marriage promises due to the woman's previous loss of honor, see ADCO B II 360 file 137, 9–16 July 1697; ADCO B II 360 file 186, 25 April 1720. For remarkably similar eighteenth-century English and sixteenth-century German experiences involving a direct calculus of honor and money, see Susan Staves, "Money for Honor: Damages for Criminal Conversation," *Studies in 18th-Century Culture* 11 (1982), 279–97, and Lyndal Roper, "Will and Honor: Sex, Words, and Power in Augsburg Criminal Trials," *Radical History Review* 43 (1989), 57.

58. ADCO B II 46 file 2, 9 March 1587.

59. Ibid., 20 March 1587.

60. Ibid., file 22, 19 June 1720.

61. "Interest" carried a number of meanings in the early modern period. In legal terminology it was synonymous with *dommages*, or damages, referring to the compensation awarded in criminal and civil matters to the wronged party; see Emile Littré, *Dictionnaire de la langue française* (Paris, 1956), "Intérêt." Less neutral meanings also existed: in his advice book published in 1662, Melchior de Marmet de Valcroissant, *Maximes pour vivre heureusement dans la monde et pour former l'honneste homme* (Paris, 1662), pp. 191–92, identified three types of interest, all intertwined: honor, family, and wealth (*d'honneur, du sang, et des biens et richesses.*) See also Albert Hirschman, *The Passions and the Interests* (Princeton, 1977).

62. See, for example, ADCO B II 360 file 103, 27 September 1680; a lower court condemned a man of *rapt* and ordered him to "dower" the plaintiff with a certain sum *par forme d'interestz*.

63. Ibid., B II 46 file 1, 5 October 1582.

64. Ibid., file 15, 12 August 1669: "to dower the said Dupuys up to the sum of 1000 *livres*" (*à dotter lad. Dupuys jusque à la somme de mil livres . . .*)

65. Ibid., B II 360 file 103, 27 September 1680: "condemned to dower Marie Gallet in the sum of 2000 *livres* . . . if he does not wish to marry her" (*condemné à dotter Marie Gallet d'une somme de deux mil livres s'il n'ayme l'espouser . . .*) See also ADSL B 663 (Comté Charolais), 1 January 1686; a plaintiff in a *rapt* case asked for 100£ from the accused for her *dotte*.

66. ADSL B 1785 file 2, 8 November 1667.

67. Muyart de Vouglans, *Institutes*, p. 488.

68. BMD MF1110, p. 427, 1 July 1643.

69. ADCO B II 360 file 65, 9 October 1648–7 September 1650.

70. BMD MF 1110, p. 422, 29 January 1609.

71. Ibid., p. 425, 28 May 1637.

72. ADCO B II 46 file 22, 17 July 1722.

73. Ibid., file 23, 20 December 1724.

74. Allain Lottin, "Naissances illégitimes et filles-mères à Lille au XVIIIe siècle," *Revue d'histoire moderne et contemporaine* 17 (1970), 309–14, found that the overwhelming majority of mothers of illegitimate children in eighteenth-century Lille, were drawn from this social stratum. See also Cissie Fairchilds, "Female Sexual Attitudes and the Rise of Illegitimacy: A Case Study," *Journal of Interdisciplinary History* 8 (Spring 1978), 627–67; and Jacques Depauw, "Illicit Sexual Activity and Society in Eighteenth-Century Nantes," in Robert Forster and Orest Ranum, eds., *Family and Society: Selections from the Annales*, trans. Elborg Forster and Patricia Ranum (Baltimore, 1976), pp. 145–91.

75. ADCO B II 46 file 10, 13 September 1646.

76. Ibid., B II 45 file 2, 12 August 1670.

77. Ibid., 11 December 1674.

78. Ibid., B II 46 file 18, 10 October 1690.

79. The literature on the European marriage pattern is extensive; for a good overview, see Jacques Dupâquier et al., eds. *Marriage and Remarriage in Populations of the Past* (New York, 1981). For Dijon, see James R. Farr, "Consumers, Commerce, and the Craftsmen of Dijon: The Changing Social and Economic Structure of a Provincial Capital, 1450–1750," in Philip Benedict, ed., *Cities and Social Change in Early Modern France* (London, 1989), pp. 158–61.

80. BMD MF 1110 p. 423, 19 December 1616.

81. ADCO B II 46 file 10, 28 July 1649.

82. BMD, MF 1110, p. 430, 7 March 1681.

83. Jean Fournel, *Traité de la séduction* (Paris, 1781), p. 61, wrote that payment of *dommages et intérêts* was always justified by the violation of a contract, including specifically a promise of marriage, reflecting for the late eighteenth century a jurisprudential trend that had been developing for over a century.

84. Isambert et al., *Recueil générale*, 21:338–39.

85. Fevret, *Traité*, 2:87, commented on this leniency by judges; "The appearance that the ravished woman or girl consented exempted the ravisher from the punishment of the law."

86. See Jean Brissaud, *History of French Private Law* (Boston, 1912), pp. 99–100. In addressing whether deflowering (*défloration*) a virgin was a mortal sin, Pierre Milhard, *La Vraye guide des curez, vicaires, et confesseurs*, (Lyon, 1604), p. 104, mentioned in passing that "justice" would constrain the man who broke a promise of marriage to "dower" the woman.

87. ADCO B II 365 file 1, 28 January 1619.

88. Declarations of pregnancies were not solely an urban phenomenon. See, for example, ADSL B 1809 file 1 (Juge Mage de Cluny), 4 June 1722, 8 December 1724, 12 January 1726, 27 October 1726, 4 March 1727, 29 January 1728; and ADSL B 663 (Juge Châtelain, Bailliage du Comté de Charollais), 28 April 1688, 5 December 1690.

89. ADCO B II 365 file 1, 11 September 1644.

90. Ibid., 14 April 1669. Two years later the syndic investigated another pregnant woman because he suspected she had plans to hide the birth and either suffocate the infant or expose it. See ibid., 30 March 1671.

91. Examples of women coming to Dijon to give birth abound, as do references to coming there to conceal unwanted pregnancies and, as one woman put it in 1724, "to avoid shame." See, for example, ADCO B II 365 file 1, 10 August 1665 (the young mother had put the newborn out to a wetnurse before the syndic arrived); ibid., 9 June 1677; ibid., 16 December 1692 (a pregnant woman confessed that she had come to Dijon *exprès pour faire ses couches*); 12 January 1702; 12 October 1708; 28 January 1712 (the syndic interrogated a woman while she was in labor); 29 November 1724; 23 February 1727. I thank Rachel G. Fuchs for informing me that this situation continued in the nineteenth century.

92. See Beatrice Gottlieb, "The Meaning of Clandestine Marriage," in Robert Wheaton and Tamara K. Hareven, eds., *Family and Sexuality in French History* (Philadelphia, 1980), pp. 49–83.

93. Francisque André, Jules-Joseph Vernier, and Pierre Pietresson de Saint-Aubin, eds., *Inventaire sommaire des archives antérieures à 1790: Aube*, sér. C, vol. 3 (Troyes, 1930), pp. 1–90, present in lengthy detail judicial proceedings before the episcopal court at Troyes between 1665 and 1730. Large numbers of females brought suits demanding the *exécution de promesses de mariage*. Not all litigants who brought such suits were female, nor did all females who brought suits demand marriage promises be enforced. Indeed, some women, as did many men, brought suit demanding that a marriage promise be broken by the court (*résolution de promesse de mariage*).

94. ADSL 8 G 2, fol. 43v., 2 June 1649.

95. See, for example, ADA G 4243, fols. 39r.–40r. (3–8 August 1675); ibid., G 4246, fols. 22v., 26 October 1686; ibid., G 4250, fol. 3r., 17 June 1690.

96. See, for example, ADA G 4239, fol. 79v., 23 March 1669.

97. See, for example, ADA G 4241, fol. 1v., 21 January 1673; G 4244, fol. 47r., 13 December 1684 (the man was ordered to marry the woman and would "be constrained [to do so] with the help of the secular arm"); ibid., fol. 3v., 12 October 1680; and G 4247 fol. 20r., 20 September 1687.

98. Secular courts also heard cases of broken marriage contracts even when pregnancy or sexual relations were not at issue. See, for example, the following cases pleaded before the mayor's court at the bailliage of Dijon: ADCO B II 360 file 137, 9–16 July 1697; 9 December 1697; file 186, 25–28 April 1720.

99. There is literary evidence that it may have been widespread: the Bishop of Montpelier issued an ordinance in 1699 stating that "the visitation we have just made of our diocese has shown us that one of the greatest disorders which holds sway there is the indulgence in those shameful intercourses which only too often precede marriage." Cited by Briggs, *Communities of Belief*, p. 271.

100. This figure is likely artificially low, given the impossibility of accounting for the numbers of infanticides, clandestine births, and abandonments.

101. See Robin Briggs, *Communities of Belief: Cultural and Social Tension in Early Modern France*, (Oxford, 1989), pp. 270–71; Jean-Louis Flandrin, *Les Amours paysannes, XVIe–XIXe siècle* (Paris, 1975), p. 225.

102. Jean-Louis Flandrin, *Les Amours paysannes*, pp. 227–29, also suggests such a calculus, but cites only an example from 1789.

103. ADSL B 1785 file 2, 8 November 1667.

104. Muyart de Vouglans, *Institutes*, p. 486.

105. ADCO B II 365 file 1, 22 December 1698.

106. For an analysis of self-serving narrative documents, see Natalie Zemon

Davis, *Fiction in the Archives* (Stanford, 1987). On declarations of pregnancy as well as how they were used, see Marie-Claude Phan, *Les Amours illégitimes: histoires de séduction en Languedoc (1676–1786)* (Paris, 1986); and Jacques Depauw. "Illicit Sexual Activity and Society in Eighteenth-Century Nantes," in Forster and Ranum, eds., *Family and Society.*

107. ADCO B II 365 file 1, 16 April 1659.

108. Ibid., 1 May 1721.

109. See, for example, BMD MF 1110, fol. 1017, 1018, 5 January 1664 (*arrêt à l'audience criminel*); ADCO B II 360 file 103, 28 July 1680.

110. ADCO B II 360 file 186, 21 February 1719 (written promise).

111. Ibid., B II 365 file 1, 9 December 1723.

112. Ibid., 25 July 1725. For similar documents, see ibid., 29 November 1724, 21 February 1726.

113. ADSL B 1265, 12 June 1634–27 July 1635.

114. ADCO B II 360 file 65, 9 October 1648–7 September 1650.

115. Ibid., file 186, 26 March 1720–26 March 1721.

116. Ibid., file 194, 21 September–10 November 1723.

117. See Phan, *Les Amours illégitimes*, p. 43. See also Sarah Maza, *Servants and Masters in Eighteenth-Century France: The Uses of Loyalty* (Princeton, 1983); and Fairchilds, "Female Sexual Attitudes."

118. Between 1619 and 1730, 274 declarations of pregnancy were noted in ADCO B II 365 file 1, the vast majority dating from the eighteenth century (only 18 survive from the seventeenth).

119. ADCO B II 360 file 76, 25 April 1660. We do not know the outcome of the case.

120. Ibid., B II 365 file 1, 15 November 1729. Alfred Soman, "Deviance and Criminal Justice in Western Europe, 1300–1800: An Essay in Structure," *Criminal Justice History* 1 (1980), 3–28, distinguishes between crimes prosecuted at public expense and those whose expenses were left to the plaintiff to assume. *Rapt* increasingly fell in the second category, and in such cases of crime, Soman suspects, out-of-court settlements arranged through notaries correspondingly increased.

121. Ibid., 18 July 1716.

122. Ibid., 12 May 1665.

123. Ibid., 29 September 1676.

124. Ibid., 28 November 1715.

125. Ibid., 15 April 1705.

126. A similar arrangement was initiated by the father of a pregnant paramour (who was also his servant) in 1667. This time Abraham Gallaud from Jallogny made Anne Ponceblanc pregnant and tried to arrange a marriage between Anne and his nephew. Rumor of her pregnancy spread quickly, however, and the nephew, getting wind of it, balked at such a plan. See ADSL B 1785 file 2, 26 July 1667.

127. Examples of declarations alleging such promises are far from rare. See, for example, ADCO B II 365 file 1, 2 March 1660, 16 December 1692, 7 October 1705, 21 April 1708, 13 November 1711, 11 April 1713, 17 March 1715, 24 January 1716, 7 January 1721, 20 September 1726, 10 September 1728.

128. ADCO B II 360 file 208, 30 November 1730–25 January 1731.

129. Ibid., B II 365 file 1, 21 February 1726.

130. As early as 1645 Mongin Chapuis, the servant of a Dijonnais notary, reported that she had become pregnant by her master. She assumed that he was

responsible for the child's support (she never mentioned marriage) and declared her intent to file a suit against him to make him support the child (*pour le rendre condamné à nourir l'enfant*): ADCO B II 365 file 1, 13 December 1645.

131. Ibid., 22 July 1728.

132. Antoine Blanchard, *Essay d'exhortation pour les états différents des malades . . . on y a joint un examen général sur tous les commandements et sur les pechés de plusieurs* (Paris, 1713).

133. ADSL B 1782, 18 June 1657.

134. ADCO B II 360 file 104, 8 May 1681.

135. Joost de Damhoudere, *Pratique judiciaire es causes criminelles* (Antwerp, 1564), p. 113.

136. See, for example, ADSL B 1265, 12 June 1634; ADCO B II 365 file 1, 6 June 1648, B II 46 file 18, 8 July 1695, file 19, 16 January 1696 (the rapt charge and a countercharge of prostitution were heard in the same case), 7 March 1698 (the male in question filed suit alleging prostitution), file 23, 17 July 1725.

137. See ADCO B II 46 file 23, 27 March 1727.

Chapter 5

1. ADCO B II 365, file 1, 30 March 1671.

2. For comparison with the German experience, see Merry Wiesner, "Early Modern Midwifery: A Case Study," in Barbara Hanawalt, ed., *Women and Work in Preindustrial Europe* (Bloomington, Ind., 1986), pp. 107–10.

3. See, for example, ADCO B II 365 file 1, 28 January 1619, B II 360 file 104, 7 February 1681.

4. Benoît Garnot, *La Population française aux XVIe, XVIIe, et XVIIIe siècles* (Paris, 1988), p. 53. On abandonment, see also Jean Meyer, "Illegitimates and Foundlings in Pre-industrial France," in Peter Laslett et al., eds., *Bastardy and Its Comparative History* (Cambridge, Mass., 1980), pp. 249–63; A. Chamoux, "Enfants illégitimes et enfants trouvés," *Annales de demographie historique* (1973), 422–29; and Claude Delasselle, "Abandoned Children in Eighteenth-Century Paris," in Robert Forster and Orest Ranum, eds., *Deviants and the Abandoned in French Society*, trans. Elborg Forster and Patricia Ranum (Baltimore, 1978), pp. 47–82. For a nineteenth-century comparison, see Rachel G. Fuchs, *Abandoned Children: Foundlings and Child Welfare in Nineteenth-Century France* (Albany, N.Y., 1984).

5. Henri II's edict of 1556 made it clear that failure to declare a pregnancy was prima facie evidence of the intention to commit infanticide, so any woman who did not declare and could be linked to a dead child would be tried for that capital offense.

6. See ADCO B II 360 file 148, 29 December 1702–2 September 1703 (the father of an abandoned infant was ordered, after investigation, to pay Saint-Esprit hospital in Dijon 35£ in *dommages et intérêts*). In the second half of the eighteenth century, Muyart de Vouglans *Institutes*, p. 534, identified two types of abandonment, both criminal but with different punishment. Abandonment with the intention to let perish was a homicide and deserved capital punishment. Abandonment to foundling hospitals, on the other hand, did not reveal homicidal intention and so warranted flogging and banishment.

7. ADCO B II 45 file 7, 15 June 1700. The appellate court, the Parlement of Burgundy, was not so sure that attempted infanticide was proved in this case,

and since the child survived, it overruled the lower court's decision, substituting a less severe but still harsh punishment of flogging and a nine year banishment.

8. J.-Henri Pignot, *Gabriel de Roquette, un évêque reformateur sous Louis XIV* (Paris, 1876), 1:318.

9. ADCO B II 46 file 10, 23 July 1649. The emphasis on avoiding ignorance of the law was first made in a royal edict by Henri III in 1586, which demanded publication of the edict of 1556 every three months by the parish priests.

10. ADCO B II 45 file 11, 19 December 1726. For other examples of reiterations of the royal edict in parlementary *arrêts*, see B II 45 file 11, 9 March 1722; 20 September 1724; and, for a late seventeenth-century example, file 6, 11 August 1689. In 1701 Dijon's town council appended a reading of the edict of 1556 to a sentence of infanticide and stipulated that the edict would be read every three months during mass in the parish churches of its jurisdiction. See B II 365 file 1, 28 December 1701.

11. Ibid., B II 45 file 11, 19 December 1726.

12. Ibid., B II 360 file 54, 18 June–27 August 1595.

13. We do not have the sentence or the appeal to Parlement, but judging from other cases with similar incriminating evidence, it would be unlikely that Gueniotte's life was spared.

14. E. de La Cuisine, *Le Parlement de Bourgogne depuis son origine jusqu'à sa chute*, (Dijon and Paris, 1864), 2:308–12; Edouard Fournier, ed., *Variétés historiques et littéraires* (Paris, 1855), 1:35–47.

15. ADSL B 1785 file 2, 3 March–7 June 1668.

16. Muyart de Vouglans, *Institutes*, p. 531, noted that the crime of "voluntary abortion," although very frequent, was not pursued in court often because of the difficulty in separating "accidents . . . of nature [miscarriage]" and homicidal intention.

17. ADCO B II 46 file 15, 10 March 1671. The only other examples I encountered in my sample of 3,024 criminal trials were the following: ibid., B II 46, file 6, 30 April 1627; file 18, 23 July 1691; and B II 45, file 11, 26 February 1726. Each of these, however, also was a trial for infanticide.

18. There are many oblique references to abortion in trials concerning *rapt*, seduction, adultery, and the like. In 1602, the Bishop of Mâcon, Gaspard Dinet, included in his *Ordonnances générales faict par Msg le reverendissime évesque de Mascon pour le réglement de son diocèse*, (Lyon, 1602), p. 63, abortion "of fruit already animated" among eleven transgressions specifically reserved (fruitlessly, as it turned out) to episcopal jurisdiction, perhaps suggesting a not infrequently practiced crime. In 1781 in his book on seduction, Jean-François Fournel, *Traité de la séduction* (Paris, 1781), p. 390, assumed that abortion was more frequently practiced than infanticide.

19. AMD I 111, 1677.

20. See, for example, ADSL B 1795 file 2, 14 March 1694; ADD G 784, April 1700–May 1702.

21. ADSL B 1262, 7 February 1616.

22. Ibid., B 1265, 11 June–1 January 1635. No sentence was rendered, perhaps because Archigny had disappeared in August. Few other cases are as complete as the Archigny trial, but some parlementary *arrêts* intimate that feigning illness to obtain *remèdes et médicaments* to abort a pregnancy was a frequently employed strategy: see, for example, ADCO B II 46 file 6, 16 July 1631.

23. ADSL B 633, 11 June 1706–8 February 1707.

24. Of a sample of 3,024 criminal trials in Parlement between 1582 and 1730, only three cases accusing abandonment (*exposition d'enfant*) turned up, and, as the words indicate, the judges may have suspected infanticide: ADCO B II 45 file 2, 20 June 1670; B II 46 file 19, 2 August 1698; and B II 45 file 7, 21 June 1700. On the Catholic Church and child abandonment, see John Boswell, *The Kindness of Strangers: The Abandonment of Children in Western Europe from Late Antiquity to the Renaissance* (New York, 1988).

25. Religious teaching on abortion during the early modern period was ambivalent when the life of the mother was in danger (some casuists believed that it was legitimate before quickening) but was categorical in its condemnation for any other reason. See John T. Noonan, "Abortion and the Catholic Church: A Summary History," *Natural Law Forum* 12 (1967), 85–131.

26. ADCO B II 46 file 18, 23 July 1691.

27. For other examples of conviction for abortion without capital punishment, see ADCO B II 46 file 1, 22 November 1585; file 10, 10 January 1646; and file 15, 10 March 1671.

28. For other examples of execution resulting from abortion and termed infanticide, see ADCO B II 46 file 6, 16 July 1631; B II 45 file 11, 26 February 1726.

29. Muyart de Vouglans, *Institutes*, p. 531, suggests that this assumption was largely followed by the second half of the eighteenth century: "Following the rules of human justice, the punishment of women and girls who procure abortions before the fruit had taken life must be less than those of whom it would be proven that the fruit was animated at the time of the abortion." Fournel, *Traité de la séduction*, pp. 395–96, confirms that this was the thinking among other jurists of the eighteenth century.

30. On infanticide, see William Langer, "Infanticide: A Historical Survey," *History of Childhood Quarterly* 1 (Winter 1974), 353–65; Richard Trexler, "Infanticide in Florence: New Sources and First Results," *History of Childhood Quarterly* 1 (Fall 1973), 98–115; Y.-B. Brissaud, "Infanticide à la fin du moyen âge, ses motivations psychologiques et sa répression," *Revue historique de droit Français et étranger* 50 (1972), 229–56; and Peter C. Hoffer and N. E. H. Hull, *Murdering Mothers: Infanticide in England and New England, 1558–1803* (New York, 1981). For a nineteenth-century comparison, see Rachel G. Fuchs, *Poor and Pregnant in Paris: Strategies for Survival in the Nineteenth-Century France*, (New Brunswick, N.J., 1992), chap. 9.

31. 1669, 1671, 1674, 1689, 1690, 1691, 1695, and 1696.

32. In 1647, 1669, 1691, 1692, 1699, 1723, and 1725.

33. ADCO B II 46 file 18, 5 December 1692.

34. Ibid., file 19, 14 July 1699.

35. Ibid., B II 45 file 11, 16 March 1723.

36. Fournel, *Traité de la séduction*, p. 3. See also Eric-Maria Benabou, *La Prostitution et la police des moeurs au XVIIIe siècle* (Paris, 1987), pp. 35–38.

37. Muyart de Vouglans, pp. 486, 489.

38. Several examples of women living as concubines in exchange for material securtity can be offered throughout our period. See, for example, ADCO B II 360 file 50, 17–25 January 1573 (a pregnant Marie Panon readily admitted that she lived with a sequence of priests in Dijon, receiving food, lodging, and even cash for her sexual favors) ibid., 11–24 April 1595 (Nicole Morisot admitted she

was a priest's concubine; she confessed that she knew it was wrong, but, being without shelter, she did it out of "necessity").

39. ADCO B II 360 file 50, 15–26 July 1572.

40. Ibid., B II 46 file 1, 10 May 1582. For similar examples of nonmarital unions with children classified as *lubricque* or *paillardise*, see ibid., 18 January 1583, 23 February 1584; file 2, 16 March 1589, 12 September 1592; ADSL 8 G 36, 12 December 1634.

41. James Brundage, "Concubinage and Marriage in Medieval Canon Law," in Vern L. Bullough and James Brundage, eds., *Sexual Practices and the Medieval Church* (Buffalo, N.Y., 1982), p. 127. In 1659 the Bishop of Mâcon, Jean de Lingendes, demanded in his *Ordonnances synodales* (Macon, 1659) p. 99, that every priest report to the bishop at each diocesan synod whether any *concubinaires* or *femmes scandaleuses et de mauvaise vie* resided in their parishes. Zamet had required the same thing earlier in the century.

42. Muyart de Vouglans, *Institutes*, p. 492; Jean Bouhier, *Commentaire sur la coutume de Bourgogne* (Dijon, 1742–46), fol. 53r.

43. Cited by Benabou, *La Prostitution*, pp. 36–37.

44. AMD B190, fol. 216v.–217v., 7 April 1553.

45. ADCO B II 46 file 18, 4 January 1695.

46. Ibid., B II 45 file 6, 13 October 1688 (*vie libertine et scandaleuse, et larrecin*); B II 46 file 18, 1 July 1695; file 19, 18 January 1697, 25 September 1697.

47. ADCO B II 360 file 148, 11–12 July 1703.

48. In seventeenth-century literature, seductions of young peasant women by men (usually seigneurs) were often accompanied by presents of a material rather than a decorative nature—fine food rather than jewelry, for example. Such an economy had become a literary topos during the *grand siècle*. See, for example, Charles Sorel, *Histoire comique de Francion* (Paris, 1973).

49. ADCO B II 360 file 50, 26 January–11 February 1573.

50. Ibid., 13–28 March 1573.

51. ADD G 609, 3 April 1713; G800, 27–29 April 1713.

52. ADCO B II 360 file 189, 15 September 1720.

53. BMD, Mss. 876, vols. A–B. The various entries to these notebooks are only occasionally dated. This poem was not.

54. Antoine Joly de Blaisy, a royal councilor from Burgundy at the Paris Parlement in the late seventeenth and early eighteenth century, reflects this ambivalence in his published recollections, *Souvenirs d'un Président au Grand Conseil sous Louis XIV*, ed. Ernest Petit (Paris and Dijon, 1899). In his youth, he wrote, he and other *enfans de famille* gave themselves over to "debauchery," something he now recalled "with regret, even with a sort of shame," although his "comrades were a bit less restrained" than he (pp. 27–28, 32–33). Judy Coffin, "Artisans of the Sidewalk," *Radical History Review* 26 (1982), 89–101, discerns a similar ambiguity in the nineteenth century, although she cautions us from viewing prostitution only from the perspective of male sexual demands. I thank Professor Coffin for this reference.

55. Sigmund Freud, *Civilization and Its Discontents* (New York, 1962); Norbert Elias, *The Civilizing Process*, trans. Edmond Jephcott (New York, 1983); Michel Foucault, *Discipline and Punish: The Birth of the Prison*, trans. Alan Sheridan (New York, 1977).

56. See, for example, Georges Vigarello, *Le Corps redressé: Histoire d'un*

pouvoir pédgogique (Paris, 1978) and *Le Propre et le sale* (Paris, 1985); Bryan S. Turner, *The Body and Society: Explorations in Social Theory* (Oxford, 1984). See also Peter E. S. Freund, "Bringing Society into the Body: Understanding Socialized Human Nature," *Theory and Society* 17 (1988), 839–64.

57. For a brilliant example, see David Sabean's analysis of the concept of *herrschaft* in *Power in the Blood* (Cambridge, 1984).

58. See Victor Turner, *The Body and Society: Explorations in Social Theory,* esp. chaps. 1 and 2; Haunani-Kay Trask, *Eros and Power: The Promise of Feminist Theory* (Philadelphia, 1986), pp. 4, 30, 35; Arthur W. Frank, "For a Sociology of the Body: An Analytical Review," in Mike Featherstone, Mike Hepworth, and Bryan S. Turner, eds., *The Body: Social Process and Cultural Theory* (London, 1991), pp. 42, 47.

59. See Mary Douglas, *Natural Symbols: Explorations in Cosmology* (New York, 1982).

60. François Isambert et al., eds. *Recueil général des anciennes lois Françaises* 39 vols. (Paris, 1833–), 14:88.

61. Benabou, *La Prostitution*, pp. 22–23.

62. Jean Fournel, *Traité de la séduction* (Paris, 1781), pp. 3, 404.

63. Benabou, *La Prostitution*, p. 30.

64. See, for example, AMD B 243, fol. 75v., 26 July 1605. ADCO B II 46 file 6, 10 July 1629; ibid., B II 360 file 58, 3 September 1641, 18 May–28 August 1642; B II 46 file 10, 16 November 1648; B II 45 file 2, 2 June 1670; B II 46 file 18, 17 April 1693; file 19, 9 August 1697.

65. ADCO B II 360 file 50, 15–26 July 1572; B II 46 file 1, 10 May 1582, 18 January 1583, 23 February 1584; file 2, 16 March 1589, 12 September 1592; ADSL 8 G 36, 12 December 1634; ADCO B II 46 file 18, 4 January 1695.

66. Benabou, *La Prostitution*, p. 33.

67. A commonplace assumption in the Middle Ages, owing to the influence of Saint Augustine. In defining respectable behavior, Olivier Maillard, *La Confession* (Paris, n.d., [1495]), fol. 9r., used prostitutes as the opposite; he assumed their existence but found them useful as a boundary marker between respectability and disgrace.

68. See Jacques Rossiaud, *Medieval Prostitution*, trans. Lydia Cochrane (Oxford, 1988); Lyndal Roper, "Discipline and Respectability: Prostitution and the Reformation in Augsburg," *History Workshop Journal* 19 (1985), 3–28.

69. Jacques-Paul Migne, ed., *Collection intégrale et universelle des orateurs sacrés du premier ordre* (Paris, 1845), 39:1348, 1354.

70. Antoine Beaugendre, *La Vie de Messire Bénigne Joly . . .* (Paris, 1854; orig. ed. 1700), pp. 71–73.

71. Joost Damhoudere, *Pratique judiciaire es causes criminelles* (Antwerp, 1564), fols. 107v.–108r.

72. Pierre-François Muyart de Vouglans, *Institutes au droit criminel* (Paris, 1757), p. 493, 495, 496; Claude-Joseph de Ferrière, *Dictionnaire de droit et de pratique* (Paris, 1749), 2:267–68.

73. The sample is based on ADCO B II 45 and 46 and copies of original *arrêts* since lost compiled by Burgundian jurists (BMD Mss. 1110).

74. Benabou, *La Prostitution*, p. 20, reports similar patterns in eighteenth-century Paris.

75. This was also true in Reformation Germany; see Lyndal Roper, "Moth-

ers of Debauchery: Procuresses in Reformation Augsburg," *German History* 6:1 (1988), 5.

76. ADCO B II 46 file 1, 7 July 1586; file 2, 17 December 1591; file 6, 17–24 July 1629.

77. Ibid., B II 45 file 2, 19 January 1672.

78. BMD Mss. MF 1110, p. 355, 11 August 1571.

79. ADCO B II 45 file 7, 16 December 1700.

80. Of the 39 cases appealed to Parlement in my sample between 1571 and 1720, 12 dated before 1645; Parlement upheld corporal punishment in all but 2 of those.

81. See, for example, ADCO B II 46 file 10, 15 June 1649; file 15, 13 August 1669; B II 45 file 2, 12 October 1669; B II 46 file 18, 19 September 1691; file 19, 23 January 1699.

82. ADCO B II 46 file 10, 16 November 1648 (*vie lubricque et scandaleuse*); 12 January 1649 (*vie lubricque et scandaleuse*); 21 January 1649 (*maquerellage public, vie lubricque et scandaleuse*); 12 March 1649 (*maquerellage et vie scandaleuse*); 15 June 1649 (*maquerellage, vie lubricque et scandaleuse*); 12 August 1649 (*maquerellage, vie lubricque et scandaleuse*); B II 360 file 65, 9 January 1649 (*maquerellage, vie lubricque et scandaleuse*).

83. Ibid., B II 46 file 10, 12 March 1649.

84. Examples abound, but see ADCO B II 46 file 2, 19 December 1588 (poisoning); 18 February 1589 (selling tainted milk); file 6, 27 April 1629 (adultery); B II 45 file 2, 7 May 1668 (concealing stolen property); 12 October 1669 (burglary, concealing stolen property); 12 January 1673 (larceny).

85. See, for example, ADCO B II 46 file 6, 24 July 1629; B II 360 file 65, 4 April 1648; B II 46 file 10, 15 June 1649; 12 August 1649; B II 45 file 2, 22 October 1667.

86. Archives Communales de Chalon-sur-Saône, Series FF, file 9, 29 October 1623; ADCO B II 360 file 58, 24 January 1631; ADSL B 1785 file 2, 7 December 1666; ADCO B II 360 file 189, 15–24 September 1720.

87. Both Rossiaud and Leah Otis, *Prostitution in Medieval Society* (Chicago, 1985), contend that the fifteenth century was marked by a notable toleration of prostitution.

88. AMD I 142, (no day or month) 1486.

89. Ibid., no date, but certainly early sixteenth century.

90. Ibid., 26 May 1508.

91. ADCO B II 360 file 48, April 1571.

92. AMD I 142, 7 August 1584.

93. Representative examples are the following: ADCO B II 360 file 54, 18 January 1595. AMD I 143, 8 February 1608; B 248, fol. 121v.–122r., 5 October 1610; I 143, 8 September 1618, n.d. but c. 1620. ADCO B II 360 file 65, 6 August–7 September 1648, 4 September 1648; file 76, 8 June 1660, 18 June 1660. AMD I 143, 7 August 1674. ADCO B II 360 file 103, 24 August 1680; file 104, 26 February 1681, 8 March 1681.

94. ACCS FF9, 30 October 1623.

95. ADCO B II 360 file 63, 8 August 1647.

96. Ibid., file 121, 13 December 1689; file 177, 25 August 1716.

97. ADSL, B 1265, 22 June 1638. For other examples of slander alleging procuring, see ADCO B II 360 file 59, 21 February 1643; file 60, 30 August 1643, 23 October 1643; file 91, 15 May 1671; file 103, 17 February 1680.

98. ADCO B II 360 file 89, 9–29 May 1670.

99. See John Bossy, *Christianity in the West, 1400–1700* (Oxford, 1985), pt. 1.

100. An overwhelming percentage of the women tried for prostitution, procuring, or "loose living" were not native to the town in which they were arrested. This was an immigrant's trade.

101. ADCO B II 360 file 65, 6 August–7 September 1648.

102. Verbal exchanges alleging that someone kept a bordello was a serious charge against a woman's honor, as was alleging that someone had been branded for illicit sexual behavior. Such slanders served to mark out in the neighborhood who had honor and belonged and who did not, because established residents assumed that engaging in the market economy of the female body placed the practitioner outside the ranks of the respectable. On the complex systems of neighborhoods and the mechanisms and discourse of inclusion and exclusion, see my *Hands of Honor: Artisans and Their World in Dijon (1550–1650)* (Ithaca, N.Y., 1988), esp. chap. 4. See also Arlette Farge, *Vivre dans la rue à Paris au XVIIIe siècle* (Paris, 1979), and David Garrioch, *Neighborhood and Community in Paris, 1740–1790* (Cambridge, 1986).

103. References to these areas as locales of procuring and prostitution abound in the criminal records: ADCO, B II 360 file 48, April 1571. AMD I 142, 7 August 1584; I 143, 8 September 1618. BMD Mss. MF 1110, p. 357. ADCO B II 360 file 63, 11 November 1647, 11 November 1647, file 76, 18 June 1660; file 103, 24 August 1680; file 121, 13 December 1689.

104. ACCS, series FF file 9, 8 May 1646.

105. See, for example, ADCO B II 46 file 18, 19 September 1691; BMD ms MF 1110, p. 359, 15 October 1693.

106. Noel Prunel, "Deux fondations de la Compagnie du Saint-Sacrement de Dijon: Le Refuge et le Seminaire," *Revue d'histoire de l'église de France* 25 (1911), 6–7.

107. The many cases from all judicial levels that I have read concerning this crime from 1500 to 1730 confirm this. The primary documentation on which this study is based amply represents rural jurisdictions, and the appeals to Parlement always state where the crime had been committed.

108. Claude Grimmer, *La Femme et le bâtard* (Paris, 1983), p. 77, finds that 80 percent of Parisian procuresses in the eighteenth century were women.

109. BMD Mss. MF 1110, p. 357, 29 July 1644; ADCO B II 45 file 7, 16 December 1700. For other examples of men complicit in their wives' procuring, see ADCO B II 46 file 2, 19 December 1588; B II 45 file 2, 5 August 1667; B II 360 file 148, 25 June 1703.

110. ADCO B II 46 file 10, 12 August 1649.

111. Ibid., B II 360 file 76, 15–31 July 1660.

112. This retort sounds remarkably like the response of a sixteenth-century Lyon woman to the Genevan Consistory. Called to account for sleeping with her fiancé, she retorted, "Paris belongs to the king and my body belongs to me." See Natalie Davis, "Boundaries and the Sense of Self in Sixteenth-Century France," in *Reconstructing Individualism: Autonomy, Individuality and the Self in Western Thought*, ed. Thomas Heller, Morton Sosna, and David Wellbury (Stanford, 1986), p. 63.

113. ADCO B II 360 file 189, 14 September 1720.

114. In 10 of the 31 extant comedies from the French Renaissance,

procuresses (*maquerelles*) were cast. They were leading characters in *Les Esbahis* (Marion), *La Veuve* (Guillemette), and *Les Contens* (Françoise); see Catherine Campbell, *The French Procuress: Her Character in Renaissance Comedies* (New York, 1985).

115. Ibid., pp. 54, 126. On abortion, see AMD I 111, 1677.

116. Campbell, *French Procuress*, p. 120.

117. Ibid., p. 65.

118. See, for example, ADCO B II 365 file 1, 5 July 1707.

119. BMD Mss. MF 1110, p. 356, 24 April 1613.

120. ADCO B II 360 file 121, 13, 15 August 1689.

121. Grimmer, *La Femme et le bâtard*, p. 77.

122. In 1647 the procuress Margueritte Pignalet, the 40-year-old unmarried daughter of a military captain, offered shelter to a woman who was fleeing her abusive husband, only to be employed as a prostitute for Pignalet: ADCO B II 360 file 63, 8 August 1647.

123. Ibid., file 137, 11 July 1697.

124. Ibid., B II 365 file 1, 5 July 1707.

125. Ibid., B II 360 file 137, 25 October 1697.

126. Michéline Baulant, "Le Salaire des ouvriers du bâtiment à Paris de 1400 à 1726," *Annales: ESC* 26:2 (1971), 475.

127. References to how much prostitutes might earn from a sexual encounter appear in ADCO B II 360 file 76, 8 June 1660 (3 gold *louis*); and ADSL Series B file 1265, 22 June 1638 (a woman prosecuted for prostitution in the royal bailliage of Mâcon claimed she earned 4 *livres*).

128. ADCO B II 360 file 76, 8 June–11 July 1660.

129. Ibid., file 104, 24 May 1681.

130. Ibid., file 137, 11 July 1697.

131. Ibid., file 65, 4 September–18 October 1648.

132. Arlette Farge, *La Vie fragile* (Paris, 1986), chap. 2.

133. ADCO B II 360 file 89, 9 May 1670; for a similar example, see file 43, 2 February 1559.

134. Ibid., file 63, 26 May–17 August 1647.

135. References to the amount paid for a sexual encounter occasionally appear in the records (58 *sous*; 1, 3, and 4 golden *louis*; 4 *livres*; 1, 2 and 3 *pistolets*), but I have found only one reference to how the payment was split between procuress and prostitute: In 1675 a prostitute said that for the sex she had with "a man with a sword from Paris," she and her procuress each received 1 *pistolet*.

136. Jacques Solé comes to similar conclusions: see "Passion charnelle et société urbaine d'ancien régime: Amour vénal, amour libre et amour fou a Grenoble au milieu de règne Louis XIV," *Annales de la faculté des lettres et science humaines, Université de Nice* 9–10 (1969), pp. 219, 221.

137. Benabou, *La Prostitution*, p. 25, noted that in eighteenth-century Paris the *lieutenant général de police* was summarily judging *en audience* en masse the *debauchées* of the streets of Paris while the Châtelet heard only a handful, the Parlement even fewer.

138. Pierre Dufour [Paul Lacroix], *Mémoires curieux sur l'histoire des moeurs et de la prostitution en France* (Brussels, 1855–61), 1:155–60.

139. Unlike in *rapt* cases, however, litigation against prostitutes and women "of lascivious ways" was always initiated by the public official, and in only six instances in my sample were these officials joined by a *partie civile*.

140. ADCO B II 360 file 121, 13 and 15 August 1689.

141. Ibid., file 148, 25 June 1703.

142. Benabou, *La Prostitution*, p. 38, notes that in Paris repression and tolerance was paradoxically mixed; the police were indulgent to the existence of the well-organized and orderly brothels and tried to repress the *petits bordels de commun*, which too frequently were sites of public *scandal*.

143. In the eighteenth century, a distinction in the hierarchy of prostitutes was well established. Ibid., p. 34. See also Grimmer, *La Femme*, pp. 79, 106.

144. See, for example, ADCO B II 360 file 103, 24 August 1680; file 121, 7 July 1689; file 137, 30 January 1697. AMD I 143, 31 January 1700. ADCO B II 360 file 148, 7 June 1703; file 189, July–September 1720.

145. ADCO B II 360 file 76, 20 July 1660.

146. AMD I 110, 25 August 1675; I 111, 10 July 1683 (abandoned woman). ADCO B II 360 file 189, 12 July 1720 (Prinstet).

147. See, for example, ADCO B II 360 file 65, 9 January 1649; file 103, 24 August 1680; file 104, 2 March 1681. AMD I 143, 31 January 1700. See also Grimmer, *La Femme*, p. 78.

148. For example, ADCO B II 360 file 65, 4 September 1648; file 189, 18 July 1720.

149. According to John A. Carey, *Judicial Reform in France before the Revolution of 1789* (Cambridge, Mass., 1981), pp. 65, 60, the noted eighteenth-century legal theoretician and reformer the Marquis d'Argenson advocated restricting parlements to "purely judicial matters" and objected strongly to "the intrusion of law courts in police matters."

150. BMD, Mss. 876, vols. T–V.

151. Ibid., vols. M–O.

Conclusion

1. For a recent discussion of these issues, see Daniel Gordon, "Philosophy, Sociology, and Gender in the Enlightenment Conception of Public Opinion," and Sarah Maza, "The Bourgeoisie, Women, and the Public Sphere: Response to Daniel Gordon and David A. Bell," *French Historical Studies* 17:4 (Fall 1992). On the scientific ideas undergirding patriarchy, see Thomas Laqueur, "Orgasm, Generation, and the Politics of Reproductive Biology," in Catherine Gallagher and Thomas Laqueur, eds., *The Making of the Modern Body* (Berkeley, 1987). Carole Pateman, *The Sexual Contract* (Stanford, 1988), argues that patriarchy has remained embedded in western law to the present, liberal contractual arguments notwithstanding.

2. See Robert Muchembled, *L'Invention de l'homme moderne: Sensibilités, moeurs et comportements collectifs sous l'Ancien Regime* (Paris, 1988), p. 426.

3. Jeffrey Merrick, *The Desacralization of the French Monarchy* (Baton Rouge, La., 1989), pp. 49, 52, 76, 167.

Bibliography

Primary Sources:
Archival Holdings and Manuscripts

Archival Holdings

A. Archives Départementales de la Côte-d'Or
   1. Archives judiciares
      a. Chambre de la Tournelle
         Régistres des audiences criminelles: B II 42
         Arrêts d'audiences au criminel: B II 45
         Arrêts definitifs criminels: B II 46
      b. Chambre des Enquêtes
         Régistres des audiences: B II 58
      c. Justice criminelle, Mairie de Dijon au bailliage
         Procédures criminelles: B II 360
         Declarations de grossesse: B II 365

B. Archives départmentales de la Saône-et-Loire
   1. Archives judiciaires
      a. Bailliage de Charolles
         Procédures criminelles: B 597, 622, 627, 633, 634, 635
      b. Prévôté royale de Mâcon
         Procédures criminelles: B 1696, 1697
      c. Bailliage royal et siège Présidial de Mâcon
         Procès criminels: B 1262, 1264, 1265
      d. Châtellenie royale de St.-Gengoux
         Procédures criminelles: B 1910, 1912, 1923, 1928, 1936, 1938

e. Justice mage de Cluny, Chevignes, Lourdon, Boutavent, and dependencies
Procédures criminelles: B 1782, 1783, 1785, 1789, 1795, 1809 1814
f. Châtellenie du comté de Charollais
Procédures criminelles: B 663, 667
2. Officialité d'Autun
Procédures: 8 G 37
Régistre d'audiences: 8 G 2-35
Monitoires separés: 8 G 66
3. Evêché d'Autun
Visites des paroisses: G 906, 909, 911, 926, 929, 935, 936

C. Archives départementales du Doubs
1. Officialité de Besançon
Requêtes à l'official: G 609
Causes matrimoniales: G 703
Procès criminels: G 784, 785, 790, 796, 800, 801

D. Archives municipales de Dijon
1. Police
Procédures: I 109, 110, 111, 113, 142, 143

E. Archives communales de Chalon-sur-Saône
1. Déliberations de la Chambre de Ville: BB 8, 10, 14, 16, 18, 23, 24, 32
2. Police
Procédures: FF 8, 9, 10

Manuscripts: Bibliothèque municipale de Dijon

"Arrêts notables du Parlement . . . [compiled by] Nicolas Perrier." 2 vols. Mss. 944–45.
"Discours et harangues prononcés par Mgr. Nicolas Brulart . . . premier président au Parlement de Dijon, 1657–1692." Mss. 319.
"Les Entretiens de table dans la serre du jardin de M. Le Loup, président en l'élection de Bresse . . . [by] Philippe Collet." Mss. 1151.
"Extraits authentiques destinés au bailliage de Charolais, 1549–1562." Mss. 960.
"Extraits des régistres du Parlement . . . 1515–1693." 6 vols. Mss. 1496–1501.
"Journal et régistre domestique de Pierre Genreau, procureur au Parlement." Mss. 1011
"Journal . . . passé au Parlement . . . 1598–1600 par Jean de Poligny, conseiller au Parlement." Mss. 763.
"Juridiction du Parlement, extraité de ses régistres." Mss. 1376–78.
"Mémoires et observations des choses plus mémorables et arrests de la cour de Parlement de Dijon, fait par Sr. [Joséph] Griguette, greffier, pour servir aux occurances." Mss. 308.
"Notes sur les ordonnances de 1667, 1669, 1670, 1673, et sur l'édit des épices de 1673, par [Jean] Melenet [in 1750]." Mss. 290.
"Recueil alphabétique d'arrêts et de deliberations secrets du Parlement de Dijon." Mss. 2292.
"Recueil d'arrest criminel . . ." Mss. 1110.

"Recueil de mémoires historiques." Mss. 911.

"Recueil des deliberations secrets du Parlement . . . [compiled by] le Président [Jean] Bouhier . . ." Mss. 1402.

"Recueil d'extraits de régistre du Parlement de Dijon . . ." Mss. 774.

"Régistre de plusieurs choses memorables . . . au Parlement . . . à 1662." Mss. 765.

"Remarques historiques . . . 1650–1669 [by] M. Gaudelet, auditeur à la Chambre des Comptes." Mss. 757

Primary Sources: Printed

Abelly, Louis, Mgr. *La Vie du venerable serviteur de dieu Vincent de Paul.* 3 vols. Paris, 1664, 1843–54, 1865.

Ancourt, L'Abbé d'. *The Lady's Preceptor; or, a Letter to a Young Lady of Distinction Upon Politeness.* London, 1745.

André, Francisque, Jules-Joseph Vernier, and Pierre Pietresson de Saint-Aubin, eds. *Inventaire sommaire des archives départementales antérieures à 1790: Aube.* Series G, vol. 3. Troyes, 1930.

Arbois de Jubainville, H. d', and Franscisque André, eds. *Inventaire sommaire des archives départementales antérieures à 1790: Aube.* Series G, vol. 2. Paris, 1896.

Argenson, René de Voyer d', ed. *Les Annales de la Compagnie du Saint-Sacrement.* Marseille, 1900.

Auboux, Jean d'. *La Véritable théorie pratique civile et criminelle des officialités.* Paris, 1648.

Ayrault, Pierre. *A Discourse for Parents' Honor and Authority Written Respectively to Reclaim a Young Man That Was a Counterfeit Iesuite, by His Father.* Trans. Io. Budden. London, 1614.

———. *L'Ordre, formalité et instruction judiciaire.* Paris, 1576.

Le Bailliage de Dijon après la bataille de Rocroy: Procès-verbaux de la visite des feux. Dijon, 1857.

Balinghem, Antoine de, S.J. *Le Vrai point d'honneur à garder en conversant, pour vivre honorablement et paisiblement avec un chacun.* St. Omer, 1618.

Bary, René. *L'Esprit de cour ou les conversations galantes.* Paris, 1662.

Beaugendre, Antoine. *La Vie de Messire Bénigne Joly, docteur de la Faculté de Paris . . . chanoine de l'église abbatiale et collégiale de Saint-Etienne de Dijon.* Paris, 1854; orig. ed. 1700.

Beaurepaire, E. de, ed. "Livre de raison de Jean Lemulier, avocat de Semur." *Bullétin de la société des antiquaires de Normandie* 6 (1870–73).

Bégat, Jean. *Remonstrances faictes au roy de France.* Anvers, 1564.

Benedicti, Jean. *La Somme des pechez.* Lyon, 1584; Paris, 1601.

Beuvelet, Mathieu. *Instructions sur le manuel par forme de demandes et responses familières pour servir à ceux qui dans les seminaires se preparent à l'administration des sacrements.* 4th ed. Paris, 1659.

Bienséance de la conversation entre les hommes. 1617.

Bignon, Jérome. *La Grandeur de nos roys et de leur souveraine puissance.* Paris, 1615.

———. *De L'excellence des roys, et du royaume de France, traitant de la preséance, premier rang et prérogatives des roys de France par dessus les autres et des causes d'icelles.* Paris, 1610.

Blanchard, Antoine. *Essay d'exortation pour les états différents des malades . . . on y a joint un examen général sur tous les commandements et sur les pechés de plusieurs estats*. 2 vols. Paris, 1713.

Bodin, Jean. *The Six Bookes of a Commonweale*. Ed. Kenneth D. McRae. Cambridge, Mass., 1962.

Boiastuau, Pierre. *Le Théatre du monde, où il est faict un ample discours des misères humaines*. Antwerp, 1580.

Boileau, Jacques. *De l'Abus des nuditez de gorge*. Paris, 1858; orig. ed. 1675.

Bonal, Raymond. *Le Cours de la théologie morale dans lequel les cas de conscience sont amplement enseignez*. 4th ed. 2 vols. Paris, 1662.

Borromeo, Saint Charles. *Instructions aux confesseurs*. Lyon, 1671; Paris, 1847.

Bossuet, Jacques-Bénigne. *Oeuvres complètes*. 10 vols. Paris, 1885.

Bouchet, Jean. *Les Triumphes de la noble et amoureuse dame et l'art de honnestement aymer*. Paris, 1536.

Boudon, Henri-Marie. *Oeuvres complètes*. 3 vols. Paris, 1856.

Bouelles, Charles de. *Proverbes et dicts sententieux, avec l'interpretation d'iceux*. Paris, 1557.

Bouhier, Jean. *Commentaire sur la coutume de Bourgogne . . .* Dijon, 1742–46.

——. *Traité des moyens qui sont en usage en France pour la preuve de l'impuissance de l'homme et quelques pièces curieuses sur le même sujet*. Paris, 1756.

Bourdaloue, Louis. *Oeuvres complètes*. 16 vols. Versailles, 1812.

Bourdoise, Adrien. *L'Idée d'un bon ecclésiastique, ou les sentences chrestiennes et cléricales*. Paris, 1667.

Bourée, Edme Bernard. *Vie de Madame de Courcelles de Pourlans*. Lyon, 1699.

——. *Homélies sur les évangiles de tous les dimanches de l'année pour l'instruction des fidèles*. 4 vols. Lyon, 1703.

Bourgeois, Louise, dite Boursier. *Observations diverses sur la sterilité, perte de fruict, foecundité, accouchements, et maladies des femmes, et enfants nouveaux-naix*. 2d ed. Rouen, 1626.

Bourgoing, François. *Homélies chrestiennes sur les évangiles des dimanches et des fêtes principales de l'année*. Paris, 1648.

Bouvot, Job. *Nouveau recueil des arrests de Bourgogne, où sont contenues diverses notables questions de droict tant coustumier que romain, controversées entre les docteurs, proposée à Me J. Bouvot, avocat au Parlement de Bourgogne, decidés par jugements et arrests de la cour souveraine du Parlement de Dijon . . .* 2 vols. Coligny, 1623; Geneva, 1628.

Brantôme, Abbé, and seigneur de [Pierre de Bourdeille]. *Les Dames galantes*. Ed. Pascal Pia. Paris, 1981.

——. *Mémoires. La vie des hommes illustrés*. Paris, 1722.

Bröe, Pierre. *Des Bonnes moeurs et honnestes contenances*. Lyon, 1555.

Bruneau, Antoine. *Observations et maximes sur les matières criminelles . . . ouvrage necéssaire à tous juges, avocats, procureurs . . . pour bien faire et instruire un procès criminel*. Paris, 1715.

Bruys, François. *The Art of Knowing Women; or, The Female Sex Dissected, in a Faithful Representation of Their Virtues and Vices*. London, 1730.

Bussy, Roger de Rabutin, comte de. *L'Histoire amoureuse des gaules*. Paris, 1966.

——. *Mémoires secrets de M. le comte de Bussy-Rabutin, contenant sa vie publique et privée, ses aventures galantes . . . et les evénements les plus intéressants de l'Europe depuis l'année 1617 jusqu'en l'année 1667*. 2 vols. Paris, 1882; 1st ed. 1696.

——. *Correspondance*. Ed. L. Lalanne. 6 vols. Paris, 1858–59.

Caillières, Jacques. *The Courtier's Calling, Shewing the Ways of Making a Fortune, and the Art of Living at Court, According to the Maxims of Policy and Morality*. London, 1675.

Callières, François de. *Des Mots à la mode et des nouvelles façons de parler*. Paris, 1692.

———. *Du Bon et du mauvais usage*. Paris, 1693.

———. *Du Bel Esprit ou sont examinés les sentiments qu'on a d'ordinaire dans le monde*. Paris, 1695.

———. *La Logique des amans, ou, L'amour logicien*. Paris, 1669.

Camus, Jean-Pierre. *The Spirit of Saint François de Sales*. Trans. C. F. Kelley. London, 1953.

———. *Homélies dominicales*. Rouen, 1624.

———. *Homélies des Etats Généraux (1614–15)*. Ed. Jean Descrains. Geneva, 1970.

Canons and Decrees of the Council of Trent. Trans. H. J. Schroeder. St. Louis and London, 1941.

Catechism of the Council of Trent for Parish Priests. Trans. John A. McHugh and Charles J. Callan. New York and London, 1947.

Chantal, Jeanne Françoise de Fremyot, baronne de. *Lettres de Mme. de Chantal*. 5 vols. Paris, 1877–79.

Chartier, Alain. *Delectable Demaundes, and Pleasant Questions, with Their Severall Answers, in Matters of Love*. London, 1596.

Chenu, Jean. *Livre des offices de France . . . des édits faits . . . réglemens notables donnez par les cours souueraines, entre ecclésiastiques, pour la célébration du seruice diuin*. Paris, 1620.

Chevassu, Joseph. *Le Missionaire paroissial*. Lyon, 1755.

Chevreul, H., ed. *Pièces sur la ligue en Bourgogne*. Dijon, 1883.

Choppin, René. *Traité de la police ecclésiastique*. Paris, 1662.

Civilité puérile et morale, pour instruire les enfans à se bien comporter. Dijon, n.d.

Clichtove, Josse. *Le Traicté de la vraye noblesse*. Paris, 1529.

Contre la médisance; dialogue et réflexions. Paris, 1693.

Corlieu, Girard. *Instruction pour tous estats. En laquelle, après une brefve description des abus qui s'y commettent, est sommairemen descrit par bons et saincts enseignemens, commen chacun se doit gouverner en l'estat auquel Dieu l'a appellé . . .* Paris, 1589.

Courtin, Antoine de. *Nouveau traité de la civilité qui se pratique en France et ailleurs, parmy les honnestes gens*. Paris, 1671.

———. *Traité de la Paresse, ou l'art de bien employer le temps en toute sorte de conditions*. Paris, 1679.

La Courtisane déchiffrée, dediée aux dames vertueuses de ce temps. Paris, 1617.

Cureau de la Chambre, Marin. *Les Caractères des passions*. Amsterdam, 1658.

Cusset, Pierre. *L'Illustre orbandale ou l'histoire ancienne et moderne de . . . Chalon-sur-Saone*. 2 vols. Lyon and Chalon, 1662.

Damhoudere, Joost de. *Pratique judiciaire es causes criminelles*. Antwerp, 1564.

Deffence du traicté du délict commun et cas privilégié en la distinction des deux puissances, ecclésiastique et seculier. Dijon, 1612.

Delamare, Nicolas. *Traité de la police*. Paris, 1722.

DeMoure, Antonio Fernandes. *L'Examen de théologie morale*. Rouen, 1638.

De Paul, Saint Vincent. *Correspondence*. Ed. Jacqueline Kilar. Trans. Helen Marie Law et al. New York, 1985.

De Sales, Saint François. *Introduction to the Devout Life*. Trans. John K. Ryan. New York, 1950.

———. *Avertissements aux confesseurs*. Paris, 1647.

———. *Les Femmes Mariées*. Paris, 1967.

———. *Les Oeuvres du bienheureux François de Sales*. Paris, 1647.

Deslandes, André François Boureau. *The Art of Being Easy at All Times, and in All Places*. Trans. Edward Combe. London, 1724.

Dictionnaire de l'Académie française. Paris, 1694.

Dinet, Gaspard. *Ordonnances générales faict par Mgr le reverendissime évesque de Mascon pour le réglement de son diocèse*. Lyon, 1602.

Dodin, André, ed. *Saint Vincent de Paul: Textes et études*. Paris, 1949.

Dôle, Michel de. *Le Miroir du pecheur penitent*. Louvain, 1627.

DuBosc, Jacques. *L'Honneste femme*. Paris, 1632.

Ducasse, François. *Pratique de la jurisdiction ecclésiastique volontaire et contentieuse*. Paris, 1702.

DuChesne, André. *Figures mystique du riche et précieux cabinet des dames . . . pompes du corps feminin*. Paris, 1605.

Dugny de Courgengouch, Philibert. *Constitutiones Synodales dioceseos Heduensis recentur*. [Manuscript]

Duguet, J.-J. *Conduite d'une dame chrétienne pour vivre saintement dans le monde*. Paris, 1724.

Du Pradel, Jean. *Traité contre le luxe*. Paris, 1705.

Duranthon, Antoine, abbé. *Des Procès-Verbaux des assemblées générales du clergé de France depuis 1560 jusqu'à present*. 9 vols. Paris, 1767–80.

Du Refuge, Eustache. *Traicté de la cour, ou l'instruction des courtisans*. Paris, 1616.

Du Rousseaud de la Combe, G. *Traité des matières criminelles suivant l'ordonnance du mois d'août 1670 . . . jusqu'à présent*. Paris, 1744.

Duval, Jacques. *Traité des hermaphrodits, parties génitales, accouchemens des femmes . . .* Rouen, 1612.

Erasmus, Desiderius. *La Civilité puérile et honnête*. Trans. A. Bonneau. Paris, 1877.

Esprit, Jacques. *Discourses on the Deceitfulness of Humane Virtues*. Trans. William Beauvoir. London, 1706.

Etat des paroisses et communautés du bailliage d'Autun en 1645, d'après le procès-verbal de la visite des feux. Autun and Paris, 1876.

Exhortation aux dames vertueuses, en laquelle est desmonstré le vray poinct d'honneur. Paris, 1597.

Faren, Antoine. *La Pratique de soy bien confesser*. Lyon, 1485?

Faret, Nicolas. *L'Honneste homme, ou, l'art de plaire à la court*. Paris, 1636.

Ferrand, Jacques. *A Treatise on Lovesickness*. Trans. Donald A. Beecher and Massimo Ciavolella. Syracuse, N.Y., 1990.

Ferrière, Claude de. *Des droits de patronage, de présentation aux benéfices, de préséances des patrons, des seigneurs, et autres*. Paris, 1686.

———. *Dictionnaire de droit et de pratique*. 2d ed. 2 vols. Paris, 1740.

Ferville, Sieur de. *La Mechancete des femmes*. Paris, 1618.

Fevret, Charles. *Traité de l'abus et du vray sujet des appellations qualifiées de ce nom d'abus*. Dijon, 1654.

Flannigan, Arthur, ed. *Les Désordres de l'amour: Madame de Villedieu: A Critical Edition*. Lanham, Md., 1986.

Fournel, Jean François. *Traité de la séduction*. Paris, 1781.

————. *Traité de l'adultère, consideré dans l'ordre judiciaire.* Paris, 1778.

Furetière, Antoine. *Dictionnaire universel.* Paris, 1682.

Gagnard, Philippe. *Histoire de l'église d'Autun.* Autun, 1774.

Garasse, François. *La doctrine curieuse des beaux esprits de ce temps contre less athées, les huguenots, les catholiques gallicans, les libertins, les voluptueux.* New York, 1971; orig. ed. Paris, 1623.

Garnier, Joseph, ed. *Correspondance de la Maire de Dijon extraité des archives de cette ville.* 3 vols. Dijon, 1868–70.

————. *Lettres d'Etienne Bernard, maire de Dijon, sur l'assemblée des Etats Généraux de la Ligue en 1593.* Paris, 1860.

Garreau, Antoine. *Description du gouvernement de Bourgogne, suivant ses principales divisions temporelles, ecclésiastiques, militaires et civiles, avec un abrège de l'histoire de la province et une description particulière de chaque pays, villes et bourgs qui en dependent.* Dijon, 1717.

Gauthier, J., ed. "Ephémerides de Jean Garinet, médécin de Besançon." *Mémoires de l'académie de Besançon* 135 (1886).

Gerbais, Jean. *Lettre d'un docteur de Sorbonne à une dame de qualité touchant les dorures des habits des femmes . . .* Paris, 1696.

————. *Traité du pouvoir de l'église et des princes sur les empeschemens de mariage.* Paris, 1646.

Gerson, Jean. *L'Instruction des curez pour instruire le simple peuple . . .* Paris, 1510?

————. *Oeuvres complètes.* Ed. Palemon Glorieux. 7 vols. Paris, Tournai, Rome, and New York, 1960–.

Godeau, Antoine. *Les Tableaux de la pénitence.* 2d ed. Paris, 1656.

Goussault, Abbé. *Le Portrait de l'honnête homme.* Paris, 1689.

Grammont, François Joseph de. *Statuta seu decreta synodalia bisuntiae . . .* Vesoul, 1707.

Grenaille, François de, Sieur de Chatounieres. *L'Honneste fille.* Paris, 1639.

————. *L'Honneste mariage.* Paris, 1640.

————. *L'Honneste veuve.* Paris, 1640.

————. *La Mode ou caractère de la religion . . . des compliments, des habits, et du style du temps.* Paris, 1642.

Habert, Louis. *Pratique du sacrement de pénitence.* Paris, 1687.

Héricourt du Vatier, Louis de. *Les Loix ecclésiastiques de France dans leur ordre naturel et une analyse des livres de droit canonique conferez avec les usages de l'église gallicane.* Paris, 1714.

Imbert, Jean. *La Pratique judiciaire, tant civile que criminelle, reçue et observée partout le royaume de France, enrichie . . . par M. Pierre Guenois . . . et B. Automne.* Coligny, 1615.

Instructions pour les confesseurs du diocèse de Chalon-sur-Saône tirée du avis de St. Charles et du Rituel du diocèse. Lyon, 1682.

Isambert, Francois et al., eds. *Recueil général des anciennes lois françaises.* 39 vols. Paris, 1833.

Jeannin, Pierre. "Discours apologétique fait par M. le Président Jeannin, de sa conduite durant les troubles de la Ligue, et depuis sous les regnes du feu Roi Henri-le-Grand, et du Rois à present règnant, 1622." In *Négociations diplomatiques et politiques du Président Jeannin.* Paris, 1819.

Jolibois, E., ed. *Les Chroniques de l'évêche de Langres.* Chaumont, 1842.

Joly de Blaisy, Antoine. *Souvenirs d'un président au Grand Conseil sous Louis XIV.* Ed. Ernest Petit. Paris and Dijon, 1899.

Jousse, Daniel. *Nouveau commentaire sur l'édit du mois d'avril 1695, concernant la jurisdiction ecclésiastique.* Paris, 1757.

———. *Traité de la jurisdiction volontaire et contentieuse des officiaux.* Paris, 1749.

———. *Nouveau commentaire sur l'ordonnance criminelle du mois d'août 1670 avec un abrège de la jurisprudence criminelle.* Paris, 1763.

———. *Traité de la justice criminelle de France.* 4 vols. Paris, 1771.

Juvernay, Pierre. *La Foudre foudroyant et ravageant contre les pechés mortels.* Paris, 1635.

———. *Discours particulier contre les femmes debraillées de ce temps.* Paris, 1637; Geneva, 1867.

L'Estoile, Pierre de. *Mémoires-Journaux.* 12 vols. Paris, 1875–76.

La Cuisine, E. de. *Choix des lettres inédites écrites par Nicolas Brulart.* 2 vols. Dijon, 1859.

La Fayette, Marie Madeleine Pioche de La Vergne, Madame de. *La Princesse de Cleves.* Paris, 1989. Eng. trans. *The Princesse de Cleves.* Trans Walter J. Cobb. New York, 1989.

———. *L'Histoire de la Princesse de Montpensier; Histoire de La Comtesse de Tende.* Geneva, 1979.

Lalourcée, C., and F. Duval, eds. *Recueil des cahiers généraux des trois ordres aux Etats-Généraux.* 4 vols. Paris, 1789.

La Primaudaye, Pierre de. *Académie françoise, en laquelle il est traitté de l'institution des moeurs* . . . Paris, 1580. English trans. *The French Academy* . . . London, 1586.

La Rochefoucauld, François, duc de. *Maxims.* Trans. Leonard Tancock. London, 1959.

Lamet, Adrien Augustin de Bussy de, and Germain Fromageau. *Dictionnaire des cas de conscience decidés suivant les principes de la morale* . . . Paris, 1733.

LaSalle, Jean-Baptiste de. *Les Régles de la bienséance et de la civilité chrétienne.* Paris, 1703.

Le Boulanger de Chalussay. *Morale galante, ou l'art de bien aimer.* Amsterdam, 1669.

Lebrun de la Rochette, Claude. *Le Procez civil et criminel.* Paris, 1623.

LeGrand, Etienne, S.J. *L'Histoire sainte de la ville de Châtillon-sur-Seine au duché de Bourgogne.* Autun, 1651.

LePicard, François. *Les Sermons et instructions chrestiennes pour tous les jours . . . et dimanches.* Paris, 1566.

Lepileur, L., ed. *La Prostitution du XIIIe au XVIe siècle. Documents tirés des archives d'Avignon, Comtat Venaissin, de la principauté d'Orange, et de la ville impériale de Besançon.* Paris, 1908.

LeRidant, Pierre. *Traité sur le mariage.* Paris, 1754.

———. *Code matrimonial ou recueil des édits, ordonnances et declarations sur le mariage, avec les décisions les plus importantes sur cette matière.* Paris, 1766.

LeSemelier, Jean Laurent. *Conférences ecclésiastiques de Paris sur le mariage.* 5 vols. Paris, 1713.

Liebault, Jean. *Trois livres de l'embellissement du corps humain.* Paris, 1582.

Lingendes, Jean de. *Ordonnances synodales* . . . Macon, 1659.

Loyseau, Charles. *Cinq livres du droit des offices.* Paris, 1613.

———. *Traité des seigneuries.* Paris, 1608.

Lurion, R. de, ed. "Etat de ce qui s'est passé à Besançon depuis 1612 jusqu'en 1721." *Mémoires de Franche-Comté* 9 (1900).

Mabillon, Jean. "Itinerarium Burgundicum." In *Ouvrages posthumes*. 3 vols. Paris, 1724.

Macheret, Clément. *Journal de ce qui s'est passé de plus mémorable à Langres et aux environs, 1628–1658*. 2 vols. Langres, 1883.

Maillard, Olivier. *La Confession*. Paris, n.d., [1495].

Marmet de Valcroissant, Melchior de. *Maximes pour vivre heureusement dans le monde et pour former l'honneste homme*. Paris, 1662.

Maupas du Tour, Henri Cauchon de. *La Vie de la venérable Mère Jeanne Françoise Frémiot de Chantal*. Paris, 1644.

Méré, Antoine Gombauld, Chevalier de. *Oeuvres complètes*. Ed. Charles-H. Boudhors. 3 vols. Paris, 1930.

Migne, Jacques-Paul, ed. *Collection intégrale et universelle des orateurs sacrés du premier ordre*. 99 vols. Paris, 1845–.

Milhard, Pierre. *La Vraye guide des curez, vicaires, et confesseurs . . .* Lyon, 1604.

———. *Inventaire des cas de conscience*. Toulouse, 1611.

Mille, Jean de. *Pratique criminelle*. Ed. Arlette Lebigre. Paris, 1983; orig, ed. 1541.

Morvan de Bellegarde, Jean-Baptiste. *Réflexions sur ce qui peut plaire ou déplaire dans le commerce du monde*. Paris, 1688.

———. *Traité de la civilité ou l'education parfaite*. Paris, 1713.

Muteau, Charles, ed. *Mémoires de Malteste, conseiller au Parlement*. Dijon, 1866.

———. *Mémoires de M. A. Millotet . . . des choses qui se sont passées en Bourgogne depuis 1650 jusqu'à 1668*. Dijon, 1866.

Muyart de Vouglans, Pierre-François. *Institutes au droit criminel*. Paris, 1757.

———. *Les Loix criminelles de France dans temps et ordres naturels*. Paris, 1780.

Nervèze, Antoine de. "La Guide des courtisans." In *Les Oeuvres morales*. Paris, 1610.

Olin, John C., ed. *Catholic Reform from Cardinal Ximenez to the Council of Trent, 1495–1563*. New York, 1990.

Olivier, Jacques. *L'Alphabet de l'imperfection et malice des femmes*. Rouen, 1634.

Papon, Jean. *Recueil d'arrests notables des cours souveraines de France*. Paris, 1563.

Perrier, François. *Arrets notables du Parlement de Dijon . . .* 2 vols. Dijon, 1735.

Perry, Claude, S.J. *Histoire civile et ecclésiastique, ancienne et moderne, de la ville et cité de Chalon-sur-Saône*. Chalon, 1659.

Philalethe, Timothée (pseud). *De la Modestie des femmes et des filles chrétiennes dans leurs habits et dans tout leur extérieur*. Liège, 1675.

Pic, Jean, Abbé. *Discours sur la bienséance, avec des maximes et des réflexions très importantes pour réduire cette vertu en usage*. Paris, 1688.

Pingaud, Léonce, ed. *Correspondance des Saulx-Tavanes au XVIe siècle*. Paris, 1877.

Polanco, Juan, S.J. *Directoire des confesseurs*. Douai, 1559.

Polman, Jean. *La Chancre ou couvre-sein feminin, ensemble, la voile ou couvre-chef feminin*. Douai, 1635.

Prunel, N., ed. *Lettres spirituelles de Sébastien Zamet*. Dijon, 1912.

Pure, Michel de la. *La Prétieuse, ou le mystère des ruelles*. Ed. Emile Magne. 2 vols. Paris, 1938–39.

Quentin, Jean. *Examen de conscience pour soy cognoistre et bien se confesser*. Paris, 1500?

Reguis, L. *La Voix du pasteur*. 2 vols. Paris, 1766.

Reims, Jean-François de. *Le Directeur pacifique des consciences*. Paris, 1645.

Remond des Cours, Nicolas. *La Véritable politique des personnes de qualité*. Paris, 1693.

Restif de la Bretonne. *Le Pornographe, ou, idées d'un honnête homme sur un projet de réglement pour les prostituées, propre à prévenir les malheurs qu'occasione le publicisme de femmes.* Vars, 1983.

Richelet, Pierre. *Dictionnaire français.* Paris, 1680.

Richelieu, Cardinal. *Instruction du chrestien.* Paris, 1640.

Le Roti-Cochon, ou méthode très-facile pour bien apprendre les enfans à lire. Dijon, n.d.

Roussel, Roy, ed. *The Conversation of the Sexes: Seduction and Equality in Selected 17th- and 18th-Century Texts.* New York, 1986.

Saint-Evremond, Charles Marguetel de Saint Denis, Seigneur de. *Oeuvres en prose.* Ed. René Ternois. 4 vols. Paris, 1962–69.

———. *The Letters of Saint Evremond.* Ed. and trans. John Hayward. London, 1930.

Sainte-Beuve, Jacques de. *Resolution de plusieurs cas de conscience touchant la morale et la discipline de l'église.* Paris, 1689.

Sanchez, Tomas. *De Sancto Matrimonii.* Lyon, 1621.

Senault, Jean-François. *L'Homme criminel.* Paris, 1644.

———. *De l'Usage des passions.* Paris, 1641.

Serpillon, François. *Code Criminelle ou commentaire de l'ordonnance de 1670.* 4 vols. Lyon, 1767.

Seyssel, Claude de. *The Monarchy of France.* Trans. J. H. Hexter. New Haven, 1981.

Sorel, Charles. *Les Recréations galantes.* Paris, 1671.

———. *Histoire comique de Francion.* Paris, 1973.

Soulatges, J. A. *Traité des crimes.* Toulouse, 1762.

Tabourot, Estienne. *Les Bigarrures du seigneur des Accords, et les escraignes Dijonnaises.* Geneva, 1970; orig. ed. 1583.

Tallement de Réaux, Gédéon. *Les Historiettes.* Paris, 1929.

Tassy, Henry Felix de. *Recueil des ordonnances sinodales du diocèse de Chalon.* Lyon, 1700.

Thésut-Niquevard, Jacques de, Abbé. *Oraison funébre de Messire Jean de Maupeou . . .* Chalon, 1677.

Toledo, Francisco. *L'Instruction des prêtres.* Lyon, 1628.

Tremblay, Jean Frain du. *Discours sur l'origine de la poésie, sur son usage et sur le bon goût.* Paris, 1711.

Trotti de La Chetartie. *Instructions pour un jeune seigneur ou l'idée d'un galant homme.* Paris, 1683.

Vallemont, Le Lorrain de, Abbé. *Du Sécret des mystères ou l'apologie de la rubrique des missels.* Paris, 1710.

Venette, Nicolas. *La Génération de l'homme ou tableau de l'amour conjugal considéré dans l'état de mariage.* Amsterdam, 1687.

Versons, André. *Declaration de l'institution de la congrégation de Notre-Dame-du-Refuge.* Paris, 1657.

Viau, Théophile de. *Oeuvres complètes.* Nandeln, Lichtenstein, 1972.

———. *Le Parnasse satyrique.* Paris, 1855; orig. ed. 1623.

Vigneulles, Philippe de. *Les Cent nouvelles nouvelles.* Ed. Charles Livingston. Geneva, 1972.

Villedieu, Madame de. *Les Désordres de l'amour.* Washington, D.C., 1982.

Xaintonge, Pierre de. *Harangues et arrests prononcez et conclusions prises aux audiances du Parlement de Bourgogne depuis l'an 1615 jusqu'en 1625.* Paris, 1631.

Zamet, Sébastien. *Statuts et ordonnances faittes en diverses assemblées synodales tenues par reverendissime père en Dieu Messire Sébastien évesque duc de Langres pair de France.* Langres, 1629.

Secondary Sources

Abbiaticci, A. et al. *Crimes et criminalitè en France, 17e et 18e siècles.* Cahiers des Annales no. 33. Paris, 1971.

Abercrombie, N., S. Hill, and B. S. Turner. *The Dominant Ideology Thesis.* London, 1980.

Abord, Hippolyte. *Histoire de la réforme et de la Ligue dans la ville d'Autun.* 3 vols. Autun, 1885–87.

Alexander, Jeffrey C., and Steven Seidman. *Culture and Society: Contemporary Debates.* Cambridge, 1990.

Alexander, Sally, and Barbara Taylor. "In Defence of 'Patriarchy.'" In *People's History and Socialist Theory.* Ed. Raphael Samuel. London, 1981.

Allier, Raoul. *La Cabale des dévots.* Paris, 1902.

Amussen, Susan D. "Gender, Family and the Social Order, 1560–1725." In *Order and Disorder in Early Modern England.* Ed. John Stevenson and Anthony Fletcher. Cambridge, 1985.

Angenot, Marc. *Les Champions des femmes: Examen du discours sur la supériorité des femmes, 1400–1800.* Montreal, 1977.

Ankarloo, B., and Gustav Henningsen, eds. *Early Modern European Witchcraft: Centers and Peripheries.* Oxford, 1989.

Apostolides, J. M. *Le Roi machine.* Paris, 1981.

Archer, John, and Barbara Lloyd. *Sex and Gender.* Cambridge, 1982.

Archer, Margaret S. *Culture and Agency: The Place of Culture in Social Theory.* Cambridge, 1988.

Ariès, Philippe, and André Béjin, eds. *Western Sexuality: Practice and Precept in Past and Present Times.* Oxford, 1985.

Ariès, Philippe, and Georges Duby, eds. *Histoire de la vie privée.* Vol. 3. Paris, 1986.

Arnold, Katherine. "The Introduction of Poses to a Peruvian Brothel and Changing Images of Male and Female." In *The Anthropology of the Body*, pp. 179–97. Ed. John Blacking. London, 1977.

Artonne, A., ed. *Repertoire des statuts synodaux des dioceses de l'ancienne France.* Paris, 1963.

Audisio, Gabriel. "Sector et sexe: Puritanisme et licence (XVI–XVII siècles)." In *Sexualité et religion.* Paris, 1988.

Bady, René. "François de Sales, maître d'honnêteté." *XVIIe siècle* 78 (1968), 3–20.

Baker, J. H. *Legal Records and the Historian.* London, 1978.

Bamford, Paul. *Fighting Ships and Prisons: The Mediterranean Galleys in the Age of Louis XIV.* Minneapolis, 1973.

Barkan, Leonard. *Nature's Work of Art: The Human Body as Image of the World.* New Haven, 1975.

Barnes, Andrew. "The Social Transformation of the French Parish Clergy, 1500–1800." In *Culture and Identity in Early Modern Europe, 1500–1800.* Ed. Barbara B. Diefendorf and Carla Hesse. Ann Arbor, 1993.

Barnes, Michael. "The Body in the *Spiritual Exercizes* of Ignatius of Loyola." *Religion* 19 (1989), 263–73.

Bart, Jean. "Coutume et droit romain dans la doctrine bourguignonne du XVIIIe siècle." *Mémoires de la société pour l'histoire du droit et des institutions des anciens pays bourguignons, comtois et romands* 28 (1967), 141–71.

Barthes, Roland. *A Lover's Discourse: Fragments.* New York, 1982.

Basdevant, Jules. *Des Rapports de l'église et de l'état dans la legislation du mariage du Concile de Trent au code civil.* Paris, 1900.

Baulant, Micheline. "Le Salaire des ouvriers du bâtiment à Paris de 1400 à 1726." *Annales: ESC* 26:2 (1971), 463–83.

Baumgartner, Frederic J. *Change and Continuity in the French Episcopate: The Bishops and the Wars of Religion, 1547–1610.* Durham, N.C., 1986.

Bayley, Peter. *French Pulpit Oratory, 1598–1650.* Cambridge, 1980.

Beattie, J. M. *Crime and the Courts in England, 1660–1800.* Princeton, 1986.

———. "Criminality of Women in Eighteenth-Century England." *Journal of Social History* 8 (1975), 80–116.

Beaumont-Maillet, Laure. *La Guerre des sexes, XVe–XIXe siècles.* Paris, 1984.

Becker, Marvin B. *Civility and Society in Western Europe, 1300–1600.* Bloomington, Ind., 1988.

Beik, William. "The Parlement of Toulouse and the Fronde." In *Society and Institutions in Early Modern France*, pp. 132–52. Ed. Mack P. Holt. Athens, Ga., 1991.

———. *Absolutism and Society in Seventeenth-Century France: State Power and Provincial Aristocracy in Languedoc.* Cambridge, 1985.

Bell, David, A. "The Public Sphere, the Law, and the State in Eighteenth-Century France." *French Historical Studies* 17:4 (Fall 1992).

Belle, Edmond. *La Réforme à Dijon des origines à la fin de la lieutenance générale de Gaspard de Saulx-Tavanes (1530–1570).* Dijon, 1911.

Benabou, Erica-Maria. *La Prostitution et la police des moeurs au XVIIIe siècle.* Paris, 1987.

Benedict, Philip. *The Huguenot Population of France.* Philadelphia, 1990.

———. *Rouen during the Wars of Religion.* Cambridge, 1981.

———. "The Catholic Response to Protestantism: Church Activity and Popular Piety in Rouen, 1560–1600." In *Religion and the People, 800–1700.* Ed. James Obelkevitch. Chapel Hill, N.C., 1979.

———, ed. *Cities and Social Change in Early Modern France.* London, 1989.

Bénichou, Paul. *Man and Ethics: Studies in French Classicism.* Trans. Elizabeth Hughes. Garden City, N.Y., 1971.

Bercé, Yves-Marie. *Révoltes et révolutions dans l'Europe moderne, XVI–XVIIIe siècles.* Paris, 1980.

———. *Fête et révolte.* Paris, 1976.

———. "Aspects de la criminalité au XVIIe siècle." *Revue historique* 239 (1968), 33–42.

Bergin, Joseph. *Cardinal de la Rochefoucauld: Leadership and Reform in the French Church.* New Haven, 1987.

———. "Henri IV and the Problem of the French Episcopate." In *From Valois to Bourbon: Dynasty, State and Society in Early Modern France.* Ed. Keith Cameron. Exeter, U.K., 1989.

———. *Cardinal Richelieu: Power and the Pursuit of Wealth.* New Haven, 1985.

Bernard, A. *Le Sermon au XVIIIe siècle.* Paris, 1901.

Bernard, Marie-Paul. *Histoire de l'autorité paternelle en France.* Paris, 1863.

Bernos, Marcel. "Le Concile de Trente et la sexualité: La doctrine et sa posterité." In *Sexualité et religion*, pp. 217–39. Paris, 1988.

———. "St Charles Boromée et ses 'Instructions aux confesseurs': Une lecture rigoriste par le clergé français (XVIe–XIXe siècles)." In *Pratiques de la confession*. Paris, 1983.

———. "Les Manuels de confession: Peuvent-ils servir à l'histoire des mentalités?" In *Histoire sociale, sensibilités collectives et mentalités: Mélanges Robert Mandrou*, pp. 87–97. Paris, 1985.

Bernot, J.-L. "La Prostitution à Dijon aux XVIIe et XVIIIe siècles." Mémoire de maîtrise, Université de Dijon, 1970.

Bernoville, Gaston. *Une Fondatrice d'ordre: Anne de Xaintonge*. Paris, 1956.

Bertelli, S., and G. Crifo, eds. *Rituale, ceremoniale, etichetta*. Milan, 1985.

Berthelot, J. M. "Sociological Discourse and the Body." In *The Body: Social Processes and Social Theory*. Ed. Mike Featherstone, Mike Hepworth, and Bryan S. Turner. London, 1991.

Bertucat, C. "La Jurisdiction municipale de Dijon: Son étendue." *Revue bourguignonne* 21 (1911), 89–235.

Blet, P. *Le Clergé de France et la monarchie. Etudes sur les assemblées générales du clergé de 1615 à 1666*. 2 vols. Rome, 1959.

Bloch, R. Howard. "Medieval Misogyny." *Representations* 20 (Fall 1987), 1–24.

Bloomfield, Morton W. *The Seven Deadly Sins*. Lansing, Mich., 1952.

Bluche, François. *La Vie quotidienne au temps de Louis XIV*. Paris, 1985.

———, ed. *Dictionnaire du Grand Siècle*. Paris, 1989.

Blumenberg, Hans. "Progress, Secularization and Modernity: The Löwith/Blumenberg Debate." *New German Critique* 18–19 (Winter 1981), 63–79.

Boglioni, Pierre, ed. *La Culture populaire au moyen age*. Montreal, 1979.

Bohanon, Donna. "The Sword as the Robe in Seventeenth-Century Provence and Brittany." In *Society and Institutions in Early Modern France*, pp. 51–62. Ed. Mack P. Holt. Athens, Ga., 1991.

Bollème, Genevieve. *Les Almanachs populaires aux XVIIe et XVIIIe siècles*. Paris, 1969.

Bonneviot, H. *Les Greffes du Parlement de Bourgogne*. Dijon, 1911.

Bonney, Richard. "Absolutism: What's in a Name?" *French History* 1 (1987), 93–117.

———. *Society and Government in France under Richelieu and Mazarin, 1624–1661*. New York, 1988.

Bossy, John. "Leagues and Associations in 16th-Century French Catholicism." In *Voluntary Religion: Studies in Church History*, 23: pp. 171–89. Oxford, 1986.

———. "Moral Arithmetic: Seven Sins into Ten Commandments." In *Conscience and Casuistry in Early Modern Europe*, pp. 214–34. Ed. Edmund Leites. Cambridge, 1988.

———. "Godparenthood: The Fortunes of a Social Institution in Early Modern Christianity." In *Religion and Society in Early Modern Europe, 1500–1800*. Ed. Kaspar von Greyerz. London, 1984.

———. *Christianity in the West, 1400–1700*. Oxford, 1985.

———. "The Counter-Reformation and the People of Catholic Europe." *Past and Present* 47 (1970), 51–70.

———. "Blood and Baptism: Kinship, Community and Christianity in Western

Europe from the Fourteenth to the Seventeenth Centuries." In *Sanctity and Secularity: The Church and the World*. Ed. Derek Baker. New York, 1973.

———. "The Mass as a Social Institution, 1200–1700." *Past and Present* 100 (1983), 29–61.

———. "Holiness and Society." *Past and Present* 75 (1977), 119–37.

———. "The Social History of Confession in the Age of the Reformation." *Transactions of the Royal Historical Society* 5th ser., 25 (1975), 21–38.

———, ed. *Disputes and Settlements: Law and Human Relations in the West*. Cambridge, 1983.

Boswell, John. *The Kindness of Strangers: The Abandonment of Children in Western Europe from Late Antiquity to the Renaissance*. New York, 1988.

———. *Christianity, Social Tolerance and Homosexuality: Gay People in Western Europe from the Beginning of the Christian Era to the Fourteenth Century*. Chicago, 1980.

Bottomley, F. *Attitudes to the Body in Western Christendom*. London, 1979.

Bouchard, Marcel. *De l'Humanisme à l'Encyclopédie: L'esprit public en Bourgogne sous l'Ancien Régime*. Paris, 1930.

Bourdieu, Pierre. "Célibat et condition paysanne." *Etudes rurales* 5 (1962), 32ff.

———. *The Logic of Practice*. Trans. Richard Nice. Stanford, 1990.

———. *Outline of a Theory of Practice*. Trans. Richard Nice. Cambridge, 1977.

Bourrée, A. *La Chancellerie près le Parlement de Bourgogne de 1476 à 1790*. Dijon, 1927.

Bouwsma, William J. "Anxiety and the Formation of Early Modern Culture." In *After the Reformation: Essays in Honor of J. H. Hexter*, pp. 215–46. Ed. Barbara C. Malament. Philadelphia, 1980.

———. "Lawyers and Early Modern Culture." *American Historical Review* 78 (1973), 303–27.

———. "The Secularization of Society in the Seventeenth Century." *Proceedings of the Thirteenth International Congress of Historical Sciences*. 5 vols. Moscow, 1970.

Braeckmans, L. *Confession et communion au Moyen Age et au Concile de Trente*. Gembloux, 1971.

Brain, R. *The Decorated Body*. London, 1979.

Brémond, Henri. *Histoire littéraire du sentiment religieux en France depuis la fin des Guerres de Religion*. 11 vols. Paris, 1967.

Briggs, Robin. *Communities of Belief: Cultural and Social Tension in Early Modern France*. Oxford, 1989.

———. "Idées and Mentalités: The Case of the Catholic Reform Movement in France." *History of European Ideas* 7:1 (1986), 9–19.

———. *Early Modern France, 1560–1715*. Oxford, 1977.

Brink, James E. "Provincial Assemblies and Parlement in Early Modern France: A Review of Historical Scholarship." *Legislative Studies Quarterly* 11:3 (August 1986), 429–53.

——— et al., eds. *The Politics of Gender in Early Modern Europe*. Kirksville, Mo., 1989.

Brissaud, Jean. *History of French Private Law*. Boston, 1912; reprint, New York, 1968.

———. *History of French Public Law*. Boston, 1915; reprint, New York, 1969.

Brissaud, Y.-B. "L'Infanticide à la fin du Moyen Age: Ses motivations psychologiques et sa répression." *Revue historique de droit français et étranger* 4th ser., 50 (1972), 229–56.

Brockliss, Lawrence, W. B. *French Higher Education in the Seventeenth and Eighteenth Centuries: A Cultural History.* Oxford, 1987.

Brooke, Rosalind, and Christopher Brooke. *Popular Religion in the Middle Ages: Western Europe, 1000–1300.* London, 1984.

Brown, Judith C. *Immodest Acts: The Life of a Lesbian Nun in Renaissance Italy.* New York, 1986.

————. "Women's Place Was in the Home: Women's Work in Renaissance Tuscany." In *Rewriting the Renaissance: The Discourses of Sexual Difference in Early Modern Europe*, pp. 206–24. Ed. Margaret W. Ferguson et al. Chicago, 1986.

Brown, Peter. *The Body and Society: Men, Women, and Sexual Renunciation in Early Christianity.* New York, 1988.

————. "Society and the Supernatural: A Medieval Change." *Daedalus* 104:2 (1975), 133–49.

————. "The Rise and Function of the Holy Man in Late Antiquity." *Journal of Roman Studies* 61 (1971), 80–101.

Brundage, James. "Sex and the Canon Law: A Statistical Analysis of Samples of Canon and Civil Law." In *Sexual Practices and the Medieval Church*, pp. 89–101. Ed. Vern L. Bullough and James Brundage. Buffalo, N.Y., 1982.

————. "Concubinage and Marriage in Medieval Canon Law." In *Sexual Practices and the Medieval Church*, pp. 118–28. Ed. Vern L. Bullough and James Brundage. Buffalo, N.Y., 1982.

————. "Adultery and Fornication: A Study in Legal Theology." In *Sexual Practices and the Medieval Church*, pp. 129–34. Ed. Vern L. Bullough and James Brundage. Buffalo, N.Y., 1982.

————. "Rape and Seduction in the Medieval Canon Law." In *Sexual Practices and the Medieval Church*, pp. 141–48. Ed. Vern L. Bullough and James Brundage. Buffalo, N.Y., 1982.

————. "Prostitution in the Medieval Canon Law." In *Sexual Practices and the Medieval Church*, pp. 149–60. Ed. Vern L. Bullough and James Brundage. Buffalo, N.Y., 1982.

————. *Law, Sex and Christian Society in Medieval Europe.* Chicago, 1987.

Bryant, Lawrence. *The French Royal Entry Ceremony.* Geneva, 1986.

Buisson, Ferdinand Edouard. *Repertoire des ouvrages pédagogiques du XVIe siècle.* Paris, 1886.

Bullough, Vern L. *Sexual Variance in Society and History.* New York, 1976.

————. "Introduction: The Christian Inheritance." In *Sexual Practices and the Medieval Church*, pp. 1–12. Ed. Vern L. Bullough and James Brundage. Buffalo, N.Y., 1982.

————. "Formation of Medieval Ideals: Christian Theory and Christian Practice." In *Sexual Practices and the Medieval Church*, pp. 14–21. Ed. Vern L. Bullough and James Brundage. Buffalo, N.Y., 1982.

————. "The Prostitute in the Early Middle Ages." In *Sexual Practices and the Medieval Church*, pp. 34–42. Ed. Vern L. Bullough and James Brundage. Buffalo, N.Y., 1982.

————. "The Sin against Nature and Homosexuality." In *Sexual Practices and the Medieval Church*, pp. 55–71. Ed. Vern L. Bullough and James Brundage. Buffalo, N.Y., 1982.

———. "Prostitution in the Later Middle Ages." In *Sexual Practices and the Medieval Church*, pp. 176–86. Ed. Vern L. Bullough and James Brundage. Buffalo, N.Y., 1982.

Bullough, Vern L., and James Brundage. "Appendix: Medieval Canon Law and Its Sources." In *Sexual Practices and the Medieval Church*, pp. 219–24. Ed. Vern L. Bullough and James Brundage. Buffalo, N.Y., 1982.

Bultot, Robert. *La Doctrine au mépris du monde*. Louvain, 1963–64.

Burguière, André. "From Malthus to Max Weber: Belated Marriage and the Spirit of Enterprise." In *Family and Society: Selections from Annales*, pp. 237–50. Ed. Robert Forster and Orest Ranum. Trans. Elborg Forster and Patricia Ranum. Baltimore, 1976.

———. "The Formation of the Couple." In *Family History at the Crossroads*, pp. 39–53. Ed. Tamara Hareven and Andrejs Plakans. Princeton, 1987.

Burke, Peter. "From Pioneers to Settlers: Recent Studies of the History of Popular Culture: A Review Article." *Comparative Studies in Society and History* 25 (1983), 181–87.

Bush, M. L., ed. *Social Orders and Social Classes in Europe since 1500: Studies in Social Stratification*. London, 1992.

Butler, Judith P. "Foucault and the Paradox of Bodily Inscriptions." *Journal of Philosophy* 86:11 (November 1989), 601–7.

———. *Gender Trouble: Feminism and the Subversion of Identity*. New York, 1990.

Bynum, Caroline Walker. *Fragmentation and Redemption: Essays on Gender and the Human Body in Medieval Religion*. Cambridge, Mass., 1992.

———. "Material Continuity, Personal Survival, and the Resurrection of the Body." *History of Religions* 30 (1990), 51–85.

Cagnac, M. *De l'Appel comme d'abus dans l'ancien droit français*. Paris, 1906.

Cahn, Susan. "Changing Conceptions of Women in 16th- and 17th-Century England." Ph.D. dissertation, University of Michigan, 1981.

Cameron, Iain A. *Crime and Repression in the Auvergne and the Guyenne, 1720–1790*. Cambridge, 1981.

Cameron, Keith, ed. *From Valois to Bourbon: Dynasty, State, and Society in Early Modern France*. Exeter, N.H., 1989.

Campbell, Catherine. *The French Procuress: Her Character in Renaissance Comedies*. New York, 1985.

Campbell, J. K. *Honour, Family and Patronage: A Study of Institutions and Moral Values in a Greek Mountain Community*. Oxford, 1964.

Camporesi, Piero. *The Incorruptible Flesh: Bodily Mutilation and Mortification in Religion and Folklore*. Trans. Tania Croft-Murray. Cambridge, 1988.

Carey, John A. *Judicial Reform in France before the Revolution of 1789*. Cambridge, Mass., 1981.

Casey, James. "Le Mariage clandestin en Andalousie à l'époque moderne." In *Amours légitimes—Amours illégitimes en Espagne*. Ed. A. Redondo. Paris, 1987.

Castan, Nicole. *Justice et répression en Languedoc à l'époque des lumières*. Paris, 1980.

Castan, Yves. *Honnêteté et relations sociales en Languedoc, 1715–1780*. Paris, 1974.

Castan, Yves, and Nicole Castan. *Vivre ensemble: Ordre et désordre en Languedoc (XVIIe–XVIIIe siècles)*. Paris, 1981.

Certeau, Michel de. *The Practice of Everyday Life*. Trans. Steven Rendall. Berkeley, 1984.

————. *The Writing of History* New York, 1968.

————. "La Formalité des pratiques: Du système religieux à l'éthique des Lumières (XVIIe–XVIIIe siècle)." In *L'écriture de l'histoire*, pp. 152–214. Paris, 1975.

————. *La Fable mystique, XVIe–XVIIe siècle.* Paris, 1982.

Certeau, Michel de, Dominique Julia, and Jacques Revel. "La Beauté du mort: Le concept de 'culture populaire.'" *Politique aujourd'hui* (December 1970), 3–23.

Chalumeau, G. "Saint Vincent de Paul et les missions en France." *XVIIe siècle* 40 (1958), 304–27.

Chamoux, A. "Enfants illégitimes et enfants trouvés." *Annales de demographie historique* 9 (1973), 422–29.

Chanock, Martin. *Law, Custom and Social Order: The Colonial Experience in Malawi and Zambia.* Cambridge, 1985.

Chapman, Terry S. "Crime in Eighteenth Century England: E. P. Thompson and the Conflict Theory of Crime." *Criminal Justice History: An International Annual* 1 (1980), 139–55.

Charpentrat, Pierre. "L'Architecture et son public: Les Eglises de la contre-réforme." *Annales: ESC* 18 (1973), 91–108.

Chartier, Roger. *Cultural History: Between Practices and Representations.* Trans. Lydia G. Cochrane. Ithaca, N.Y., 1988.

————. "Culture as Appropriation: Popular Cultural Uses in Early Modern France." In *Understanding Popular Culture*, pp. 229–54. Ed. Steven L. Kaplan. Berlin, Ger., 1984.

————. *The Cultural Uses of Print in Early Modern France.* Trans. Lydia G. Cochrane. Princeton, 1988.

Chatellier, Louis. *Tradition chrétienne et renouveau catholique dans l'ancien diocèse de Strasbourg, 1660–1770.* Strasbourg, 1981.

————. *L'Europe des dévots.* Paris, 1987.

Chaunu, Pierre. *L'Europe des deux réformes.* Paris, 1981.

Chevrier, Georges. "Les Rapports entre la justice seculière et la justice ecclésiastique dans le comté de Bourgogne pendant la première moitié du XVI siècle." *Mémoires de la société pour l'histoire du droit et des institutions des anciens pays bourguignons, comtois et romands* 24 (1963), 197–225.

————. "Le Régime matrimonial en Mâconnais aux XVIIe et XVIIIe siècles." *Mémoires de la société pour l'histoire du droit et des institutions des anciens pays bourguignons, comtois et romands* 25 (1964), 77–95.

Chiffoleau, Jacques, et al. *Du Christianisme flamboyant à l'aube des lumières.* Paris, 1988.

Chill, Emmanuel. "Religion and Mendicity in Seventeenth-Century France." *International Review of Social History* 7:3 (1962), 400–425.

————. "The Company of the Holy Sacrament, 1660–1666: Social Aspects of the French Counter-Reformation." Ph.D. dissertation, Columbia University, 1960.

Church, William Farr. "The Decline of the French Jurists as Political Theorists, 1660–1789." *French Historical Studies* 5 (1967), 1–16.

————. *Richelieu and Reason of State.* Princeton, 1972.

Clare, Lucien. "Les Triomphes du corps ou la noblesse dans la paix, XVIIe siècle." *Histoire, économie, société* 3 (1984), 339–80.

Clifford, James, and George E. Marcus, eds. *Writing Culture: The Poetics and Politics of Ethnography.* Berkeley, 1986.

Cockburn, J. S., ed. *Crime in England, 1550–1800.* London, 1977.

Coffin, Judy. "Artisans of the Sidewalk." *Radical History Review* 26 (1982), 89–101.

Coleman, Emily R. "L'Infanticide dans le haut Moyen Age." *Annales: ESC* 29 (1974), 315ff.

Collins, James B. "The Economic Role of Women in Seventeenth-Century France." *French Historical Studies* 16:2 (Fall, 1989), 436–70.

Collins, Stephen L. *From Divine Cosmos to Sovereign State: An Intellectual History of Consciousness and the Idea of Order in Renaissance England.* Oxford, 1989.

Comaroff, John L., and Simon Roberts. *Rules and Processes: The Cultural Logic of Dispute in an African Context.* Chicago, 1981.

Conley, John M., and William M. O'Barr. *Rules versus Relationships: The Ethnography of Legal Discourse.* Chicago, 1990.

Connor, Paul. "Patriarchy: Old World and New." *American Quarterly* 17 (1965), 48ff.

Cook, Alexandra Parma, and Noble David Cook. *Good Faith and Truthful Ignorance: A Case of Transatlantic Bigamy.* Durham, N.C., 1991.

Coquille, Jean-Baptiste Victor. *Les Legistes: Leur influence politique et religieuses.* Paris, 1863.

Corbin, Alain. *Les Filles de noce.* Paris, 1983.

Il Corpo delle donne. Ancona, 1988.

Couliano, Ioan P. "A Corpus for the Body." *Journal of Modern History* 63 (March 1991), 61–80.

———. *Eros and Magic in the Renaissance.* Trans. Margaret Cook. Chicago, 1987.

Crouzet, Denis. *Les Guerriers de Dieu: La Violence au temps des troubles de religion, vers 1525–vers 1610.* 2 vols. Seyssel, 1990.

———. "La Ligue (1588–1589): Un enracinement panique?" In *La Guerra del sale,* pp. 255–73. Ed. Giorgio Lombardi. Milan, 1986.

———. "Les Fondements idéologiques de la royauté d'Henri IV." In *Avénément d'Henri IV, Quatrième centénaire,* pp. 165–94. Pau, 1989.

Cummings, Mark. "Elopement, Family, and the Courts: The Crime of 'Rapt' in Early Modern France." *Proceedings of the Annual Meeting of the Western Society for French History* 4 (1976), 118–25.

Curtin, M. "A Question of Manners: Status and Gender in Etiquette and Courtesy." *Journal of Modern History* 57 (1985), 395–423.

Curtis, Timothy. "Explaining Crime in Early Modern England." *Criminal Justice History* 1 (1980), 117–37.

Dargan, Edwin C. *A History of Preaching.* 2 vols. New York, 1912.

Dargin, Edward V. "Reserved Cases According to the Code of Canon Law." Dissertation in Canon Law, Catholic University of America, 1924.

Darnton, Robert. "The Symbolic Element in History." *Journal of Modern History* 58 (March 1986), 218–34.

Davis, Andrew McFarland. *The Law of Adultery and Ignominius Punishments.* Worcester, Mass., 1895.

Davis, Natalie Z. "From 'Popular Religion' to Religious Cultures." In *Reformation Europe: A Guide to Research,* pp. 321–41. Ed. Steven Ozment. St. Louis, 1982.

———. "Boundaries and the Sense of Self in Sixteenth-Century France." In *Reconstructing Individualism: Autonomy, Individuality and the Self in Western*

Thought. Ed. Thomas Heller, Morton Sosna, and David Wellberry. Stanford, 1986.

———. *Fiction in the Archives*. Stanford, 1987.

———. "Women in the Crafts in Sixteenth-Century Lyon." In *Women and Work in Preindustrial Europe*, pp. 167–97. Ed. Barbara B. Hanawalt. Bloomington, 1986.

———. "Charivari, Honor, and Community in Seventeenth-Century Lyon and Geneva." In *Rite, Drama, Festival, Spectacle: Rehearsals toward a Theory of Cultural Performance*, pp. 42–57. Ed. John J. MacAloon. Philadelphia, 1984.

———. *Society and Culture in Early Modern France*. Stanford, 1975.

———. "Ghosts, Kin, and Progeny: Some Features of Family Life in Early Modern France." *Daedalus* (Spring 1977), 87–114.

———. "The Sacred and the Body Social in Sixteenth-Century Lyon." *Past and Present* 90 (1980), 40–70.

Dawson, John P. *A History of Lay Judges*. Cambridge, Mass., 1960.

Deconchy, J.-P. *L'Orthodoxie religieuse: essai de logique psycho-sociale*. Paris, 1971.

Delannoy, P. *La Juridiction ecclésiastique en matière bénéficiale sous l'ancien régime en France*. Louvain, 1910.

Delasselle, Claude. "Abandoned Children in Eighteenth-Century Paris." In *Deviants and the Abandoned in French Society*, pp. 47–82. Ed. Robert Forster and Orest Ranum. Trans. Elborg Forster and Patricia Ranum. Baltimore, 1978.

Delcambre, Etienne. "Witchcraft Trials in Lorraine: Psychology of the Judges." In *European Witchcraft*, pp. 88–95. Ed. E. William Monter. New York, 1969.

Delumeau, Jean. *Naissance et affirmation de la Réforme*. Paris, 1968.

———. *Sin and Fear: The Emergence of a Western Guilt Culture, 13th–18th Centuries*. Trans. Eric Nicholson. New York, 1990.

———. *Un Chemin d'histoire: Chrétienté et christianisation*. Paris, 1981.

———. *Protéger et rassurer*. Paris, 1986.

———. *La Peur en occident (XIVe–XVIIIe siècles): Une cité assiégée*. Paris, 1978.

———. *La Mort des pays de cocagne*. Paris, 1976.

———. *Le Catholicisme entre Luther et Voltaire*. Paris, 1985.

Demey, Julien. *La Notion actuelle du devoir conjugal et le but du mariage devant les tribunaux civils et les officialités*. Paris, 1931.

Dens, Jean-Pierre. *Honnête homme et la critique du goût: Esthétique et société au XVIIe siècle*. Lexington, Ky., 1981.

Depauw, Jacques. "Illicit Sexual Activity and Society in Eighteenth-Century Nantes." In *Family and Society*, pp. 141–91. Ed. Robert Forster and Orest Ranum. Trans. Elborg Forster. Baltimore, 1976.

Descimon, Robert. "La Ligue à Paris (1585–1594): Une révision." *Annales: ESC* 37 (1982), 72–111.

———. *Qui étaient les seize?* Paris, 1983.

Dessert, Daniel. *Argent, pouvoir, et société au Grand Siècle*. Paris, 1984

Detourbet, Edmond. *La Procédure criminelle au XVIIe siècle. Histoire de l'ordonnance du 28 août 1670; son influence sur les législations qui l'ont suivie et notamment sur celle qui nous régit actuellement*. Paris, 1881.

Devries, Jan. *European Urbanization, 1500–1800*. Cambridge, Mass., 1984.

Dewald, Jonathan. *The Formation of a Provincial Nobility: The Magistrates of the Parlement of Rouen, 1499–1610*. Princeton, 1980.

———. "The Perfect Magistrate: Parlementaires and Crime in Sixteenth-Century Rouen." *Archiv für Reformationsgeschichte* 67 (1976), 285–99.

Deyon, Pierre. "La Propagande religieuse au 16e siècle." *Annales: ESC* (1981), 16–25.

——. *Le Temps des prisons. Essai sur l'histoire de la délinquance et les origines du système pénitentiaire.* Lille, 1975.

Dhetel, P. *Annales historiques de la ville de Saint-Jean de Losne.* 2 vols. Paris, 1908.

Dhotel, Jean-Claude. *Les Origines du catéchisme moderne.* Paris, 1967.

Diefendorf, Barbara B. *Paris City Councillors in the Sixteenth Century: The Politics of Patrimony.* Princeton, 1983.

——. *Beneath the Cross: Catholics and Huguenots in Sixteenth-Century Paris.* New York, 1991.

Diefendorf, Barbara B., and Carla Hesse, eds. *Culture and Identity in Early Modern Europe, 1500–1800: Essays in Honor of Natalie Zemon Davis.* Ann Arbor, 1993.

Doherty, Dennis. *The Sexual Doctrine of Cardinal Cajetan.* Regensburg, 1966.

Dompnier, Bernard. "Pastorale de la peur et pastorale de la séduction: La Méthode de conversion des missionaires capucins." In *La Conversion au 17e siècle*, pp. 257–73. Actes du Colloque du CMR 17. Marseille, 1983.

——. "Missions et confession au 17e siècle." In *Pratiques de la confession*, pp. 201–22. Paris, 1983.

——. "Les Missions des capucins et leur empreinte sur la réforme catholique en France." *Revue d'histoire de l'église de France* 70 (1984), 127–47.

Donahue, Charles. "The Canon Law on the Formation of Marriage and Social Practice in the Later Middle Ages." *Journal of Family History* 8 (Summer 1983), 141–58.

Donzelot, Jacques. *La Police des familles.* Paris, 1977.

Doucet, Roger. *Les Institutions de la France au XVIe siècle.* 2 vols. Paris, 1948.

Douglas, Mary. *Purity and Danger: An Analysis of the Concepts of Pollution and Taboo.* London, 1985.

——. *Natural Symbols: Explorations in Cosmology.* New York, 1982.

Doyle, William O. "The Parlements of France and the Breakdown of the Old Regime." *French Historical Studies* 6:4 (1970), 415–58.

Drouot, Henri. *Mayenne et la Bourgogne: Etude sur la Ligue (1587–1596).* 2 vols. Dijon, 1937.

Dufour, Pierre [Paul Lacroix]. *Mémoires curieux sur l'histoire des moeurs et de la prostitution en France.* 2 vols. Brussels, 1855–61.

Duggan, Lawrence G. "Fear and Confession on the Eve of the Reformation." *Archiv fur Reformationsgeschichte* 75 (1984), 153–75.

Duguit, Léon. "Etude historique sur le rapt de séduction." *Nouvelle revue historique de droit français et étranger* 10 (1886), 587–625.

Dumonceaux, P. *Langue et sensibilité au 17e siècle: L'Evolution du vocabulaire affectif.* Geneva, 1975.

Dupâquier, Jacques, et al., eds. *Marriage and Remarriage in Populations of the Past.* New York, 1981.

Dupont-Ferrier, Gustave. *Les Officiers royaux des bailliages et senéchaussées et les institutions monarchiques locales en France à la fin du Moyen Age.* Paris, 1903.

Easlea, Brian. *Science and Sexual Oppression: Patriarchy's Confrontation with Woman and Nature.* London, 1981.

Ehrard, Jean. *L'Idée de nature en France dans la première moitié du XVIIIe siècle.* 2 vols. Paris, 1963.

Ehrenreich, Barbara, and Dierdre English. *Witches, Midwives and Nurses: A History of Women Healers.* New York, 1973.

Eisenstadt, S. N., ed. *The Protestant Ethic and Modernization.* New York, 1968.

Eisenstadt, S. N., and Louis Roniger. *Patrons, Clients and Friends: Interpersonal Relations and the Structure of Trust in Society.* Cambridge, 1984.

Elias, Norbert. *The Court Society.* Trans. Edmund Jephcott. New York, 1983.

———. *The Civilizing Process.* Trans. Edmund Jephcott. 2 vols. New York, 1978, 1982.

Ellen, Roy F. "Anatomical Classification and the Semiotics of the Body." In *The Anthropology of the Body,* pp. 343–73. Ed. John Blacking. London, 1977.

Emmison, F. G. *Elizabethan Life: Morals and the Church Courts.* Chelmsford, U.K., 1973.

Epstein, A. L., ed. *Contention and Dispute: Aspects of Law and Social Control in Melanesia.* Canberra, 1974.

Erikson, Kai. *Wayward Puritains: A Study in the Sociology of Deviance.* New York, 1966.

Esmein, Adhemar. *A History of Continental Criminal Procedure with Special Reference to France.* Trans. John Simpson. Boston, 1913; reprint 1968.

———. *Le Mariage en droit canonique.* 2 vols. New York, 1968.

Estes, Leland L. "The Medical Origins of the European Witch-Craze: A Hypothesis." *Journal of Social History* 17 (1983), 271–84.

Estignard, A. *Le Parlement de Franche-Comté.* Paris and Besançon, 1892.

Evennett, H. Outram. *The Spirit of the Counter-Reformation.* Cambridge, 1968.

Ewald, François. "Norms, Discipline, and the Law." *Representations* 30 (Spring 1990), 138–61.

Ezell, Margaret J. M. *The Patriarch's Wife: Literary Evidence and the History of the Family.* Chapel Hill, N.C., 1987.

Fairchilds, Cissie. "Female Sexual Attitudes and the Rise of Illegitimacy: A Case Study." *Journal of Interdisciplinary History* 8 (Spring 1978), 627–67.

Faire Croire: Modalités de la diffusion et de la réception des messages religieux du XIIe au XVe siècle. Rome, 1981.

Farge, Arlette. *Vivre dans la rue à Paris au XVIIIe siècle.* Paris, 1979.

———. *La Vie fragile.* Paris, 1986.

———. *Déliquance et criminalité: Le Vol d'aliments à Paris au XVIII siècle.* Paris, 1974.

———, ed. *Le Miroir des femmes.* Paris, 1982.

Farge, Arlette, and A. Zysberg. "Géographie de la violence à Paris au XVIIIe siècle." *Annales: ESC* (1979), 984–1015.

Farge, Arlette, and Michel Foucault. *Le Désordre des familles: Lettre de cachet des archives de la Bastille.* Paris, 1982.

Farge, Arlette, and Jacques Revel. "Les Règles de l'émeute: L'Affaire des élèvements d'enfants, Paris, mai 1750." In *Mouvements populaires et conscience sociale, XVIe–XIXe siècle,* pp. 635–46. Paris, 1985.

Farr, James R. *Hands of Honor: Artisans and Their World in Dijon, 1550–1650.* Ithaca, N.Y., 1988.

———. "The Pure and Disciplined Body: Hierarchy, Morality, and Symbolism in France during the Catholic Reformation." *Journal of Interdisciplinary History* 21:3 (1991), 391–414.

———. "Consumers, Commerce, and the Craftsmen of Dijon: The Changing

Social and Economic Structure of a Provincial Capital, 1450–1750." In *Cities and Social Change in Early Modern France*, pp. 134–73. Ed. Philip Benedict. London, 1989.

———. "Crimine nel vicinato: Ingiurie, matrimonio e onore nella Digione del XVIe e XVIIe secolo." *Quaderni storici* 22:3 (1987), 839–54.

———. "Parlementaires and the Paradox of Power: Sovereignty, Law, and Justice in Early Modern Burgundy." Forthcoming.

Feher, Michel, et al., eds. *Fragments for a History of the Human Body*. New York, 1989.

Ferté, J. *La Vie religieuse dans les campagnes parisiennes, 1622–1695*. Paris, 1962.

Figes, E. *Patriarchal Attitudes*. London, 1978.

Finely-Crosswhite, Annette. "Henry IV and the Towns: Royal Authority and Municipal Autonomy, 1589–1610." Ph.D. dissertation, Emory University, 1991.

Fineman, Martha Albertson, and Nancy Sweet Thomadsen, eds. *At the Boundaries of Law: Feminism and Legal Theory*. New York, 1991.

Flandrin, Jean-Louis. *Families in Former Times: Kinship, Household and Sexuality*. Trans. Richard Southern. Cambridge, 1979.

———. *Les Amours paysannes: Amour et sexualité dans les campagnes de l'ancienne France (XVIe–XIXe siècles)*. Paris, 1975.

———. *Le Sexe et l'occident: Evolution des attitudes et des comportments*. Paris, 1981.

———. "Repression and Change in the Sexual Life of Young People in Medieval and Early Modern Times." *Journal of Family History* 2 (1977), 196ff.

———. "L'Attitude à l'égard du petit enfant et les conduites sexuelles dans la civilisation occidentale." *Annales de demographie historique* 9 (1973), 143ff.

———. "Contraception, Marriage and Sexual Relations in the Christian West." In *Biology of Man in History*. Ed. Robert Forster and Orest Ranum. Trans. Elborg Forster and Patricia Ranum. Baltimore, 1975.

———. *L'Eglise et le contrôle des naissances*. Paris, 1970.

Flannigan, Arthur. *Mme de Villedieu's "Les Désordres de l'amour": History, Literature, and the "Nouvelle Historique."* Washington, D.C., 1982.

Fleury, Vindry. *Les Parlementaires français au XVIe siècle*. 2 vols. Paris, 1909–1912.

Flinn, Michael W. *The European Demographic System, 1500–1820*. Baltimore, 1981.

Fogel, Michele. *Les Cerémonies de l'information dans la France du XVIe au XVIIIe siècle*. Paris, 1989.

Forster, Robert, and Orest Ranum, eds. *Ritual, Religion, and the Sacred*. Trans. Elborg Forster and Patricia Ranum. Baltimore, 1982.

Foucault, Michel. *The Order of Things: An Archaeology of the Human Sciences*. New York, 1973.

———. *Discipline and Punish: The Birth of the Prison*. Trans. Alan Sheridan. New York, 1977.

———. "The Discourse on Language." In *Archaeology of Knowledge*. New York, 1972.

———. *L'Histoire de la sexualité*. 3 vols. Paris, 1984.

Fournier, Edouard, ed. *Variétés historiques et littéraires*. Paris, 1855.

Frank, Arthur W. "For a Sociology of the Body: An Analytical Review." In *The Body: Social Process and Cultural Theory*. Ed. Mike Featherstone, Mike Hepworth, and Bryan S. Turner. London, 1991.

French, Roger, and Andrew Wear, eds. *The Medical Revolution of the Seventeenth Century*. Cambridge, 1989.

Freud, Sigmund. *Civilization and Its Discontents.* New York, 1962.

Freund, Peter E. S. "Bringing Society into the Body: Understanding Socialized Human Nature." *Theory and Society* 17 (1988), 839–64.

———. *The Civilized Body: Social Domination, Control and Health.* Philadelphia, 1982.

Frijhoff, W. "Official and Popular Religion in Christianity: The Late Middle Ages and Early Modern Times." In *Official and Popular Religion: Analysis of a Theme for Religious Studies.* Ed. P. H. Vrijhof and J. Waardenburg. The Hague, 1979.

Froeschlé-Chopard, Marie-Hélène. *La Religion populaire en Provence orientale au XVIIIe siècle.* Paris, 1980.

Fuchs, Rachel G. *Poor and Pregnant in Paris: Strategies for Survival in the Nineteenth Century.* New Brunswick, N.J., 1992.

———. *Abandoned Children: Foundlings and Child Welfare in Nineteenth-Century France.* Albany, 1984.

Fumaroli, Marc. *L'Age de l'éloquence: Rhétorique et "res literaria" de la Renaissance au seuil de l'époque classique.* Geneva, 1980.

Funck-Brentano, F. *Les Lettres de cachet.* Paris, 1903, 1926.

Gadille, J., D. Julia, and M. Venard. "Pour un repertoire des visites pastorales." *Annales: ESC* (1970), 561–66.

Gallagher, Catherine, and Thomas Laqueur, eds. *The Making of the Modern Body.* Berkeley, 1989.

Galpern, A. N. *Religions of the People in Sixteenth-Century Champagne.* Cambridge, Mass., 1976.

Garnot, Benoît. *La Population française aux XVIe, XVIIe, XVIIIe siècles.* Paris, 1988.

Garretta, Jean-Claude. "Les Archives du Parlement de Dijon, étude des sources." *Mémoires de la société pour l'histoire du droit et des institutions des anciens pays bourguignons, comtois et romands* 23 (1962), 203–44.

Garrioch, David. *Neighborhood and Community in Paris, 1740–1790.* Cambridge, 1986.

Gascon, Richard. *Le Grand commerce et la vie urbaine au 16e siècle.* 2 vols. Paris, 1971.

Gaudemet, J. "Législation canonique et attitudes seculières à l'égard du lien matrimonial au XVIIe siècle." *XVIIe siècle* 102–3 (1974), 15–30.

Gay, Peter. *The Bourgeois Experience: Victoria to Freud.* 3 vols. Oxford, 1984.

Geertz, Clifford. *Local Knowledge.* New York, 1983.

———. *Interpretation of Cultures.* New York, 1973.

Gélis, Jacques. *History of Childbirth: Fertility, Pregnancy and Birth in Early Modern Europe.* Trans. Rosemary Morris. Boston, 1991.

Genestral, Robert. *Les Origines de l'appel comme d'abus.* Paris, 1950.

Geremek, Bronislaw. *Inutiles au monde: Truands et misérables.* Paris, 1980.

———. *The Margins of Society in Late Medieval Paris.* Trans. Jean Birrell. Cambridge, 1988.

Germain, E. *Langages de la foi à travers l'histoire: Mentalités et catechèse.* Paris, 1972.

Gibbs, J., and M. Erickson. "Major Developments in the Sociological Study of Deviance." *Annual Review of Sociology* 1 (1975), 21–42.

Gibson, Mary. *Prostitution in Italy.* New Brunswick, N.J., 1986.

Giddens, Anthony. *Central Problems in Social Theory: Action, Structure and Contradiction in Social Analysis.* Berkeley, 1979.

Giesey, Ralph E. *Ceremonial et puissance souveraine: France, XVe–XVIIe siècles.* Paris, 1987.

———. "Rules of Inheritance and Strategies of Mobility in Prerevolutionary France." *American Historical Review* 82 (1977), 271–89.

———. "State-Building in Early Modern France: The Role of Royal Officialdom." *Journal of Modern History* 55 (1983), 191–207.

———. "Modèles de pouvoir dans les rites royaux en France." *Annales: ESC* (May–June 1986), 579–99.

Ginzburg, Carlo. "High and Low: The Theme of Forbidden Knowledge in the Sixteenth and Seventeenth Centuries." *Past and Present* 73 (1976), 28–41.

Girard, René. *La Violence et le sacre.* Paris, 1980.

Godard de Donville, Louise. *Signification de la mode sous Louis XIII.* Aix-en-Provence, 1978.

Gold, Penny S. "The Marriage of Mary and Joseph in the Twelfth-Century Ideology of Marriage." In *Sexual Practices and the Medieval Church.* Ed. Vern L. Bullough and James Brundage. Buffalo, N.Y., 1982.

Golden, Richard M., ed. *Church, State, and Society under the Bourbon Kings of France.* Lawrence, Kan., 1982.

Goldstone, Jack A. *Revolution and Rebellion in the Early Modern World.* Berkeley, 1991.

Gordon, Daniel. "Philosophy, Sociology, and Gender in the Enlightenment Conception of Public Opinion." *French Historical Studies* 17:4 (1992), 882–911.

Gottlieb, Beatrice. "The Meaning of Clandestine Marriage." In *Family and Sexuality in French History,* pp. 49–83. Ed. Robert Wheaton and Tamara K. Hareven. Philadelphia, 1980.

Goubert, Pierre. "Les Officiers royaux des présidiaux, bailliages, et élections dans la société française du XVIIe siècle." *XVIIe siècle* 42–43 (1959), 54–75.

Goulemot, J. M. "Demons, merveilles et philosophie à l'age classique." *Annales: ESC* 35 (1980), 1223–50.

Graff, Harvey J. *The Legacies of Literacy: Continuities and Contradictions in Western Culture and Society.* Bloomington, Ind., 1987.

Grandet, J. *Les Saints prêtres français du XVIIe siècle.* 3 vols. Angers, 1897.

Gras, Pierre, ed. *Histoire de Dijon.* Toulouse, 1980.

Greenblatt, Stephen. "Fiction and Friction." In *Reconstructing Individualism: Autonomy, Individuality, and the Self in Western Thought.* Ed. Thomas Heller, Morton Sosna, and David Wellbery. Stanford, 1986.

———. *Shakespearean Negotiations: The Circulation of Social Energy in Renaissance England.* Berkeley, 1988.

———. *Renaissance Self-Fashioning, from More to Shakespeare.* Chicago, 1980.

Greengrass, Mark, *France in the Age of Henri IV: The Struggle for Stability.* London, 1986.

Greenshields, Malcolm. "An Introduction to the Pastoral Visit Project: Between Two Worlds, 1560–1720." *Proceedings of the Annual Meeting of the Western Society for French History* 15 (1988), 51–60.

Gresset, Maurice. "Les Juridictions ecclésiastiques bisontines à la fin du XVIIe siècle." *Mémoires de la société pour l'histoire du droit et des institutions des anciens pays bourguignons, comtois et romands* 35 (1978), 85–93.

Grimmer, Claude. *La Femme et le bâtard: Amours illégitimes et secrètes dans l'ancienne France.* Paris, 1983.

Gros, L. "Le Parlement et la ligue en Bourgogne." *Revue bourguignonne.* 20:3–4 (1910), pp. 1ff.

Gueudre, M.-C. "La Femme et la vie spirituelle." *XVIIe siècle* 62–63 (1964), 47–77.

Guichard, Georges. *La Juridiction des prévôts du connétable et des maréchaux de France.* Lille, 1926.

Guillais, Joelle. *La Chair de l'autre: Le Crime passionel au XIXe siècle.* Paris, 1986.

Guillemot, P. *Histoire de Seurre.* Beaune, 1859.

Gutierrez, Ramon A. "Honor, Ideology, Marriage Negotiation, and Class-Gender Domination in New Mexico, 1698–1846." *Latin American Perspectives* 44:12 (1985), 81–104.

Gutton, Jean-Pierre. *La Société et les pauvres: L'Exemple de la généralité de Lyon, 1534–1789.* Paris, 1974.

Hagstrum, Jean H. *Sex and Sensibility: Ideal and Erotic Love from Milton to Mozart.* Chicago, 1980.

Hallpike, C. R. "Social Hair." *Man* n.s., 4:2 (1969), 256–67.

Hamscher, Albert N. *The Conseil Privé and the Parlements in the Age of Louis XIV: A Study in French Absolutism.* Philadelphia, 1987.

———. *The Parlement of Paris after the Fronde, 1653–1673.* Pittsburgh, 1976.

Hanawalt, Barbara A. *Crime and Conflict in English Communities, 1300–1348.* Cambridge, Mass., 1979.

Hanley, Sarah. "Family and State in Early Modern France: The Marriage Pact." In *Connecting Spheres: Women in the Western World, 1500 to the Present,* pp. 53–63. Ed. Marilyn J. Boxer and Jean H. Quataert. New York, 1987.

———. "Engendering the State: Family Formation and State Building in Early Modern France." *French Historical Studies* 16:1 (Spring 1989), 4–27.

———. *The Lit de Justice of the Kings of France: Constitutional Ideology in Legend, Ritual and Discourse.* Princeton, N.J., 1983.

Harding, Robert J. *Anatomy of a Power Elite: The Provincial Governors of Early Modern France.* New Haven, 1978.

———. "Revolutions and Reform in the Holy League: Angers, Rennes, Nantes." *Journal of Modern History* 53 (1981), 376–416.

Harding, Sandra, ed. *Feminism and Methodology.* Bloomington, Ind., 1987.

Harsin, Jill. *Policing Prostitution in Nineteenth-Century Paris.* Princeton, 1986.

Harth, Erica. *Ideology and Culture in Seventeenth-Century France.* Ithaca, N.Y., 1983.

Hartmann, Heidi. "Capitalism, Patriarchy and Job Segregation by Sex." *Signs* 1 (1976), 137ff.

Hayden, J. Michael. *France and the Estates General of 1614.* Cambridge, 1974.

———. "The Pastoral Visit Project Phase I: The Dioceses of Coutances and Avranches." *Proceedings of the Annual Meeting of the Western Society for French History* 15 (1988), 61–70.

Hazard, Paul. *The European Mind, 1680–1715.* Trans. J. Lewis May. New York, 1963.

Headley, John, and John Tomaro, eds. *San Carlo Borromeo.* Cranbury, N.J., 1988.

Heath, Anthony. *Rational Choice and Social Exchange: A Critique of Exchange Theory.* Cambridge, 1976.

Heller, Henry. *Iron and Blood: Civil Wars in Sixteenth-Century France.* Montreal, 1991.

Hepp, N., and J. Hennequin, eds. *Les Valeurs chez les mémorialistes français du XVIIe siècle*. Paris, 1979.

Hepworth, Mike, and Bryan S. Turner. *Confession: Studies in Deviance and Religion*. London, 1982.

Herrup, Cynthia B. "Law and Morality in Seventeenth-Century England." *Past and Present* 106 (1985), 102–23.

———. *The Common Peace: Participation and the Criminal Law in Seventeenth-Century England*. Cambridge, 1987.

Heyd, Michael. "The Reaction to Enthusiasm in the Seventeenth Century: Towards an Integrative Approach." *Journal of Modern History* 53 (1981), 258–63.

Hirschman, Albert. *The Passions and the Interests*. Princeton, 1977.

Hoffer, Peter C., and N. E. H. Hull. *Murdering Mothers: Infanticide in England and New England, 1558–1803*. New York, 1981.

Hoffman, Philip. *Church and Community in the Diocese of Lyon, 1500–1789*. New Haven, 1984.

Holt, Mack P., ed. *Society and Institutions in Early Modern France*. Athens, Ga., 1991.

Horowitz, Louise K. *Love and Language: A Study of the Classical French Moralist Writers*. Columbus, Ohio, 1977.

Houdaille, J. "Le Mouvement saisonier des naissances dans la France rurale de 1640 à 1869." *Population* 40 (1985), 360–62.

Houlbrooke, Ralph. *Church Courts and the People during the English Reformation, 1520–1570*. Oxford, 1979.

Howard, Leon. "In Rightly Dividing the Word of Truth: Ramean Hermeneutics and the Commandment against Adultery." In *Renaissance Uses of Ramean Logic*. Albuquerque, N.M., 1972–77.

Hsia, R. Po-chia. *Social Discipline in the Reformation*. London, 1989.

———. *Society and Religion in Munster, 1535–1618*. New Haven, 1984.

Hudson, L. *Bodies of Knowledge: The Psychological Significance of the Nude in Art*. London, 1982.

Hufton, Olwen. "Attitudes toward Authority in Eighteenth-Century Languedoc." *Social History* 3 (1978), 281–302.

Hufton, Olwen. "Begging, Vagrancy, Vagabondage, and the Law: An Aspect of the Problem of Poverty in Eighteenth-Century France." *European Studies Review* 2 (1972), 97–123.

Hughes, Diane Owen. "La Moda proibita: La Legislazione suntuaria nell Italia rinascimentale." *Memoria: Rivista distoria delle donne* 11–12 (1984), 82–105.

———. "Kinsmen and Neighbors in Medieval Genoa." In *The Medieval City*. Ed. Harry A. Miskimin, David Herlihy, and A. L. Udovitch. New Haven, 1977.

Huguet, Edmond. *Dictionnaire de la langue française du seizième siècle*. 7 vols. Paris, 1925–66.

Hunt, Lynn, ed. *Eroticism and the Body Politic*. Baltimore, 1990.

———. *The New Cultural History*. Berkeley, 1989.

Huppert, George. *Public Schools in Renaissance France*. Urbana, Ill., 1984.

———. *Les Bourgeois Gentilshommes: An Essay on the Definition of Elites in Renaissance France*. Chicago, 1977.

Ingram, Martin. *Church Courts, Sex and Marriage in England, 1570–1640*. Cambridge, 1988.

Ingrid, Merkel, and Allen Debus, eds. *Hermeticism and the Renaissance: Intellectual History and the Occult in Early Modern Europe.* Washington, D.C., 1988.

Jacquart, Danielle, and Claude Thomasset. *Sexuality and Medicine in the Middle Ages.* Princeton, 1989.

Jacquinet, P. *Des Prédicateurs du XVIIe siècle avant Bossuet.* Paris, 1885.

Jahan, R. *Etude historique sur l'appel comme d'abus.* Laval, 1888.

James, Mervyn E. "Ritual, Drama, and Social Body in the Late Medieval English Town." *Past and Present* 98 (1983), 3–29.

Jeay, Madeleine. "Sexuality and Family in Fifteenth-Century France." *Journal of Family History* 4 (1979), 328ff.

Jedin, Hubert. *A History of the Council of Trent.* Trans. Dom Ernest Graf. 2 vols. St. Louis, 1957.

Johnson, Mark. *The Body in the Mind: The Bodily Basis of Meaning, Imagination, and Reason.* Chicago, 1987.

Jones, Ann Rosalind. *The Currency of Eros: Women's Love Lyric in Europe, 1540–1620.* Bloomington, Ind., 1990.

Jouanna, Arlette. *Le Devoir de révolte: La Noblesse française et la gestation de l'état moderne, 1559–1661.* Paris, 1989.

———. *L'Ordre social dans la France du seizième siècle.* Paris, 1977.

Joyce, G. H. *Christian Marriage: An Historical and Doctrinal Study.* London, 1948.

Julia, Dominique. "Discipline ecclésiastique et culture paysanne au XVIIIe siècle." In *La Religion populaire.* Paris, 1979.

———. "La Réforme posttridentine en France d'après les procès-verbaux de visites pastorales: Ordre et résistances." *La Società religiosa nell'éta moderna.* Naples, 1973.

———. "Le Prêtre au XVIIIe siècle: La théologie et les institutions." *Recherches de science religieuse* 58 (1970), 521–34.

Julia, Dominique, and D. McKee. "Le Clergé paroissial dans le diocèse de Reims sous l'episcopat de Charles-Maurice Le Tellier: Origine et carrières." *Revue d'histoire moderne et contemporaine* 29 (1982), 529–83.

Kaiser, Colin. "The Deflation in the Volume of Litigation at Paris in the Eighteenth Century and the Waning of the Old Judicial Order." *European Studies Review* 10 (1980), 309–36.

Kamenka, Eugene, and Alice Erh-Soon Tay, eds. *Law and Social Control.* New York, 1980.

Kaplan, Steven L., ed. *Understanding Popular Culture.* New York, 1984.

Kavolis, Vytautas. "Logics of Selfhood and Modes of Order: Civilizational Structures for Individual Identities." In *Identity and Authority: Exploration in the Theory of Society*, pp. 40–60. Ed. Roland Robertson and Burkart Holzner. Oxford, 1980.

Kelley, Donald R. *Foundations of Modern Historical Scholarship: Language, Law, and History in the French Renaissance.* New York, 1970.

———. *The Human Measure: Social Thought in the Legal Tradition.* Cambridge, Mass., 1990.

———. *History, Law, and the Human Sciences.* London, 1984.

Keohane, Nannerl O. *Philosophy and the State in France: The Reniassance to the Enlightenment.* Princeton, 1980.

Kertzer, David, I., ed. *Ritual, Politics, and Power.* New Haven, 1988.

Kettering Sharon. *Patrons, Brokers and Clients in Seventeenth-Century France.* New York, 1986.

―――. "Clientage during the French Wars of Religion." *Sixteenth Century Journal* 20:2 (1989), 221–39.

―――. *Judicial Politics and Urban Revolt in Seventeenth-Century France: The Parlement of Aix, 1629–1659.* Princeton, 1978.

King, Preston. *The Ideology of Order: A Comparative Analysis of Jean Bodin and Thomas Hobbes.* New York, 1974.

Klaits, Joseph. *Servants of Satan.* Bloomington, Ind., 1985.

Klaniczay, Gabor. *The Uses of Supernatural Power: The Transformation of Popular Religion in Medieval and Early Modern Europe.* Princeton, 1990.

Kolakowski, L. *Chrétiens sans église: La Conscience religieuse et lien confessionel au XVIIe siècle.* Paris, 1966.

Kors, Alan C. *Atheism in France, 1650–1729. Vol. 1: The Orthodox Sources.* Princeton, 1990.

Kunzle, David. *Fashion and Fetishism: A Social History of the Corset, Tight-Lacing, and Other Forms of Body-Sculpture in the West.* Totowa, N.J., 1982.

La Buissiere, P. de. *Le Bailliage de Mâcon: Etude sur l'organisation judiciaire du Mâconnais sous l'Ancien Régime.* Dijon, 1914.

La Cuisine, E. de. *Le Parlement de Bourgogne depuis son origine jusqu'à sa chute.* 3 vols. Dijon and Paris, 1864.

Labrousse, Elisabeth. *Une Foi, une loi, un roi? La Revocation de l'édit de Nantes.* Paris, Geneva, 1985.

Lacapra, Dominick. *Rethinking Intellectual History: Texts, Contexts, Language.* Ithaca, N.Y., 1983.

Lafayette, Madame de. *The Princess of Cleves.* Trans. Walter J. Cobb. New York, 1989.

Lajeunie, E.-J. *Saint François de Sales: L'Homme, la pensée, l'action.* 2 vols. Paris, 1966.

Lakoff, George. *Women, Fire, and Dangerous Things: What Categories Reveal about the Mind.* Chicago, 1987.

Laloy, P., ed. *Le Présidial de Besançon.* Villefranche, 1926.

Landes, Joan B. *Women and the Public Sphere in the Age of the French Revolution.* Ithaca, N.Y., 1988.

Langbien, John. *Torture and the Law of Proof.* Chicago, 1977.

―――. *Prosecuting Crime in the Renaissance.* Cambridge, Mass., 1974.

Langer, William. "Infanticide: A Historical Survey." *History of Childhood Quarterly* 1 (Winter 1974), 353–65.

Langlois, Monique, et al. *Guide des recherches dans les fonds judiciaires de l'Ancien Régime (aux Archives Nationales).* Paris, 1958.

Lanhers, Yvonne. "Crimes et criminels au XIVe siècle." *Revue historique* 240 (1968), 325–38.

Laqueur, Thomas. *Making Sex: Body and Gender from the Greeks to Freud.* Cambridge, Mass., 1990.

―――. "Orgasm, Generation, and the Politics of Reproductive Biology." In *The Making of the Modern Body.* Ed. Catherine Gallagher and Thomas Laqueur. Berkeley, 1987.

Larner, Christina. *Witchcraft and Religion: The Politics of Popular Belief.* Oxford, 1984.

Lascoumes, Pierre, Pierrette Poncela, and Pierre Le noel. *Au Nom de l'ordre: Une Histoire politique du code pénal.* Paris, 1989.

Laslett, Peter, ed. *Bastardy and Its Comparative History.* London, 1980.

Laslett, Peter, and Richard Wall. *Family Life and Illicit Love in Earlier Generations.* Cambridge, 1977.

Latreille, A. *Histoire du catholicisme en France.* Vol. 2. Paris, 1960.

Laurain, Ernest. "Essai sur les présidiaux." *Nouvelle revue historique de droit français et étranger* 20 (1896), 74–76.

Law and Society Review 25:2 (1991), 219–410. Special issue on gender.

Le Roy Ladurie, Emmanuel. *Carnival in Romans.* Trans. Mary Feeney. New York, 1979.

———. *The Peasants of Languedoc.* Trans. John Day. Urbana, Ill., 1974.

Lea, Henry Charles. *The History of Sacerdotal Celibacy in the Christian Church.* New York, 1957.

———. *Superstition and Force.* New York, 1971; orig ed. 1870.

Lears, T. J. Jackson. "The Concept of Cultural Hegemony: Problems and Possibilities." *American Historical Review* 90 (June 1985), 567–93.

Lebigre, Arlette. *La Justice du Roi: La Vie judiciaire dans l'ancienne France.* Paris, 1988.

LeBras, Gabriel. "La Doctrine du mariage chez les théologiens et les canonistes depuis l'an mille." *Dictionnaire de théologie catholique,* vol. 9, pt. 2. Paris, 1927.

———. "Le Contrôle canonique de la vie chrétienne dans le diocèse d'Auxerre sous Louis XIV." *Mémoires de la société pour l'histoire du droit et des institutions des anciens pays bourguignons, comtois et romands* 2 (1935), 141–56.

———. *Introduction à l'histoire de la pratique religieuse en France.* 2 vols. Paris, 1942–45.

LeBras, Gabriel, et al. "Pratique religieuse et religion populaire." *Archives des sciences sociales religieuses* 43 (1977), 7–22.

Le Breton, David. *Corps et sociétés: Essai de sociologie et d'anthropologie du corps.* Paris, 1985.

Lebrun. François. *La Vie conjugale sous l'ancien régime.* Paris, 1975.

———. "Demographie et mentalités: Le Mouvement de conception sous l'ancien régime." *Annales de demographie historique* 10 (1974), 45ff.

Lebrun, François, Marc Venard, and Jean Quéniart. *L'Histoire générale de l'enseignement et de l'education en France.* Paris, 1981.

Lebrun, Francois, ed. *Histoire des catholiques en France.* Paris, 1980.

Lecuir, Jean. "Criminalité et 'mortalité': Montyon, statisticien du Parlement de Paris." *Revue d'histoire moderne et contemporaine* 21 (1974), 445–93.

Lefebvre-Teillard, Anne. "Les Officialités à la veille du concile de Trente." *Bibliothèque d'histoire du droit et droit romain* 19 (1973).

LeGoff, Jacques. *The Birth of Purgatory.* Trans. Arthur Goldhammer. Chicago, 1985.

Leites, Edmund. *Puritan Conscience and Modern Sexuality.* New Haven, 1986.

———, ed. *Conscience and Casuistry in Early Modern Europe.* Cambridge, 1988.

Lemaître, Nicole. "Confession privée et confession publique dans les paroisses du XVIe siècle." *Revue de l'histoire de l'église de France* 69 (1983), 189–208.

———. "Un Prédicateur et son public: Les Sermons du père Lejeune et le Limousin, 1653–1672." *Revue d'histoire moderne et contemporaine* 30 (1983), 33–65.

Lemay, Helen Rodnite. "Human Sexuality in Twelfth- through Fifteenth-Century Scientific Writings." In *Sexual Practices and the Medieval Church.* Ed. Vern L. Bullough and James Brundage. Buffalo, N.Y., 1982.

Lemercier, Pierre. *Les Justices seigneuriales de la region Parisienne de 1580 à 1789.* Paris, 1933.

Lenman, Bruce, and Geoffrey Parker. "The State, the Community and Criminal Law in Early Modern Europe." In *Crime and the Law: The Social History of Crime in Western Europe since 1500.* Ed. V. A. C. Gatrell, Bruce Lenman, and Geoffrey Parker. London, 1980.

Lettman, R. *Die Diskussion uber di klandestinen Ehen und die Einfurhung einer zur Gultikeit verplichtenden Eheschliessungsform auf den Konzil von Trent.* Munster, 1967.

Levack, Brian P. *The Witch-Hunt in Early Modern Europe.* London, 1987.

Levi, Anthony. *French Moralists: The Theory of the Passions, 1585 to 1649.* Oxford, 1964.

Levi, Giovanni. *Inheriting Power: The Story of an Exorcist.* Chicago, 1988.

Levy, Jean-Philippe. "L'Officialité de Paris et les questions familiales à la fin du XIVe siècle." In *Etudes d'histoire du droit canonique dediées à Gabriel Le Bras.* 2 vols. Paris, 1965.

Lewis, I. M. *Ecstatic Religion.* Baltimore, 1971.

Ligeron, Louis. "La Jurisprudence du Parlement de Dijon en matière de sorcellerie au debut du 17e siècle." *Mémoires de la société pour l'histoire du droit et des institutions des anciens pays Bourguignons, Comtois et Romands* 33 (1975–76), 281–89.

Little, Lester K. "Pride goes before Avarice: Social Change and Vices in Latin Christendom." *American Historical Review* 76 (1971), 16–49.

Littré, Emile. *Dictionnaire de la langue française.* 7 vols. Paris, 1956.

Lorde, Audre. *Sister Outsider.* Trumansburg, N.Y., 1984.

Lottin, Alain. "Naissances illégitimes et fille-mères à Lille au XVIIIe siècle." *Revue d'histoire moderne et contemporaine* 17 (1970), 278–322.

Lougee, Carolyn. *Le Paradis des femmes: Women, Salons, and Social Stratification in Seventeenth-Century France.* Princeton, 1976.

Lough, J. *France Observed in the Seventeenth Century by English Travellers.* London, 1984.

Loustaunau, Joseph. *Etude sur l'adultère au point de vue pénal en droit romain et en droit français.* Paris, 1889.

Lowith, Karl. *Meaning in History: The Theological Implications of the Philosophy of History.* Chicago, 1949.

Loye, L. *Histoire de l'église de Besançon.* 3 vols. Besançon, 1901–3.

Luhmann, Niklaus. *Love as Passion: The Codification of Intimacy.* Trans. Jeremy Gaines and Doris L. Jones. Cambridge, Mass., 1986.

Luria, Keith. *Territories of Grace: Cultural Change in the Seventeenth-Century Diocese of Grenoble.* Berkeley, 1990.

Maccubbin, Robert Purks, ed. *'Tis Nature's Fault: Unauthorized Sexuality during the Enlightenment.* Cambridge, 1985.

MacDonald, Michael. *Mystical Bedlam: Madness, Anxiety, and Healing in Seventeenth-Century England.* Cambridge, 1981.

McDonough, R., and R. Harrison. "Patriarchy and Relations of Production." In *Feminism and Materialism: Women and Modes of Production*, pp. 11–41. Ed. A. Kuhn and A. M. Wolpe. London, 1978.

McGowan, Margaret M. "Pierre de Lancre's 'Tableau.'" In *The Damned Art: Essays in the Literature of Witchcraft.* Ed. Sydney Anglo. London, 1977.

McGuire, Meredith. "Religion and the Body: Rematerializing the Human Body in the Social Sciences of Religion." *Journal for the Scientific Study of Religion* 29:3 (1990), 283–96.

McKnight, Stephen A. *Sacralizing the Secular: The Renaissance Origins of Modernity.* Baton Rouge, La., 1989.

McLaren, Angus. "Some Secular Attitudes toward Sexual Behavior in France, 1760–1860." *French Historical Studies* 8 (1974), 604ff.

———. *Reproductive Rituals: The Perception of Fertility in England from the Sixteenth Century to the Nineteenth Century.* London, 1984.

MacLean, Ian. *Woman Triumphant: Feminism in French Literature, 1610–1652.* Oxford, 1977.

———. *The Renaissance Notion of Women.* Cambridge, 1980.

McManners, John. *French Ecclesiastical Society under the Ancien Regime.* Manchester, 1960.

McNamara, Jo Ann. "Chaste Marriage and Clerical Celibacy." In *Sexual Practices and the Medieval Church.* Ed. Vern L. Bullough and James Brundage. Buffalo, N.Y., 1982.

MacRae, D. G. "The Body and Social Metaphor." In *The Body as a Medium of Expression*, pp. 59–73. Ed. J. Benthall and T. Polhemus. New York, 1975.

McWhorter, Ladelle. "Culture or Nature? The Function of the Term 'Body' in the Work of Michel Foucault." *Journal of Philosophy* 86:11 (November 1989), 608–14.

Magendie, Maurice. *La Politesse mondaine et les théories de l'honnêteté en France au XVIIe siècle, de 1600 à 1650.* 2 vols. Geneva, 1970; orig. ed. 1925.

Makowski, Elizabeth M. "The Conjugal Debt and Medieval Canon Law." *Journal of Medieval History* 3 (1977), 99–114.

Mâle, Emile. *L'Art religieux après le Concile de Trente.* Paris, 1932.

Mandrou, Robert. *From Humanism to Science, 1480–1700.* Trans. Brian Pearce. Harmondsworth, 1978.

———. *Magistrats et sorciers en France au XVIIe siècle.* Paris, 1968.

Manselli, Raoul. *La Religion populaire au moyen âge.* Montreal, 1975.

———. "Vie familiale et éthique sexuelle dans les penitentiels." In *Famille et parenté dans l'occident mediévale.* Ed. Georges Duby and Jacques LeGoff. Rome, 1977.

Maravall, José Antonio. *The Culture of the Baroque: Analysis of a Historical Structure.* Trans. Terry Cochran. Minneapolis, 1986.

Marcel, Louis. *Le Cardinal de Givry, évêque de Langres (1529–1561).* 2 vols. Author, 1926.

Marion, Marcel. *Dictionnaire des institutions de la France aux XVIIe et XVIIIe siècles.* Paris, 1923, 1979.

———. "A Propos de la géographie judiciaire de la France sous l'Ancien Régime: La Question de ressort des présidiaux." *Revue historique* 89 (1905), 80–88.

Marly, Diana de. *Costume and Civilization: Louis XIV and Versailles.* London, 1987.

Martin, A. Lynn. *The Jesuit Mind: The Mentality of an Elite in Early Modern France.* Ithaca, N.Y., 1988.

Martin, Hervé. "Confession et contrôle social à la fin du moyen âge." In *Pratiques de la confession des pères du desert à Vatican II.* Paris, 1983.

Martin, Victor. *Le Gallicanisme politique et le clergé de France.* Paris, 1929.

———. *Les Origines du gallicanisme.* 2 vols. Paris, 1938–39.

———. *Le Gallicanisme et la réforme catholique.* Paris, 1919.

Maury, Alfred. "La Legislation criminelle sous l'Ancien Regime." *Revue des deux mondes* 23 (1877), 241–78, 580–617.

Mauss, Marcel. "Techniques of the Body." *Economy and Society* 2:1 (1973), 70–88.

Mauzi, Robert. *L'Idée du bonheur dans la littérature et la pensée Françaises au XVIIIe siècle*. Paris, 1960.

Maza, Sarah. "The Bourgeoisie, Women, and the Public Sphere." *French Historical Studies* 17:4 (Fall 1992), 935–50.

———. *Servants and Masters in Eighteenth-Century France: The Uses of Loyalty*. Princeton, 1983.

Medick, Hans. "Plebeian Culture in the Transition to Capitalism Culture." In *Ideology and Politics*. Ed. Raphael Samuel. London, 1982.

Medick, Hans, and David Warren Sabean. "Interest and Emotion in Family and Kinship Studies: A Critique of Social History and Anthropology." In *Interest and Emotion: Essays on the Study of Family and Kinship*, pp. 9–27. Cambridge, 1984.

Meillassoux, Claude. *Femmes, greniers, et capitaux*. Paris, 1975.

Mennell, Stephen. *Norbert Elias: Civilization and the Human Self-Image*. Oxford, 1989.

Mentzer, Raymond A. *Heresy Proceedings in Languedoc, 1500–1560*. Transactions of the American Philosophical Society, vol. 74. Philadelphia, 1984.

———. "The Self-Image of the Magistrate in Sixteenth-Century France." *Criminal Justice History* 5 (1984), 23–43.

Merrick, Jeffrey. *The Desacralization of the French Monarchy*. Baton Rouge, La., 1989.

Mettam, Roger. "Power, Status, and Precedence: Rivalries among the Provincial Elites of 17th-century France." *Transactions of the Royal Historical Society* 5th series, 38 (1988), 43–62.

———. *Power and Faction in Louis XIV's France*. Oxford, 1988.

Mettam, Roger, ed. *Government and Society in Louis XIV's France*. London, 1977.

Meyer, Jean. "Illegitimates and Foundlings in Pre-industrial France." In *Bastardy and Its Comparative History*, pp. 249–63. Ed. Peter Laslett. Cambridge, Mass., 1980.

Michaud-Quantin, Pierre. *Sommes de casuistique et manuels de confession au moyen âge (XIIe–XVIe siècles)*. Analecta Medievalia Namurcensia, 13. Louvain, Lille, and Montreal, 1962.

Milhaven, John Giles. "A Medieval Lesson on Bodily Knowing: Women's Experience and Men's Thought." *Journal of the American Academy of Religion* 57:2 (Summer 1989), 341–72.

Miller, Nancy K. Introduction to *The Princess of Cleves*. New York, 1989.

Mollat, Michel. "Les Formes populaires de la piété au moyen âge." *Etudes sur l'économie et la société de l'occident mediéval XII–XV*. London, 1977.

Monter, E. William. *Enforcing Morality in Early Modern Europe*. London, 1987.

———. *Ritual, Myth and Magic in Early Modern Europe*. Athens, Ohio, 1983.

———. *Frontiers of Heresy: The Spanish Inquisition from the Basque Lands to Sicily*. Cambridge, 1990.

———. "Crime and Punishment in Calvin's Geneva." *Archiv fur reformationsgeschichte* 64 (1973), 281–87.

———. "La Sodomie à l'époque moderne en Suisse Romande." *Annales: ESC* 29 (1974), 1023–33.

Montuclard, M. "Les Limites épistémologiques du système orthodoxe." *Archives de sciences sociales des religions* (1983), 107–21.

Moogk, Peter. "Thieving Buggers and Stupid Sluts: Insults and Popular Culture in New France." *William and Mary Quarterly* 3d ser., 36 (1979), 524–47.

Moore, Sally Falk. *Law as Process.* Cambridge, Mass., 1977.

Moote, A. Lloyd. *The Revolt of the Judges: The Parlement of Paris and the Fronde, 1643–1652.* Princeton, 1971.

———. *Louis XIII, The Just.* Berkeley, 1989.

Morey, J. *Le Diocèse de Besançon au XVIIe siècle.* Besançon, 1869.

Morgan, Robin. *Going Too Far: The Personal Chronicle of a Feminist.* New York, 1977.

Moriarty, Michael. *Taste and Ideology in Seventeenth Century France.* Cambridge, 1988.

Morrill, John S. "French Absolutism as Limited Monarchy." *Historical Journal* 21:4 (1978), 961–72.

Motley, Mark. *Becoming a French Aristocrat: The Education of the Court Nobility, 1580–1715.* Princeton, 1990.

Mousnier, Roland. *La Venalité des offices sous Henri IV et Louis XIII.* Paris, 1971.

———. *Les Fureurs paysans: Les Paysans dans les révoltes du XVIIe siècle.* Paris, 1967.

———. "Les Concepts d''ordres,' d''états,' de 'fidelité,' et de 'monarchie absolu' en France, de la fin du 15e siècle à la fin du 18e." *Revue historique* 247 (1972), 289–312.

———. *The Institutions of France under the Absolute Monarchy, 1598–1789.* Trans. Brian Pierce and Arthur Goldhammer. 2 vols. Chicago, 1979, 1984.

Moxey, Keith. *Peasants, Warriors, and Wives: Popular Imagery in the Reformation.* Chicago, 1989.

Muchembled, Robert. "Mentalités, cultures, sociétés: Jalon pour un débat." *Mentalités: histoire des cultures et des sociétés* 1 (1988), pp. 1ff.

———. *Société et mentalités dans la France Moderne, XVIe–XVIIIe siècle.* Paris, 1990.

———. *L'Invention de l'homme moderne: Sensibilités, moeurs et comportements collectifs sous l'Ancien Régime.* Paris, 1988.

———. "Lay Judges and the Acculturation of the Masses (France and the Southern Low Countries, Sixteenth to Eighteenth Centuries)." In *Religion and Society in Early Modern Europe*, pp. 56–65. Ed. Kaspar von Greyerz. London, 1984.

———. "Famille, amour et mariage: Mentalités et comportements des nobles artésiens à l'époque de Philippe II." *Revue d'histoire moderne et contemporaine* 22 (1975), 233–61.

Muchembled, Robert, ed. *Culture et mentalités sous l'ancien régime.* Paris, 1990.

Muir, Edward. "The Virgin on the Street Corner: The Place of the Sacred in Italian Cities." In *Religion and Culture in the Renaissance and Reformation.* Ed. Steven Ozment. Kirksville, Mo., 1989.

Muir, Edward, and Guido Ruggiero, eds. *Sex and Gender in Historical Perspective.* Baltimore, 1990.

Mukerji, Chandra, and Michael Schudson, eds. *Rethinking Popular Culture: Contemporary Perspectives in Cultural Studies.* Berkeley, 1991.

Mullett, Michael A. "Popular Culture and the Counter-Reformation." *History of European Ideas* 11 (1989), 493–99.

Neuschel, Kristin B. *Word of Honor: Interpreting Noble Culture in Sixteenth-Century France.* Ithaca, N.Y., 1989.

Nicholls, Jonathan. *The Matter of Courtesy: Medieval Courtesy Books and the Gawain-Poet.* Woodbridge, Suffolk, U.K., 1985.

Noel, P. *Monographie de la ville de Seurre.* Dijon, 1887.

Noonan, John T. "Abortion and the Catholic Church: A Summary History." *Natural Law Forum* 12 (1967), 85–131.

———. *Contraception: A History of Its Treatment by the Catholic Theologians and Canonists.* Cambridge, Mass., 1966.

———. *Power to Dissolve: Lawyers and Marriages in the Courts of the Roman Curia.* Cambridge, Mass., 1972.

Norberg, Kathryn. *Rich and Poor in Grenoble, 1600–1814.* Berkeley, 1985.

O'Malley, John. *The Catholic Reformation: A Guide to Research.* St. Louis, 1988.

Obelkevitch, J., L. Roper, and R. Samuel, eds. *Disciplines of Faith: Studies in Religion, Politics and Patriarchy.* London, 1986.

Oestreich, Gerhard. *Neostoicism and the Early Modern State.* Trans. David McLintock. Cambridge, 1982.

Orcibal, Jean. *Le Premier Port-Royal: Reforme ou Contre-Reforme?* Paris, 1956.

———. "Richelieu, homme d'église, homme d'état." *Revue d'histoire de l'église de France* 34 (1948), 94–101.

Orgel, Stephen. *The Illusion of Power: Political Theater in the English Renaissance.* Berkeley, 1975.

Ortner, Sherry B. "Is Female to Male as Nature Is to Culture?" In *Women, Culture and Society,* pp. 67–87. Ed. M. A. Rosaldo and L. Lamphere. Stanford, 1974.

Ortner, Sherry B., and Harriet Whitehead, eds. *Sexual Meanings: The Cultural Construction of Gender and Sexuality.* Cambridge, 1986.

Otis, Leah. *Prostitution in Medieval Society: The History of an Urban Institution in Languedoc.* Chicago, 1985.

Ourliac, Paul, and J. de Malafosse. *Le Droit familial.* Paris, 1968.

Ourliac, Paul, and Jean-Louis Gazzaniga. *Histoire du droit privé Français de l'an mil au Code Civil.* Paris, 1985.

Outram, Dorinda. *The Body and the French Revolution: Sex, Class, and Political Culture.* New Haven, 1989.

Ozment, Steven. *When Fathers Ruled: Family Life in Reformation Europe.* Cambridge, Mass., 1983.

Pacilly, G. "Contribution à l'histoire de la théorie du rapt de séduction: Etude de jurisprudence." *Tijdschrift voor rechtsgeschiedenis* 13 (1934), 306–18.

Pagden, Anthony, ed. *The Languages of Political Theory in Early Modern Europe.* Cambridge, 1987.

Pannet, R., and Bernard Plongeron, eds. *La Religion populaire dans l'Occident Chrétien.* Paris, 1976.

Parker, David. "Law, Society and the State in the Thought of Jean Bodin." *History of Political Thought* 2:2 (Summer 1981), 253–85.

———. *The Making of French Absolutism.* New York, 1983.

———. "Sovereignty, Absolutism, and the Function of the Law in Seventeenth-Century France." *Past and Present* 122 (1989), 36–74.

Pateman, Carole. *The Sexual Contract.* Stanford, 1988.

Pelikan, Jaroslav. *Reformation of Church and Dogma (1300–1700).* Chicago, 1984.

Perouas, Louis. *Le Diocèse de La Rochelle de 1648 à 1724: Sociologie et pastorale.* Paris, 1964.

Perronet, Michel. *Les Évêques de l'ancien France.* 2 vols. Paris, 1978.

Perry, Mary E. *Gender and Disorder in Early Modern Seville.* Princeton, 1990.

Petrovitch, P. *Crime et criminalité en France: XVIIe–XVIIIe siècles.* Paris, 1971.

Phan, Marie-Claude. *Les Amours illégitimes: Histoires de séduction en Languedoc, 1676–1786.* Paris, 1986.

Philips, Susan U., Susan Steele, and Christine Tanz, eds. *Language, Gender, and Sex in Comparative Perspective.* Cambridge, 1987.

Picot, M. G. *Histoire des états généraux.* 4 vols. Paris, 1872.

Pieri, Georges. "Les Particularités de la puissance paternelle." *Mémoires de la société pour l'histoire du droit et des institutions des anciens pays bourguignons, comtois et romands* 26 (1965), 51–90.

Pignot, J.-Henri. *Gabriel de Roquette, un évêque réformateur sous Louis XIV.* 2 vols. Paris, 1876.

Pillorget, René. "Vocation religieuse et état en France aux XVIe et XVIIe siècles." In *La Vocation religieuse et sacerdotale en France (XVII–XIX siècles)*, pp. 9–18. Angers, 1979.

Pintard, René. *Le Libertinage érudit dans la première moitié du XVIIe siècle.* Geneva, 1983; orig. ed. 1943.

Pisani, P. *Les Compagnies de prêtres des XVIIe et XVIIIe siècles.* Paris, 1928.

Pitt-Rivers, Julian. *The Fate of Schechem, or the Politics of Sex.* Cambridge, 1977.

———. "Honor and Social Status." In *Honor and Shame: The Values of Mediterranean Society.* Ed. J. G. Peristiany. London, 1965.

Piveteau, Cécile. *La Pratique matrimoniale d'après les statuts synodaux du concile de Trente à la Révolution.* Le Puy, 1957.

Plessix-Buisset, Christiane. *Le Criminel devant ses juges en Bretagne aux 16e et 17e siècle.* Paris, 1988.

Pocock, J. G. A. "Virtues, Rights, and Manners: A Model for Historians of Political Thought." In *Virtue, Commerce, and History: Essays on Political Thought and History, Chiefly in the Eighteenth Century*, pp. 37–50. Cambridge, 1985.

Polhemus, Ted. *Body Styles.* Luton, 1988.

———. "Social Bodies." In *The Body as a Medium of Expression*, pp. 11–35. Ed. Jonathan Benthall and Ted Polhemus. New York, 1975.

Porchnev, Boris. *Les Soulèvements populaires en France au XVIIe siècle.* Paris, 1972.

Portemer, Jean. "Le Statut de la femme en France (XVIe–XVIIIe siècles)." In *Recueil de la Société Jean Bodin.* Paris, 1962.

———. "La Femme dans la législation royale des deux derniers siècles de l'ancien régime." In *Etudes d'histoire du droit privé offertes à Pierre Petot*, pp. 441–54. Paris, 1959.

———. "Réflexion sur les pouvoirs de la femme selon le droit Français au XVIIe siècle." *XVIIe siècle* 114 (1984), 189–202.

Pospisil, L. *Anthropology of Law: A Comparative Theory.* New York, 1971.

Poulle, August. *Le Parlement de Bourgogne* Dijon, 1902.

Poutet, Y. *Le 17e siècle et les origines Lasalliennes.* Rennes, 1970.

Powis, Jonathan. "Order, Religion, and the Magistrates of a Provincial Parliament in Sixteenth-Century France." *Archiv für Reformationsgeschichte* 71 (1980), 180–97.

———. "Officiers and Gentilhommes: A Parlementaire Class in Sixteenth-Century Bordeaux?" In *Bordeaux et les Iles Britanniques*, pp. 27–36. Bordeaux, 1973.

Pred, Alan. "Power, Everyday Practice and the Discipline of Human Geography." In *Space and Time in Geography: Essays Dedicated to T. Hagerstrand.* Lund, Sweden, 1981.

Prunel, Noel. *Sébastien Zamet: Évêque-duc de Langres*. Paris, 1912.

———. "Deux fondations de la Compagnie du Saint-Sacrement de Dijon: Le Refuge et le Seminaire, 1653–1660." *Revue d'histoire de l'église de France* 25 (1911), 5–16.

Quaife, G. R. *Wanton Wenches and Wayward Wives: Peasants and Illicit Sex in Early Seventeenth-Century England*. New Brunswick, N.J., 1979.

Quéniart, Jean. *La Revocation de l'édit de Nantes: Protestants et Catholiques français de 1598 à 1685*. Paris, 1985.

———. *Les Hommes, l'église et Dieu dans la France du XVIIIe siècle*. Paris, 1978.

Quitard, M. *Proverbes sur les femmes, l'amitié, l'amour et le mariage*. Paris, 1861.

Rabb, Theodore K. *The Struggle for Stability in Early Modern Europe*. Oxford, 1975.

Racinet, A. *Le Costume historique*. 6 vols. Paris, 1824–88.

Raitt, Janet. *Madame de Lafayette and "La Princesse de Cleves"*. London, 1971.

Ranum, Orest. "Courtesy, Absolutism, and the Rise of the French State, 1630–1660." *Journal of Modern History* 52 (1980), 426–51.

———. "Money, Dignity, and Self-Esteem in the Relations between Judges and Great Nobles of the Parlement of Paris during the Fronde." In *Society and Institutions in Early Modern France*, pp. 117–31. Ed. Mack P. Holt. Athens, Ga., 1991.

———. *Richelieu and the Councillors of Louis XIII*. Oxford, 1963.

Ranum, Orest, and Patricia Ranum, eds. *Popular Attitudes toward Birth Control in Pre-Industrial France and England*. New York, 1972.

Rapley, Elizabeth. *The Dévotes: Women and Church in Seventeenth Century France*. Montreal, 1990.

Rapp, Francis. "Réflexions sur la religion populaire au Moyen Age." *La Religion populaire* (1976), 51–98.

Rateau, Marguerite. "Les Peines capitales et corporelles en France sous l'ancien régime (1670–1789)." *Annales internationales de criminologie* (1963), 276–308.

Ravitch, Norman. *Sword and Mitre: Government and Episcopate in France and England in the Age of Aristocracy*. The Hague, 1966.

Raynal, Jean. *Histoire des institutions judiciaires*. Paris, 1964.

Reinhard, Wolfgang. "Gegenreformation als Modernisierung?" *Archiv fur Reformationsgeschichte* 68 (1977), 226–52.

Reinhardt, Steven G. "Crime and Royal Justice in Ancien Régime France: Modes of Analysis." *Journal of Interdisciplinary History* 13:3 (1983), 437–60.

———. *Justice in the Sarladais, 1770–1790*. Baton Rouge, La., 1991.

Rey, Maurice, ed. *Histoire des diocèses de Besançon et de Sainte-Claude*. Paris, 1977.

Rich, Adrienne. *Of Woman Born*. New York, 1976.

Richet, Denis. "Aspects socioculturels des conflits religieux à Paris dans la seconde moitié du 16e siècle." *Annales: ESC* 32:4 (1977), 764–89.

Ricoeur, Paul. *The Conflict of Interpretations*. Evanston, Ill., 1974.

———. *Interpretation Theory: Discourse and the Surplus of Meaning*. Fort Worth, Tex., 1976.

Riollot, Jean. *Le Droit de prévention des juges royaux sur les juges seigneuriaux*. Paris, 1931.

Robert, Philippe, and René Levy. "Histoire et question pénale." *Revue d'histoire moderne et contemporaine* 32 (1985), 481–526.

Rogers, Susan Carol. "Woman's Place: A Critical Review of Anthropological Theory." *Comparative Studies in Society and History* 20:1 (1978), 123–62.

Roper, Lyndal. *The Holy Household: Women and Morals in Reformation Augsburg.* Oxford, 1989.

———. "Will and Honor: Sex, Words and Power in 16th-Century Augsburg Criminal Trials." *Radical History Review* 43 (1989), 45–71.

———. "Mothers of Debauchery: Procuresses in Sixteenth-Century Augsburg." *German History* 6:1 (1988).

———. "The Common Man, the Common Good, the Common Woman: Gender and Meaning in the German Reformation Commune." *Social History* 12:1 (1987), 1–22.

———. "Discipline and Respectability: Prostitution and the Reformation in Augsburg." *History Workshop Journal* 19 (1985), 3–28.

Rosaldo, M. A., and L. Lamphere, eds. *Women, Culture and Society.* Stanford, 1974.

Ross, Ellen, and Rayna Rapp. "Sex and Society: A Research Note from Social History and Anthropology." *Comparative Studies in Society and History* 23:1 (1981), 51–72.

Rossiaud, Jacques. "Prostitution, Youth, and Society in the Towns of Southeastern France in the Fifteenth Century." In *Deviants and the Abandoned in French Society.* Ed. Robert Forster and Orest Ranum. Trans. Elborg Forster and Patricia Ranum. Baltimore, 1978.

———. "Fraternités de jeunesse et niveaux de culture dans les villes du sud-est à la fin du Moyen Age." *Cahiers d'histoire* 1 (1976), 67–102.

———. *Medieval Prostitution.* Trans. Lydia G. Cochrane. Oxford, 1988.

Rosso, Jeannette Geffriaud. *Etudes sur la féminité aux XVII et XVIII siècles.* Paris, 1984.

Rothkrug, Lionel. "German Holiness and Western Sanctity in Medieval and Modern History." *Historical Reflections/Réflexions historiques* 15 (1988).

———. "Religious Practices and Collective Perceptions: Hidden Homologies in the Renaissance and Reformation." *Historical Reflections/Réflexions historiques* 7 (1980), 3–254.

Roupnel, Gaston. *La Ville et la campagne au XVIIe siècle: Etude sur les populations du pays Dijonnais.* Paris, 1955.

Rousseau, G. S., and Roy Porter, eds. *Sexual Underworlds of the Enlightenment.* Chapel Hill, N.C., 1988.

Rowbotham, Sheila. "The Trouble with 'Patriarchy.'" In *People's History and Socialist Theory.* Ed. Raphael Samuel. London, 1981.

Rubin, Gayle. "The Traffic in Women." In *Toward an Anthropology of Women.* Ed. Rana Reiter. New York, 1975.

Rudé, George. *Criminal and Victim.* Oxford, 1986.

Ruff, Julius R. *Crime, Justice and Public Order in Old Regime France: The Senechaussées of Libourne and Bazas, 1696–1789.* London, 1984.

Ruggiero, Guido. *Binding Passions.* New York, 1993.

———. *Violence in Early Renaissance Venice.* New Brunswick, N.J., 1980.

———. *The Boundaries of Eros: Sex Crime and Sexuality in Renaissance Venice.* New York, 1985.

Sabatier. *Histoire de la législation sur les femmes publiques.* Paris, 1828.

Sabean, David. *Power in the Blood.* Cambridge, 1984.

Sahlins, Marshall. *Islands of History*. Chicago, 1985.

Saint-Germain, J. de. *La Reynie et la police au 17e siècle*. Paris, 1962.

Saint-Jacob, Pierre de. "Mutations économiques et sociales dans les campagnes bourguignonnes à la fin du XVIe siècle." *Etudes rurales* 1 (1961): 34–49.

Salmon, John H. M. *Renaissance and Revolt: Essays in the Intellectual and Social History of Early Modern France*. Cambridge, 1987.

———. *Society in Crisis: France in the Sixteenth Century*. London, 1975.

Samaha, Joel. "Gleanings from Local Criminal Court Records: Sedition amongst the 'Inarticulate' in Elizabethan England." *Journal of Social History* 8 (1975), 61–79.

Sanday, Peggy Reeves. *Female Power and Male Dominance: On the Origins of Sexual Inequality*. Cambridge, 1987.

Sanders, E. K. *Vincent De Paul: Priest and Philanthropist, 1576–1660*. New York, 1913.

Sauzet, Robert. "Le Milieu dévot tourangeau et les débuts de la Reforme catholique." *Revue d'histoire de l'église de France* 75 (1989), 159–66.

———. "Les Résistances au catéchisme au XVIIe siècle." In *Aux origines du catéchisme en France*. Paris, 1989.

———. "Dieu et mammon: Les Réformes et la richesse." *History of European Ideas* 9:4 (1988), 443–45.

———. "La Lente mise en place de la réforme tridentine." In *L'Eglise Gallicane au temps du Roi-Soleil*. Paris, 1988.

———. *Les Visites pastorales dans le diocèse de Chartres pendant la première moitié du XVIIe siècle*. Paris, 1970.

Savonnet, Bernard. "Fluctuations économiques et évolution de la criminalité: L'Exemple de Dijon à la fin du XVIIe siècle." *Economie du centre-est* 79 (1978), 87–107.

Sawyer, Jeffrey K. "Judicial Corruption and Legal Reform in Early Seventeenth-Century France." *Law and History Review* 6:1 (1988), 95–117.

Sceaux, Raoul de. "Le Père Honoré de Cannes, Capucin missionaire." *XVIIe siècle* 40 (1958), 349–74.

Schalk, Ellery. *From Valor to Pedigree*. Princeton, 1986.

Schama, Simon. "The Unruly Realm: Appetite and Restraint in Seventeenth-Century Holland." *Daedalus* 108:3 (1979), 103–23.

Schiffman, Zachary. *On the Threshold of Modernity*. Baltimore, 1991.

Schilling, Heinz. "'History of Crime' or 'History of Sin'?—Some Reflections on the Social History of Early Modern Church Discipline." In *Politics and Society in Reformation Europe*, pp. 289–310. Ed. E. I. Kouri and Tom Scott. New York, 1987.

Schmitt, Jean-Claude. "Les Traditions folkloriques dans la culture mediévale: Quelques réflexions de méthode." *Archives de sciences sociales des religions* 52 (1981), 5–20.

———. *The Holy Greyhound*. Cambridge, 1983.

———. "Gestures." *History and Anthropology* 1 (1984), 1–18.

Schmitt, Thérèse-Jean. *L'Organisation ecclésiastique et la pratique religieuse dans l'archidiaconé d'Autun de 1650 à 1750*. Autun, 1957.

Schnapper, Bernard. "La Répression pénale au XVIe siècle: L'Exemple du Parlement de Bordeaux (1510–1565)." In *Recueil de mémoires et travaux publié par la société d'histoire du droit et des institutions des anciens pays de droit ecrit* 8 (1971), 13–20.

————. "La Justice criminelle rendue par le Parlement de Paris sous le règne de François Ier." *Revue historique de droit français et étranger* 52 (1974), 252–84.

Schneider, Jane. "Of Vigilance and Virgins: Honor, Shame and Access to Resources in Mediterranean Societies." *Ethnology* 10:1 (1971), 1–24.

Schneider, Peter. "Honor and Conflict in a Sicilian Town." *Anthropological Quarterly* 42:3 (1969), 130–54.

Schneider, Robert A. "Mortification on Parade: Penitential Processions in Sixteenth- and Seventeenth-Century France." *Renaissance and Reformation*, 10:1 (1986), 123–46.

Schochet, Gordon J. *Patriarchalism in Political Thought.* New York, 1975.

Scholer, Robert. "Uncoding Mama: The Female Body as Text." In *Semiotics and Interpretation.* New Haven, 1982.

Scott, Joan W. "Gender: A Useful Category of Historical Analysis." *American Historical Review* 91 (1986), 1053–75.

Scribner, Robert W. "Is a History of Popular Culture Possible?" *History of European Ideas* 10 (1989), 175–91.

————. "Oral Culture and the Transmission of Reformation Ideas." In *The Transmission of Ideas in the Lutheran Reformation.* Ed H. Robinson-Hammerstein. Dublin, 1989.

————. "Religion, Society, and Culture: Reorienting the Reformation." *History Workshop Journal* 14 (1982), 2–22.

————. "Cosmic Order and Daily Life: Sacred and Secular in Pre-Industrial German Society." In *Religion and Society in Early Modern Europe, 1500–1800.* Ed. Kaspar von Greyerz. London, 1984.

————. "Ritual and Popular Religion in Catholic Germany at the Time of the Reformation." *Journal of Ecclesiastical History* 35 (January, 1984), 47–77.

Sedgwick, Alexander. *Jansenism in Seventeenth-Century France.* Charlottesville, Va., 1977.

Séguin, Jean-Pierre. *L'Information en France avant le périodique.* Paris, 1964.

Seguy, J. "The Marxist Classics and Asceticism." *Annual Review of the Social Sciences of Religion* 1 (1977), 94–101.

Sensibilité religieuse et discipline ecclésiastique. Strasbourg, 1975.

Serbat, L. *Les Assemblées du clergé de France: Origines, organisation, developpement (1561–1615).* Paris, 1906.

Sharpe, James A. *Crime in Early Modern England, 1550–1750.* London, 1984.

————. *Defamation and Sexual Slander in Early Modern England: The Church Courts at York.* Borthwick Papers no. 58. York, 1980.

————. "'Such Disagreement Betwyx Neighbors': Litigation and Human Relations in Early Modern England." In *Disputes and Settlements: Law and Human Relations in the West.* Ed. John Bossy. Cambridge, 1983.

Shorter, Edward. "Capitalism, Culture and Sexuality: Some Competing Models." *Social Science Quarterly* 53 (1972), 338ff.

————. "Illegitimacy, Sexual Revolution and Social Change in Modern Europe." *Journal of Interdisciplinary History* 2 (1971), 237ff.

Slack, Paul. "Mortality Crises and Epidemics, 1485–1610." In *Health, Medicine and Mortality in the Sixteenth Century.* Ed. Charles Webster. Cambridge, 1979.

Smart, B. "Foucault, Sociology and the Problem of Human Agency." *Theory and Society* 11 (1982), 121–41.

Solé, Jacques. "Passion charnelle et société urbaine d'ancien régime: Amour vénal, amour libre et amour fou à Grenoble au milieu du règne Louis XIV." *Annales de la faculté des lettres et science humaines, Université de Nice* 9–10 (1969), 211–32.

———. *L'Amour en occident à l'époque moderne.* Paris, 1976.

Solnon, Jean-François. *La Cour de France.* Paris, 1987.

Soman, Alfred. "Les Procès de sorcellerie au Parlement de Paris (1565–1640)." *Annales: ESC* 32 (1977), 790–814.

———. "Press, Pulpit and Censorship in France before Richelieu." *Proceedings of the American Philosophical Society* 120:6 (1976), 439–63.

———. "Criminal Jurisprudence in Ancien Regime France: The Parlement of Paris in the Sixteenth and Seventeenth Centuries." In *Crime and Criminal Justice in Europe and Canada,* pp. 43–75. Ed. Louis Knafla. Waterloo, Ontario, 1981.

———. "La Decriminalisation de la sorcellerie en France." *Histoire, économie et société* 4 (1985), 179–201.

———. "Deviance and Criminal Justice in Western Europe, 1300–1800: An Essay in Structure." *Criminal Justice History* 1 (1980), 3–28.

Soman, Alfred, and Elisabeth Labrousse. "La Querelle de l'antimoine: Guy Patin sur la sellette." *Histoire, économie et société* 5 (1986), 31–45.

Soulet, Jean-François. *Traditions et réformes religieuses dans les Pyrenées centrales au XVIIe siècle.* Pau, 1974.

Sourieau, Robert. "L'Organisation intérieure du Parlement de Dijon." *Mémoires de la société pour l'histoire du droit et des institutions des anciens pays bourguignons, comtois et romands* 6 (1939), 238–46.

Spicker, S. F., ed. *The Philosophy of the Body.* Chicago, 1970.

Spierenburg, Pieter. *The Spectacle of Suffering: Executions and the Evolution of Repression.* Cambridge, 1984.

Stallybrass, Peter. "Patriarchal Territories: The Body Enclosed." In *Rewriting the Renaissance: The Discourses of Sexual Difference in Early Modern Europe,* pp. 123–42. Ed. Margaret W. Ferguson et al. Chicago, 1986.

Stallybrass, Peter, and Alton White. *The Politics and Poetics of Transgression.* Ithaca, N.Y., 1982.

Stanton, Domna C. *The Aristocrat as Art: A Study of the "Honnête Homme" and the Dandy in Seventeenth- and Nineteenth-Century French Literature.* New York, 1980.

Starr, June, and Jane F. Collier, eds. *History and Power in the Study of Law: New Directions in Legal Anthropology.* Ithaca, N.Y., 1989.

Staves, Susan. "Money for Honor: Damages for Criminal Conversation." *Studies in Eighteenth-Century Culture* 11 (1982), 279–97.

Stone, Lawrence. *Family, Sex and Marriage in England, 1500–1800.* New York, 1977.

Strauss, Gerald. *Law, Resistance and the State.* Princeton, 1987.

Strosetzski, Christoph. *Rhétorique de la conversation: Sa Dimension littéraire et linguistique dans la société française du XVIIe siècle.* Trans. Sabine Suebert. Paris, 1984.

Sueur, Philippe. *Histoire du droit public français, XVe–XVIII siècle.* 2 vols. Paris, 1989.

Suleiman, Susan R. *The Female Body in Western Culture: Contemporary Perspectives.* Cambridge, Mass., 1986.

Tackett, Timothy. *Priest and Parish in Eighteenth-Century France: A Social and Political Study of the Curés in a Diocese of Dauphiné, 1750–1791.* Princeton, 1977.

Tackett, Timothy, and Claude Langlois. "Ecclesiastical Structures and Clerical Geography on the Eve of the French Revolution." *French Historical Studies* 11 (1980), 352–70.

Tapié, Victor-L. "Les Officiers seigneuriaux dans la société provinciale du XVIIe siècle." *XVIIe siècle* 42–43 (1959), 118–40.

Tentler, Thomas N. *Sin and Confession on the Eve of the Reformation.* Princeton, 1977.

Therborn, G. *The Ideology of Power and the Power of Ideology.* London, 1980.

Thomas, Alexandre. *Une Province sous Louis XIV.* Paris, 1844.

Thomas, Keith. "The Puritans and Adultery: The Act of 1650 Reconsidered." In *Puritans and Revolutionaries: Essays in Seventeenth-Century History Presented to Christopher Hill.* Ed. Donald Pennington and Keith Thomas. Oxford, 1978.

Thomas, M. *Sainte Chantal.* Paris, 1953.

Thompson, E. P. *Whigs and Hunters: The Origin of the Black Act.* New York, 1975.

Thore, Luc. "Langage et sexualité." In *Sexualité humaine*, pp. 65–96. Paris, 1970.

Tilly, Charles. *The Contentious French.* Cambridge, Mass., 1986.

Tobias, J. J. *Crime and Police in England, 1700–1900.* New York, 1979.

Torre, Angelo. "Il Consumo di devozioni: Rituali e potere nelle campagne Piemontesi nella prima meta del Settecento." *Quaderni storici* 20 (1985), 181–223.

Traer, James F. *Marriage and the Family in Eighteenth-Century France.* Ithaca, N.Y., 1980.

Trask, Haunani-Kay. *Eros and Power: The Promise of Feminist Theory.* Philadelphia, 1986.

Trexler, Richard. "Infanticide in Florence: New Sources and First Results." *History of Childhood Quarterly* 1 (1973), 98–115.

———. "La Prostitution florentine au XVe siècle: patronages et clientèles." *Annales: ESC* 26:6 (1981), 983–1015.

Trinkaus, Charles, and Heiko Oberman, eds. *The Pursuit of Holiness in Late Medieval and Renaissance Religion.* Leiden, 1974.

Tuchle, H., C. A. Bouman, and J. Lebrun. *Nouvelle histoire de l'église: Réforme et contre-réforme.* Paris, 1966–68.

Turlan, Juliette M. "Recherches sur le mariage dans la pratique coutumière (XIIe–XVIe s.)." *Revue historique de droit français et étranger* 35 (1957), 477–528.

Turner, Bryan S. "The Body and Religion: Towards an Alliance of Medical Sociology and Sociology of Religion." *Annual Review of the Social Sciences of Religion* 4 (1980), 247–86.

———. "Recent Developments in the Theory of the Body." In *The Body: Social Process and Cultural Theory.* Ed. Mike Featherstone, Mike Hepworth, and Bryan S. Turner. London, 1991.

———. *Religion and Social Theory: A Materialist Perspective.* London, 1983.

———. *The Body and Society: Explorations in Social Theory.* Oxford, 1984.

Turner, Victor. *The Anthropology of Performance.* New York, 1987.

———. *From Ritual to Theatre: The Human Seriousness of Play.* New York, 1982.

———. *Dramas, Fields and Metaphors: Symbolic Action in Human Society.* Ithaca, N.Y., 1974.

————. *The Ritual Process: Structure and Anti-Structure*. Chicago, 1968.

————. *Image and Pilgrimage in Christian Culture*. Oxford, 1978.

Ulrich, Daniel. "La Répression en Bourgogne au XVIII siècle." *Revue historique de droit français et étranger* 50 (1972), 398–437.

Valensisse, Marina. "Le Sacre du roi: Stratégie symbolique et doctrine politique de la monarchie Française." *Annales: ESC* (May–June 1986), 543–77.

Van Shaick, P.-J. "Le Coeur et la tête: Une Pédagogie par l'image populaire." *Revue d'histoire de la spiritualité* 50 (1974), 457–78.

Viard, Georges. "Les Visites pastorales dans l'ancien diocèse de Langres: La Réglementation episcopale et sa mise en oeuvre." *Revue d'histoire de l'église de France* 63 (July–December 1977), 235–72.

Vigarello, Georges. *Le Corps rédressé: Histoire d'un pouvoir pédagogique*. Paris, 1978.

————. *Le Propre et le sâle: L'Hygiene du corps depuis le Moyen Age*. Paris, 1985.

Vignier, Françoise. "La Justice de Magny-sur-Tille, XVe–XVIIIe siècles." *Mémoires de la société pour l'histoire du droit et des institutions des anciens pays bourguignons, comtois et romands* 23 (1962), 278–88.

Viguerie, Jean de. *Une Oeuvre d'education sous l'ancien régime: Les Pères de la doctrine chrétienne en France et en Italie, 1592–1792*. Paris, 1976.

————. "La Vocation sacerdotale et religieuse aux XVIIe et XVIIIe siècles: La Théorie et la réalité." In *La Vocation religieuse et sacerdotale en France (XVIIe–XIXe siècles)*, pp. 27–39. Angers, 1979.

————. "Les Fondations et la foi du peuple chrétien: Les Fondations de messes en Anjou au XVIIe siècle." *Revue historique* 256 (1976), 289–320.

Von Greyerz, Kaspar. "Sanctity, Deviance and the People of Late Medieval and Early Modern Europe." *Comparative Studies in Society and History* 27:2 (1985), 280–90.

Vovelle, Michel. *Piété baroque et déchristianisation en Provence au XVIIIe siècle*. Paris, 1978.

Walker, D. P. *The Decline of Hell: Seventeenth-Century Discussions of Eternal Torment*. Chicago, 1964.

Walle, Etienne van de. "Marriage and Marital Fertility." *Daedalus* 97 (1968), 468ff.

Watson, Alan. *The Evolution of Law*. Baltimore, 1985.

Weaver, F. Ellen. "Erudition, Spirituality, and Women: The Jansenist Contribution." In *Women in Reformation and Counter-Reformation Europe*. Ed. Sherrin Marshall. Bloomington, Ind., 1989.

Weeks, Jeffrey. *Against Nature: Essays on History, Sexuality, and Identity*. London, 1991.

Weisser, Michael R. *Crime and Punishment in Early Modern Europe*. Brighton, 1982.

Weitman, S. "Intimacies: Notes towards a Theory of Social Inclusion and Exclusion." *Archives européenes de sociologie* 11 (1970), 348–67.

Wheaton, Robert, and Tamara Hareven, eds. *Family and Sexuality in French History*. Philadelphia, 1980.

White, James Boyd. *When Words Lose Their Meaning: Constitutions and Reconstitutions of Language, Character, and Community*. Chicago, 1984.

Whyte, Martin King. *The Status of Women in Preindustrial Societies*. Princeton, 1978.

Wiesner, Merry. "Early Modern Midwifery: A Case Study." In *Women and Work in Preindustrial Europe*. Ed. Barbara Hanawalt. Bloomington, Ind., 1986.

———. "Paternalism in Practice: The Control of Servants and Prostitutes in Early Modern German Cities." In *The Process of Change in Early Modern Europe: Essays in Honor of Miriam Chrisman.* Ed. Philip N. Bebb and Sherrin Marshall. Athens, Ohio, 1989.

———. *Working Women in Renaissance Germany.* New Brunswick, N.J., 1986.

Wilentz, Sean, ed. *Rites of Power: Symbolism, Ritual, and Politics since the Middle Ages.* Philadelphia, 1985.

Willaert, Leopold. *La Restauration catholique (1563–1648).* Paris, 1960.

Williams, Charles E. *The French Oratorians and Absolutism, 1611–1641.* New York, 1990.

Wills, Antoinette. *Crime and Punishment in Revolutionary Paris.* Westport, Conn., 1981.

Wirth, Jean. "Against the Acculturation Thesis." In *Religion and Society in Early Modern Europe*, pp. 66–78. Ed. Kaspar von Greyerz. London, 1984.

Wood, James B. *The Nobility of the Election of Bayeux, 1463–1666: Continuity through Change.* Princeton, 1980.

Wright, Gordon. *Between the Guillotine and Liberty: Two Centuries of the Crime Problem in France.* New York, 1983.

Wrightson, Keith. "Infanticide in European History." *Criminal Justice History* 3 (1982), 1–20.

Wrightson, Keith, and David Levine. *Poverty and Piety in an English Village.* New York, 1979.

Yardeni, Myriam. *La Conscience nationale en France pendant les guerres de religion, 1559–1598.* Louvain, 1971.

Yeo, Eileen, and Stephen Yeo, eds. *Popular Culture and Class Conflict, 1590–1914: Explorations in the History of Labor and Leisure.* Brighton, 1981.

Yver, Jean. *Egalité entre héritiers et exclusion des enfants dotés: Essai de géographie coutumier.* Paris, 1966.

Zagorin, Perez. *Ways of Lying: Dissimulation, Persecution and Conformity in Early Modern Europe.* Cambridge, Mass., 1990.

———. *Rebels and Rulers, 1500–1660.* Cambridge, 1982.

Zysberg, Andre. *Les Galériens: Vies et destins de 60,000 forçats sur les galères de France, 1680–1748.* Paris, 1987.

Index

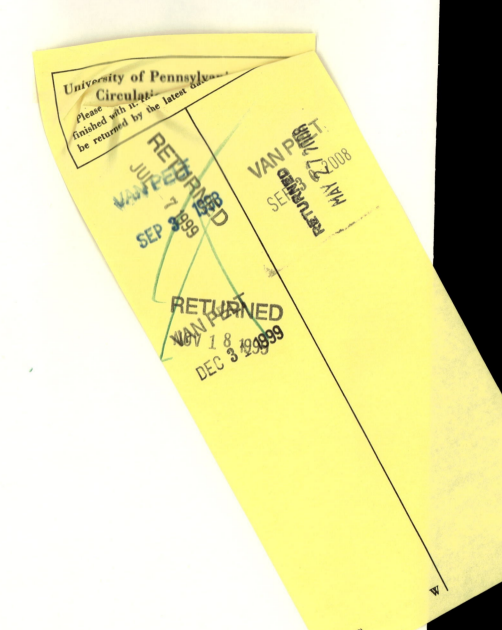